Emergency Preparedness

Emergency Preparedness

A Safety Planning Guide for
People, Property, and Business Continuity

2ND EDITION

Don Philpott

Bernan Press

Lanham • Boulder • New York • London

Published by Bernan Press
An imprint of The Rowman & Littlefield Publishing Group, Inc.
4501 Forbes Boulevard, Suite 200, Lanham, Maryland 20706
www.rowman.com
800-865-3457; info@bernan.com

Unit A, Whitacre Mews, 26-34 Stannary Street, London SE11 4AB

British Library Cataloguing in Publication Information Available

Library of Congress Cataloging-in-Publication Data

Names: Philpott, Don, 1946– author.
Title: Emergency preparedness : a safety planning guide for people, property,
    and business continuity / Don Philpott.
Other titles: Emergency preparedness for facilities
Description: Second edition. | Lanham : Bernan Press, [2016] | Earlier
    edition published as: Emergency preparedness for facilities : a guide to
    safety planning and business continuity / David A. Casavant. | Includes
    bibliographical references and index.
Identifiers: LCCN 2015051282 (print) | LCCN 2016006258 (ebook) | ISBN
    9781598887914 (pbk. : alk. paper) | ISBN 9781598887921 (electronic)
Subjects: LCSH: Emergency management. | Business planning.
Classification: LCC HD49 .C38 2016 (print) | LCC HD49 (ebook) | DDC
    658.4/77—dc23
LC record available at http://lccn.loc.gov/2015051282

∞™ The paper used in this publication meets the minimum requirements of
American National Standard for Information Sciences—Permanence of Paper
for Printed Library Materials, ANSI/NISO Z39.48-1992.

Printed in the United States of America

Contents

Introduction vii

Part I: Emergencies and Disasters: Natural and Non-natural Events

Chapter One: 1. Understanding Emergencies and Disasters.................................. 3

Chapter Two: Tornadoes, Hurricanes, Thunderstorms, and Floods 11

Chapter Three: Earthquakes, Tsunamis, Volcanoes, and Landslides....................... 43

Chapter Four: Fire and Wildfire, Drought and Extreme Heat,
and Blizzards and Avalanches.. 65

Chapter Five: Bomb Threats, Chemical Warfare, and Bioterrorism...................... 95

Chapter Six: Chemical Spills, Contamination, and Household Emergencies...... 123

Chapter Seven: Nuclear Threat and Exposure 131

Chapter Eight: Workplace Violence and Workplace Medical Emergencies.......... 137

Chapter Nine: More Non-natural Events: Civil Disturbances, Blackouts,
Structural Collapse 145

Part II: Planning, Procedures, Mitigation, and Recovery

Chapter Ten: The Emergency Action Plan, Part One: Laying the Groundwork 155

Chapter Eleven: The Emergency Action Plan, Part Two: Creating the Plan 179

Chapter Twelve: Training, Drills, and Evacuations.. 207

Chapter Thirteen: Basic First Aid and Medical Care in the Workplace
or Anyplace 233

Chapter Fourteen: Post-event Restoration 241

Chapter Fifteen: Guidelines for Emergency Mitigation 271

Chapter Sixteen: Emergency Preparedness: Hospitals and
Healthcare Facilities 297

Chapter Seventeen: Emergency Preparedness: Schools 317

Appendices

Emergency Action Plan Template 345

Storm Preparations Activities List 352

Post Event Restoration Activities List 381

Administrative Issues—Annual Audit 387

Emergency Plan Issues—Annual Audit 389

General Building Issues—Annual Audit 392

Health-Related Issues—Annual Audit 401

Specific Threats—Annual Audit 402

Resources 404

Glossary 413

Index 437

Introduction to the Second Edition

There is no doubt that the world is a dangerous place. Overseas we have terror groups and rogue governments that threaten global peace. At home, there are daily reminders of the violence in our streets and even our schools are no longer the safe havens they should be.

Of course, it is not just the threat of violence that concerns us. There is always the danger of natural disasters and we have to be prepared for them. Emergency preparedness planning is essential if you want to protect your company, your employees, family, and friends.

No one knows when they might be a victim of violence or a casualty of a natural disaster. It makes sense, therefore, to prepare for the unthinkable. It is always better to be prepared than not.

Despite the events of 9/11, Hurricane Katrina, and tropical storm Sandy there are still companies that have not developed an emergency preparedness plan. They still cling to the mindset that "it will not happen to us." This is dangerously flawed thinking.

Almost as bad are those companies that have taken the trouble to develop a plan and then kept it locked away in a drawer for years without revising it or keeping it up-to-date.

Emergency preparedness planning serves many functions. It allows us to identify all the threats we face, both manmade and natural, and to take steps to mitigate the effects should a disaster or emergency strike.

At the same time, by identifying all risks and vulnerabilities, we can initiate immediate actions to overcome them. This remedial action may help increase productivity, reduce costs, and improve the health and safety of employees.

Being prepared and understanding what to do can reduce fear, anxiety, and the losses that accompany disasters. Businesses, communities, families, and individuals should know what to do in the event of an emergency.

You should know how to respond to severe weather or any disaster that could come in your area, such as hurricanes, earthquakes, wildfires, flooding, and extreme cold. You should also be ready to be self-sufficient for at least three days. Immediately following a disaster you cannot expect first responders and other emergency personnel to help you—they will have more urgent things to attend to. This may mean that you will have to provide your own shelter, first aid, food, water, and sanitation.

Being prepared, understanding your risks, and taking all steps to reduce those risks can reduce the damages caused by emergencies and disasters. This book aims to help you identify those risks and be prepared for them. Now is the time to create your emergency preparedness plan. Do not put it off.

*   *   *

This second edition of *Emergency Preparedness* expands the scope of the first edition, authored by David Casavant, which looked at facility management and business continuity. This edition, while retaining that information, also offers emergency preparedness useful to individuals, families, communities, schools, healthcare organizations—anyone who could be caught up in a crisis situation. All the resources and urls of the first edition have been updated and added to. Additional information on natural and non-natural events has been added. There is new information on extreme heat and landslides, new chapters focusing on schools and hospitals, as well as additional case studies. The appendices include a sample Emergency Plan as well as checklists for annual audits, storm activities (before and after the event), contractor availability, and such. A new addition to this book is a thorough glossary of terms.

EMERGENCIES AND DISASTERS:
NATURAL AND NON-NATURAL EVENTS

I

Understanding Emergencies and Disasters

Every year, millions of people around the world lose their lives or have them seriously disrupted because of floods, tsunamis, wildfires, earthquakes, blizzards, hurricanes, and other extreme events. In today's troubled world, we face even greater threats from terrorism, civil unrest, explosions, and the possibility of chemical, biological, or even nuclear attack.

In the United States, the terrorist threat is not only from overseas groups; domestic terrorism has been with us for decades, and violence in the workplace and schools is a serious area of concern. In the last twenty-five years, according to the FBI, there have been 327 domestic terrorist incidents and suspected incidents—that averages out at more than one every month during this period. In the last five years alone 108 students, teachers, and custodians have been shot dead at incidents in schools. The threat is real and growing.

More than half the businesses in the United States do not have an emergency preparedness plan—what to do in the event of a crisis or disaster—and many of those that do have one do not keep it up to date. Even fewer businesses and organizations have a physical security plan to protect their property and people who work in it.

In the United States there are more than 1,800 government-owned buildings and more than 6,200 leased locations throughout the fifty states and Washington, D.C. They employ almost a million federal workers and host tens of millions of visitors.

There are 327,000 education buildings in the fifty states and Washington, D.C. There are 87,630 schools with 47 million children enrolled and employing around 3 million teachers.

There are 7,569 hospitals nationwide employing 2.4 million registered nurses, 1.8 million nursing aides, 819,000 physicians and surgeons, and 350,000 therapists. On any given day there are 539,000 hospital inpatients plus visitors. There are 127,000 additional health care facilities nationwide offering inpatient/outpatient treatment.

There are 133,000 malls and strip malls, 534,000 large stores, 349,000 food-service facilities, and 153,000 hotels and motels nationwide.

Throughout the United States, there are more than 1 million office buildings and 603,000 warehouses and storage facilities. There are more than 307,000 churches nationwide and more than 305,000 public assembly buildings. And, there are more than 110 million households.

On December 1, 2014, the Federal Bureau of Investigation (FBI) warned that there was a serious threat of an Islamic State (IS) terrorist attack within the United States. Terrorism is not a new challenge, and it is not going to go away any time soon so we have a duty to our families, friends, and loved ones to ensure that the places where we live, work, learn, and play are secure, and that the people using them are safe.

What Exactly Is an Emergency?

Let's start with the basics. Is an emergency not the same as a disaster? Although these two terms are often used interchangeably they mean something quite different. An **emergency** can be defined as any event that negatively impacts a community or organization's production, safety, or personnel. That's a wide-open definition that encompasses many events.

The caution is to not view an emergency as a disaster. A **disaster** describes an emergency that has devolved into something with much greater impact. An emergency imposes a negative impact while a disaster's impact is both negative and severe. By concentrating on disasters, we overlook the more common and often more costly emergencies that affect us all. Disaster planning is fine and quite necessary; however, the purpose of this book is to identify *any* event that might cause disruption in your life, your community, or your organization.

When we think of disasters, we tend to envision naturally occurring events such as hurricanes and tornadoes. However, emergency preparedness and planning must take into account all emergencies. These include manmade emergencies, whether accidental like a chemical spill or deliberate acts such as a terrorist or arson attack.

Never ever discount something in your planning on the basis that it will not happen to you. No matter how remote the possibility of something happening, plan and be prepared for it.

Another point worth making is that the terms *emergency* and *disaster* are very elastic terms. What might be considered a disaster for one organization might be just an inconvenience for another. For this reason, this book will generally use *emergency* to describe disruptive events.

Interestingly, all disasters start out as emergencies. It is not until the event has transpired that the emergency becomes viewed as a disaster. Think about large-scale emergencies such as the Louisiana Flood of May 1995.

This single event brought up to twenty inches of rain to New Orleans in a two-day period and caused nearly $350 million dollars in damage (damage total for all of southern Louisiana was more than $7 billion). During the course of the event, it was considered a definite emergency; some people even called it a disaster. However, federal disaster assistance was not available until the president surveyed the damage and declared it a disaster. Compare that with Hurricane Katrina, which slammed into New Orleans a decade later killing almost 1,800 people and causing more than $100 billion in damage. That was an immediate and very obvious disaster. However, more than 90 percent of the floods that occur, although quite disruptive, are never declared disasters.

The fact is that emergencies occur much more frequently than do disasters; therefore, an emergency is more likely to affect you or your business. While planning for emergencies, we are encouraged to ask the question: "What is the worst that can happen?" Planning for a worst-case scenario is essential; however, we need to spend quality time performing a true risk analysis by asking, "What events are most likely to happen?"

Typically, emergency events can be classified into two separate groups, natural events and non-natural events. When considering possible emergencies, remember to think about all events that might occur. As you read this book, you'll learn that many events we believe may have little chance of occurring could actually befall us.

With proper planning, you can significantly reduce the impact of disaster or emergency events on your business. In many instances, with proper planning, you can even prevent the emergency from occurring in the first place.

Natural Events

Tornado	Hurricane
Earthquake	Fires and wildfires
Blizzard and ice storms	Floods
Tsunamis	Drought
Volcanic eruptions	Landslides, mudflow, and debris flow

Non-Natural Events

Loss of utility	Loss of communications
Loss or theft of computer data	Arson
Water leak	Chemical spill
Terrorist attack	Act of war
Riot or demonstration	Bomb threat
Medical emergency	Workplace violence
Nuclear accident	

Billion-Dollar U.S. Weather Disasters

The United States has endured 178 weather-related disasters since 1980 in which the overall damages exceeded $1 billion per event. Hurricane Katrina cost an estimated $100 billion in damage and Superstorm Sandy in 2012 caused almost $70 billion in damage.

The National Climatic Data Center (NCDC) is responsible for monitoring and assessing both national and international climate. Additionally, the NCDC identifies weather trends and provides summaries and comparisons with a historical perspective. Their interesting Web page, "Billion-Dollar Weather and Climate Disasters" (www.ncdc.noaa.gov/billions), tracks weather-related disasters—drought, tornadoes, flooding, ice storms, and more—and their costs. This sobering information should be an eye opener for those who place low priority on emergency-planning activities.

The NOAA Weather Radio

Your greatest source of information prior to or during any emergency event is the radio. During and after a major disaster, all radio stations drop their usual format and deliver helpful post-disaster information. It is critical to have a battery-powered or hand-cranked radio to listen for storm warnings and advisories. Don't forget to have extra batteries; you may be using the radio for quite some time after the storm has passed. Don't make the mistake of depending on electricity to power your radio: electricity may not be available.

NOAA Weather Radios

The following are just a few of the companies that manufacture NOAA weather radios. For more manufacturers—and resellers such as WeatherRadios.com (www.weatherradios.com)—see the NOAA Web site (www.nws.noaa.gov/nwr).

Alert Works
www.alertworks.com

Homesafe, Inc.
www.homesafeinc.com

Midland Radio
www.midlandradio.com

Giant International Ltd/Motorola Weather Products
http://shop.giantintl.com/WeatherProducts.aspx

Radio Shack
www.radioshack.com

The National Weather Service (NWS) broadcasts weather advisories and updates as received from the National Oceanic and Atmospheric Administration (NOAA). These broadcasts are available on NOAA weather radio, twenty-four hours a day. The advisories cover both natural events and non-natural events such as chemical spills and biological threats. NOAA weather radio has been created as an "all hazards" radio network, available to national, state, and local emergency management agencies. It is the most comprehensive emergency information source available to the general public.

Currently the NOAA radio network has more than 1,028 stations covering all fifty states, Puerto Rico, the U.S. Virgin Islands, American Samoa, Guam, and the Northern Mariana Islands, including adjacent waterways and coastal waters. The cost of the NOAA weather radio ranges from $20 to $200 or more, depending on the strength of the receiver and other features. Extra features include an alarm tone that allows you to keep the radio on but quiet unless a special signal is received by the national weather service. When this occurs, the radio will transmit the advisory. Another excellent feature, especially if you work in one area and live in another, is the SAME (Specific Area Message Encoding) feature. This option allows you to receive only those transmissions that relate to the areas important to you. Other features are available for those who are hearing or visually impaired. These options include attention-getting devices such as text printers, monitors, strobe lights, and even bed shakers.

Disaster Warning

Effective emergency planning and accurate warning information coupled with speedy response have proven instrumental in saving lives and reducing losses. In particular, quick dissemination of warning information is essential to saving lives. For example, the use of Doppler radars has increased lead-time and accuracy of tornado warnings. Prior to 1990, the average lead-time for a tornado was two or three minutes and accuracy was low. The average lead-time for the years 1993 to 1999 was about nine minutes with an accuracy of about 58 percent. Today, warnings are often given thirty minutes out although the nationwide average lead-time for tornado warnings is thirteen minutes—still enough time for most people to take shelter.

Unfortunately, on February 22 and 23, 1998, forty-two people were killed when a series of strong tornadoes swept through central Florida in the middle of the night. The National Weather Service issued fourteen tornado warnings and those warnings were widely broadcast via news media, but most people were asleep and didn't hear them. In this scenario, a tone-alert NOAA weather radio could have awoken these people and saved their lives.

Effective warning depends upon both a public and private partnership. Most emergency warnings are delivered by government agencies, but the information is usually disseminated by public avenues such as radio and television. In 1963, the Emergency Broadcast System (EBS) was established to provide a vehicle for warning the public about national disasters. In 1994 the Emergency Alert System (EAS) replaced the Emergency Broadcast System. The EAS is the national warning system designed to allow the president of the United States to address the nation in a reliable manner during and after a major national emergency.

At a national level, the EAS can only be activated by the president of the United States or his constitutional successor. After the president has used the system, it may be used by other federal agencies, such as the Federal Emergency Management Agency (FEMA). At a local level, the EAS can also be used by state and local agencies to release emergency notifications. In fact, the EAS is activated more than one hundred times per month at state and local levels. These messages may be originated by the National Weather Service, police, governors, or emergency managers. The EAS will interrupt normal television programming and provide an appropriate verbal warning or text "crawl" located at the bottom of the screen.

FEMA's Impact

A good record of major emergencies that have affected the country is the Federal Emergency Management Agency records. For the 1990 to 1999 period, FEMA spent more than $25.4 billion for declared disasters and emergencies. This is in comparison to $3.9 billion (current dollars) in disaster aid for the 1980 to 1989 period. This increase in spending can be attributed to a number of factors including public awareness of FEMA, increased population in trouble areas, and increased funding by the federal government. FEMA spent more than $60 billion in 2005 alone following Hurricane Katrina.

The Disaster Aid Process and Programs

First response to an emergency is the responsibility of the local and state government emergency services and various volunteer agencies. If the emergency is of large scale, the affected state's governor may request federal resources, which can be mobilized through the Federal Emergency Management Agency. FEMA may provide search and rescue assistance, electrical power, food, water, shelter, and other basic human needs.

Usually, if the emergency has a short-term effect, FEMA assistance is not required; however the long-term recovery phase of a disaster can place severe financial strain on a local or state government. Even a large city with significant resources may be in need of federal assistance if the damage is severe. Of course, the infusion of federal funds requires the affected state to commit considerable funds as well. If the president determines the disaster to be of greater scope than the state can handle, a presidentially declared disaster is acknowledged and funding comes from the President's Disaster Relief Fund, which is managed by FEMA.

There exist two major categories of disaster aid:

- **Individual Assistance**—for damage to residences and businesses or personal property losses.
- **Public Assistance**—for repair of infrastructure, public facilities, and debris removal.

In the event of an emergency event where the president officially declares a disaster, FEMA disaster workers will arrive and set up a central field office to coordinate the recovery effort. Shortly thereafter a toll-free telephone number will be established for use by affected residents and business owners. Additionally, disaster recovery centers will be opened where disaster victims can meet FEMA representatives to obtain information and apply for federal assistance.

Disaster aid to individuals generally falls into the following categories:

Housing may be available for up to eighteen months for displaced persons whose residences were heavily damaged or destroyed. Funding also can be provided for housing repairs and replacement of damaged items to make homes habitable.

Grants are available to help meet other serious disaster-related expenses not covered by insurance. These expenses may include replacement of personal property, transportation, and medical, dental, and funeral expenses.

Low-Interest Loans are available after a disaster for homeowners and renters from the U.S. Small Business Administration (SBA) to cover uninsured property losses. Loans may be for repair or replacement of homes, automobiles, clothing, or other damaged personal property. Loans are also available to businesses for property loss and economic injury.

Other Aid Programs include crisis counseling, disaster-related unemployment assistance, legal aid, and assistance with income tax, Social Security benefits, and Veterans' benefits.

In addition to individual assistance, FEMA offers public assistance to assist state or local governments in rebuilding a community's damaged infrastructure. Typically, FEMA's public assistance programs pay for 75 percent of the approved project costs. Projects may include debris removal and repair of damaged public property, in addition to other public concerns.

Where To Start

Whether speaking of disasters or emergencies, businesses, communities, and individuals must be prepared. Those businesses unprepared for emergency events will experience costly business interruption. More importantly, lives are at stake. History has shown that billions of dollars are lost each year due to emergency and disaster events and many organizations are ill-prepared to survive an extended period of downtime.

Organizations exist that can offer assistance during and after an emergency event. In the event of a costly or long-term emergency, the governor of a state may petition the federal government for assistance. When this occurs, the Federal Emergency Management Agency quickly moves to provide assistance to individuals, businesses, and public entities.

Being prepared and understanding what to do can reduce the fear, anxiety, and loss that accompany disasters. Businesses, communities, families, and individuals should know what to do in a fire and where to seek shelter from a tornado. They should be ready to evacuate their homes, take refuge in public shelters, and know how to care for their basic medical needs.

Individuals can also reduce the impact of disasters (flood proofing, elevating a home or moving it out of harm's way, securing items that could shake loose in an earthquake) and sometimes avoid the danger altogether.

You should know how to respond to severe weather or any disaster that could occur in your area—hurricanes, earthquakes, extreme cold, or flooding. You should also be ready to be self-sufficient for at least three days. This may mean providing for your own shelter, first aid, food, water, and sanitation.

This book focuses on the physical hazards of emergencies and disasters and how to prepare for them, but there are also the emotional effects of losing a loved one, a home, a business, or treasured possessions. When under stress, people can become irritable, fatigued, hyperactive, angry, and withdrawn. Children and older adults are especially vulnerable to post-disaster psychological effects.

You need to plan because you need to be prepared. Planning will also help you be more self-sufficient after the event. Immediately after an emergency, essential services may be cut-off and local disaster relief and government responders may not be able to reach you right away. Even if they can reach you, knowing what to do to protect yourself, your business, and your household is essential.

2

Tornadoes, Hurricanes, Thunderstorms, and Floods

As already discussed, most people think of emergencies and disasters as naturally occurring events. Natural events do tend to occur more frequently than non-natural events (such as nuclear exposure or loss of utility) but all potential causes should be factored in when planning. In the next several chapters, we focus on the natural events.

Tornadoes

Tornadoes are nature's most violent storms. Spawned from powerful thunderstorms, tornadoes are rapidly rotating columns of air that can uproot trees, destroy buildings, and turn harmless objects into deadly missiles. They can devastate a neighborhood in seconds. A tornado appears as a rotating, funnel-shaped cloud that extends to the ground with whirling winds that can reach 300 miles per hour. Damage paths can be in excess of one mile wide and fifty miles long. Because of the destructive nature of tornadoes, hundreds of millions of dollars annually are lost to its effects, and on average forty-two people die from tornadoes each year.

In the United States, tornadoes are more frequent in the Southeast and Midwest but can occur anywhere. Like hurricanes, tornadoes have a season which runs from March through August, but tornadoes can occur anytime if the weather conditions are just right. Every state is at some risk from this hazard.

Ten Tornado Facts

1. A tornado is a violently rotating column of air extending from a thunderstorm to the ground.
2. Tornadoes are capable of destroying homes and vehicles and can cause fatalities.
3. Tornadoes may strike quickly, with little or no warning.
4. Tornadoes may appear nearly transparent until dust and debris are picked up or a cloud forms in the funnel. The average tornado moves SW to NE but tornadoes have been known to move in any direction.

5. The average forward speed is thirty mph but may vary from stationary to seventy mph with rotating winds that can reach 300 miles per hour.
6. Tornadoes can accompany tropical storms and hurricanes as they move onto land.
7. Waterspouts are tornadoes that form over water.
8. Tornadoes are most frequently reported east of the Rocky Mountains during spring and summer months, but can occur in any state at any time of year.
9. In the southern states, peak tornado season is March through May, while peak months in the northern states are during the late spring and early summer.
10. Tornadoes are most likely to occur between 3 p.m. and 9 p.m., but can occur at any time of the day or night.

Case Study 1: Super Outbreak, 1974

The Super Outbreak of 1974 was aptly named. Within a sixteen-hour period 148 tornadoes touched down in thirteen states. At one point fifteen tornadoes had touched down at the same time. The path of destruction covered more than 2,500 miles and irreversibly changed the lives of thousands of people.

Xenia, Ohio, was the location of the deadliest of all the twisters. This particular tornado was particularly violent and reached an F-5 rating on the Fujita scale (see table 2.1).

Table 2.1. The Fujita Scale*

Category F0	Gale tornado <72 mph	Light damage. Some sign damage. Tree branches broken and shallow-rooted trees will be toppled.
Category F1	Moderate tornado 73–112 mph	Moderate damage. Roofing tiles loosen and take flight. Moving automobiles pushed off roads. Mobil homes may come off foundations.
Category F2	Significant Tornado 113–157 mph	Significant damage. Large trees are uprooted. Mobil homes are demolished. Roofs are torn off of some homes.
Category F3	Severe Tornado 158–206 mph	Severe damage. Cars can be lifted into the air and thrown about. Small missiles are generated. Roofs on well-constructed buildings are torn off.
Category F4	Devastating Tornado 207–260 mph.	Devastating damage. Large missiles are generated. Well-constructed buildings are demolished.
Category F5	Incredible Tornado 261–318 mph.	Incredible damage. Trees will be debarked. Well-constructed buildings will be lifted off their foundations and travel until they break apart. Automobile-sized missiles will travel in excess of 100 yards.

* See http://www.spc.noaa.gov/faq/tornado/ef-scale.html for a more detailed scale, the Enhanced Fujita Scale developed in 2007.

Winds reached speeds upward of 318 mph. On Thursday, April 4, when the winds had calmed, people emerged from their homes in a state of shock. Large tanker trucks had been tossed about like leaves. Large trees had been uprooted and tossed thousands of feet away. Roofs were torn off of buildings. Hundreds of buildings were leveled. In just twenty or thirty seconds, the tornado took the lives of thirty-three people and leveled half the city. More than 1,300 buildings were destroyed, including four schools.

Know the Terminology

Tornado Watch: Tornadoes are possible in the given area of the watch.

Tornado Warning: A tornado has actually been sighted by a spotter or by radar and is occurring or is imminent in the warning area.

Fujita Scale: Scale measuring the intensity and damage extent of tornadoes.

Xenia was not the only town to experience a deadly and rare F-5 tornado. During the Super Outbreak a record seven F-5 tornados developed. The 148 tornados that made up the Super Outbreak combined to take 315 lives and injure 5,484 people. Damages totaled $600 million, making April 4, 1974, one of the deadliest and most expensive days of tornadoes ever.

Case Study 2: Oklahoma/Kansas, 1999

On Monday evening, May 3, 1999, a devastating tornado developed and quickly gained strength. In fact, the tornado clocked the highest ever-recorded wind speed—318 mph. This distinction earned it an F-5 rating on the Fujita scale. Interestingly, if the tornado winds were just one mph faster, the tornado would have been classified an F-6, the highest rating on the Fujita scale and previously thought to be an unreachable milestone.

Oklahoma City was hit particularly hard by this wave of violence, enduring fifty-two tornadoes in a very short period of time. The largest of these tornadoes stayed on the ground for nearly four hours as it cut a path of destruction across the infamous "Tornado Alley."

Tornado Alley

"Tornado Alley" is commonly used to describe the states from Texas north to the Dakotas. The region's geographic makeup and climate is conducive to the production of most of the nation's tornadoes. Dry air from the Rockies to the west collides with warm air from the Gulf of Mexico, and the union is anything but pleasant. These conditions create violent thunderstorms that spawn the tornadoes that are so prevalent in the region.

By the time the estimated seventy-six tornadoes had ended, more than fifty-five deaths and 675 injuries were recorded. More than 8,000 buildings were damaged or destroyed, which contributed to over $1.2 billion in damages.

What To Do Before Tornadoes Threaten

Because of the "surprise" element of tornadoes, advance preparation is a must. Basic to this preparation is an understanding of exactly where designated shelters are located. This includes not just at the workplace but at home as well. Here are other crucial preparation guidelines:

1. Know the terms used to describe tornado threats: **Tornado Watch** and **Tornado Warning** (see above).
2. Know the county or parish in which you live. Counties and parishes are used in Watches and Warnings to identify the location of tornadoes.
3. Ask your local emergency management office or American Red Cross chapter about the tornado threat in your area. Ask about community warning signals. Ask if there are any public safe rooms or shelters nearby.
4. Purchase a NOAA Weather Radio with a battery backup and tone-alert feature that automatically alerts you when a watch or warning is issued (tone alert is not available in some areas). Purchase a battery-powered commercial radio and extra batteries as well.
5. Determine places to seek shelter, such as a basement or storm cellar. If an underground shelter is not available, identify an interior room or hallway on the lowest floor.
6. Practice going to your shelter with your household.
7. Know the locations of designated shelters in places where you and your household spend time, such as public buildings, nursing homes, and shopping centers. Ask local officials whether a registered engineer or architect has inspected your children's schools for shelter space.
8. Assemble a disaster supply kit. Keep a stock of food and extra drinking water.
9. Make a record of your personal property. Take photographs or videos of your belongings. Store these documents in a safe place.

A good source of tornado information can be found on the FEMA Web site at www.fema. gov. This site offers a publication that shows how you can protect yourself from tornadoes while at home. Within the pages of this publication, you will find a Wind Zone Map, which graphically shows the frequency and strength of storms across the country. This map includes over forty years of tornado history and one hundred years of hurricane history.

Another great source of historical information can be found at www.tornadoproject.com. This site allows you to drill down to a county level and lists all occurrences and the magnitudes of hurricanes since 1950.

Wind "Safe Room and Shelter"

Extreme windstorms in many parts of the country pose a serious threat to buildings and their occupants. Your residence may be built "to code," but that does not mean that it can withstand winds from extreme events like tornadoes or major hurricanes.

The purpose of a wind shelter or "Safe Room" is to provide a space where you and your household can seek refuge that provides a high level of protection. You can build a shelter in one of the several places in your home:

- In your basement
- Beneath a concrete slab-on-grade foundation or garage floor
- In an interior room on the first floor

Shelters built below ground level provide the greatest protection, but a shelter built in a first-floor interior room can also provide the necessary protection. Below-ground shelters must be designed to avoid accumulating water during the heavy rains that often accompany severe windstorms.

To protect its occupants, an in-house shelter must be built to withstand high winds and flying debris, even if the rest of the residence is severely damaged or destroyed. Therefore:

- The shelter must be adequately anchored to resist overturning and uplift.
- The walls, ceiling, and door of the shelter must withstand wind pressure and resist penetration by windborne objects and falling debris.
- The connections between all parts of the shelter must be strong enough to resist the wind.
- If sections of either interior or exterior residence walls are used as walls of the shelter, they must be separated from the structure of the residence, so that damage to the residence will not cause damage to the shelter.

If you are concerned about wind hazards where you live, especially if you live in a high-risk area, you should consider building a shelter. Publications are available from FEMA to assist in determining if you need a shelter and how to construct one. Contact the FEMA distribution center for a copy of "Taking Shelter from the Storm" (L-233 for the brochure and FEMA-320 for the booklet with complete construction plans).

What To Do During a Tornado Watch

1. Listen to NOAA Weather Radio or to commercial radio or television newscasts for the latest information.
2. Be alert for approaching storms. If you see any revolving funnel-shaped clouds, immediately call 911 to report it.
3. Watch for tornado danger signs:

   - Dark, often greenish sky
   - Large hail
   - A large, dark, low-lying cloud (called a "wall cloud")—particularly if rotating
   - Loud roar, similar to a freight train

Caution:

- Some tornadoes are clearly visible, while rain or nearby low-hanging clouds obscure others.
- Occasionally, tornadoes develop so rapidly that little, if any, advance warning is possible.
- Before a tornado hits, the wind may die down and the air may become very still.
- A cloud of debris can mark the location of a tornado even if a funnel is not visible.
- Tornadoes generally occur near the trailing edge of a thunderstorm. It is not uncommon to see clear, sunlit skies behind a tornado.

4. Avoid places with wide-span roofs, such as auditoriums, cafeterias, large hallways, supermarkets, or shopping malls.
5. Be prepared to take shelter immediately. Gather household members and pets. Assemble supplies to take to the shelter, such as flashlight, battery-powered radio, water, and first-aid kit.

If you do not have a designated shelter nearby or the close proximity of a tornado precludes you from accessing the shelter, you must be aware of areas of safe refuge available within the building.

What To Do During a Tornado Warning

When a tornado has been sighted, go to your shelter immediately.

1. In a residence or small building, move to a predesignated shelter, such as a basement, storm cellar, or "Safe Room or Shelter."
2. If there is no basement, go to an interior room on the lower level (closets, interior hallways). Put as many walls as possible between you and the outside. Get under a sturdy table and use arms to protect your head and neck. Stay there until the danger has passed.
3. Do not open windows. Use the time to seek shelter.
4. Stay away from windows, doors, and outside walls. Go to the center of the room. Stay away from corners because they attract debris.
5. In a school, nursing home, hospital, factory, or shopping center, go to predetermined shelter areas. Interior hallways on the lowest floor are usually safest. Again, stay away from windows and open spaces.
6. In a high-rise building, go to a small, interior room or hallway on the lowest floor possible.

7. Get out of vehicles, trailers, and mobile homes immediately and go to the lowest floor of a sturdy nearby building or a storm shelter. Mobile homes, even if tied down, offer little protection from tornadoes.
8. If caught outside with no shelter, lie flat in a nearby ditch or depression and cover your head with your hands. Be aware of the potential for flooding.
9. Do not get under an overpass or bridge. You are safer in a low, flat location.
10. Never try to outrun a tornado in urban or congested areas in a car or truck; instead, leave the vehicle immediately for safe shelter. Tornadoes are erratic and move swiftly.
11. Watch out for flying debris. Flying debris from tornadoes causes most fatalities and injuries.
12. Stay tuned to the television or radio for further instructions.
13. Have access to a first aid kit and stored food and water.

What To Do After a Tornado

1. Look out for broken glass and downed power lines.
2. Check for injuries. Do not attempt to move seriously injured people unless they are in immediate danger of death or further injury. If you must move an unconscious person, first stabilize the neck and back, and then call for help immediately.

   ⅄ If the victim is not breathing, carefully position the victim for artificial respiration, clear the airway, and commence mouth-to-mouth resuscitation.

   ⅄ Maintain body temperature with blankets. Be sure the victim does not become overheated.

   ⅄ Never try to feed liquids to an unconscious person.

3. Use caution when entering a damaged building. Be sure that the walls, ceiling, and roof are in place and that the structure rests firmly on the foundation. Wear sturdy work boots and gloves.
4. See the chapter "Post-Event Restoration" for more important information.

Hurricanes

Hurricanes are one of the most devastating and costly of all natural weather events. This phenomenon thrives in the warm waters of the Atlantic Ocean and Caribbean Sea as well as in the Gulf of Mexico. In its early stages, this tropical disturbance is quite harmless. As it matures, however, an area of low pressure develops, winds begin a counter-clockwise rotary circulation, and wind speeds up to thirty-five mph are clocked. At this point the tropical disturbance is identified as a **tropical depression**. As the winds grow yet stronger (thirty-six to seventy-three mph), the depression is categorized as a **tropical storm**. Once the wind velocity exceeds seventy-three mph, the storm graduates into an officially named **hurricane**.

A hurricane is a type of **tropical cyclone**, the generic term for a low-pressure system that generally forms in the tropics. The ingredients for a hurricane include a preexisting weather disturbance, warm tropical oceans, moisture, and relatively light winds aloft. A typical cyclone is accompanied by thunderstorms, and in the Northern Hemisphere, a counter-clockwise circulation of winds near the earth's surface.

Know the Terminology

Tropical cyclones are classified as follows:

Tropical Depression An organized system of clouds and thunderstorms with a defined surface circulation and maximum sustained winds of thirty-eight mph (thirty-three knots) or less. Sustained winds are defined as one-minute average wind measured at about thirty-three feet (ten meters) above the surface.

Tropical Storm An organized system of strong thunderstorms with a defined surface circulation and maximum sustained winds of thirty-nine to seventy-three mph (thirty-four to sixty-three knots).

Hurricane An intense tropical weather system of strong thunderstorms with a well-defined surface circulation and maximum sustained winds of seventy-four mph (sixty-four knots) or higher. All Atlantic and Gulf of Mexico coastal areas are subject to hurricanes and tropical storms. Although rarely struck by hurricanes, parts of the southwest United States and the Pacific Coast experience heavy rains and floods each year from hurricanes spawned off Mexico.

The U.S. hurricane season as defined by NOAA's National Hurricane Center lasts from June 1 through November 30. During an average year, approximately ten tropical storms develop over the Atlantic Ocean and Gulf of Mexico. Typically six of these storms develop into hurricanes, and every three years about five hurricanes reach the United States. Two of these five hurricanes are usually considered major hurricanes with a Saffir-Simpson hurricane intensity scale rating of Category 3 or stronger.

Hurricanes are classified into five categories based on their wind speed, central pressure, and damage potential. Category 3 and higher are considered major hurricanes, though Category 1 and 2 are still extremely dangerous and warrant your full attention.

Saffir-Simpson Rating and Storm Categories

1. **Minimal**—Winds of 74 to 95 mph. Damage is minimal, usually limited to trees and power lines.
2. **Moderate**—Winds of 96 to 110 mph. Some roof damage may occur. Trees can be uprooted and power poles can be downed. Windows and storefronts can be damaged.
3. **Extensive**—Winds of 111 to 130 mph. Roofs are badly damaged or lost. Structural damage is common.
4. **Extreme**—Winds of 131 to 155 mph. Damage to most structures is severe. Extreme flooding can occur along and near the coast. Loss of life is common.
5. **Catastrophic**—Winds in excess of 155 mph. Damage is total in many places. Many structures are destroyed. Severe flooding is common several miles inland.

Dangerous Hurricane Byproducts

Although the strong winds of a hurricane cause incredible damage, often it is the byproducts of the hurricane that inflict the greatest damage. The following severe weather watches and warnings may be issued during a hurricane event:

- **Flood Watch**: Floodwaters are possible in the given area of the watch and during the time frame identified in the flood watch. Flood watches are usually issued for flooding that is expected to occur at least six hours after heavy rains have ended.
- **Flood Warning**: Flooding is actually occurring or is imminent in the warning area.
- **Flash Flood Watch**: Flash flooding is possible in the given area. Flash flood watches are usually issued for flooding that is expected to occur within six hours after heavy rains have ended.
- **Flash Flood Warning**: Flash flooding is actually occurring or is imminent in the warning area.
- **Tornado Watch**: Tornadoes are possible in the given area of the watch.
- **Tornado Warning**: A tornado has actually been sighted by a spotter or by radar and is occurring or is imminent in the warning area.

As we all have seen from hurricanes like Andrew and Katrina, they can cause catastrophic and deadly damage to coastlines and several hundred miles inland. Winds can exceed 155 miles per hour. Hurricanes and tropical storms can also spawn tornadoes and microbursts, create a surge along the coast, and cause extensive damage due to inland flooding from trapped water.

Tornadoes most often occur in thunderstorms embedded in rain bands well away from the center of the hurricane; however, they also occur near the eye-wall. Typically, tornadoes produced by tropical cyclones are relatively weak and short-lived but still pose a threat.

A **storm surge** is a huge dome of water pushed on-shore by hurricane and tropical storm winds. Storm surges can reach twenty-five feet high and be fifty to one hundred miles wide. Storm tide is a combination of the storm surge and the normal tide (i.e., a fifteen-foot storm surge combined with a two-foot normal high tide over the mean sea level creates a seventeen-foot storm tide). These phenomena cause severe erosion and extensive damage to coastal areas.

Hurricanes can produce widespread torrential rains. Floods are the deadly and destructive result. Excessive rain can also trigger landslides or mudslides, especially in mountainous regions. Flash flooding can occur due to the intense rainfall. Flooding on rivers and streams may persist for several days or more after the storm. (See also chapter 3 on Floods, Landslides, Mudflow, and Debris Flow.)

The speed of the storm and the geography beneath the storm are the primary factors regarding the amount of rain produced. Slow moving storms and tropical storms moving into mountainous regions tend to produce more rain.

Time to Prepare

Most emergencies or disasters happen without advance notice. Earth's tectonic plates suddenly shift and an earthquake results. A dam bursts and water floods a low-lying valley, catching the inhabitants by surprise. A tornado quickly develops and touches down while a community sleeps. Hurricanes, however, are unique because of their advance notice. We have the ability to track them as they develop. We can forecast their paths days in advance. You would have thought, therefore, that their effects could be mitigated and few lives lost. Two factors keep hurricanes in the headlines and cause them to continue to take lives.

First, people like living on the coast. Building codes require hurricane-proofing construction but the homes and offices built in these locations are larger and more costly than years past. So when a major storm sweeps through it inflicts great damage and replacement costs quickly soar.

The second factor is complacency. Residents of coastal areas become accustomed to numerous tropical storms and hurricanes that develop only to fizzle before they hit land. Those that do touch U.S. soil usually end up somewhere else, never in one's own backyard. This fact is made evident each year as hurricane season begins and the first storm approaches. The day prior to the storm, people flock to lumber yards waiting hours for overpriced plywood for shut-

The areas most often affected by hurricanes are usually coastal towns and cities with high populations and dense development. However, inland areas can also be damaged. In 1989, Hurricane Hugo, a Category-4 storm, made a direct hit on Charleston, South Carolina, but caused damage as far inland as Charlotte, North Carolina, more than 200 miles inland. Windows were broken in downtown office buildings and air handler units were blown off rooftops.

tering doors and windows. Many people are content to ride the storm out instead of heading inland or to the emergency shelters. Each time a near miss occurs, it simply reinforces that complacency.

Despite improved warnings and a decrease in the loss of life, property damage continues to rise because an increasing number of people are living or vacationing near coastlines. Those in hurricane-prone areas need to be prepared for hurricanes and tropical storms.

Case Study 1: Hurricane Andrew, 1992

The classic example of the destructive force of a hurricane occurred on August 24, 1992, in Homestead, Florida. Hurricane Andrew caused an estimated $26 billion in damages in the United States alone, making it the most expensive natural disaster in U.S. history at that time. Fortunately, Hurricane Andrew hit southern Dade County, a less populated and developed area, thereby lessening the economic impact of the disaster. If Hurricane Andrew had touched down just fifty miles to the north, billions of dollars more damage would have certainly been inflicted.

Hurricane Andrew had maximum sustained winds of 145 mph and gusts of 175 mph. Additionally, Hurricane Andrew brought with it a 16.9-foot storm surge. Andrew destroyed 25,524 homes and damaged an additional 101,241. Twenty-three people died directly as a result of Andrew and thirty-eight others died from secondary causes. The hurricane disrupted electrical service to 1.4 million customers; many of these customers went weeks without electrical service.

As devastating as Hurricane Andrew was, it never achieved Category-5 status. Through 2015, thirty-three Atlantic storms have reached Category-5 strength, and of these thirty-three, only two made landfall in the United States: the 1935 Florida Keys hurricane (not named) and Hurricane Camille, which pummeled the Mississippi coastline in 1969. (The rest of the Caribbean and Central America have been punished by Category-5 hurricanes more often with thirteen landfalls.)

Case Study 2: Hurricane Katrina, 2005

Hurricane Katrina was the third-strongest and one of the deadliest storms to hit the United States and ten years later, there is still recovery work to be done. Katrina formed over the Bahamas on August 23, 2005, and became a tropical storm the next day. It gained intensity as it moved across the Gulf of Mexico and was eventually upgraded to a Category-5 hurricane with winds of 160 mph. By the time it made landfall in Louisiana Katrina had weakened to a Category-4 storm but still had winds of up to 155 mph. The area was pounded for hours by high winds, storms, and torrential rain. The levees protecting New Orleans failed and 80 percent of the city was flooded: about 300,000 homes were destroyed. The storm caused major damage in Alabama, Louisiana, and Mississippi. The official death toll in Florida,

Louisiana, and Mississippi was 1,836. There was huge environmental and economic damage. With costs at $148 billion, Katrina is currently the most expensive U.S. natural disaster.

Fact: It was estimated that if all the debris left behind by the destruction was stacked on a football field, the pile would be ten-and-a-half miles high.

What To Do Before a Hurricane

As mentioned above, hurricanes present a unique situation because of their advance notice. So take the time given to prepare and plan. Proper planning prevents pain and panic. Although we can't eliminate storms, there are a number of proactive things that can be done that will decrease the impact.

1. Learn the difference between "Watch" and "Warning"—see above.
2. Listen for local radio or television weather forecasts. If you haven't already, purchase a NOAA Weather Radio with battery backup and a tone-alert feature that automatically alerts you when a Watch or Warning is issued (tone alert is not available in some areas). Purchase a battery-powered commercial radio and extra batteries, because the media will be broadcasting information on other events as well.
3. Ask your local emergency management office about community evacuation plans relating to your neighborhood. Learn evacuation routes. Determine where you would go and how you would get there if you needed to evacuate. Sometimes alternate routes are desirable.
4. Talk to your household/employees about hurricane issues. Create a household/business disaster plan. Plan to meet at a place away from your residence in case you are separated. Choose an out-of-town contact for everyone to call to say they are safe. (See the later chapters on preparing an Emergency Plan.)
5. Determine the needs of your household members who may live elsewhere but need your help in a hurricane. Consider the special needs of neighbors, such as people who are disabled or those with limited sight or vision problems.
6. Prepare to survive on your own for at least three days. Assemble a disaster supply kit. Keep a stock of food and extra drinking water.
7. Make plans to secure your property. Permanent storm shutters offer the best protection for windows. A second option is to board up windows with 5/8-inch marine plywood, cut to fit and ready to install. Tape does not prevent windows from breaking.
8. Learn how to shut off utilities and where gas pilots and water mains are located.
9. Have your home inspected for compliance with local building codes. Many of the roofs destroyed by hurricanes have not been constructed or retrofitted according to building codes. Installing straps or additional clips to securely fasten your roof to the frame structure will substantially reduce roof damage.

10. Be sure trees and shrubs around your home are well trimmed. Dead limbs or trees could cause personal injury or property damage. Clear loose and clogged rain gutters and downspouts.
11. If you have a boat, determine where to secure it in an emergency.
12. Consider flood insurance. Purchase insurance well in advance: there is a thirty-day waiting period before flood insurance takes effect.
13. Make a record of your personal property. Take photographs or videos of your belongings. Store these documents in a safe place.

Your local emergency management office or the Red Cross can inform you of approved evacuation routes and established shelters. Additionally, they can assist in creating an actual emergency plan and conducting dry runs. Another great resource is FEMA.

As mentioned, your local emergency management agency will assist you in finding nearby shelters. Understand that not every "well-built" building constitutes a safe haven from a storm. Large gymnasiums, metal buildings, and other long-span buildings provide little protection from a storm of significant magnitude. Additionally, structures built without proper hurricane strapping are susceptible to wind lift. A reinforced concrete structure might seem like a great storm shelter, but if the roof isn't properly attached to the walls, there's a good chance it may take flight during the storm. This was a common problem in Dade County during Hurricane Andrew. Many structures were still intact, but the roofs came off and became dangerous missiles. Because of this, numerous revisions to the South Florida Building Code were made, and these standards became a model for many at-risk communities across the county.

In addition to identifying safe shelters, your local emergency management agency will also outline the proper evacuation routes to be used in the event of a storm. Sometimes evacuations are optional, while other times they are mandatory. Either way, you'll need to know the best and safest route out of town, especially if you are in a low-lying coastal area and a storm

> Evacuation routes should take you a minimum of fifty miles inland, and depending on the storm, that may not be enough. Hurricanes tend to weaken as they pass over land, but a large hurricane can be 600 miles in diameter.

is imminent. The problem begins when you (and everybody else) wait until the very last moment to evacuate. Imagine thousands of cars clogging the one or two evacuation routes hours prior to a storm making landfall.

Storm Activities

Immediately prior to, during, and after any emergency it is often difficult to think clearly and rationally. The time before a hurricane strikes affords you the ability to use a checklist to ensure all critical issues are dealt with. Don't leave storm preparation and recovery steps to chance! As depicted in figure 2.1, a storm activity list specifically addresses issues that must be addressed prior to the storm's arrival. The beauty of this list is its format. It identifies critical tasks that must be completed at the following time increments:

- ⋏ Seventy-two hours prior to the storm's arrival
- ⋏ Thirty-six hours prior to the storm's arrival
- ⋏ Twenty-four hours prior to the storm's arrival
- ⋏ After the storm has passed

The activity list also identifies the responsible employee or contractor and includes space for their phone numbers. As each activity is completed, simply highlight (electronically or manually) and move on to the next activity. This activity list should be distributed to all of your emergency management team. This form works well as a discussion base during conference calls before and after the storm.

Storm Activities	(72 Hours) Before	(36 Hours) Before	(24 Hours) Before	Responsible Employee	Contractor/Company	Office Phone	Cell Phone
Grounds							
Shrubs and hedges	Survey/Trim as needed		Bring all planters into the building				
Trees	Trim all broken/dead limbs						
Light and flag poles			Remove all flags				
Newspaper stands		Bring into building or call newspaper vendor					
Drainage		Clear all drains of debris					
Parking			Remove vehicles from areas near trees				
Access		Make sure manual override on gates are funtional					
Vehicle Fuel Tanks			Top off fuel tanks				
Building Exterior							
Shutters	Inventory all detachable shutters to verify completeness.		Close and secure all shutters				
Window Leaks		If appropriate seal leak. Indicate location on building floor plan. Move any materials/equipment away from leak area.	Same as 36Hrs before				
Rain Gutters		Remove debris from gutter	Remove debris from gutter				
Sand Bags	Notify sand supplier for delivery	Fill and place sand bags in low lying areas (doorways)					
Water Pumps	Notify rental company of impending need	Request pump(s) delivered. (250' - 500' hose)					
Building Interior							
Water System	Notify bottled water contractor of impending need.	Place order for 25 5-gallon water bottles					
Sewer System	Notify Port-o-Pottie of impending need	Request Port-o-Potties. (Store or have delivered post storm)					
A/C System	Inventory portable fans on hand	Rent any additional portable fans necessary					
Generator System	Notify generator maintenance contractor and top off fuel	Contractor check all operations. (Test WITH Building Load)	Contractor MUST have completed all checks and have generator operational.				
UPS System	(Do preventative maintenance check prior to storm season)						
Telephone System	Notify all people on the storm call list. Verify all phone numbers on list.	Make corrections to phone numbers when they are reported	Make corrections to phone numbers when they are reported				
Radio	Set up a radio distribution list. Test all radios and batteries. Repair/replace as needed.	Distribute all radios per distribution list	All radio operators check in				
Garbage Pickup/Removal	Call for a pickup for all Dumpsters						
Food Operations	Notify food service management. Inventory food stocks (for 2-day supply, 4 meals per day). Place order for shortages.	Notify food service staff	Food service manager contact departments to verify meal schedule				
Refrigerators			Set to a colder setting and limit access				
TV & Cable Systems	Check all monitors for proper channel and operations		If antennas used, take down				
Fire Alarm System	Update callout list with monitoring contractor		Remove locks on shut-off valves				
Security System	Check all electro/mechanical locks for proper function. Repair any problems. Notify security contractor to determine personnel status.	Meet with departments to determine the number of people that will be on site DURING storm.	Security guards are briefed on their role and given specific instructions. Security contractor places all guards (including any additional				
Storm Supply Storage	Identify (on map) potential staging areas for supplies to be stored during the storm		Clear out staging area of any non-storm material				
Miscellaneous							
Critical documents	Identify critical documents		Pack documents and move 50 to 75 miles inland away from storm				
Insurance	Review policy. Take video of interior and exterior						
Inventory List	Complete and replinish where necessary						
Contractor Avaliability	Call contractors to ensure availability		Call key contractors again				

Figure 2.1. Storm Activities List: Before the Storm (see Appendix for full view).

Storm Activities	After	Responsible Employee	Contractor Company	Office Phone	Cell Phone
Grounds					
Shrubs and hedges	Survey site. Indicate all damage on site map. Report to landscape contractor				
Trees	Survey site. Indicate all damage on site map. Report to landscape contractor				
Light Poles & Flag Poles	Survey site. Indicate all damage on site map. Report to electrical contractor				
Newspaper stands	Return to original location				
Drainage	Unclog all drains				
Parking	Remove all debris. Indicate helicopter landing areas				
Access	Check all gates for proper operation				
Vehicle Fuel Tanks	Order fuel, if needed				
Building Exterior					
Shutters	Open/Remove all shutters. Store removable shutters in designated area. Open windows to air				
Window Leaks	Report all damage to Window contractor				
Rain Gutters	Remove all debris from gutter				
Sand Bags	Remove sand bags after water has subsided				
Water Pumps	Set-up and run until water subsides				
Building Interior					
Water System	Repair all damages to water system. Disperse water bottles. Replenish water bottles until water system				
Sewer System	Schedule pickups of Port-o-Potties until sewer system is operational				
A/C System	Repair all damage. (Check roof top units visually)				
Generator System	If activated, monitor operations. Check usage and refuel if necessary				
UPS System	Report all irregularities to UPS maintenance contractor				
Telephone System	Inform telecommunications contractor of any irregularities.				
Radio	Radio operators check in per schedule or as needed to report any concerns.				
Garbage Pickup/Removal	Call for pickups as needed during restoration period.				
Food Operations	Feed employees per schedule for duration of restoration process. Restock supplies as needed.				
Refrigerator	If no electricity, open only when needed. When electricity restored, set controls to normal position				
TV and Cable Systems	Repair any damage				
Fire Alarm System	Repair all damage. Replace locks on shut-off valves. Notify monitoring contractor when repairs are complete.				
Security System	Guards monitor buildings and report any irregularities.				
Storm Supply Storage	Facilitate smooth transition of storm material from staging area to area where needed				
Miscellaneous					
Critical Documents	Bring back once building is dry and secure				
Insurance	Take video of interior and exterior				
Inventory List	Replinish used stock after hurricane.				
Contractor Avaliability Li	Call contractors to assign tasks				

Figure 2.2. Storm Activities List: After the Storm (see Appendix for full view).

Figure 2.2 depicts the same storm activity list, except this version is to be used after the storm has passed. Again, as each of the activities is completed, simply highlight and move on to the next task.

What To Do Before a Hurricane Lands and During the Storm

You will be limited in what you can do during the storm. If you followed your plan, now is the time to ride out the storm in a safe shelter or an area out of the storm path. Now is not the time to let your guard down when it comes to safety. Be especially cautious when using candles or kerosene lamps. Many buildings (and people) have survived a storm but died in a fire resulting from carelessness with lamps or candles.

If electrical power is lost, turn off major appliances at the breaker panel to avoid a power surge. Unplug sensitive equipment such as televisions and computers. If possible, move these items to upper level floors and away from windows and doors. As a side note, make sure data from your computer is properly backed up and perhaps even stored offsite or in the "cloud."

- Listen to radio or television newscasts. If a hurricane "Watch" is issued, you typically have twenty-four to thirty-six hours before the hurricane hits land.
- Talk with household members. Make sure everyone knows where to meet and who to call, in case you are separated. Consider the needs of relatives and neighbors with special needs.
- Secure your home. Close storm shutters. Secure outdoor objects or bring them indoors. Moor your boat if time permits. If instructed, turn off utilities at the main valves.
- Gather several days' supply of water and food for each household member. Water systems may become contaminated or damaged. Sterilize (with diluted bleach solution of one part bleach to ten parts water) and fill the bathtub to ensure a supply of safe water in case you are unable or told not to evacuate.
- Be sure to pack bug spray and sunscreen for post-storm conditions.
- If you are evacuating, take your disaster supply kit with you to the shelter. Remember that alcoholic beverages and weapons are prohibited within shelters. Also, pets are not usually allowed in a public shelter due to health reasons. (Contact your local humane society for additional information on pets.)
- Prepare to evacuate. Fuel your car—service stations may be closed after the storm. If you do not have a car, make arrangements for transportation with a friend or relative.
- Review evacuation routes.
- Evacuate to an inland location if:

    Local authorities announce an evacuation and you live in an evacuation zone.

    You live in a mobile home or temporary structure—they are particularly hazardous during hurricanes no matter how well fastened to the ground.

    You live in a high-rise. Hurricane winds are stronger at higher elevations.

You live on the coast, on a floodplain near a river or inland waterway. You feel you are in danger.

▲   When authorities order an evacuation:

Leave immediately.
Follow evacuation routes announced by local officials.
Stay away from coastal areas, riverbanks, and streams.
Tell others where you are going.

▲   If you are not required or are unable to evacuate, stay indoors during the hurricane and away from windows and glass doors. Keep curtains and blinds closed. Do not be fooled if there is a lull, it could be the eye of the storm—winds will pick up again.

Turn off utilities if told to do so by authorities.
If not instructed to turn off, turn the refrigerator to its coldest setting and keep closed.
Turn off propane tanks.

▲   In strong winds, follow these rules:

Take refuge in a small interior room, closet, or hallway.
Close all interior doors. Secure and brace external doors.
In a two-story residence, go to an interior first-floor room, such as a bathroom or closet.
In a multiple-story building, go to the first or second floors and stay in interior rooms away from windows.
Lie on the floor under a table or another sturdy object.

▲   Avoid using the phone except for serious emergencies. Local authorities need first priority on telephone lines.
▲   See the "Evacuation" sections for important information.

Windows, skylights, doors, and other building openings often represent the weakest link in a building; therefore, it would be prudent to avoid such areas during a storm. Instead, take refuge in a closet or bathroom near the center of a building and away for exterior openings such as windows and doors.

When the storm is passing through, beware of misinterpreting the eye of the storm as the end of the storm. Remember, a hurricane is produced when winds begin a counter-clockwise rotary circulation around a center point. Within this center point or eye, hurricane strength winds are absent, and as this eye passes over, you may be fooled into thinking the storm has passed. Again, don't go outside until the National Weather Service has given the all-clear.

What to Do After a Hurricane

At some point the storm will have passed and efforts to begin restoration should be started. The best source of information concerning the storm status is the NOAA radio or local media.

When the storm has passed, the first responsibility is to assist those injured. The first hours immediately following a hurricane are usually chaotic. Many buildings will be without utilities including water, telephone, and electricity. Having a plan in place will help you to remain calm and focused on the most important tasks. The "Storm Activities List: After the Storm" (figure 2.2, above) is an example of an audit that will help to focus your recovery efforts.

If you were evacuated prior to the storm, you may not be able to immediately return to your home or place of business. In these affected areas, access is often restricted by local police and National Guard. Keep this in mind if you leave your property. Will you be able to conduct business away from the office? Have you thought about a remote location for conducting business and staging?

When you do finally return to your home or business, beware of snakes and other animals that may have been driven to higher ground because of flooding. Bugs and mosquitoes will be attracted to the wet conditions, so make sure you have packed adequate protection. Also be sure to pack adequate sunscreen. You'll be spending more time outdoors while trying to evaluate the damage and make repairs. Many natural shade providers such as trees and brush will be ripped out and displaced by the velocity of the winds. The sun will do more than give you a nasty burn.

Working in the sun will quickly dehydrate the body as well. Take care to listen to your body, hydrate when necessary, and take breaks whenever you feel the need. Protect yourself from the elements early on, and you'll be able to successfully move from the chaotic post-storm phase to controlled and productive recovery stage.

After a hurricane, water seems to be everywhere. Whether from a storm surge or relentless rains, there is a good chance you will be surrounded by standing water. One of the best steps to solve this problem is to begin pumping water from the premises and into other areas such as retention ponds or off-site locations. Don't forget to unclog roof drains, gutters, and catch basins that might be impeding the flow of water from your surrounding area as well. If water has made its way into your building, and if it is not currently raining, open the windows to ventilate and dry the building.

General Post-Storm Guidelines

    ⌄   Stay where you are if you are in a safe location until local authorities say it is safe to leave. If you evacuated the community, do not return to the area until authorities say it is safe to return.

- Keep tuned to local radio or television stations for information about caring for your household, where to find medical help, how to apply for financial assistance, and so on.
- Drive only when necessary. Streets will be filled with debris. Roads may have weakened and could collapse. Do not drive on flooded or barricaded roads or bridges. Closed roads are for your protection. As little as six inches of water may cause you to lose control of your vehicle—two feet of water will carry most cars away.
- Do not drink or prepare food with tap water until notified by officials that it is safe to do so.
- Consider your family's health and safety needs. Be aware of symptoms of stress and fatigue. Keep your household together and seek crisis counseling if you have need.
- Talk with your children about what has happened and how they can help during the recovery. Being involved will help them deal with the situation.
- Consider the needs of your neighbors. People often become isolated during hurricanes.
- Stay away from disaster areas unless local authorities request volunteers. If you are needed, bring your own drinking water, food, and sleeping gear.
- Stay away from riverbanks and streams until potential flooding has passed. Do not allow children, especially under the age of thirteen, to play in flooded areas. There is a high risk of injury or drowning in areas that may appear safe.
- Stay away from moving water. Moving water only six inches deep can sweep you off your feet. Standing water may be electrically charged from underground or downed power lines.
- Stay away from downed power lines and report them to the power company. Report to local officials any broken gas, sewer, or water mains.
- Don't use candles or other open flames indoors. Use a flashlight to inspect damage.
- Set up a manageable schedule to repair property.
- Contact your insurance agent. An adjuster will be assigned to visit your home. To prepare:

> Take photos of your belongings and your home or video them.
> Separate damaged and undamaged belongings.
> Locate your financial records.
> Keep detailed records of cleanup costs.

- See the "Post-Event Restoration" chapter for more important information.

Contractor Availability

If you are a business owner or manager, your company probably will have key people assigned to lend their assistance during storm mode. Business units such as human resources, procurement, engineering, and facility management will play an important role in preparation and recovery. No doubt outside assistance will be needed as well. With this in mind, create a list of available contractors. The "Contractor Availability Form" depicted in figure 2.3 works well for this task.

Seventy-two hours prior to the storm's predicted landfall, contractors should be contacted and their availability pre- and post-storm confirmed. This critical step must be completed prior to the storm. Understand that contractors may agree to offer assistance after the storm, but because of circumstances out of their control, they may not be available. Access roads could be blocked, their offices could be heavily damaged, or some other problem might exist. For this reason, you need to have alternate contractors available. The "Contractor Availability Form" (figure 2.3) includes tabs for alternate contractors.

Contractor Availability Form: First Alternate

Issue	Contractor	Contact	Office Phone	Cell Phone	AVAILABLE	NOT AVAILABLE	LEFT MESSAGE	Comments
Generator								
Landscaper								
Sign Maker								
Parking Lot Sweeper								
Barricade Supplier								
Tool Rental								
Security Guard Service								
Motorized Gate								
Fence Contractor								
Roofing Contractor								
Ice Machine								
Ice Supplier								
Dumpster Rental								
Refuse Company								
Trash Hauler								
Port-O-Pottie Supplier								
Computer Systems								
Computer Network Tech								
Phone Technician								
HVAC Contractor								
Electrical Contractor								
Engineering								
Architect								
Plumber								
Locksmith								
Glass Company								
Movers								
Carpet Cleaner								
Janitorial								
Laundry Services								
Elevator Service								
Fire Protection Vendor								
Security System								
Electric Utility								
Gas Utility								
Water Utility								
Phone Company								

Figure 2.3. Contractor Availability Form.

Post-Storm Inventory of Materials

Recovery from a storm occurs more quickly if you have an inventory of equipment and tools to work with. Again, don't leave the creation of this inventory up to chance. In addition to the typical emergency inventory, employees involved in storm recovery should be responsible for their own "survival" package. Necessary items include:

- Two pairs of sturdy shoes
- Multiple changes of clothes
- Toiletries
- Sunblock and hat
- Essential medicines (especially prescription)
- Replacement glasses or extra contact lenses
- Cell phone including extra batteries and car charger
- Automobile with fuel topped off
- Food and drink for the first day

While conducting audits of your building and grounds, be aware of downed power lines and broken water or sewer lines. Report these problems immediately to the proper utility company, police, or fire department. Don't try to negotiate around downed electrical lines. Be safe—and smart!

Remember: For areas susceptible to storms, keeping a stockpile of food and other necessities is essential. If you keep a supply of necessities, don't forget that most of these items have a limited shelf life. Plan to rotate items such as food and batteries on an annual basis.

Thunderstorms

Thunderstorms are very common and affect great numbers of people each year. Despite their small size in comparison to hurricanes and winter storms, all thunderstorms are dangerous. Every thunderstorm produces lightning. Other associated dangers of thunderstorms include tornadoes, strong winds, hail, and flash flooding. Flash flooding is responsible for more fatalities—more than 140 annually—than any other thunderstorm-associated hazard.

Some thunderstorms do not produce rain that reaches the ground. These are generically referred to as dry thunderstorms and are most prevalent in the western United States. Known to spawn wildfires, these storms occur when there is a large layer of dry air between the base of the cloud and the ground. The falling raindrops evaporate, but lightning can still reach the ground.

Thunderstorm Facts

- ▲ Thunderstorms may occur singly, in clusters, or in lines.
- ▲ Some of the most severe weather occurs when a single thunderstorm affects one location for an extended time.
- ▲ Thunderstorms typically produce heavy rain for a brief period, anywhere from thirty minutes to an hour.
- ▲ Warm, humid conditions are very favorable for thunderstorm development.
- ▲ A typical thunderstorm is fifteen miles in diameter and lasts an average of thirty minutes.
- ▲ Of the estimated 100,000 thunderstorms each year in the United States, about 10 percent are classified as severe.
- ▲ A thunderstorm is classified as severe if it produces hail at least three-quarters of an inch in diameter, has winds of fifty-eight miles per hour or higher, or produces a tornado.

Lightning

The ingredient that defines a thunderstorm is lightning. Since lightning creates thunder, a storm producing lightning is called a thunderstorm. Lightning occurs during all thunderstorms. Lightning results from the buildup and discharge of electrical energy between positively and negatively charged areas. The unpredictability of lightning increases the risk to individuals and property. On average, in the United States, 300 people are injured and eighty people are killed each year by lightning. Although most lightning victims survive, people struck by lightning often report a variety of long-term, debilitating symptoms, including memory loss, attention deficits, sleep disorders, numbness, dizziness, stiffness in joints, irritability, fatigue, weakness, muscle spasms, depression, and an inability to sit for a long period of time.

Know the Terminology

Severe Thunderstorm Watch: Tells you when and where severe thunderstorms are likely to occur. Watch the sky and stay tuned to radio or television to know when warnings are issued.

Severe Thunderstorm Warning: Issued when severe weather has been reported by spotters or indicated by radar. Warnings indicate imminent danger to life and property to those in the path of the storm.

What to Do Before Thunderstorms Approach

1. Know the calculation to determine how close you are to a thunderstorm:

   Count the number of seconds between a flash of lightning and the next clap of thunder. Divide this number by five to determine the distance to the lightning in miles.

2. Remove dead or rotting trees and branches that could fall and cause injury or damage during a severe thunderstorm.

3. When a thunderstorm approaches, secure outdoor objects that could blow away or cause damage. Shutter windows, if possible, and secure outside doors. If shutters are not available, close window blinds, shades, or curtains.

What to Do During a Thunderstorm

When thunderstorms threaten your area, get inside a home, building, or hard-top automobile (not a convertible) and stay away from metallic objects and fixtures.

If you are inside a home:

- Avoid showering or bathing. Plumbing and bathroom fixtures can conduct electricity.
- Avoid using a corded telephone, except for emergencies. Cordless and cellular telephones are safe to use.
- Unplug appliances and other electrical items, such as computers, and turn off air conditioners. Power surges from lightning can cause serious damage.
- Use your battery-operated NOAA Weather Radio for updates from local officials.

If you are outside, with no time to reach a safe location, follow these recommendations:

- In a forest, seek shelter in a low area under a thick growth of small trees.
- In open areas, go to a low place, such as a ravine or valley. Be alert for flash floods.
- Do not stand under a natural lightning rod, such as a tall, isolated tree in an open area.
- Do not stand on a hilltop, in an open field, on the beach, or in a boat on the water.
- Avoid isolated sheds or other small structures in open areas.
- Get away from open water. If you are boating or swimming, get to land and find shelter immediately.
- Get away from anything metal: tractors, farm equipment, motorcycles, golf carts, golf clubs, bicycles, and such.
- Stay away from wire fences, clotheslines, metal pipes, rails, and other metallic paths that could carry lightning to you from some distance away.
- If you feel your hair stand on end (which indicates that lightning is about to strike), squat low to the ground on the balls of your feet. Place your hands over your ears and your head between your knees.
- Make yourself the smallest target possible and minimize your contact with the ground. DO NOT lie flat on the ground.

Remember the following facts and safety tips about lightning:

- ▲ Lightning often strikes outside of heavy rain and may occur as far as ten miles away from any rainfall.
- ▲ "Heat lightning" is actually lightning from a thunderstorm too far away for thunder to be heard. However, the storm may be moving in your direction!
- ▲ Most lightning deaths and injuries occur when people are caught outdoors in the summer months during the afternoon and evening.
- ▲ Lightning starts many fires in the western United States and Alaska.
- ▲ Lightning can occur from cloud-to-cloud, within a cloud, cloud-to-ground, or cloud-to-air.
- ▲ Your chances of being struck by lightning are estimated to be 1 in 600,000 but could be better by following safety tips.

Lightning Injuries

Contact your local emergency management office or American Red Cross chapter for information on CPR and first-aid classes. Points to remember if you encounter a lightning-strike injury:

- ▲ Lightning-strike victims carry no electrical charge and should be attended to immediately.
- ▲ If breathing has stopped, begin mouth-to-mouth resuscitation. If the heart has stopped, a trained person should administer CPR.
- ▲ If the victim has a pulse and is breathing, look for other possible injuries. Check for burns where the lightning entered and left the body. Be alert also for nervous system damage, broken bones, and loss of hearing or eyesight.

General Thunderstorm Safety Tips

- ▲ Postpone outdoor activities if thunderstorms are likely.
- ▲ Remember the 30/30 lightning safety rule: go inside if, after seeing lighting, you cannot count to thirty before hearing thunder. Stay indoors for thirty minutes after hearing the last clap of thunder.
- ▲ Rubber-soled shoes and rubber tires provide NO protection from lightning.
- ▲ The steel frame of a hard-topped vehicle provides increased protection if you are not touching metal.

Although you may be injured if lightning strikes your car, you are much safer inside a vehicle than outside.

Floods

Floods are among the most common hazards in the United States. However, all floods are not alike. **Riverine floods** develop slowly, sometimes over a period of days. **Flash floods** can develop quickly, sometimes in just a few minutes, without any visible signs of rain. Flash floods often have a dangerous wall of roaring water that carries a deadly cargo of rocks, mud, and other debris and can sweep away most things in its path. Overland flooding occurs outside a defined river or stream, such as when a levee is breached, but still can be destructive. Flooding can also occur from a dam break producing effects similar to flash floods.

Flood effects can be very local, impacting a neighborhood or community, or very large, affecting entire river basins and multiple states. Be aware of flood hazards no matter where you live, but especially if you live in a low-lying area, near water, or downstream from a dam. Even very small streams, gullies, creeks, culverts, dry streambeds, or low-lying ground that appear harmless in dry weather can flood. Snowmelt, broken water pipes, breached dams, tsunamis, hurricanes, excessive rain, or even lack of permeable soil (i.e., in parking lots) can trigger a flood. Every state is at risk from this hazard.

Floods kill an average of 150 people per year and cause billions of dollars in damage. Approximately 9 million people currently reside in identified floodplains.

In addition to the actual danger created by a flood, additional danger exists from water contamination, electrocution, structural instability, and drowning. Based on the likelihood of a flood affecting your property—commercial or residential—it is wise to include flood risks in your emergency planning efforts.

Case Study 1: The Great Chicago Flood, 1992

One of the more unusual floods in the United States occurred in Chicago in an event that became known as the Great Chicago Flood. This flood was not the result or storms or snowmelt. It was the result of millions of gallons of water from the Chicago River pouring into the basements of more than 500 buildings in Chicago's downtown Loop. The river water was able to enter the basements because a contractor driving pilings around the Kinzie Street Bridge penetrated an abandoned tunnel system, which once provided downtown buildings with coal during the early part of the century. The tunnel system was largely forgotten and unused except by utility workers who used the tunnel system to run cables and conduits. When the lining of the tunnel system was penetrated, water filled the tunnels, which in turn filled the basements connected to the intricate tunnel system. During the early stages of the flooding, water began to rise at nearly four feet per hour.

The economic loss, including repairs, cleanup, and lost business exceeded $2 billion. This flood proved costly because basement areas traditionally house the mechanical heart of buildings. Vital and expensive equipment such as electrical centers, generators, elevator rooms, chillers, and boilers are housed in basements. Thanks to the flooded basements, much of this equipment was rendered useless. Although no deaths were caused by this emergency, some 250,000 people were impacted by the flood. Hundreds of buildings were shut down temporarily, some up to three weeks.

What made this emergency so frustrating is the fact that the tunnels did not flood until six months after the pilings were driven. Engineers had noted some unusual activity in the tunnel and even provided an estimate of $10,000 to make the needed repairs! Obviously, the needed repairs didn't happen in time and the results were disastrous.

Case Study 2: New Orleans Flood, 1995

During the spring of 1995, heavy thunderstorms drenched Louisiana and the Mississippi Delta. During a sixteen-day spree, parts of Louisiana recorded twelve to seventeen inches of rain. A period of normalized weather extended for the next three weeks and then the severe rain began to fall again. In many areas the rain fell quickly and resulted in flash flooding. From May 8 to May 10, 1995, up to twenty-six inches of rain fell on portions of southeastern Louisiana and other coastal areas extending all the way to the Florida Panhandle. In just eight hours, more than fifteen inches of rain fell at the National Weather Service's Slidell Office.

Know the Terminology

Flood Watch: Flooding is possible. Stay tuned to NOAA Weather Radio or commercial radio or television for information. Watches are issued twelve to thirty-six hours in advance of a possible flooding event.

Flash Flood Watch: Flash flooding is possible. Be prepared to move to higher ground. A flash flood could occur without any warning. Listen to NOAA Weather Radio or commercial radio or television for additional information.

Flood Warning: Flooding is occurring or will occur soon. If advised to evacuate, do so immediately.

Flash Flood Warning: A flash flood is occurring. Seek higher ground on foot immediately.

Severe flooding was reported in Slidell, which borders Lake Pontchartrain, causing many homes to be evacuated. Flooding continued to New Orleans, which is particularly susceptible to flooding because it is, on average, six feet below sea level and is bordered by Lake Pontchartrain and the Mississippi River.

Neighboring states Texas, Oklahoma, and Mississippi were also hit hard by the continued rainfall. Some areas received twenty-five inches of rainfall in a five-day period. More than thirty-two deaths were recorded and damages of more than $5 billion were assessed.

Identifying Your Flood Risk

Find out if you live in a flood plain or if there is a history of flooding in the area. The Federal Emergency Management Agency (FEMA) has mapped most of the floodplains and determined the risk for those areas. FEMA's Flood Insurance Study (FIS) contains a Flood Insurance Rate Map (FIRM), which will be key in identifying your risk. The Flood Insurance Rate Map (FIRM) identifies Special Flood Hazard Areas (SFHAs), designates flood zones, and establishes Base Flood Elevations (BFE). The Base Flood Elevation is the elevation of water that results from a "100-year Flood."

For more information on flood zones and maps, go to FEMA's Flood Map Service Center at msc.fema.gov/portal. For information on FIRMs, go to www.fema.gov/flood-insurance -rate-map-firm.

The next step is to examine the FIRM to determine your exposure. If the exposure is great, a specific flood plan should be created for your property.

When evaluating your exposure to flood emergencies, the one hundred–year flood zone is the standard benchmark. If you fall within this zone, you should plan for the inevitable flood emergency. The one hundred–year flood is often misunderstood. In reality, the one hundred–year flood has a 1 percent chance of occurring in any given year. Such a flood may, however, occur two years in a row or multiple times during a one hundred–year time frame.

Your property insurance provider will have access to FEMA's flood zone maps. When evaluating insurance, remember most policies do not include damage that occurs as a result of floods. A separate flood policy must be purchased.

When looking at purchasing flood insurance consider these points:

- Flood losses are not covered under homeowners' insurance policies.
- FEMA manages the National Flood Insurance Program, which makes federally backed flood insurance available in communities that agree to adopt and enforce floodplain management ordinances to reduce future flood damage.
- There is a thirty-day waiting period before flood insurance goes into effect, so don't delay.
- Flood insurance is available whether the building is in or out of the identified flood-prone area.

What to Do Before a Flood

When a flood threatens, your best source of information is the NOAA radio. If you do not have a NOAA radio, watch the television or dial into a local radio station and stay tuned for more information and further instructions. Most smartphones have a facility for text alerts on flash floods and other emergencies. Remember to have a battery-powered radio and additional fresh batteries because electrical service may be interrupted during the emergency.

Dams and Flood Risk

If you are located near a river and within fifty miles of a dam, you are exposed to an elevated risk of flooding. If the dam were breached, the water could be released and could cause an emergency. Check with your local planning agencies for their emergency action plans. If you are uncertain about the existence of dams, visit the Association of State Dam Safety Officials (ASDSO) at www.damsafety.org or e-mail at info@damsafety.org.

Another resource is the National Inventory of Dams (NID) at nid.usace.army.mil/cm_apex /f?p=838:12. The NID database is updated every two years and includes more than 76,000 dams in the country. Unfortunately, due to the potential for terrorist activities, the Web site is not open to the general public. You may visit the site and leave contact information for the site administrators. They will help you determine the state official who will be able to answer your questions.

In the United States, thousands of dams exist and over half of them have Emergency Action Plans that identify areas downstream that would be flooded in the event of a breach.

Here are a few of the guidelines for before a flood threat:

1. Become familiar with local emergency agencies and their plans and official flood warning signals. Local officials are good sources to find out how you can protect your home from flooding.
2. Identify dams in your area and determine whether they pose a hazard to you.
3. Purchase a NOAA Weather Radio with battery backup and a tone-alert feature that automatically alerts you when a watch or warning is issued (tone alert is not available in some areas). Purchase a battery-powered commercial radio and extra batteries.
4. Be prepared to evacuate. Learn your community's flood evacuation routes and where to find high ground.
5. Talk to your household about flooding. Plan a place to meet your household in case you are separated from one another in a disaster and cannot return home. Choose an out-of-town contact for everyone to call to say they are okay. In some emergencies, calling out-of-state is possible even when local phone lines are down.
6. Determine how you would care for household members who may live elsewhere but might need your help in a flood. Determine any special needs your neighbors might have.
7. Prepare to survive on your own for at least three days. Assemble a disaster supply kit. Keep a stock of food and extra drinking water.
8. Keep a supply of sandbags for creating water barriers and lumber for repairs.
9. Move valuables to higher ground (or higher floors).
10. Know how to shut off electricity, gas, and water at main switches and valves. Know where gas pilot lights are located and how the heating system works.

11. Consider purchasing a generator for power and water portable pumps with discharge hoses to remove water from building after the event.
12. Consider options for protecting your property:

    ✕   Make a record of your personal property. Take photographs or videos of your belongings. Store these documents in a safe place.

    ✕   Keep insurance policies, deeds, property records, and other important papers in a safe place away from your home.

    ✕   Elevate furnace, water heater, and electric panel to higher floors or the attic if they are susceptible to flooding.

    ✕   Install "check valves" in sewer traps to prevent floodwater from backing up into the drains of your home.

    ✕   Construct barriers, such as levees, berms, and floodwalls to stop floodwater from entering the building.

    ✕   Seal walls in basements with waterproofing compounds to avoid seepage.

    ✕   Call your local building department or emergency management office for more information.

Danger: Flash Floods

According to FEMA, nearly half of all flash flood fatalities are automobile related. When a vehicle stalls in floodwaters, the water's momentum is transferred to the car. For each foot that water rises, 500 pounds of lateral force is applied to the car; however, the biggest factor is buoyancy. For each foot the water rises up the side of the car, the car displaces 1,500 pounds of water. In effect, the car weighs 1,500 pounds less for each foot the water rises. A depth of two feet of water will carry away most automobiles.

What to Do During a Flood

1. Be aware of flash flooding. *If there is any possibility of a flash flood, move immediately to higher ground. Do not wait for instructions to move.*
2. Listen to radio or television stations for local information.
3. Be aware of streams, drainage channels, canyons, and other areas known to flood suddenly. Flash floods can occur in these areas with or without such typical warning signs as rain clouds or heavy rain.
4. If local authorities issue a flood watch, prepare to evacuate:

    ✕   Secure your home. If you have time, tie down or bring outdoor equipment and lawn furniture inside. Move essential items to the upper floors.

    ⅄   If instructed, turn off utilities at the main switches or valves. Disconnect electrical appliances. Do not touch electrical equipment if you are wet or standing in water.

    ⅄   Fill the bathtub with water in case water becomes contaminated or services are cut off. Before filling the tub, sterilize it with a diluted bleach solution.

5. Do not walk through moving water. Six inches of moving water can knock you off your feet. If you must walk in a flooded area, walk where the water is not moving. Use a stick to check the firmness of the ground in front of you.

6. Always watch for downed electrical lines (report immediately).

7. Do not drive into flooded areas. Six inches of water will reach the bottom of most passenger cars causing loss of control and possible stalling. A foot of water will float many vehicles. Two feet of water will wash away almost all vehicles. If floodwaters rise around your car, abandon the car and move to higher ground, if you can do so safely. You and your vehicle can be quickly swept away as floodwaters rise.

8. Beware of using fire (candle or cooking) because gas may escape from ruptured lines.

What to Do After a Flood

1. Avoid floodwaters. The water may be contaminated by oil, gasoline, or raw sewage. The water may also be electrically charged from underground or downed power lines.

2. Avoid moving water. Moving water only six inches deep can sweep you off your feet.

3. Be aware of areas where floodwaters have receded. Roads may have weakened and could collapse under the weight of a car.

4. Stay away from downed power lines and report them to the power company.

5. Stay away from designated disaster areas unless authorities ask for volunteers.

6. Return home only when authorities indicate it is safe. Stay out of buildings if they are surrounded by floodwaters. Use extreme caution when entering buildings. There may be hidden damage, particularly in foundations.

7. Consider your family's health and safety needs:

    ⅄   Wash hands frequently with soap and clean water if you come in contact with floodwaters.

    ⅄   Throw away food that has come in contact with floodwaters.

    ⅄   Listen for news reports to learn whether the community's water supply is safe to drink.

        ⅄   Listen to news reports for information about where to get assistance for housing, clothing, and food.

        ⅄   Seek necessary medical care at the nearest medical facility.

8. Service damaged septic tanks, cesspools, pits, and leaching systems as soon as possible. Damaged sewage systems are serious health hazards.
9. Use water portable pumps with discharge hoses to remove water from building.
10. Remember to properly dehumidify the building after cleanup.
11. Contact your insurance agent. If your policy covers your situation, an adjuster will be assigned to visit your home. To prepare:

        ⅄   Take photos of your belongings and your home or video them.

        ⅄   Separate damaged and undamaged belongings.

        ⅄   Locate your financial records.

        ⅄   Keep detailed records of cleanup costs.

12. If your residence has been flooded obtain a copy of "Repairing Your Flooded Home" from the local American Red Cross chapter.

3

Earthquakes, Tsunamis, Volcanoes, and Landslides

Earthquakes

When you think of earthquakes, chances are you think of California. True, the Pacific Coast seems to be particularly susceptible to earthquakes. Earthquakes are most likely to occur west of the Rocky Mountains, although forty states have been identified as having at least a moderate earthquake risk. Even areas not typically thought of as susceptible to earthquakes such as Boston, Massachusetts, and Charleston, South Carolina, have experienced seismic activity.

Earthquakes occur without warning as the earth's tectonic plates stress and shift. An earthquake is a sudden shaking of the earth caused by the breaking and shifting of rock beneath the earth's surface. Earthquakes can result in fires, explosions, and landslides. Earthquakes can also cause huge ocean waves, called tsunamis, which travel long distances over water until they crash into coastal areas.

Although earthquakes typically last only seconds, they can inflict tremendous damage. At their worst and most violent, earthquakes can cause buildings and highways to collapse. Even if a total collapse does not occur, people can be injured by falling objects and flying glass. Additionally, downed power lines and ruptured gas lines add to the casualties. Fire sprinklers are often triggered by earthquakes, which results in even more property damage.

After the earthquake has occurred, it is not uncommon to experience multiple aftershocks. These aftershocks are particularly dangerous because they may occur days later when unsuspecting people are engaged in emergency recovery efforts.

Case Study 1: Loma Prieta, 1989

At 5:04 p.m. on October 17, 1989, an earthquake measuring 7.1 on the Richter scale rocked the California Coast. The epicenter of this powerful quake was approximately sixty miles south of San Francisco, but the greatest impact occurred in the heavily populated San Francisco/Oakland Bay areas. The shockwaves were felt as far south as San Diego and west to Nevada.

Many people will remember the horror of seeing an elevated section of Interstate 880 in Oakland that had collapsed onto the lower section below. The majority of the sixty-two fatalities caused by the Loma Pricta earthquake occurred in this location. Also notable was the postponement of the third game of the World Series that was to be held that evening at Candlestick Park in the Bay area.

Damage and economic impact was estimated at about $10 billion. Most of the damaged and destroyed structures were residential homes, but more than 2,500 commercial buildings were damaged and 147 were totally destroyed. Sixty-two people died and more than 3,700 were injured. Thankfully, these numbers were lower than they might have been considering the timing of the earthquake. Many people were just leaving work. If Candlestick Park, with its arriving fans, had been hit more intensely, one fears to think about the loss of life that may have occurred.

Case Study 2: Northridge, California, 1994

The Loma Prieta earthquake of 1989 was fresh in the minds of many Californians when their worst fears were realized once again. At 4:31 a.m. on January 17, 1994, a quake measuring 6.8 on the Richter scale struck Southern California. This earthquake became known as the Northridge earthquake. Although not as intense as the earlier Loma Prieta quake, the Northridge earthquake caused a greater economic impact. Thousands of aftershocks, many measuring 5.0 on the Richter scale, continued to rock the area, further destroying properties and making the recovery effort even more difficult.

The cost was high, both in lives and property damage. Fifty-seven people lost their lives and more than 8,700 were injured, 1,500 of those seriously. Well over 100,000 structures were damaged, while nearly 4,000 of these structures were severely damaged and tagged for condemnation. Many properties were without electricity, water, or gas for an extended period of time. Fires started as a result of the earthquake, which added to the damage. In retail businesses and warehouses, large inventories were lost due to earthquake damage, fire, or water from fire sprinkler systems. All told, the economic impact of this twenty-second event and its aftershocks reached an estimated $20 billion.

Although the cost of the quake was large, California is no stranger to the devastating effects of earthquakes, and certainly past experiences helped to reduce the negative effects and recovery time necessary. Many of the properties destroyed were between thirty and forty years old, built prior to stricter building codes. Response teams were able to quickly provide relief and ascertain the extent of damage. Additionally the early pre-dawn timing of this quake, no doubt, preserved the lives of people who might have otherwise been traveling on roads and bridges that collapsed.

Know the Terminology

Aftershock: an earthquake of similar or lesser intensity that follows the main earthquake.

Earthquake: a sudden slipping or movement of a portion of the earth's crust accompanied and followed by a series of vibrations.

Epicenter: the area of the earth's surface directly above the origin of an earthquake.

Fault: the earth's crust slips along a fault, an area of weakness where two sections of crust have separated. The crust may only move a few inches to a few feet in a severe earthquake.

Magnitude: indicates how much energy was released. This energy can be measured on a recording device and graphically displayed through lines on a Richter Scale. A magnitude of 7.0 on the Richter Scale would indicate a very strong earthquake. Each whole number on the scale represents an increase of about 30 times the energy released. Therefore, an earthquake measuring 6.0 is about thirty times more powerful than one measuring 5.0.

Seismic Waves: vibrations that travel outward from the center of the earthquake at speeds of several miles per second. These vibrations can shake some buildings so rapidly that they collapse.

What to Do Before an Earthquake

The first step is to determine the probability of an earthquake affecting your location. This can be accomplished by visiting the U.S. Geological Survey's Earthquake Hazards Program Web site to find their Seismic Hazard Maps and Data at earthquake.usgs.gov/hazards/products/conterminous/index.php#2014. Many maps detailing earthquake probability similar to the one shown in figure 3.1 are available at this site.

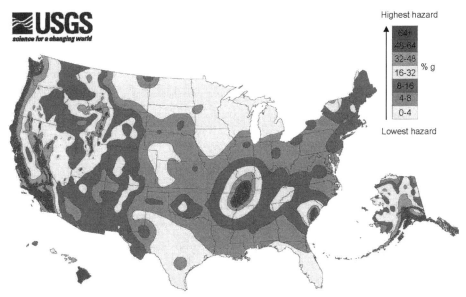

Figure 3.1. USGS National Seismic Hazard Map.

If you are located in an area identified as 2 percent g (peak acceleration due to gravity) or less, you have a relatively low probability of an earthquake occurrence and may elect not to spend time on this hazard. Conversely, if you are located in an area of 3 percent g or more, you have a greater probability of an earthquake occurrence and should plan for earthquake emergencies.

Prior to an earthquake you should have a detailed plan for handling the emergency both during and after. Also:

1. Look for elements in your home that could become a hazard in an earthquake:

    ⋏ Repair defective electrical wiring, leaky gas lines, and inflexible utility connections.

    ⋏ Bolt down water heaters and gas appliances (have an automatic gas shut-off device installed that is triggered by an earthquake).

    ⋏ Place large or heavy objects on lower shelves. Fasten shelves to walls. Brace high and top-heavy objects.

    ⋏ Store bottled foods, glass, china, and other breakables on low shelves or in cabinets that can fasten shut.

    ⋏ Anchor overhead lighting fixtures.

    ⋏ Check and repair deep plaster cracks in ceilings and foundations. Get expert advice, especially if there are signs of structural defects.

    ⋏ Be sure the residence is firmly anchored to its foundation.

    ⋏ Install flexible-pipe fittings to avoid gas or water leaks. Flexible fittings are more resistant to breakage.

2. Know where and how to shut off electricity, gas, and water at main switches and valves. Check with your local utilities for instructions.

3. Hold earthquake drills with your household:

    ⋏ Locate safe spots in each room under a sturdy table or against an inside wall. Reinforce this information by physically placing yourself and your household in these locations.

    ⋏ Identify danger zones in each room—near windows where glass can shatter, bookcases or furniture that can fall over, or under ceiling fixtures that could fall down.

4. Develop a plan for reuniting your household after an earthquake. Establish an out-of-town telephone contact for household members to call to let others know that they are okay.

5. Review your insurance policies. Some damage may be covered even without specific earthquake insurance.

6. Protect important home and business documents.

7. Prepare to survive on your own for at least three days. Assemble a disaster supply kit. Keep a stock of food and extra drinking water.

8. An emergency survival kit should include:

- Water for three days
- Nonperishable food for three days
- Portable battery-powered radio
- Extra batteries
- Basic tools (for utility shut-off)
- Personal medicine
- General first aid kit
- Clothing
- Money

What to Do During an Earthquake

During an earthquake it is imperative that you remain calm.

If you are outdoors, move away from buildings, radio towers, light poles, and overhead utility lines. In a high rise building, stay off of elevators. If you are on an elevator when an earthquake occurs, stay calm. The elevator may quit working. If power is lost, most elevators will automatically go to the lowest level. Don't be surprised if fire alarms or fire sprinkler systems go off.

Stay inside until the shaking stops and it is safe to go outside. Most injuries during earthquakes occur when falling objects hit people as they enter or exit buildings.

Remember these guidelines:

1. **Drop, Cover, and Hold On!** Minimize your movements during an earthquake to a few steps to a nearby safe place. Stay indoors until the shaking has stopped and you are sure exiting is safe.

2. If you are indoors, take cover under a sturdy desk, table, or bench, or against an inside wall, and hold on. Stay away from glass, windows, outside doors, or walls, and anything that could fall, such as lighting fixtures or furniture. If you are in bed, stay there, hold on, and protect your head with a pillow, unless you are under a heavy light fixture that could fall.

3. If there isn't a table or desk near you, cover your face and head with your arms and crouch in an inside corner of the building. Doorways should only be used for shelter if they are in close proximity to you and if you know that they have a strongly supported load-bearing doorway.

4. If you are outdoors, stay there. Move away from buildings, streetlights, and utility wires.

5. If you live in an apartment building or other multihousehold structure with many levels, consider the following:

   ⋏ Stay in the building (many injuries occur as people flee a building and are struck by falling debris from above).
   ⋏ Get under a desk and stay away from windows and outside walls.
   ⋏ Be aware that the electricity may go out and sprinkler systems may come on.
   ⋏ DO NOT use the elevators.

6. If you are in a crowded indoor public location:

   ⋏ Stay where you are. Do not rush for the doorways.
   ⋏ Move away from tall shelves, cabinets, and bookcases containing objects that may fall.
   ⋏ Take cover and grab something to shield your head and face from falling debris and glass.
   ⋏ Be aware that the electricity may go out or the sprinkler systems or fire alarms may turn on.
   ⋏ DO NOT use elevators.

7. In a moving vehicle, stop as quickly as safety permits, and stay in the vehicle. Avoid stopping near or under buildings, trees, overpasses, or utility wires. Then, proceed cautiously, watching for road and bridge damage.

8. If you become trapped in debris:

   ⋏ Do not light a match.
   ⋏ Do not move about or kick up dust.
   ⋏ Cover your mouth with a handkerchief or clothing.
   ⋏ Tap on a pipe or wall so rescuers can locate you. Use a whistle if one is available. Shout only as a last resort—shouting can cause you to inhale dangerous amounts of dust.

9. Again, stay indoors until the shaking has stopped and you are sure exiting is safe.

Because of subterranean damage that occurs during an earthquake, electrical utilities, gas lines, and water lines are often ruptured and rendered useless. Although it creates an uncomfortable situation, a lack of utilities is a survivable event. A lack of water, however, is more than just a nuisance. As we know, water is essential to life. This must be considered when planning for an earthquake. The average person consumes between two to two-and-a-half quarts of water per day. If limited water exists, do not ration the water to amounts less than one quart per person per day. Instead, provide each person with adequate water and immediately find more water! Here are a few of the "hidden" sources of water:

- ⅄ Water in hot water tank (twenty to sixty gallons)
- ⅄ Water in toilet flush tanks (not the bowl!)
- ⅄ Ice cubes
- ⅄ Other liquids such as juice, soda, and fruits
- ⅄ Water pipes

What to Do After an Earthquake

It is important to understand that immediately after an earthquake, all emergency personnel will be reacting to critical crises. For this reason you should be able to be self-sufficient for at least seventy-two hours. Keep this in mind when preparing your plan and survival kit.

Remember these guidelines:

1. Listen to news reports for the latest emergency information.
2. Be prepared for aftershocks. These secondary shock waves are usually less violent than the main quake but can be strong enough to do additional damage to weakened structures.
3. Check for injuries. Do not attempt to move seriously injured people unless they are in immediate danger of death or further injury. If you must move an unconscious person, first stabilize the neck and back, and then call for help immediately.

    - ⅄ If the victim is not breathing, carefully position the victim for artificial respiration, clear the airway and start mouth-to-mouth resuscitation.
    - ⅄ Maintain body temperature with blankets. Be sure the victim does not become overheated.
    - ⅄ Never try to feed liquids to an unconscious person.

4. If the electricity goes out, use flashlights or battery powered lanterns. Do not use candles, matches, or open flames indoors after the earthquake because of possible gas leaks.
5. In areas covered with fallen debris and broken glass, wear sturdy shoes.
6. Check your home for structural damage. If you have any doubts about safety, have your home inspected by a professional before entering.
7. Check chimneys for visual damage; however, have a professional inspect the chimney for internal damage before lighting a fire.
8. Clean up spilled medicines, bleaches, gasoline, and other flammable liquids. Evacuate the building if gasoline fumes are detected and the building is not well ventilated.
9. Visually inspect utility lines and appliances for damage.

- If you smell gas or hear a hissing or blowing sound, open a window and leave. Shut off the main gas valve. Report the leak to the gas company from the nearest working phone or cell phone available.
- Stay out of the building. If you shut off the gas supply at the main valve, you will need a professional to turn it back on.
- Switch off electrical power at the main fuse box or circuit breaker if electrical damage is suspected or known.
- Shut off the water supply at the main valve if water pipes are damaged.
- Do not flush toilets until you know that sewage lines are intact.

10. Open cabinets cautiously. Beware of objects that can fall off shelves.
11. Use the phone only to report life-threatening emergencies.
12. Stay off the streets. If you must go out, watch for fallen objects, downed electrical wires, and weakened walls, bridges, roads, and sidewalks.
13. Stay away from damaged areas unless your assistance has been specifically requested by police, fire, or relief organizations.
14. If you live in coastal areas, be aware of possible tsunamis, sometimes mistakenly called tidal waves. When local authorities issue a tsunami warning, assume that a series of dangerous waves is on the way. Stay away from the beach. See the "Tsunamis" section in this chapter for more information.

After the earthquake local authorities may advise you to turn off the main water valves that serve your buildings. If this occurs, follow the instructions. It will prevent water from evacuating your water pipes. To capture the water in your pipes, turn on the faucet at the highest point in your building. This lets air into the system. Next, draw water from the faucet located in the lowest point of your building.

When all clean sources of water are exhausted, you must turn your efforts toward water that is considered unclean. This water must be purified prior to drinking. To properly purify the water, here are a few guidelines:

- Strain the water. Use cloth or paper towels if a filtration system is not available.
- Boil the water for three to five minutes.
- If boiling is not feasible, use purification tablets.

As in many emergencies, many injuries occur as a result of the aftereffects, not directly as a result of the emergency itself. Many problems are a result of improper food storage, preparation, and handling.

- Don't forget normal hygiene practices. Wash hands when preparing food.
- Use clean utensils and cutting surfaces.
- Keep food in covered containers.
- If in doubt about whether food is spoiled, avoid it.

Tsunamis

Tsunamis are large waves that are the result of a disturbance in the water. Often incorrectly referred to as tidal waves, tsunamis have no association with the tides or any weather phenomenon. A tsunami usually occurs as a result of an underwater earthquake; however, the violent agitation can also be caused by volcanic eruptions and even large landslides. Much like a rock dropped in a pond which sends ripples in all directions, in this case, the ripples are caused by a very large disturbance. The waves of a tsunami can travel at speeds over 500 mph and reach heights of 100 feet! For obvious reasons, low-lying coastal planes are at greatest risk, particularly land situated less than fifty feet above sea level and within a mile of the shore.

The nature of a tsunami is not to pound the shore with a single wave. Instead, a series of waves will hit land at a frequency between five minutes and ninety minutes. In open water the waves of a tsunami may appear to be normal and not of great concern; but as they approach the shallower water near the shore, they quickly grow in size and strength.

Tsunamis could occur in any of the major oceans of the world but they are most prevalent in the Pacific Ocean. The Pacific Ocean is home to more active volcanoes than any other location on the planet; for this reason the area is aptly named the "Ring of Fire." Coastal areas that border the Pacific Ocean and the many islands found within the ring of fire are particularly susceptible to the threat of tsunamis. Although rare, tsunamis can occur in the Atlantic Ocean due to earthquakes, landslides, and volcanic disruptions.

One byproduct of an earthquake, especially in areas with hilly terrain, is a landslide. In a coastal area, soil could become unstable and slide into the ocean. If the landslide is large, the resulting disruption in the ocean could very easily result in a tsunami. In a similar scenario, flank failure of a volcano could also produce a tsunami. Even meteorites can cause a tsunami.

Because of the large waves that are produced as a result of a tsunami, the majority of fatalities are caused by drowning. Other injuries and deaths are the result of flooding, debris, downed power lines, broken gas lines, and polluted water supplies. For these reasons, care must be taken after a tsunami to avoid danger.

Case Study 1: Hilo, Hawaii, 1946

On April 1, 1946, a tsunami with waves of twenty to thirty-two feet crashed into Hilo, Hawaii, flooding the downtown area and killing more than 159 people. The tsunami was a result of an earthquake in the Aleutian islands of Alaska. The earthquake measured 8.6 on the Richter scale, and within five hours the tsunami traveled from Alaska to the Hawaiian Islands. This proved to be one of the most deadly and destructive tsunamis in recorded history. Water reached more than one-half-mile inland and property damage reached more than $26 million.

One of the telltale signs preceding a tsunami is the receding water at a beach. This curious phenomenon often leaves reefs exposed and onlookers will walk out to the reefs. This happened in Hilo, and many people, especially school children, were killed by the approaching tsunami as they stood on the exposed reefs. Hilo, Hawaii, is now home to the Pacific Tsunami Museum, a memorial to all those who died in this tragic event.

On May 23, 1960, another tsunami destroyed much of downtown Hilo. This century there have been more than a dozen significant tsunamis that have impacted the vulnerable Hawaiian Islands. As a result, an early warning system was created. Hawaii is home to the Pacific Tsunami Warning Center, established in 1949.

Case Study 2: Indian Ocean, 2004

Although most of the case studies in this book are related to the United States, the Indian Ocean tsunami must be mentioned simply because of the staggering loss of life and damage. On December 26, 2004, a massive 9.3 magnitude undersea earthquake (the third-largest ever recorded) off the west coast of Sumatra, Indonesia, triggered a series of tsunamis that raced across the Indian Ocean. About 280,000 people in fourteen countries died in what was one of the deadliest natural disasters in recorded history. Indonesia was the hardest hit, followed by Sri Lanka, India, and Thailand. Local economies—especially fishing and tourism—were devastated. Even South Africa was affected, with at least eight deaths attributed to the abnormally high sea levels. The earthquake literally caused the entire planet to vibrate and triggered other earthquakes as far away as Alaska.

What to Do Before a Tsunami

The logical starting point for tsunami preparation is to first determine if you are in an area that is susceptible to tsunamis. A good Web site that provides general and historical information is that of the International Tsunami Information Center (itic.ioc-unesco.org/index. php). This site includes links to databases of historical tsunamis. If tsunamis have occurred in your area, local communities will have a warning system in place. Take time to learn about these early warning systems. The Pacific Tsunami Warning Center has a page for Hawaii residents to plot both risk and evacuation routes (ptwc.weather.gov/ptwc/hawaii.php).

In both case studies above, damage and death was high because of a lack of an early warning system. In the mid-1960s formal agreements were made between a number of tsunami-tracking agencies, including the Alaska-based tsunami warning center and the Hawaii-based tsunami warning center. Today, these centers are operated through the National Oceanic and Atmospheric Administration's (NOAA) National Weather Service. The Alaskan center, renamed the National Tsunami Warning Center in 2013, serves as an early warning resource for Alaska, U.S. Atlantic and Gulf of Mexico coasts, Puerto Rico, the Virgin Islands, and the Atlantic coast of Canada. The Hawaiian center serves as an early warning center for Hawaii and other Pacific-specific areas. The International Tsunami Information Center (ITIC) provides tsunami preparedness information to all of the Pacific Ocean nations.

These three early warning centers can be reached at:

National Tsunami Warning Center (NTWC)
(Formerly the West Coast and Alaska Tsunami Warning Center)
910 South Felton Street
Palmer, AK 99645
(907) 745-4212
E-mail: ntwc@noaa.gov
www.tsunami.gov

Pacific Tsunami Warning Center (PTWC)
91-270 Fort Weaver Road
Ewa Beach, HI 96706-2928
(808) 689-8207
ptwc.weather.gov/ptwc/

International Tsunami Information Center (ITIC)
1845 Wasp Boulevard, Building 176
Honolulu, HI 96818
(808) 725-6050
itic.ioc-unesco.org/index.php

Know the Terminology

These are the tsunami-related terms used by the National Tsunami Warning Center and the Pacific Tsunami Warning Center.

Advisory: An earthquake has occurred in the Pacific basin, which might generate a tsunami. NTWC and PTWC will issue hourly bulletins advising of the situation.

Watch: A tsunami was or may have been generated, but is at least two hours travel time to the area in Watch status.

Warning: A tsunami was or may have been generated, which could cause damage; therefore, people in the warning area are strongly advised to evacuate.

A Tsunami Watch is automatically declared when an earthquake occurs that meets certain criteria. The earthquake must be in an area that is likely to trigger a tsunami and it must have a magnitude of 7.5 or greater on the Richter scale. For those earthquakes originating in the Aleutian Islands of Alaska, an earthquake 7.0 or greater will automatically trigger a Tsunami Watch.

At this point, notification of various agencies begins, and a limited public announcement is made. The progress of the tsunami is monitored and readings from various tidal gauges are examined. If a tsunami can be confirmed, a Tsunami Warning is given. If the tsunami cannot be confirmed, the Tsunami Watch is canceled. Because of the quick-moving nature of the tsunami, a Tsunami Warning warrants quick action. The public will be warned via the emergency broadcast system and evacuation will be implemented.

The next logical step in planning for possible tsunamis is to map out an elevated evacuation route. Because of the size of a tsunami, you should move to an elevation at least fifty feet above sea level and one mile inland. Don't limit yourself to a single evacuation path because that road may be blocked or unavailable during an evacuation. In Hawaii, predetermined evacuation routes have been established using historical and predictive data. These routes are easily identified with prominent signage and can be found in map form in local telephone books and through the Hawai'i Emergency Management Agency (www.scd.hawaii.gov/).

When a tsunami occurs in open water, it can be tracked and early warnings can be given to those in its path. The NOAA weather radio is a great source for these warnings. If you are in an area susceptible to tsunamis or if you experience an earthquake, be ready to tune into your weather radio and evacuate to higher ground if instructed.

Other guidelines to prepare for a tsunami:

1. Learn evacuation routes. Determine where you would go and how you would get there if you needed to evacuate.
2. Prepare a survival kit. This survival kit might include

   ⋏   Water
   ⋏   Nonperishable food
   ⋏   Portable battery-powered radio
   ⋏   Flashlight
   ⋏   Extra batteries
   ⋏   Nonelectric/manual can opener
   ⋏   Basic tools for utility shut-off
   ⋏   Personal medicine
   ⋏   General first aid kit
   ⋏   Clothing, including sturdy shoes
   ⋏   Money

3. Develop an emergency communication plan that will allow you to contact family, employers, or employees immediately before and after the emergency event.
4. Listen to radio or television for more information and follow the instructions of your local authorities. If you feel an earthquake in a coastal area, turn on your radio to learn if there is a tsunami warning.

What to Do During a Tsunami

1. If you are advised to evacuate, do so immediately.
2. Immediate warning of tsunamis sometimes comes in the form of a noticeable recession in water away from the shoreline. This is nature's tsunami warning, and it should be heeded by moving inland to higher ground immediately.
3. Stay away from the area until local authorities say it is safe. Do not be fooled into thinking that the danger is over after a single wave—a tsunami is not a single wave but a series of waves that can vary in size.
4. Do not go to the shoreline to watch for a tsunami. When you can see the wave, it is too late to escape.
5. A tsunami may generate more than one wave. Do not let the modest size of one wave allow you to forget how dangerous a tsunami is. The next wave may be bigger.
6. Know that a small tsunami at one beach can be a giant wave a few miles away. The topography of the coastline and the ocean floor will influence the size of the wave.

What to Do After a Tsunami

After the tsunami has reached land and the danger has passed, the first responsibility is to assist those injured. Do not attempt to move those seriously injured unless their location places them in additional danger.

The following tasks should be addressed as well:

- Tune into your radio for further information.
- Check for gas and water leaks. Turn off or report to utility company immediately.
- Check for downed power lines. Report to utility company.
- Examine the building for obvious structural damage. Warn others.
- Cooperate fully with public safety officials.
- Avoid flooded and damaged areas until officials say it is safe to return.
- Stay away from debris in the water; it may pose a safety hazard to boats and people.
- If possible stay off the roads. Emergency personnel should be given first priority.

And after any emergency event, employees, employers, and family members should contact one another—hopefully through a planned contact system. Any delay in doing so might result in unnecessary search and concern.

Tsunamis have been known to attract surfers and other curious onlookers to the beach. Make no mistake; the beach is the wrong place to be during a tsunami. As tsunamis get closer to shore, they often double in size and quickly overtake the beach area. Do not attempt to return to the beach after the initial impact of the tsunami. The waves travel in groups, and often the secondary waves are greater than the first. An extended period of time may elapse between the waves. Return to your buildings only when advised to do so by authorities.

After the tsunami has passed and you are given permission to return to your buildings, immediately evaluate the building's condition. If any doubt exists as to the safety or structural integrity of the building, do not enter it until professional advice has been given. If the building is safe to enter, you should open all doors and windows to dry out the building. If water has saturated the carpets, have them cleaned and treated immediately. If water is still standing onsite, set up sump pumps to evacuate the water. If extensive water damage has occurred, aggressive cleanup steps must be taken, followed by testing for indoor air quality. If the damp environment remains, mold and mildew could develop, creating unwanted health problems and even greater cleanup costs.

Volcanoes

A volcano is a mountain that has an opening (vent) above a large pool of molten lava deep beneath the earth's surface. In its dormant state, little or no danger exists; however, that can quickly change. An eruption occurs when pressure builds up and the opening to the earth's surface provides the quickest escape route for the built-up pressure. The magma begins to rise and gasses begin to spew forth. A violent eruption will cause large rocks to explode, thereby becoming missiles traveling dangerously through the air.

Explosive eruptions can shoot columns of gases and rock fragments tens of miles into the atmosphere, spreading ash hundreds of miles downwind. Lateral blasts can flatten trees for miles. Hot, sometimes poisonous, gases may flow down the sides of the volcano.

As rocks begin to fracture and shift, earthquakes can occur. In many cases, flank failure happens as well. Flank failure occurs when a large portion of the volcanic mountain slips away from the rest of the mountain, much like a huge avalanche. If the volcano is situated near the ocean and debris from this failure lands in the ocean, a tsunami is likely to occur.

Although hot lava and exploding rocks pose the obvious danger, debris flow can be equally devastating. Debris flow occurs when water, ash, rock, trees, and other items begin to slide down the volcano side. As the debris gains momentum and grows larger, it takes over everything in its path. The debris flow can be deceiving. It may develop in an area totally unaffected by lava flow that destroys everything in its path. This is when onlookers get hurt. Volcanoes are very serious, very dangerous, and should be respected. Some eruptions are relatively quiet, producing lava flows that creep across the land at two to ten miles per hour.

Fresh volcanic ash, made of pulverized rock, can be harsh, acidic, gritty, glassy, and odorous. While not immediately dangerous to most adults, the combination of acidic gas and ash could cause lung damage to small infants, the elderly, or those suffering from severe respiratory illnesses. Volcanic ash can also damage machinery, including engines and electrical equipment. Ash accumulations mixed with water become heavy and can collapse roofs.

Because of the makeup of the earth, the area of the United States most likely to experience volcanic activity includes Hawaii, Alaska, California, Oregon, and Washington. This area, minus Hawaii, makes up half of the "Ring of Fire." The second half of the Ring of Fire extends across the Pacific Ocean to Asia. Hawaii is situated in the center of the Ring of Fire.

Volcanic eruptions can be accompanied by other natural hazards: earthquakes, mudflows and flash floods, rock falls and landslides, acid rain, fire, and (under special conditions) tsunamis.

Case Study 1: Mount St. Helens, 1980

On May 18, 1980, Mount St. Helens in Washington State violently erupted after more than a century of dormancy. Mount St. Helens quickly gained recognition as the most destructive volcano in the history of the United States. It caused more than $1 billion in property damage and took the lives of fifty-eight people.

Typical of most volcanoes, most deaths were not the result of burning lava but instead were the result of the massive mud and debris flow. The enormous landslide filled the valley area below, moving some thirteen miles down the Toutle River and covering twenty-four square miles.

By the next day the volcano was no longer erupting but it continued to spew volcanic ash. The ash quickly traveled over the state of Washington, inducing darkness in many areas. In fact, roosters were fooled into thinking it was morning as they crowed in the mid-afternoon. The ash continued to travel over the central and northern United States. Within two weeks, a small trace of volcanic ash had drifted completely around the earth.

Case Study 2: Kilauea Volcano, Hawaii, 1983 to Present

Kilauea has been erupting on and off since 1960. The latest eruption started in 1983. It has a large summit caldera with a central crater (home of the fire goddess Pele according to Hawaiian legend). The latest eruption is from two flank vents with lava flows running down to the sea. In the last thirty years the lava has covered more than 100 square miles, destroyed more than 200 homes and added new coastline. In the summer of 2014 a new vent opened and the lava flow forced the evacuation of villages in its path. At the time of writing the volcano was still active with lava flowing.

What to Do Before an Eruption

The logical starting point for volcano preparation is to first determine if you are in a danger zone. The U.S. Department of the Interior, U.S. Geological Survey's Volcano Hazards Program contains a U.S. active volcano map at volcanoes.usgs.gov with color-coded alerts. If volcanoes are present in your area, local communities will have a warning system in place. Take time to learn about these early warning systems.

1. Sign up for the Volcano Notification Service at the U.S. Geological Survey's volcano site (volcanoes.usgs.gov/vns/). This free service offers e-mail alerts about volcanic activity that are customizable to your needs.

2. Make evacuation plans. If you live in a known volcanic hazard area, plan a route out and have a backup route in mind. Don't limit yourself to a single exit path, because that road may be blocked or unavailable during an eruption. Avoid low-lying areas and, if possible, travel to higher regions. This suggestion will keep you from land that could quickly be filled with water or debris during a flash flood, but also realize that travel to higher areas may place you closer to the danger zone.

3. Develop a household disaster plan. In case household members are separated from one another during a volcanic eruption (a real possibility during the day when adults are at work and children are at school), have a plan for getting back together. Ask an out-of-town relative or friend to serve as the "household contact" because, after a disaster, it's often easier to call long distance. Make sure everyone knows the name, address, and phone number of the contact person.

4. Get a pair of goggles and a throwaway breathing mask for each member of the household in case of ash-fall.

5. Do not visit an active volcano site unless officials designate a safe-viewing area.

6. Assemble a disaster supply kit, which might include:

   - Water
   - Nonperishable food
   - Manual can opener
   - Goggles and throwaway breathing masks
   - Portable battery-powered radio
   - Flashlight
   - Extra batteries
   - Basic tools for utility shut-off
   - Personal medicine
   - General first aid kit
   - Clothing, including sturdy shoes
   - Money

What to Do During an Eruption

1. If close to the volcano, evacuate immediately away from the volcano to avoid flying debris, hot gases, lateral blast, and lava flow.

2. Avoid areas downwind from the volcano to avoid volcanic ash.

3. Be aware of mudflows. The danger from a mudflow increases as you approach a stream channel and decreases as you move away from a stream channel toward higher ground. In some parts of the world (Central and South America, Indonesia, the Philippines), this danger also increases with prolonged heavy rains. Mudflows can move faster than you can walk or run. Look upstream before crossing a bridge, and do not cross if the mudflow is approaching. Avoid river valleys and low-lying areas.

4. Stay indoors until the ash has settled unless there is danger of the roof collapsing.

5. During an ash fall, close doors, windows, and all ventilation in the house (chimney vents, furnaces, air conditioners, fans, and other vents).

6. Avoid driving in heavy dust unless absolutely required. If you do drive in dense dust, keep your speed down to thirty-five mph or slower.

7. Remove heavy ash from flat or low-pitched roofs and rain gutters.

8. Volcanic ash is actually fine, glassy fragments and particles that can cause severe injury to breathing passages, eyes, and open wounds, and irritation to skin. Follow these precautions to keep yourself safe from ash-fall:

   ⚞ Wear long-sleeved shirts and long pants.
   ⚞ Use goggles and wear eyeglasses instead of contact lenses.
   ⚞ Use a dust mask or hold a damp cloth over your face to help breathing.
   ⚞ Keep car or truck engines off. Driving can stir up volcanic ash that can clog engines and stall vehicles. Moving parts can be damaged from abrasion, including bearings, brakes, and transmissions.

It is difficult to predict the volcano's path and reach; therefore, you should listen to your radio for instructions from the authorities. They will provide guidance concerning safe evacuation routes. Since a volcano's danger area is considered to be a twenty-mile radius, those in the danger zone will likely be instructed to evacuate. If you are instructed to evacuate, do so. Don't assume that your building will provide adequate shelter. A violent volcanic eruption will send large boulders flying through the air. If these rocks were to hit your building, the structure will not likely provide you with a safe haven. If you are unable to evacuate, or if you are instructed to remain in place, you should close all windows, dampers, chimney flues, and doors. Extra precaution should be taken by placing wet towels under doors and window openings.

Since a volcano releases toxic fumes and glass-containing particles, you should avoid areas downwind of the volcano. If you are in an area where the breathing of fumes cannot be avoided, protect yourself with a respirator. If a respirator is not readily available, a dust mask might be used as a temporary solution while evacuating. If you are outdoors during a volcanic eruption and you are unable to immediately seek shelter, you should fashion a breathing mask using a shirt or other material. If water is available, soak the shirt first. Beware of low-lying areas where flash floods could occur. If the volcanic explosion produces a hail of rocks and debris, immediately search for an area that may provide relief from the rock storm.

What to Do After the Eruption

After the initial eruption, danger is still present from the volcanic ash and poisonous gasses. Stay tuned to your radio for further instructions. Do not attempt to reenter the danger zone until the all clear has been given by the authorities. Because the volcanic ash may continue to flow even after you are allowed to reenter your location, you must take safety precautions. Always wear a respirator and have extra filter cartridges. Since our eyes are perhaps the most sensitive organs we have, be sure to wear safety goggles at all times. Hard-soled shoes, long pants, and long-sleeved shirts are also recommended for safety reasons. For those with allergies or asthma, it would be advisable to not enter the affected areas until the ash flow has ceased and the surrounding areas have been cleaned.

Although the danger area around a volcano usually covers about a twenty-mile radius, disruptive volcanic ash can travel hundreds of miles.

Further guidelines:

1. Avoid ash-fall areas if possible. If you are in an ash-fall area, cover your mouth and nose with a mask, keep skin covered, and wear goggles to protect the eyes.
2. Clear roofs of ash-fall because it is very heavy and can cause buildings to collapse. But exercise great caution when working on a roof.
3. Avoid driving through ash-fall that is easily stirred up and can clog engines, causing vehicles to stall.
4. If you have a respiratory ailment, avoid contact with any amount of ash. Stay indoors until local health officials advise it is safe to go outside.

Landslides, Mudflow, and Debris Flow

Landslides occur all over the United States and its territories. They occur when masses of rock, earth, or debris move down a slope. Landslides may be small or large, and can move at slow or very high speeds. They are activated by storms, earthquakes, volcanic eruptions, fires, and by human modification of the land.

Debris flow and **mudflows** are rivers of rock, earth, and other debris saturated with water. They develop when water rapidly accumulates in the ground, during heavy rainfall or rapid snowmelt, changing the earth into a flowing river of mud or "slurry." They can flow rapidly down slopes or through channels, and can strike with little or no warning at avalanche speeds. They can also travel several miles from their source, growing in size as they pick up trees, large boulders, cars, and other materials along the way.

Landslide, mudflow, and debris-flow problems are occasionally caused by land mismanagement. Improper land-use practices on ground of questionable stability, particularly in mountain, canyon, and coastal regions, can create and accelerate serious landslide problems. Land-use zoning, professional inspections, and proper design can minimize many landslide, mudflow, and debris-flow problems.

What to Do Before a Landslide or Debris Flow

1. Contact your local emergency management office or American Red Cross chapter for information on local landslide and debris flow hazards.
2. Get a ground assessment of your property: County or state geological experts, local planning department or departments of natural resources may have specific information on areas vulnerable to landslides. Consult an appropriate professional expert for advice on corrective measures you can take.
3. Familiarize yourself with your surrounding area:

   - Small changes in your local landscape could alert you to the potential of greater future threat.
   - Observe the patterns of storm-water drainage on slopes and especially the places where runoff water converges.
   - Watch for any sign of land movement, such as small slides, flows, or progressively leaning trees, on the hillsides near your home.

4. Be particularly observant of your surrounding area before and during intense storms that could heighten the possibility of landslide or debris flow from heavy rains. Many debris-flow fatalities occur when people are sleeping.
5. Minimize home hazards by having flexible-pipe fittings installed to avoid gas or water leaks. Flexible fittings are more resistant to breakage. Only the gas company or its professionals should install gas fittings.
6. Learn to recognize landslide-warning signs.

   - Doors or windows stick or jam for the first time.
   - New cracks appear in plaster, tile, brick, or foundations.
   - Outside walls, walks, or stairs begin pulling away from the building.
   - Slowly developing, widening cracks appear on the ground or on paved areas, such as streets or driveways.
   - Underground utility lines break.
   - Bulging ground appears at the base of a slope.
   - Water breaks through the ground surface in new locations.

- The ground slopes downward in one specific direction and may begin shifting in that direction under your feet.
- Fences, retaining walls, utility poles, or trees tilt or move.
- You hear a faint rumbling sound that increases in volume as the landslide nears.

7. Talk to your insurance agent. Debris flow may be covered by flood insurance policies from the National Flood Insurance Program (NFIP).

What to Do During a Heightened Threat (Intense Storm) of Landslide or Debris Flow

1. Listen to radio or television for warnings of intense rainfall:

   - Be prepared to evacuate if instructed by local authorities or if you feel threatened.
   - Should you remain at home, move to a second story if possible to distance yourself from the direct path of debris flow and landslide debris.

2. Be alert when intense, short bursts of rain follow prolonged heavy rains or damp weather, which increases the risk of debris flows.

3. Listen for any unusual sounds that might indicate moving debris, such as trees cracking or boulders knocking together. A trickle of flowing or falling mud or debris may precede larger landslides. Moving debris can flow quickly and sometimes without warning.

4. If you are near a stream or channel, be alert for sudden increases or decreases in water flow and for a change from clear to muddy water. Such changes may indicate landslide activity upstream. Be prepared to move quickly.

5. Be especially alert when driving. Embankments along roadsides are particularly susceptible to landslides. Watch for collapsed pavement, mud, fallen rocks, and other indications of possible debris flows.

6. Evacuate when ordered by local authorities.

What to Do During a Landslide or Debris Flow

1. Quickly move away from the path of a landslide or debris flow.
2. Areas generally considered safe include:

   - Areas that have not moved in the past.
   - Relatively flat-lying areas away from drastic changes in slope.
   - Areas at the top of or along ridges set back from the tops of slopes.

3. If escape is not possible, curl into a tight ball and protect your head.

What to Do After a Landslide or Debris Flow

1. Listen to local radio or television stations for the latest emergency information.
2. Stay away from the slide area. There may be danger of additional slides.
3. Check for injured and trapped people near the slide, without entering the direct slide area, and direct rescuers to them.
4. Help neighbors who may require special assistance: large families, children, elderly people, and people with disabilities.
5. Landslides and flows can provoke associated dangers, such as broken electrical, water, gas and sewage lines, and disrupt roadways and railways: Look for and report broken utility lines to appropriate authorities. Reporting potential hazards will get the utilities turned off as quickly as possible, preventing further hazard and injury.
6. Check the building foundation, chimney, and surrounding land for damage. Damage to foundations, chimneys, or surrounding land may help you assess the safety of the area.
7. Watch for flooding, which may occur after a landslide or debris flow. Floods sometimes follow landslides and debris flows because they may both be started by the same event.
8. Replant damaged ground as soon as possible since erosion caused by loss of ground cover can lead to flash flooding and additional landslides in the near future.
9. Seek the advice of a geotechnical expert for evaluating landslide hazards or designing corrective techniques to reduce landslide risk. A professional will be able to advise you of the best ways to prevent or reduce landslide risk, without creating further hazard.
10. See the "Post-Event Restoration" chapter for more information.

4

Fire and Wildfire, Drought and Extreme Heat, and Blizzards and Avalanches

Fire and Wildfire

A fire is started every eighteen seconds on average. Each year more than 4,000 Americans die and more than 25,000 are injured in fires, many of which could be prevented. Public fire departments attend to over 1.7 million fires in a typical year—about 85 percent occur in homes. In 2010, someone died in a fire every 169 minutes and more than 22,000 people were injured. Direct property loss due to fires is estimated at $8.6 billion annually.

To protect yourself, it's important to understand the basic characteristics of fire. Fire spreads quickly. There is no time to gather valuables or make a phone call. In just two minutes a fire can become life threatening. In five minutes a residence can be engulfed in flames.

Heat and smoke from fire can be more dangerous than the flames. Inhaling the super-hot air can sear your lungs. Fire produces poisonous gases that make you disoriented and drowsy. Instead of being awakened by a fire, you may fall into a deeper sleep. Asphyxiation is the leading cause of fire deaths, exceeding burns by a three-to-one ratio.

There are two distinct categories of fire. The first category is fire that occurs within a building. These fires are usually started by a secondary source, such as faulty electrical wiring, carelessness, or flammables. Smoking is the leading cause of fire-related deaths and cooking is the primary cause of residential fires (36.8 percent of residential fires).

The second category of fire is the wildfire. The wildfire is fueled by vegetation. If the wildfire is not controlled, it can quickly consume buildings as well. People start more than 80 percent of the wildfires that occur. Lightning strikes usually cause the remainder. Each of these types of fires presents its own unique challenges and solutions. We will examine case studies and consider possible mitigation steps for both types.

Case Study 1: Beverly Hills Supper Club, 1977

On the evening of May 28, 1977, a festive crowd of nearly 2,800 gathered at the popular Beverly Hills Supper Club in Southgate, Kentucky, to enjoy an evening of good food, friends, and entertainment. No one could have predicted that 165 of those nightclub patrons would not come out of the club alive. At around 9 p.m., a smoldering fire in the infrastructure burst into a ravaging flame and within minutes engulfed the entertainment complex, blocking key exits. Ten minutes into the blaze the power went out and fleeing patrons were left in darkness.

The most often cited reasons for the fire and its devastation were faulty aluminum wire, inadequate exits, and lack of minimum firewall-rated materials used in construction. Many of those who died were not burned or even covered in soot. They appeared as if asleep, dead due to smoke inhalation. The fire burned for five long hours before it was extinguished. One hundred sixty-five people were dead, and all that remained of the Beverly Hills Supper Club was the front façade and a few partially standing walls.

Case Study 2: Western United States Wildfires, 2000

During the spring and summer months of 2000, nearly 7 million acres of land in the western United States was burned. The magnitude of these fires can be blamed on the unusually dry, hot summer and the presence of strong winds. These winds helped to fuel the fires and increased the speed at which they expanded. Lightning storms without the benefit of rainfall appeared to be the root cause of most of the wildfires. Because of the severe drought gripping the western United States, much of the vegetation had dried up and provided the fires with additional fuel.

By the time the raging fires were extinguished and the economic impact was calculated, an estimated $2 billion was spent. Fortunately, no lives were reported lost; however, hundreds were injured, including many of those assisting in efforts to contain the fires.

What to Do Before a Building Fire Occurs

We will discuss wildfire preparation and mitigation below, but first, let's look at fires that start in buildings. You can prepare by being sure your building, home, or workplace isn't a contributing factor itself to a fire. Ask your local fire department to inspect your residence for fire safety and prevention. Then you can practice personal safety measures.

Preparing Your Residence

1. Check the **electrical wiring** in your home:

   ⚞   Inspect extension cords for frayed or exposed wires or loose plugs.

   ⚞   Outlets should have cover plates and no exposed wiring.

✗ Make sure wiring does not run under rugs, over nails, or across high-traffic areas.

✗ Do not overload extension cords or outlets. If you need to plug in two or three appliances, get a UL-approved unit with built-in circuit breakers to prevent sparks and short circuits.

✗ Make sure home insulation does not touch electrical wiring.

✗ For further security, have an electrician check the electrical wiring in your home.

2. Check **heating sources**. Many home fires are started by faulty furnaces or stoves, cracked or rusted furnace parts and chimneys with creosote build-up. Have chimneys, wood stoves, and all home-heating systems inspected and cleaned annually by a certified specialist.

3. Insulate **chimneys** and place spark arresters on top. The chimney should be at least three feet higher than the roof. Remove branches hanging above and around the chimney.

4. Clean out storage areas. Don't let trash, such as old newspapers and magazines, accumulate.

5. Know the locations of the gas valve and electric fuse or circuit-breaker box and how to turn them off in an emergency. If you shut off your main gas line for any reason, allow only a gas company representative to turn it on again.

6. Install A-B-C type **fire extinguishers** in the home and teach household members how to use them.

✗ Type A: wood or papers fires only

✗ Type B: flammable liquid or grease fires

✗ Type C: electrical fires

✗ Type A-B-C: rated for all fires and recommended for the home

7. Consider installing an automatic fire sprinkler system in your home.

Personal Safety Measures

1. **Install smoke alarms**. Working smoke alarms decrease your chances of dying in a fire by half:

✗ Place smoke alarms on every level of your residence: outside bedrooms on the ceiling or high on the wall, at the top of open stairways or at the bottom of enclosed stairs, and near (but not in) the kitchen.

✗ Test and clean smoke alarms once a month and replace batteries at least once a year. Replace smoke alarms once every ten years.

2. With your household, plan **two escape routes** from every room in the residence. Practice with your household escaping from each room:

⋏ Make sure windows are not nailed or painted shut. Make sure security gratings on windows have a fire safety-opening feature so that they can be easily opened from the inside.

⋏ Consider escape ladders if your home has more than one level and ensure that burglar bars and other anti-theft mechanisms that block outside window entry are easily opened from inside.

⋏ Teach household members to stay low to the floor (where the air is safer in a fire) when escaping from a fire.

⋏ Pick a place outside your home for the household to meet after escaping from a fire.

3. Teach children how to report a fire and when to use 911.

4. Never use gasoline, benzene, naphtha, or similar liquids indoors:

⋏ Store flammable liquids in approved containers in well-ventilated storage areas.

⋏ Never smoke near flammable liquids.

⋏ After use, safely discard all rags or materials soaked in flammable material.

5. Take care when using **alternative heating sources**, such as wood, coal, and kerosene heaters, and electrical space heaters:

⋏ Check with your local fire department on the legality of using kerosene heaters in your community. Be sure to fill kerosene heaters outside after they have cooled.

⋏ Place heaters at least three feet away from flammable materials. Make sure the floor and nearby walls are properly insulated.

⋏ Use only the type of fuel designated for your unit and follow manufacturer's instructions.

⋏ Store ashes in a metal container outside and away from the residence.

⋏ Keep open flames away from walls, furniture, drapery, and flammable items. Keep a screen in front of the fireplace.

⋏ Have chimneys and wood stoves inspected annually and cleaned, if necessary.

⋏ Use portable heaters only in well-ventilated rooms.

6. Keep matches and lighters up high, away from children, and if possible, in a locked cabinet.

7. Do not smoke in bed, or when drowsy or medicated. Provide smokers with deep, sturdy ashtrays. Douse cigarette and cigar butts with water before disposal.

8. Safety experts recommend that you sleep with your door closed.

9. To support insurance claims in case you do have a fire, conduct an inventory of your property and possessions and keep the list in a separate location. Photographs and videos are also helpful.

What to Do During a Fire

1. Use water or a fire extinguisher to put out small fires. Do not try to put out a fire that is getting out of control. If you're not sure if you can control it, get everyone out of the residence and call the fire department from a neighbor's residence.
2. Never use water on an electrical fire. Use only a fire extinguisher approved for electrical fires.
3. Smother oil and grease fires in the kitchen with baking soda or salt, or put a lid over the flame if it is burning in a pan. Do not attempt to take the pan outside.
4. If your clothes catch fire, **stop, drop, and roll** until the fire is extinguished. Running only makes the fire burn faster.
5. If you are escaping through a closed door, use the back of your hand to feel the top of the door, the doorknob, and the crack between the door and doorframe before you open it. Never use the palm of your hand or fingers to test for heat: burning those areas could impair your ability to escape a fire (i.e., ladder use and crawling):

    ⚐   If the door is cool, open slowly and ensure fire or smoke is not blocking your escape route. If your escape route is blocked, shut the door immediately and use an alternate escape route, such as a window. If clear, leave immediately through the door. Be prepared to crawl. Smoke and heat rise. The air is clearer and cooler near the floor.

    ⚐   **If the door is warm or hot, do not open**. Escape through a window. If you cannot escape, hang a white or light-colored sheet outside the window, alerting firefighters to your presence.

6. If you must exit through smoke, crawl low under the smoke to your exit—heavy smoke and poisonous gases collect first along the ceiling.
7. Close doors behind you as you escape to delay the spread of the fire.
8. Once you are safely out, stay out and call 911.

What to Do after a Fire

1. Give first aid where needed. After calling 911 or your local emergency number, cool and cover burns to reduce chance of further injury or infection.
2. Do not enter a fire-damaged building unless authorities say it is OK.
3. If you must enter a fire-damaged building, be alert for heat and smoke. If you detect either, evacuate immediately.

4. Have an electrician check your household wiring before the current is turned on.
5. Do not attempt to reconnect any utilities yourself. Leave this to the fire department and other authorities.
6. Beware of structural damage. Roofs and floors may be weakened and need repair.
7. Contact your local disaster relief service, such as the American Red Cross or Salvation Army, if you need housing, food, or a place to stay.
8. Call your insurance agent:

  - Make a list of damage and losses. Pictures are helpful.
  - Keep records of cleanup and repair costs. Receipts are important for both insurance and income tax claims.
  - Do not throw away any damaged goods until an official inventory has been taken. Your insurance company takes all damages into consideration.

9. If you are a tenant, contact the landlord. It's the property owner's responsibility to prevent further loss or damage to the site.
10. Secure personal belongings or move them to another location.
11. Discard food, beverages, and medicines that have been exposed to heat, smoke, or soot. Refrigerators and freezers left closed hold their temperature for a short time. Do not attempt to refreeze food that has thawed.
12. If you have a safe or strong box, do not try to open it. It can hold intense heat for several hours. If the door is opened before the box has cooled, the contents could burst into flames.
13. If a building inspector says the building is unsafe and you must leave your home:

  - Ask local police to watch the property during your absence.
  - Pack identification, medicines, glasses, jewelry, credit cards, checkbooks, insurance policies, and financial records, if you can reach them safely.
  - Notify friends, relatives, police and fire departments, your insurance agent, the mortgage company, utility companies, delivery services, employers, schools, and the post office of your whereabouts.

Wildfires

Although not necessarily predictable, the probability of a wildfire can be deduced. If you are located in an area with a history of wildfires or if you are located near dense brush or forests, you should consider your risk to be escalated. Additionally, if you are currently experiencing extended drought, this condition increases the risk of wildfires.

To view the current threat of wildfires, visit the U.S. Fire Safety's (USFS) Wildland Fire Assessment System (WFAS) Web site for fire weather and fire danger maps at www.wfas .net. This site includes Google Earth map data. The information here will help you to determine possible impending threats to your location from wildfire. The National Weather Service also includes fire weather information at www.weather.gov/ctp/FireWeather and www.srh.noaa.gov/abq/?n=forecasts-fireweather-firedanger. The National Park Service has in-depth information on fire danger at www.nps.gov/fire/wildland-fire/learning-center/fire-in-depth/understanding-fire-danger.cfm.

If you live on a remote hillside, in a valley, prairie, or forest where flammable vegetation is abundant (i.e., fuels the fire), your residence could be vulnerable to wildfire. These fires are usually triggered by lightning or accidents.

These are the realities about fire and rural living:

- Once a fire starts outdoors in a rural area, it is often hard to control. Firefighters dealing with such fires are trained to protect natural resources, not homes and buildings.
- Many homes are located far from fire stations. The result is longer emergency response times. Within a matter of minutes, an entire home may be destroyed by fire.
- Limited water supply in rural areas can make fire suppression difficult.

If you live remotely, ask the nearest fire authorities for information about wildfires in your area. Request that they inspect your residence and property for hazards.

Preparing Your Residence before a Wildfire Strikes

Following are tips for making your property fire resistant. The philosophy behind most of these tips is to reduce the fuel that can feed a wildfire.

- Keep lawns trimmed, leaves raked, and the roof and rain-gutters free from debris, such as dead limbs and leaves.
- Stack firewood at least thirty feet away from your home.
- Store flammable materials, liquids, and solvents in metal containers outside the home, at least thirty feet away from structures and wooden fences.
- Create defensible space by thinning trees and brush within thirty feet around your home. Beyond thirty feet, remove dead wood, debris, and low tree branches.
- Landscape your property with fire-resistant plants and vegetation to prevent fire from spreading quickly. For example, hardwood trees are more fire resistant than pine, evergreen, eucalyptus, or fir trees.
- Make sure water sources, such as hydrants, ponds, swimming pools and wells, are accessible to the fire department.

In addition to reducing vegetative fuel on your property, here are ways to protect your home and make it more fire-resistant:

- Use fire-resistant, protective roofing and materials like stone, brick, and metal to protect your home. Avoid using wood materials, which offer the least fire protection.
- Cover all exterior vents, attics, and eaves with metal mesh screens no larger than six millimeters or a quarter-inch to prevent debris from collecting and to help keep sparks out.
- Install multipane windows, tempered safety glass, or fireproof shutters to protect large windows from radiant heat.
- Use fire-resistant draperies for added window protection.
- Have chimneys, wood stoves, and all home-heating systems inspected and cleaned annually by a certified specialist.
- Insulate chimneys and place spark arresters on top. Chimney should be at least three feet above the roof.
- Remove branches hanging above and around the chimney.

Personal Safety Measures for before a Wildfire Strikes

It is essential that you and your family/community have a fire safety and evacuation plan—one that has been practiced.

1. Create a fire safety and evacuation plan and practice it!
2. Know which local emergency services are available and have their phone numbers posted near telephones and saved in cellphone contact lists.
3. Make it easy for emergency services to reach you:

   - Mark the entrance to your property with address signs that are clearly visible from the road.
   - Provide emergency-vehicle access through roads and driveways at least twelve feet wide with adequate turnaround space.

4. Follow local burning laws:

   - Do not burn trash or other debris without proper knowledge of local burning laws, techniques, and the safest times of day and year to burn.
   - Before burning debris in a wooded area, make sure you notify local authorities and obtain a burning permit.
   - Use an approved incinerator with a safety lid or covering with holes no larger than three-quarters of an inch.
   - Create at least a ten-foot clearing around the incinerator before burning debris.
   - Have a fire extinguisher or garden hose on hand when burning debris.

What to Do When Faced with a Wildfire

If wildfire threatens your home and time permits, consider the following:

Inside

- Shut off gas at the meter. Turn off pilot lights.
- Open fireplace damper. Close fireplace screens.
- Close windows, vents, doors, blinds, or noncombustible window coverings and heavy drapes.
- Remove flammable drapes and curtains.
- Move flammable furniture into the center of the home away from windows and sliding-glass doors.
- Close all interior doors and windows to prevent drafts.
- Place valuables that will not be damaged by water in a pool or pond.
- Gather pets into one room. Make plans to care for your pets if you must evacuate.
- Back your car into the garage or park it in an open space facing the direction of escape. Shut doors and roll up windows. Leave the key in the ignition and the car doors unlocked. Close garage windows and doors, but leave them unlocked. Disconnect automatic garage door openers.

> If advised to evacuate, do so immediately. Choose a route away from the fire hazard. Watch for changes in the speed and direction of fire and smoke.

Outside

- Seal attic and ground vents with pre-cut plywood or commercial seals.
- Turn off propane tanks.
- Take combustible patio furniture inside.
- Connect garden hoses to outside taps. Place lawn sprinklers on the roof and near aboveground fuel tanks. Wet the roof.
- Wet or remove shrubs within fifteen feet of the home.
- Gather fire tools, such as a rake, axe, handsaw or chainsaw, bucket, and shovel.

Businesses and Fire

The Occupational Safety and Health Act (OSHA) requires that employers protect employees from fire and other emergencies. Part 1910 of the OSHA addresses general industry, which covers most operating facilities. Specifically 1910.38 (b) (1-5) requires the following components:

    ▲   A list of all the major workplace fire hazards and their proper handling and storage requirements

    ▲   Potential ignition sources (i.e., welding, smoking)

    ▲   Type of fire protection available to control each hazard

    ▲   Names of personnel responsible for maintenance of equipment installed to prevent or control fires

    ▲   Names of personnel responsible for controlling ignition sources

    ▲   Maintenance plan for fire equipment or systems (i.e., inspections and certifications)

    ▲   Housekeeping procedures to ensure that work area is kept free from accumulation of flammable and combustible materials

In addition to these distinct requirements, OSHA requires employers to provide adequate training to employees. The training must apprise employees of the fire hazards of the materials and processes to which they are exposed. A written plan must be available for all employees to review.

If you utilize a "fire brigade," employees who are assigned to assist others during a fire, their responsibilities must be set out in writing and included in the fire emergency plan, and those employees must be trained in their responsibilities. Their responsibilities might include:

    ▲   Providing first aid to those injured (as well as moving them to safety)

    ▲   Controlling spectators and those not involved in the fighting of the fire

    ▲   Meeting the fire department and giving them information as requested

    ▲   Ensuring that the alarm is given throughout the building and all people, including those with disabilities, are able to evacuate the building

    ▲   Providing communication between various staging areas and central command

    ▲   Using fire extinguishers as needed

    ▲   Communicating information about missing people to the fire department

    ▲   Turning off gas lines, machinery, blowers, and other equipment that may make the fire more dangerous

If you have difficulty determining what might constitute a fire hazard, meet with your local fire department and ask for its assistance. The firefighters will be happy to visit your facility and assist in identifying processes or materials that could cause a fire. Additionally, they will identify chemicals or other substances that will fuel a fire or contaminate the building during a fire.

A water sprinkler system is the most effective method of controlling fires automatically. These systems can be expensive to install and are usually required in new commercial construction, but the peace of mind they provide and the reduction in insurance premiums are well worth the cost. Three types of automatic sprinkler systems exist:

⋏   **Wet Pipe System**—Water is held in pipes that are located in the building. When heat from a fire is present, the seals in the sprinkler heads are ruptured and the water is able to flow and douse the fire.

⋏   **Dry Pipe System**—Instead of water in the pipes, air is present. When a sprinkler head is ruptured, the air rushes out and water flows through the pipes and to the fire. This application is useful when the possibility of frozen water in the pipes exists.

⋏   **Deluge System**—This system is similar to a dry pipe system except that some of the sprinkler heads remain in the open position to facilitate water flow in a chosen direction. Because some of the valves do not have a heat seal and remain open, this system can be operated manually or automatically.

Drought and Extreme Heat

A **drought** is a period of abnormally dry weather that persists long enough to produce serious effects (crop damage, water supply shortages, etc.). The severity of the drought depends upon the degree of moisture deficiency, the duration, and the size of the affected area. Drought can affect vast territorial regions and large population numbers. In effect, drought is a silent but very damaging phenomenon that is rarely lethal but enormously destructive. Drought can ruin local and regional economies that are agricultural and tourism-based. Drought also creates environmental conditions that increase risk of other hazards, such as fire, flash flood, and possible landslides or debris flow.

Between 1980 and 1999, the United States endured forty-six extreme weather events which each resulted in damage of $1 billion or greater. The cost of the forty-six events exceeded $275 billion.

Drought was responsible for nearly half of those losses: $120 billion. In addition to the economic losses, the toll on human life was large as well, exceeding 10,000 deaths as a result of drought and heat-related stress. Since January 2000 half of the country has experienced drought. During that same period California experienced extreme or severe drought for 9 percent of that time. At the time of writing moderate drought covered a large area of the United States from the West Coast to the central and southern Great Plains

> Emergency water shortages can also be caused by contamination of a water supply. A major spill of a petroleum product or hazardous chemical on a major river can force communities to shut down water treatment plants. Although typically more localized, the contamination of ground water or an aquifer can also disrupt the use of well water.

and New Mexico. There were two areas of extreme to exceptional drought: one covering California, Nevada, and Oregon, and the other centered in the southern Plains around North Texas and Oklahoma.

Drought is one of those conditions that can affect just about any region of the country, even land that is surrounded by water. Drought is often accompanied by severe heat, which can complicate recovery as well. If the drought lasts a long time, vegetation will dry up and fires can easily be started. When drought conditions exist, wildfires can become difficult to control and extinguish. Drought can have a dramatic effect on the environment as well. Without a doubt, drought can cause serious interruption in both business and personal life.

Case Study 1: California's Seven-Year Drought, 1987–1994

The worst drought in fifty years affected not just California but thirty-four other states as well. Some areas did not seen rain for four years. Nearly half of Yellowstone National Park—more than two million acres—burned as a result of the drought. Many homes were destroyed by the wildfires and billions of dollars in damage was assessed due to direct effects of the drought. In many areas, mandatory water restrictions were enforced. Some communities even began to reward homeowners who removed the grass from their yards and planted vegetation that required little irrigation. This form of landscaping became known as "xeriscape" and produced a new industry. The drought even had an impact on the cost of electricity. Because of the reduction in hydroelectricity, a significant increase in the cost of electricity was absorbed by Californians.

Case Study 2: Southern Drought, 1998–2000

A significant drought impacted Alabama, Georgia, Florida, Louisiana, and Mississippi beginning in mid-1998 and extending through 2000. And during a twelve-month period starting in September 1999 and ending in August 2000, this region experienced the driest period ever recorded in the southern United States since records began being kept in 1895. In Florida, forestry officials estimated four million trees were lost in 2000 alone. Mandatory water restrictions were enacted in many Florida counties. The restrictions were based on addresses. If your address, business or residential, was an even number, you were only allowed to irrigate your lawns on selected days for a limited period of time. Odd numbered addresses were permitted to irrigate their lawns on other specific days. Washing automobiles was strictly prohibited. Those breaking the drought law were subject to fines.

Heat Index and Drought Monitor Information

In a typical year, about 175 people die due to extreme heat. In an effort to save lives, the National Weather Service has developed the Heat Index (HI), an accurate measure of how hot it feels based on actual temperature plus the relative humidity. Think of it as wind chill factor in reverse. For example, in a very humid area such as Florida, a temperature of 94 degrees with 75 percent humidity actually feels like 124 degrees. Figure 4.1 shows the heat index. Table 4.1 indicates the possible dangers as the Heat Index increases.

National Weather Service
Heat Index Chart

Temperature (°F)

Relative Humidity (%)	80	82	84	86	88	90	92	94	96	98	100	102	104	106	108	110
40	80	81	83	85	88	91	94	97	101	105	109	114	119	124	130	136
45	80	82	84	87	89	93	96	100	104	109	114	119	124	130	137	
50	81	83	85	88	91	95	99	103	108	113	118	124	131	137		
55	81	84	86	89	93	97	101	106	112	117	124	130	137			
60	82	84	88	91	95	100	105	110	116	123	129	137				
65	82	85	89	93	98	103	108	114	121	128	136					
70	83	86	90	95	100	105	112	119	126	134						
75	84	88	92	97	103	109	116	124	132							
80	84	89	94	100	106	113	121	129								
85	85	90	96	102	110	117	126	135								
90	86	91	98	105	113	122	131									
95	86	93	100	108	117	127										
100	87	95	103	112	121	132										

Likelihood of Heat Disorders with Prolonged Exposure and/or Strenuous Activity

Caution ▪ Extreme Caution ▪ Danger ▪ Extreme Danger

Figure 4.1. National Weather Service Heat Index (www.weather.gov/media/unr/heatindex.pdf).

Table 4.1. Heat Index Dangers

Heat Index	Possible Heat Disorder
80°F–90°F	Fatigue possible with prolonged exposure and physical activity.
90°F–105°F	Sunstroke, heat cramps, and heat exhaustion possible.
105°F–130°F	Sunstroke, heat cramps, and heat exhaustion likely, and heat stroke possible.
130°F or greater	Heat stroke highly likely with continued exposure.

If, based on the heat index, the National Weather Service deems the heat excessive, they will issue a warning to the public. A common benchmark for excessive heat is a sustained daytime heat index equal to or greater than 105 degrees Fahrenheit, and a nighttime sustained temperature of 80 degrees Fahrenheit for two or more consecutive days. When this occurs, the National Weather Service broadcasts warnings via the NOAA weather radio.

Obviously, if the National Weather Service deems it necessary to inform the public of excessive heat, employers should do the same, especially if their employees are working outdoors.

The Drought Monitor Web site (available at droughtmonitor.unl.edu) is the result of a partnership between federal and academic scientists. The two main federal partners are the U.S. Department of Agriculture (USDA) and the National Oceanic and Atmospheric Administration (NOAA). These two agencies have joined forces with the National Drought Mitigation Center of the University of Nebraska–Lincoln. Current drought information is gathered and released each Thursday at 8:30 a.m. (EST). A map (see figure 4.2) is posted and drought conditions are graphically represented using the following indicators:

D0 – Abnormally dry
D1 – Drought Moderate
D2 – Drought Severe
D3 – Drought Extreme
D4 – Drought Exceptional

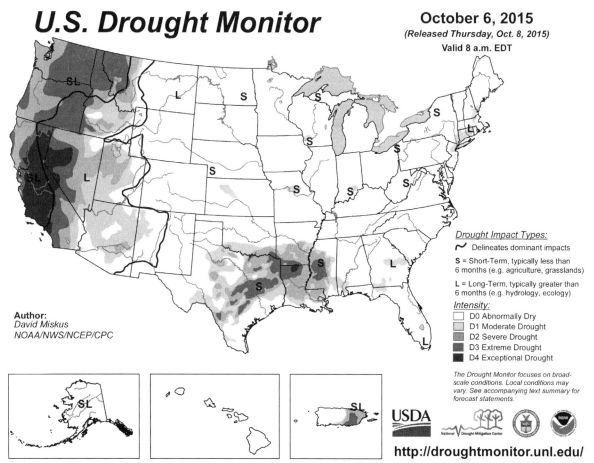

Figure 4.2. The U.S. Drought Monitor is jointly produced by the National Drought Mitigation Center at the University of Nebraska–Lincoln, the U.S. Department of Agriculture, and the National Oceanic and Atmospheric Administration. Map courtesy of NDMC-UNL

Also, regions that are susceptible to wildfire as a result of drought are identified. From this Web site (droughtmonitor.unl.edu) you can view drought forecasts, historical data, and a written synopsis of the current conditions.

Drought Planning for Businesses

The United States does not have a cohesive national water policy. Instead, each state or local municipality has taken the lead in developing proactive mitigation and conservation policies. As recently as the U.S. drought of 1977, no state had a formal drought plan. In 2002, only ten states did *not* have a formal drought plan. Based on this fact, the first source for drought-related planning for businesses should be your state or local municipality.

The National Drought Mitigation Center

The National Drought Mitigation Center (NDMC) was established in 1995 and is based in the School of Natural Resource Sciences at the University of Nebraska–Lincoln. The NDMC provides drought monitoring, planning, and mitigation. They also maintain a database of historical drought occurrences. They work with various governmental agencies to create drought policies and answer frequently asked questions. The NDMC conducts workshops and conferences that address the problems of drought. They are an excellent source of information for drought planning and recovery.

Here is a step-by-step method for developing an effective drought plan:

Step 1

Consult your local municipality or state for an established plan. If they do have a formal plan, use it to develop your plan in parallel.

Step 2

Conduct a historical drought analysis for your location. Do this by visiting the Drought Monitor Web site at drought.unl.edu.

Step 3

Categorize the risk. If your historical analysis identifies a high probability of drought, proceed with the drought plan.

Step 4

Identify specific areas that are drought prone. This might include large areas of vegetation or property that borders on wooded areas. Non-irrigated properties might pose a cosmetic problem as well.

Step 5

Establish terms that identify the severity of the drought such as:
- Advisory
- Alert
- Emergency
- Ration

These terms are more effective than numbers to identify the severity.

Step 6

Based on the severity and the term assigned, develop steps for each. For instance, when an "advisory" is announced, steps might include reduction of water use and a visual inspection of the premises to identify potential fire hazards.

Step 7

During and after the drought, be certain to evaluate what worked and what didn't work. Revise your drought plan accordingly.

Here are a few other ideas that may assist in your drought mitigation efforts:

- Always be aware of and obey the water rationing laws.
- Train employees in water conservation activities and set expectations for compliance.
- Trim back vegetation from the building and premises that could dry out and catch fire.
- Be aware of work that could cause fires such as welding, roofing, and grinding. Take precautions to protect against these potential fire triggers.
- Be aware of chemical storage and spills that could cause fires.
- Ensure that fire systems and fire extinguishers are working properly.
- Provide employees with training for proper fire control and building evacuation.

A prolonged drought, poor water supply management, or contamination of a surface water supply source or aquifer can cause an emergency water shortage.

Water Conservation

Conserving water is very important during emergency water shortages. Water saved by one user may be enough to protect the critical needs of others. Irrigation practices can be changed to use less water, and crops that use less water can be planted. Cities and towns can ration water, factories can change manufacturing methods, and individuals can practice water-saving measures to reduce consumption. If everyone reduces water use during a drought, more water will be available to share.

Practice Indoor Water Conservation

General

- Check all plumbing for leaks. Have leaks repaired by a plumber.
- Repair dripping faucets by replacing washers. One drop per second wastes 2,700 gallons of water per year!

▲   Never pour water down the drain when there may be another use for it. Use it to water your indoor plants or garden.

Bathroom

▲   Don't let the water run while brushing your teeth, washing your face, or shaving.

▲   Install a toilet displacement device to cut down on the amount of water needed to flush. Place a one-gallon plastic jug of water into the tank to displace toilet flow (do not use a brick, it may dissolve and loose pieces may cause damage to the internal parts). Be sure installation does not interfere with the operating parts.

▲   Consider purchasing a low-volume toilet that uses less than half the water of older models. NOTE: The law requires low-volume units in many areas.

▲   Don't flush the toilet unnecessarily. Dispose of tissues, insects, and other similar waste in the trash rather than the toilet.

▲   Replace your showerhead with an ultra-low-flow version.

▲   Do not take baths—take short showers—only turn on water to get wet and lather and then again to rinse off.

▲   Place a bucket in the shower to catch excess water for watering plants.

Kitchen

▲   Operate automatic dishwashers only when they are fully loaded. Use the "light wash" feature if available to use less water.

▲   Hand-wash dishes by filling two containers—one with soapy water and the other with rinse water containing a small amount of chlorine bleach.

▲   Most dishwashers can clean soiled dishes very well, so dishes do not have to be rinsed before being placed in the dishwasher. Just remove large particles of food, and put the soiled dishes in the dishwasher.

▲   Store drinking water in the refrigerator. Don't let the tap run while you are waiting for water to cool.

▲   Do not waste water waiting for it to get hot. Capture it for other uses, such as plant watering or heat it on the stove or in a microwave.

▲   Do not use running water to thaw meat or other frozen foods. Defrost food overnight in the refrigerator, or use the defrost setting on your microwave.

▲   Clean vegetables in a pan filled with water rather than running water from the tap.

▲   Kitchen sink disposals require a lot of water to operate properly. Start a compost pile as an alternate method of disposing of food waste, or simply dispose of food in the garbage.

Laundry

▲   Operate automatic clothes washers only when they are fully loaded or set the water level for the size of your load.

Long-term indoor water conservation

▲   Retrofit all household faucets by installing aerators with flow restrictors.

▲   Consider installing an instant hot water heater on your sink.

▲   Insulate your water pipes to reduce heat loss and prevent them from breaking if you have a sudden and unexpected spell of freezing weather.

▲   If you are considering installing a new heat pump or air-conditioning system, the new air-to-air models are just as efficient as the water-to-air type, and they do not waste water.

▲   Install a water-softening system only when the minerals in the water would damage your pipes. Turn the softener off while on vacation.

▲   When purchasing a new appliance, choose one that is more energy and water efficient.

Practice Outdoor Water Conservation

General

▲   If you have a well at home, check your pump periodically. If the automatic pump turns on and off while water is not being used, you have a leak.

Lawn-care

▲   Don't over-water your lawn. A heavy rain eliminates the need for watering for up to two weeks. Most of the year, lawns only need one inch of water per week.

▲   Water in several short sessions rather than one long one in order for your lawn to better absorb moisture.

▲   Position sprinklers so water lands on the lawn and shrubs and not on paved areas.

▲   Avoid sprinklers that spray a fine mist. Mist can evaporate before it reaches the lawn. Check sprinkler systems and timing devices regularly to be sure they operate properly.

▲   Raise the lawn-mower blade to at least three inches, or to its highest level. A higher cut encourages grass roots to grow deeper, shades the root system, and holds soil moisture.

▲   Plant drought-resistant lawn seed.

- Avoid over-fertilizing your lawn. Applying fertilizer increases the need for water. Apply fertilizers that contain slow-release, water-insoluble forms of nitrogen.
- Use a broom or blower instead of a hose to clean leaves and other debris from your driveway or sidewalk.
- Do not leave sprinklers or hoses unattended. A garden hose can pour out 600 gallons or more in only a few hours.

Car washing

- Use a shut-off nozzle on your hose that can be adjusted down to a fine spray, so that water flows only as needed.
- Consider using a commercial car wash that recycles water. If you wash your own car, park on the grass so that you will be watering it at the same time.

Pool

- Consider installing a new water-saving pool filter. A single back flushing with a traditional filter uses 180 to 250 gallons of water.
- Cover pools and spas to reduce evaporation of water.

Long-term outdoor conservation

- Plant native or drought-tolerant grasses, groundcovers, shrubs, and trees. Once established, they do not need water as frequently and usually will survive a dry period without watering. Small plants require less water to become established. Group plants together based on similar water needs.
- Install irrigation devices that are the most water efficient for each use. Micro and drip irrigation and soaker hoses are examples of efficient devices.
- Use mulch to retain moisture in the soil. Mulch also helps control weeds that compete with landscape plants for water.
- Avoid purchasing recreational water toys that require a constant stream of water.
- Avoid installing ornamental water features (such as fountains) unless they use recycled water.

Participate in public water-conservation programs of your local government, utility, or water management district. Follow water conservation and water shortage rules in effect. Remember, you are included in the restrictions even if your water comes from a private well. Be sure to support community efforts that help develop and promote a water-conservation ethic. Contact your local water authority, utility district, or local emergency management agency for information specific to your area.

Poor water-quality management can result in the demand for water exceeding the available supply. This can be exacerbated by fluctuations in regional precipitation, excessive water demand, or rapid residential development.

Extreme Heat

Heat kills by pushing the human body beyond its limits. Under normal conditions, the body's internal thermostat produces perspiration that evaporates and cools the body. However, in extreme heat and high humidity, evaporation is slowed and the body must work extra hard to maintain a normal temperature. Most heat disorders occur because the victim has been overexposed to heat or has over-exercised for his or her age and physical condition. The elderly, young children, and those who are sick or overweight are more likely to succumb to extreme heat.

Conditions that can induce heat-related illnesses include stagnant atmospheric conditions and poor air quality. Consequently, people living in urban areas may be at greater risk from the effects of a prolonged heat wave than those living in rural areas. Also, asphalt and concrete store heat longer and gradually release heat at night, which can produce higher nighttime temperatures known as the "urban heat island effect."

Know the Terminology

Heat wave: Prolonged period of excessive heat, often combined with excessive humidity.

Heat index: A number in degrees Fahrenheit (F) that tells how hot it *feels* when relative humidity is added to the air temperature. Exposure to full sunshine can increase the heat index by fifteen degrees.

Heat cramps: Muscular pains and spasms due to heavy exertion. Although heat cramps are the least severe, they are often the first signal that the body is having trouble with the heat.

Heat exhaustion: Typically occurs when people exercise heavily or work in a hot, humid place where body fluids are lost through heavy sweating. Blood flow to the skin increases, causing blood flow to decrease to the vital organs. This results in a form of mild shock. If not treated, the victim's condition will worsen. Body temperature will keep rising and the victim may suffer heat stroke.

Heat stroke: Heat stroke is life-threatening. The victim's temperature-control system, which produces sweating to cool the body, stops working. The body's temperature can increase so high that brain damage and death may result if the body is not cooled quickly.

Sun stroke: Another term for heat stroke.

What to Do Before an Extreme Heat Emergency

Consider the following preparedness measures when faced with the possibility of extreme heat:

- Install window air conditioning units snugly in the window frame, insulate if necessary.
- Close any floor heat registers nearby, and use a circulating or box fan to spread cool air.
- Check air-conditioning ducts for proper insulation.
- Install temporary reflectors, such as aluminum foil covered cardboard, to reflect heat back outside and be sure to weather-strip doors and sills to keep cool air in.
- Cover windows that receive morning or afternoon sun with drapes, shades, awnings, or louvers.
- Outdoor awnings or louvers can reduce the heat that enters a home by up to 80 percent. Consider keeping storm windows up all year.

What to Do During Extreme Heat or a Heat-wave Emergency

1. Stay indoors as much as possible:
   - If air conditioning is not available, stay on the lowest floor out of the sunshine.
   - Remember that electric fans do not cool; they just blow hot air around.
2. Eat well-balanced, light, and regular meals. Avoid using salt tablets unless directed to do so by a physician.
3. Drink plenty of water regularly even if you do not feel thirsty:
   - People who have epilepsy or heart, kidney, or liver disease, are on fluid-restrictive diets, or have a problem with fluid retention should consult a doctor before increasing liquid intake.
4. Limit intake of alcoholic beverages. Although beer and alcoholic beverages appear to satisfy thirst, they actually cause further body dehydration.
5. Never leave children or pets alone in closed vehicles.
6. Dress in loose clothes that cover as much skin as possible. Lightweight, light-colored clothing reflects heat and sunlight and helps maintain normal body temperature.
7. Protect your face and head by wearing a wide-brimmed hat.

8. Avoid too much sunshine. Sunburn slows the skin's ability to cool itself. Use a sunscreen lotion with a high SPF (sun protection factor) rating (i.e., 15 or greater) and reapply frequently.

9. Avoid strenuous work during the warmest part of the day. Use a buddy system when working in extreme heat and take frequent breaks.

10. Spend at least two hours per day in an air-conditioned place. If your home is not air conditioned, consider spending the warmest part of the day in public buildings, such as libraries, schools, movie theaters, shopping malls, and other community facilities. Your city may have a designated public cooling center (call 311 for information).

11. Check on family, friends, and neighbors who do not have air conditioning and who spend much of their time alone.

First Aid for Heat-induced Illnesses

Sunburn

▲   Symptoms: Skin redness and pain, possible swelling, blisters, fever, headaches.

▲   First aid: Take a shower, using soap, to remove oils that may block pores, preventing the body from cooling naturally. If blisters occur, apply dry, sterile dressings and get medical attention.

Heat cramps

▲   Symptoms: Painful spasms, usually in leg and abdominal muscles. Heavy sweating.

▲   First aid: Get the victim to a cooler location. Lightly stretch and gently massage affected muscles to relieve spasm. Give sips of up to a half glass of cool water every fifteen minutes. Do not give liquids with caffeine or alcohol. If victim feels nauseous, discontinue liquids.

Heat exhaustion

▲   Symptoms: Heavy sweating. Skin may be cool, pale, or flushed. Weak pulse. Normal body temperature is possible but temperature will likely rise. Fainting or dizziness, nausea or vomiting, exhaustion, and headaches are possible.

▲   First aid: Get victim to lie down in a cool place. Loosen or remove clothing. Apply cool, wet cloths. Fan or move victim to air-conditioned place. Give sips of water if victim is conscious. Be sure water is consumed slowly. Give half a glass of cool water every fifteen minutes. If nausea occurs, discontinue. If vomiting occurs, seek immediate medical attention.

Heat stroke (sun stroke)

- ⅄ Symptoms: High body temperature (105+). Hot, red, dry skin. Rapid, weak pulse and rapid, shallow breathing. Possibly unconsciousness. Victim will likely not sweat unless victim was sweating from recent strenuous activity.
- ⅄ First aid: Heat stroke is a severe medical emergency. Call 911 or emergency medical services or get the victim to a hospital immediately. Delay can be fatal. Move victim to a cooler environment. Remove clothing. Try a cool bath, sponging, or wet sheet to reduce body temperature. Watch for breathing problems. Use extreme caution. Use fans and air conditioners.

Blizzards and Avalanches

Each year winter storms disrupt our daily activities. At their worst severe winter storms can result in blizzards and avalanches, which can cause death and property damage. In storms of lesser severity, transportation routes may be closed, communications may be cut off, and water pipes may freeze or even burst. The accumulation of snow and ice creates dangers for pedestrians and commuters alike. The cost of snow removal and the loss the business may have great negative economic impact on the area as well.

Many areas in the United States are susceptible to severe winter weather. For instance, from the Middle Atlantic coast up to the New England coast, you might experience storms that originate off of the Carolina coast and move northward. These storms are commonly known as Nor'easters. These storms can be very intense and include ice storms, strong winds, and flooding. The northeastern United States is also susceptible to severe winds originating from Canada. The Rocky Mountains tend to create severe weather as well, with cool air flowing eastward from the mountains meeting cool air from Canada and the Great Lakes. This places the Midwest at risk for winter storm events. The impacts include flooding, storm surge, closed highways, blocked roads, downed power lines, and hypothermia.

Even those areas such as southern California or northern Florida, which do not typically experience severe winter weather conditions, are at risk for winter dangers. Because of the rarity of severe weather in these more temperate areas, many people are not properly prepared. Weather dipping into the twenties or thirties may present a mere inconvenience in South Dakota, while in Florida it creates an emergency condition. The important point to understand is severe winter weather can occur in just about any region in the country; therefore, preparations should be made prior to the event.

Case Study 1: Great Appalachian Blizzard, 1996

The Great Appalachian Blizzard of 1996 began on Sunday, January 7, and didn't stop until Friday, January 12. What made the impact of this storm so great is the effect it had on the nation's capital. Just before the blizzard struck, the Republican congress and the

Democratic president had been squabbling over the federal budget for an extended period of time. Due to this political impasse, government offices were shut down for nearly a month into early January. Finally, both sides reached a palatable consensus and thousands of federal workers were ready to go back to work on Monday, January 8. But the extreme weather did not cooperate.

On Monday morning, the citizens of the District of Columbia awoke to a city buried beneath seventeen to twenty-one inches of snow. The nation's capital was paralyzed. Other locations were hit even harder. Baltimore was sacked by two feet of snowfall, and nearly three feet of snow fell over Maryland's Frederick and western Loudoun counties. Road crews worked hard to clear Monday's snow. As these road crews cleared the major arteries and began to tackle the secondary roads, a second storm blew through the District of Columbia, dumping an additional three to five inches of snow. The snowplows assigned to clear the secondary and residential roads now had to go back and hit the main roads again.

Just as the population was beginning to sense relief and the completion of the blizzard, a third storm struck on Friday, January 12, dumping another four to six inches over the Washington, D.C., metropolitan area. By late Friday afternoon, the entire area was buried under two to three feet of snow. Because of this incredible week of severe weather, the government did not open its doors. It remained closed for most of the week while many schools and businesses gave up and closed their doors for the entire week.

Case Study 2: Groundhog Day Blizzard, 2011

This huge winter storm, fueled by moisture from the Gulf of Mexico, started in Texas and marched north to the Great Lakes dumping up to two feet of snow over many states. Winds of up to seventy miles per hour were recorded along the shores of Lake Michigan, which caused major drifting in the Milwaukee and Chicago areas. Snow drifts of up to ten feet were reported, closing interstates and stranding thousands of motorists. Many cities declared states of emergency as public transport was suspended for several days to allow cleanup crews in to open up main highways. On top of snow, up to three feet thick in many places along the Mid-Atlantic Coast and New England, freezing rain added to the problems. Boston and Baltimore both recorded record snowfalls. Most highways were closed and some secondary roads were unpassable for a week or more. A second storm hit immediately after the first and, taking the same route, dumped an additional foot or two of snow, compounding the problem. Chicago was brought to a virtual standstill and total insured losses topped $1.8 billion. At least thirty-six deaths were attributed to the storm, according to the NOAA.

Know the Terminology

Freezing rain: Rain that freezes when it hits the ground, creating a coating of ice on roads, walkways, trees, and power lines

Sleet: Rain that turns to ice pellets before reaching the ground. (Sleet also causes roads to freeze and become slippery.)

Frost/Freeze Warning: Below-freezing temperatures are expected.

Winter Storm Watch: A winter storm is possible in your area.

Winter Storm Warning: A winter storm is occurring, or will soon occur, in your area.

Blizzard Warning: Sustained winds or frequent gusts to thirty-five miles-per-hour or greater and considerable falling or blowing snow (reducing visibility to less than a quarter mile) are expected to prevail for a period of three hours or longer.

What to Do Before a Winter Storm Threatens

1. Prepare to survive on your own for at least three days. Assemble a disaster supply kit. Be sure to include winter-specific items, such as rock salt to melt ice on walkways, sand to improve traction, snow shovels, and other snow removal equipment. Keep a stock of food and extra drinking water.

2. Prepare for possible isolation in your home:

   - Have sufficient heating fuel; regular fuel sources may be cut off.
   - Have emergency heating equipment and fuel (a gas fireplace or a wood-burning stove or fireplace) so you can keep at least one room of your residence livable. (Be sure the room is well ventilated.) If a thermostat controls your furnace and your electricity is cut off by a storm, you will need emergency heat.
   - Kerosene heaters are another emergency-heating option.
   - Store a good supply of dry, seasoned wood for your fireplace or wood-burning stove.
   - Keep fire extinguishers on hand, and make sure your household knows how to use them.

3. Winterize your home to extend the life of your fuel supply:

   - Insulate walls and attics.
   - Caulk and weather-strip doors and windows.
   - Install storm windows or cover windows with plastic.

4. Maintain several days' supply of medicines, water, and food that needs no cooking or refrigeration.

What to Do During a Winter Storm

1. Listen to the radio or television for weather reports and emergency information.
2. Eat regularly and drink ample fluids, but avoid caffeine and alcohol.
3. Dress for severe cold:

   - Wear several layers of loose fitting, lightweight, and warm clothing rather than one layer of heavy clothing. The outer garments should be tightly woven and water repellent.
   - Mittens are warmer than gloves.
   - Wear a hat; most body heat is lost through the top of the head if the head is uncovered.
   - Cover your mouth with a scarf to protect your lungs.

4. Be careful when shoveling snow. Over-exertion can bring on a heart attack—a major cause of death in the winter. If you must shovel snow, stretch before going outside and don't overexert yourself.
5. Watch for signs of **frostbite**: loss of feeling and white or pale appearance in extremities, such as fingers, toes, ear lobes, or the tip of the nose. If symptoms are detected, **get medical help immediately**.
6. Watch for signs of **hypothermia**: uncontrollable shivering, memory loss, disorientation, incoherence, slurred speech, drowsiness, and apparent exhaustion. If symptoms of hypothermia are detected, get the victim to a warm location, remove any wet clothing, warm the center of the body first, and give warm, non-alcoholic beverages if the victim is conscious. Get medical help as soon as possible.
7. When at home:

   - Conserve fuel if necessary by keeping your residence cooler than normal. Temporarily "close off" heat to some rooms.
   - When using kerosene heaters, maintain ventilation to avoid build-up of toxic fumes. Refuel kerosene heaters outside and keep them at least three feet from flammable objects.

8. **Never burn charcoal indoors**.

Business Preparation for Severe Winter Storms

Severe weather can be very dangerous and may impede your company's production. Because of this, you should have procedures in place to reduce or eliminate the negative effects of severe winter storms. For instance, a de-icing schedule and procedures should be written for your parking areas, loading dock, employee access areas, and other important locations. Create a process for removing snow from walkways. Timing is important; don't clear the snow too early or the pathways will be covered with snow before employees and visitors visit your buildings.

In addition to de-icing, here are a few other proactive measures for effectively dealing with severe winter weather:

- Keep snow removal tools (shovels, salt, etc.) on hand.
- Create a rotating schedule for maintenance employees to be on call after hours in the event of an emergency.
- Consider using outside vendors for snow removal.
- Have a NOAA radio on site to monitor conditions.
- If you have a generator on site, remember to perform preventative maintenance on it, including startup and run.
- Beware of snow accumulation on roofs, which may become heavy and cause roofs to collapse.
- Check roof drains, gutters, catch basins, and other areas that can freeze or get clogged and impede the flow of melted snow.
- Winterize HVAC, fire sprinkler, and irrigation systems during the fall.

Equipment Maintenance

1. Lawn irrigation

   - Turn off the water to the irrigation system at main valve.
   - Turn the automatic irrigation controller to the "off" setting.
   - Turn on each of the valves to release pressure in the pipes.
   - Drain all of the water out of any irrigation components that might freeze.
   - Drain water out of the components and irrigation lines using compressed air.

2. Boilers

   - Drain idle equipment.
   - Check all service lines for freezing.
   - Elevate dead ends and low points.
   - Install heat tracing around control-line transmitter boxes and piping that carries water glass.

3. HVAC Cooling Coils

   - Valve off coil and drain to level recommended by manufacturer.
   - If an automatic freeze protection system is in use, test it for its proper use.
   - Add a mixture of water and glycol, as recommended by manufacturer to coils where water cannot be drained.

Fire Sprinklers

Fire sprinkler systems freeze faster and therefore are at greater risk than standard plumbing pipe because the water doesn't flow unless there's a fire. In a dry pipe system, low points are susceptible to freezing due to the collection of condensation. Low points in a dry pipe sprinkler system where condensation can collect are susceptible to freezing. In wet pipe systems, the use of anti-freeze can be a deterrent to freezing. Also, the size of the pipe plays a role in its likelihood to freeze. A smaller diameter pipe will freeze much more quickly than a larger diameter pipe. Remember, fire sprinkler pipes cannot be insulated or heated. If you utilize either of these methods you will defeat the purpose of the system or accidentally trigger the release of water.

The best advice for keeping fire sprinkler systems operational during the winter months is to keep the heat on. It is recommended that all rooms with sprinklers be maintained at 40 degrees Fahrenheit or warmer to avoid the possibility of pipes freezing. If you have concerns about the possibility of your sprinkler system failing as a result of cold weather, call your contractor and get professional advice.

Antifreeze loops or dry pipe applications are a simple solution for small unheated areas. It is recommended that you consult with your fire safety engineer or contractor.

Sometimes it will be advisable to let your building occupants leave work early so they can get home safely. Create a process for making this happen. How will you communicate this? Who will be required to remain? Who will shut down the building? Will anyone stay on site and monitor the site during the storm? If yes, will they be able to keep warm and fed? The time to create this process is *before* the severe weather sets in, not during.

Winter Driving

About 70 percent of winter deaths related to snow and ice occur in automobiles. Consider public transportation if you must travel. If you travel by car, travel in the day, don't travel alone, and keep others informed of your schedule. Stay on main roads; avoid back-road shortcuts.

1. Winterize your car. This includes a battery check, antifreeze, wipers and windshield-washer fluid, ignition system, thermostat, lights, flashing hazard lights, exhaust system, heater, brakes, defroster, oil level, and tires. Consider snow tires, snow tires with studs, or chains. Keep your car's gas tank full.
2. Carry a "winter car kit" in the trunk of your car. The kit should include:

   - Shovel
   - Windshield scraper
   - Battery-powered radio
   - Flashlight
   - Extra batteries

⅄ Water and snack food
⅄ Mittens and hat
⅄ Blanket
⅄ Tow chain or rope
⅄ Tire chains
⅄ Bag of road salt and sand
⅄ Fluorescent distress flag
⅄ Booster cables
⅄ Road maps
⅄ Emergency flares
⅄ Cellular telephone or two-way radio, if available

If a Blizzard Traps You in Your Car

⅄ Pull off the highway. Turn on hazard lights and hang a distress flag from the radio aerial or window.

⅄ Remain in your vehicle where rescuers are most likely to find you. Do not set out on foot unless you can see a building close by where you know you can take shelter. Be careful: distances are distorted by blowing snow. A building may seem close but be too far to walk to in deep snow.

⅄ Run the engine and heater about ten minutes each hour to keep warm. When the engine is running, open a window slightly for ventilation. This will protect you from possible carbon monoxide poisoning. Periodically clear snow from the exhaust pipe.

⅄ Exercise to maintain body heat, but avoid overexertion. In extreme cold, use road maps, seat covers and floor mats for insulation. Huddle with passengers and use your coat for a blanket.

⅄ Take turns sleeping. One person should be awake at all times to look for rescue crews.

⅄ Drink fluids to avoid dehydration.

⅄ Be careful not to waste battery power. Balance electrical energy needs—the use of lights, heat, and radio—with supply.

⅄ At night, turn on the inside light so work crews or rescuers can see you.

⅄ If stranded in a remote area, spread a large cloth over the snow to attract attention of rescue personnel who may be surveying the area by airplane.

⅄ Once the blizzard passes, you may need to leave the car and proceed on foot.

5

Bomb Threats, Chemical Warfare, and Bioterrorism

Non-natural emergencies and disasters can take many forms from bomb threats, terrorist activities, and nuclear accidents to building collapse, chemical spills, and workplace violence. These events usually involve some form of human interaction and therefore have some predictability. Unfortunately, we often don't read the signs that precede the emergency. A disgruntled employee makes violent comments, but we simply shrug them off. Terrorists plant a bomb in the bowels of the World Trade Center in a semi-successful operation, but come back nine years later to finish the job. Not all non-natural events are predictable, but many of them are. And many of these events can be mitigated. Contingency plans can—and must—be created. Recovery and continuity plans can be written. The goal of the following chapters is to identify non-natural events and discuss the proactive steps we can take to eliminate or minimize their occurrences.

Bomb Threats

Thousands of bomb attacks occur each year in the United States. Many of these bombs are crude, cause minimal damage, and are instigated by amateur criminals. Many of these attacks are small, localized in nature, and target property rather than people. For these reasons, most of these events do not make the national news. If the United States experiences thousands of bomb attacks per year, we can surmise that tens of thousands of bomb threats occur annually.

Obviously, bomb threats that are carried out are very costly, both in terms of the loss of human life and property damage. However, even the threat of a bomb can interrupt work, introduce fear into the workplace, and, if the employer is perceived to handle the threat carelessly, erode employee confidence. Based on recent experiences, the threat of bomb attack—particularly those attributed to international terrorists—gives cause for great concern.

On December 2, 2014, intelligence services in the United Kingdom confirmed that the Islamic State (IS) terrorist group had made threats to detonate a dirty bomb in London. A dirty bomb combines radioactive materials and conventional explosives. When detonated it causes localized destruction but radioactivity is spread over a wide area. It is believed that IS acquired radioactive uranium from Mosul University in Mosul, Iraq, when they overran the city in June 2014. The Iraqi government has confirmed the theft of the uranium but was unable to say who had taken it. If IS does possess the wherewithal to make a dirty bomb it is thought more likely that they would detonate it in Syria or Iraq rather than transport it—but the mere threat of such a possibility is enough to put intelligence and security forces around the globe on alert.

Iraq is not the only source of radioactive materials. With the fall of the Soviet Union large quantities of radioactive material are held, often with little security, in many of the former satellite states. Terrorist groups are very anxious to get their hands on this material and may have already done so.

The following three case studies of bomb attacks were watershed events, each of which grew progressively more deadly.

Case Study 1: World Trade Center, 1993

In retrospect, the 1993 World Trade Center bombing served as an eerie precursor to the 2001 attack that brought the World Trade Center towers down. The World Trade Center served as an attractive target, as the twin towers were immediately recognized the world over as a symbol of American capitalism and were located in the world's greatest city—New York City. In the case of the 1993 World Trade Center bombing, the perpetrators were able to hide a bomb in a vehicle and park it two stories below the ground level in the parking garage. Six people lost their lives and more than a thousand were injured, mostly from smoke inhalation.

This scenario could have been much worse if the building structure was not as solid as it was and if the bomb used was greater in size. The bomb used 1,000 pounds of urea nitrate and a few cylinders of hydrogen gas. It was believed that the terrorists responsible for this attack had planned for a larger bomb but did not have the financial resources to make it a reality. In fact, the terrorists were caught because they attempted to get their rental deposit back from the van rental company. Many believe that this bombing, although limited in success, proved to various terrorist cells that the United States was not untouchable and that, if adequate funds were available, the towers could be brought down.

Case Study 2: Alfred P. Murrah Building, Oklahoma City, 1995

One of the best defenses against a bomb attack is distance. If you can keep distance between the bomb and the building (and personnel), you can limit the effects of the bomb. In 1995 a domestic terrorist was able to park a moving-van full of explosives within twenty feet of the Alfred P. Murrah Federal Building in Oklahoma City. The violent explosion resulted in a significant building collapse and the death of 168 people, including fifteen children in the building's daycare center. Glass was broken more than a mile away. If the Murrah Federal Building had had greater standoff areas around the building (in other words, if vehicle access had been limited near the building), the effects of the bomb might not have been as severe.

Two interesting facts became apparent with this event. First, a domestic terrorist was the mastermind of this attack. Usually, we fear international terrorists and give little concern to the actions of our own disgruntled citizens. Second, this attack did not occur in a large metropolitan area such as New York or Los Angeles. The attack occurred in the less-populated heartland of the United States. Who would have thought that a federal building in Oklahoma City would become an attractive target for a terrorist, domestic or otherwise? Any preconceived notions we may have had about terrorism had been shattered.

Case Study 3: Attacks of September 11, 2001

September 11, 2001—a day that will "live in infamy." That phrase was used once before, on December 7, 1941, immediately after the Japanese attacked Pearl Harbor. The attacks of September 11, 2001, would eclipse even that infamous day.

At 8:45 a.m. American Airlines Flight 11 out of Boston was hijacked and flown into the World Trade Center North Tower. All eighty-one passengers and eleven crew members were killed. The explosion was tremendous and left a gaping hole in the tower, taking the lives of many more inside the tower. Just minutes later, at 9:03 a.m., a second hijacked airliner, United Airlines Flight 175, was flown into the South Tower, killing all fifty-six passengers and nine crewmembers. Within a half hour, the FAA shut down all air traffic throughout the country. At 9:43 a.m., American Airlines Flight 77 was hijacked and flown into the Pentagon, severely damaging the two outermost rings and immediately killing all fifty-eight passengers and six crewmembers aboard. Within a half hour a large portion of the damaged area collapsed.

At 10:05 a.m., the South Tower of the World Trade Center experienced total collapse. At 10:10 a.m., the final hijacked flight, United Airlines Flight 93, crashed in a field southeast of Pittsburgh, Pennsylvania. At 10:28 a.m. the World Trade Center's North Tower collapsed. At 5:20 p.m., the forty-seven-story Building 7 of the World Trade Center collapsed as a result of damage sustained earlier when the North and South Towers collapsed. In the next few days and weeks, the grisly task of searching for bodies and cleanup began. The final tally of the attacks included 2,888 confirmed deaths. If you include the missing and presumed dead from the air attacks, the number of deaths rises past 3,000.

Aside from the great loss of human life, the emotional impact on survivors, families, and American citizens was heavy. The economic impact of the September 2001 attacks was phenomenal. From a real estate standpoint, tens of millions of square feet of prime office space was lost in a day. Organizations were required to move to other sites or go out of business altogether.

Never before had the United States had to be concerned with terrorism on such a large scale. Nor had the world, for that matter. Obviously the rules had changed. Whether the threat is a suicide bomber or a hijacked airplane, an anthrax laden letter or a crude nuclear device hidden in a suitcase, domestic terrorist or foreign, we must be aware of the possibilities.

Preparing for a Bomb Threat

The best defense against a bomb attack is preparation. People who have a plan for the eventuality of a bomb threat are in the best position to survive the threat of attack. Even if your facility is ultra-secure, it remains impossible to eliminate bomb threats. Threats can be carried out by anyone with access to a telephone.

You must take time to develop procedures prior to a bomb threat occurring. When developing these procedures, consult with your local fire and police departments. They will be able to provide suggestions and possibly even training.

Upon establishing procedures for handling bomb threats and evacuations, share these procedures with your employees. They will be eager to hear your plan for dealing with these threats. An organization without bomb threat procedures stands the risk of losing the confidence of its employees. Worse still is the organization that has no plan and hides the occurrence of threats from its employees.

Under the Department of Justice, the Bureau of Alcohol, Tobacco, Firearms, and Explosives (ATF) is tasked with regulating explosives and disseminating education about them. Some years ago, they prepared a "Bomb Threat Checklist" for threats received by phone that is still useful now (see figure 5.1). See the online form at www.doe.in.gov/sites/default/files/safety/caller-checklist.pdf.

Even if an actual attack never materializes, the threat can cause major disruptions and expense. Upon receiving a threat, one must be prepared for some sort of action. The usual first course of action is evaluation. You must be prepared to evaluate the threat and its legitimacy. This is not an exact science and is open to interpretation, but without some standard method of evaluation you will be ill-prepared for the threat.

The Bomb Threat Checklist

This checklist gives the recipient of a bomb threat a list of questions to ask the caller. If you receive a bomb threat, get as much information from the caller as possible. Keep the caller on the line and record everything that is said. Then notify the police and the building management.

Some questions are obvious such as "When is the bomb going to explode?" and "Where is the bomb located?" while other questions seem less obvious. Questions such as "What is your name?" and "Where are you calling from?" might not be answered by the caller, but stranger things have happened! Even if all of the questions on this checklist are not answered,

ATF BOMB THREAT CHECKLIST

Exact time of call _____

Exact words of caller _____
_____
_____

QUESTIONS TO ASK

1. When is bomb going to explode? _____

2. Where is the bomb? _____

3. What does it look like? _____

4. What kind of bomb is it? _____

5. What will cause it to explode? _____

6. Did you place the bomb? _____

7. Why? _____

8. Where are you calling from? _____

9. What is your address? _____

10. What is your name? _____

CALLER'S VOICE (circle)

Calm	Disguised	Nasal	Angry	Broken
Stutter	Slow	Sincere	Lisp	Rapid
Giggling	Deep	Crying	Squeaky	Excited
Stressed	Accent	Loud	Slurred	Normal

If voice is familiar, whom did it sound like? _____

Were there any background noises? _____

Remarks: _____
_____

Person receiving call: _____

Telephone number call received at: _____

Date: _____

Report call immediately to: _____
(Refer to bomb incident plan)

Figure 5.1. Bomb Threat Checklist

Detach and place by each telephone. Duplicate as necessary.

it keeps the caller on the phone line for an extended period of time, and that may assist the authorities in tracing the call. Another section of the checklist is designed so the recipient can circle a description of the caller's voice. This may help to identify the caller and may assist you in determining the legitimacy of the threat. For instance, if the caller sounds stressed and is crying, you might decide the threat is a real one. However, if the caller sounds young and is giggling while speaking, you may determine that the call is a prank.

This bomb threat checklist should be copied onto a bright colored paper that stands out amid the typical clutter in an office. In the event of a threat by telephone, the recipient can quickly find the checklist and take the appropriate notes.

When a Bomb Threat Is Made

If you receive a bomb threat, do not touch any suspicious packages. Clear the area around suspicious packages and notify the police immediately. Around your building, keep all streets and sidewalks clear for emergency vehicles and have a member of your search team wait for the authorities to arrive and provide an escort to the location in question. Because of increased demands on local police departments and other related agencies, the police may not be able to attend straight away and the decision to search for a bomb and the call for an evacuation is one that will be made by you, the building owner, or manager.

Whether to Evacuate

In the event a bomb threat has been received, a decision to evacuate or remain will need to be made quickly. The basis for this decision will often depend on the perceived credibility of the caller. When faced with a bomb threat, you have three basic options:

1. Ignore the threat
2. Evacuate immediately
3. Search for the bomb and evacuate if necessary

Obviously each of these options presents its own pros and cons.

In many cities across the country, your local police or fire department will not conduct a bomb search if you receive a threat. They will expect your organization to make the decision to evacuate. They will often expect your organization to perform the actual bomb search. This may seem unfair or even dangerous but it underscores the need for a game plan when dealing with these issues. If you do happen to find a bomb or something unusual, the police or fire department will defuse and remove the bomb, but again, this is after you find it! By consulting with your local fire department and police department, you'll likely be able to predetermine their level of involvement in a search as well.

The Bomb Search

At some point, especially if the threat seems to have merit, the decision to conduct a search for the bomb will need to be made. As mentioned previously, the actual bomb search will likely be conducted by the building manager or owner. If this describes your situation, now is the time to identify processes and procedures and communicate them to the responsible parties. Here are a few steps that must be addressed prior to the actual search:

- Train employees how to evacuate the building in a calm and orderly fashion.
- Determine if a bomb squad is available to assist you and how they will respond. Police and fire departments are a good starting place.
- Designate search team members (include someone who works in the department or floor being searched).
- Have a set of floor plans available for the search team and authorities.
- Practice efficient search techniques.
- Establish a command center outside of the building.
- Establish a procedure to report progress back to authorities.
- Establish a process to allow employees back into the building.

The building search should be conducted in an orderly and thorough fashion. If a building search is to be conducted, the following tools should be made available and used:

Keys: Some rooms may be locked and require a unique key. This is usually not a problem during regular operating hours but could be a real problem after hours.

Stepladder: Many of the areas to be searched are above eye level and cannot be examined properly without a small step ladder.

Flashlight: Not every area will be well lit, so be sure to have a flashlight handy.

Mirrors: Mirrors are critical for gaining visual access to certain areas. Check with your local law enforcement agency for suppliers of such mirrors.

Floor plan: A floor plan can be instrumental in conducting a bomb search. Be sure to have highlighters on hand to mark areas on the floor plan after they are searched. If an actual sweep and search of the premises becomes necessary, it should be conducted in an efficient and safe manner. The ATF prepared an excellent procedure for sweeping and searching buildings (see figures 5.2 through 5.6). This procedure entails five steps:

1. Enter the room. Stop, look, and listen.
2. Divide the room by height for search.

> Zone 1: Floor to waist
> Zone 2: Waist to chin
> Zone 3: Chin to ceiling
> Zone 4: Above false (drop) ceiling

3. Search room by zone and assigned area. Overlap if necessary.
4. Search the interior public areas.
5. Search the outside areas.

Figure 5.2. Bomb Search: Stop, Listen.

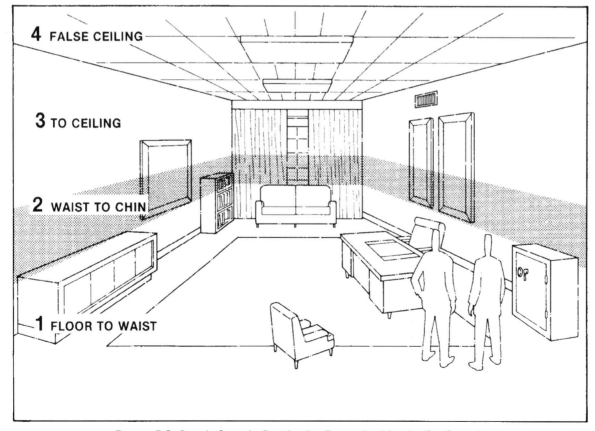

4 FALSE CEILING

3 TO CEILING

2 WAIST TO CHIN

1 FLOOR TO WAIST

Figure 5.3. Bomb Search: Divide the Room by Height for Search.

Figure 5.4. Bomb Search: Search Room by Height and Assigned Area. Overlap for Better Coverage.

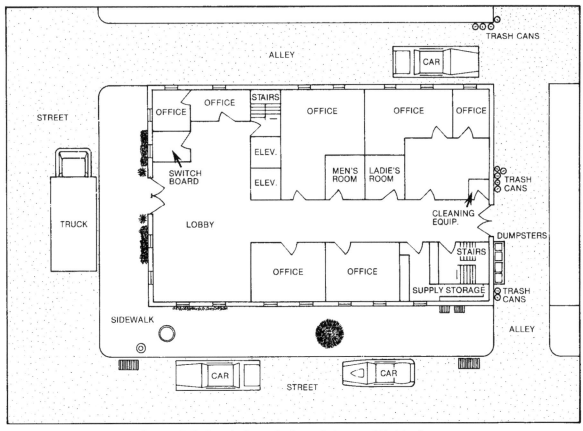

Figure 5.5. Bomb Search: Search Internal Public Areas.

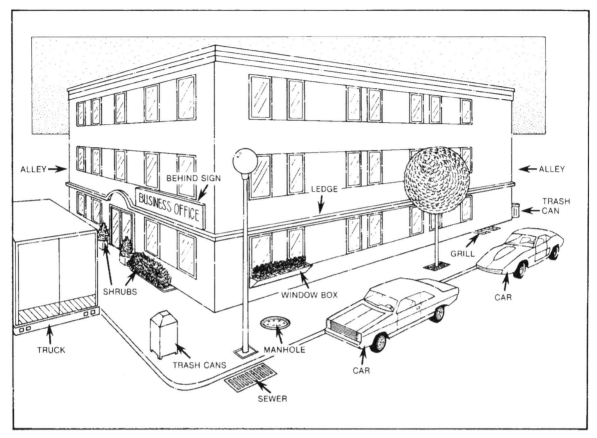

Figure 5.6. Bomb Search: Search Outside Areas.

Step number two is critical. A minimum of two people should enter a room and walk to one end of the room. The two employees will stand back to back and proceed around the perimeter of the room, limiting their observations to "Zone 1," which is from the floor to waist height. This might entail looking underneath desks, in garbage cans, behind plants, and other such areas. As the two employees complete their sweep of the perimeter of the room, they will eventually meet back at the starting point. This completes the wall sweep of Zone 1. Next, the employees would turn around, back to back again, and repeat the perimeter sweep once more. This time however, the two employees will observe all items in "Zone 2," which is waist height to chin height. Each step is repeated for each zone, and finally a sweep of the middle area of the room should be completed. This logical process should be completed in each room to ensure the absence of an explosive device.

When using a search team for the building sweep, it is recommended that you have an employee who works in that specific area on the team. That employee is most likely to know what belongs and what is out of place. When a specific department, floor, or common area has been completely searched, highlight that area on your floor plan and communicate back to central command that the area has been searched.

A **command center** must always be set up to help handle the evacuation, search, communication, and eventual reentry into the building. The command center would include an employee with a floor plan stationed outside of the building structure. This person would keep track of the employees and visitors evacuated and the areas searched. They would serve as the liaison between the authorities and the search and sweep team. The command center would give the employees and visitors the "green light" to reenter the building. For this reason, the command center must be staffed by a person(s) who has the authority to make "re-enter or go home" decisions. A definite chain of command must be established prior to attempting a sweep and search of evacuation. Without these critical issues being resolved, the process will be sloppy, chaotic, and will likely not be completed properly, thus placing employees at risk.

> A word of warning: When searching a building for a bomb, beware of using two-way radios as a means of communication because these devices can cause a premature detonation of an electronic blasting cap! Instead of radios and cell phones, use a runner to communicate progress back to the command center.

Suspicious Parcels and Letters

Be wary of suspicious packages and letters. They can contain explosives or chemical or biological agents. Be particularly cautious at your place of employment. The U.S. Postal Service has created posters to educate us about suspicious packages and how to handle them. One of the telltale signs of a potentially dangerous package is the use of excessive stamps. This may seem trivial, but most letters and packages sent for legitimate business purposes use metered mail and not stamps. The metered mail can be traced to its origin, something that stamps do not allow. In an effort to mail the piece, the sender will often put more stamps on the package than necessary.

Some typical characteristics postal inspectors have detected over the years, which ought to trigger suspicion, include parcels that:

- Are unexpected or from someone unfamiliar to you.
- Have no return address, or have one that can't be verified as legitimate.
- Show a city or state in the postmark that doesn't match the return address.
- Are addressed to someone no longer with your organization or are otherwise outdated.
- Are addressed to a title (i.e., CEO) instead of a personal name.
- Similarly, have incorrect titles or title without a name.
- Are marked with restrictive endorsements, such as "Personal," "Confidential," or "Do Not X-ray."
- Have protruding wires or aluminum foil, strange odors, or stains.
- Are of unusual weight, given their size, or are lopsided or oddly shaped.

    ⋏   Are marked with any threatening language.

    ⋏   Have inappropriate or unusual labeling.

    ⋏   Have excessive postage or excessive packaging material, such as masking tape and string.

    ⋏   Have misspellings of common words.

    ⋏   Have handwritten or poorly typed addresses.

    ⋏   Are from a foreign country of origin.

    ⋏   Have warnings not to x-ray (i.e., film enclosed).

With suspicious envelopes and packages other than those that might contain explosives, take these additional steps against possible biological and chemical agents:

    ⋏   Refrain from eating or drinking in a designated mail-handling area.

    ⋏   Place suspicious envelopes or packages in a plastic bag or some other type of container to prevent leakage of contents. Never sniff or smell suspect mail.

    ⋏   If you do not have a container, then cover the envelope or package with anything available (e.g., clothing, paper, trashcan, etc.) and do not remove the cover.

    ⋏   Leave the room and close the door, or section off the area to prevent others from entering.

    ⋏   Wash your hands with soap and water to prevent spreading any powder to your face.

    ⋏   If you are at work, report the incident to your building security official or an available supervisor, who should notify police and other authorities without delay.

    ⋏   List all people who were in the room or area when this suspicious letter or package was recognized. Give a copy of this list to both the local public health authorities and law enforcement officials for follow-up investigations and advice.

    ⋏   If you are at home, report the incident to local police.

Many businesses have opted to open mail off site or to outsource mailroom operations altogether. If a letter containing anthrax is received, exposure would be limited to the off-site location.

What to Do When There Is an Explosion

Leave the building as quickly as possible. Do not stop to retrieve personal possessions or make phone calls. If things are falling around you, get under a sturdy table or desk until they stop falling. Then leave quickly, watching for weakened floors and stairs and falling debris as you exit.

After evacuating a building, don't stand in front of windows, glass doors or other potentially hazardous areas. Do not block sidewalk or streets to be used by emergency officials or others still exiting the building.

> If a bomb does explode, many employees will be disoriented and panicked. Instruct the search team to assist the employees in evacuating in an orderly fashion. Be prepared to isolate the damaged area and do not allow employees to enter the building until it has been inspected for structural integrity.

If there is a fire

- Stay low to the floor and exit the building as quickly as possible.
- Cover your nose and mouth with a wet cloth.
- When approaching a closed door, use the back of your hand to feel the lower, middle, and upper parts of the door. Never use the palm of your hand or fingers to test for heat: burning those areas could impair your ability to escape a fire (i.e., using ladders and crawling).
- If the door is NOT hot, open slowly and ensure fire or smoke is not blocking your escape route. If your escape route is blocked, shut the door immediately and use an alternate escape route, such as a window. If clear, leave immediately through the door. Be prepared to crawl. Smoke and heat rise. The air is clearer and cooler near the floor.
- If the door is hot, do not open it. Escape through a window. If you cannot escape, hang a white or light-colored sheet outside the window, alerting fire fighters of your presence.
- Heavy smoke and poisonous gases collect first along the ceiling. Stay below the smoke at all times.

If you are trapped in debris

- Do not light a match or ignite a lighter.
- Do not move about or kick up dust. Cover your mouth with a handkerchief or clothing.
- Rhythmically tap on a pipe or wall so that rescuers can hear where you are. Use a whistle if one is available. Shout only as a last resort when you hear sounds and think someone will hear you—shouting can cause a person to inhale dangerous amounts of dust.

TERRORISM

Americans face threats posed by hostile governments or extremist groups. These threats to national security include acts of terrorism and acts of war.

Terrorism is the use of force or violence against people or property in violation of the criminal laws of the United States for purposes of intimidation, coercion, or ransom. Terrorists often use threats to create fear among the public, to try to convince citizens that their government is powerless to prevent terrorism, and to get immediate publicity for their causes.

Acts of terrorism can range from threats of terrorism to assassinations, kidnappings, hijackings, cyber-attacks (computer-based), bomb scares and bombings, and the use of chemical, biological, and nuclear weapons.

High-risk targets include military and civilian government facilities, international airports, large cities, and high-profile landmarks. Terrorists might also target large public gatherings, water and food supplies, utilities, and corporate centers. Further, they are capable of spreading fear by sending explosives or chemical and biological agents through the mail.

In the immediate area of a terrorist event, you would need to rely on police, fire, and other officials for instructions. However, you can prepare in much the same way you would prepare for other crisis events.

Preparing for Terrorism

1. Wherever you are, be aware of your surroundings. The very nature of terrorism suggests there may be little or no warning.
2. Take precautions when traveling. Be aware of conspicuous or unusual behavior. Do not accept packages from strangers. Do not leave luggage unattended. Unusual behavior, suspicious packages, and strange devices should be promptly reported to the police or security personnel.
3. Do not be afraid to move or leave if you feel uncomfortable or if something does not seem right.
4. Learn where emergency exits are located in buildings you frequent. When you enter unfamiliar buildings, notice where exits and staircases are located. Plan how to get out of a building, subway, or congested public area or traffic. Notice heavy or breakable objects that could move, fall or break in an explosion.
5. Assemble a disaster supply kit at home and learn first aid. Separate the supplies you would take if you had to evacuate quickly, and put them in a backpack or container, ready to go.
6. Be familiar with different types of fire extinguishers and how to locate them. Know the location and availability of hard hats in buildings in which you spend a lot of time.

Chemical and Biological Weapons (CBR) or Threats

Not so long ago, this section might not have been included, because the threat of chemical warfare or bioterrorism on American soil seemed so remote. Words such as *anthrax* and *biotoxins* were foreign to us just a short time ago. Today we enter a new reality, one in which we must be concerned about the use of biological organisms as weapons of mass destruction.

Chemical and biological agents can be delivered in a number of ways. From anthrax in an envelope to smallpox injected into another human, these kinds of threats are very real. Making these threats even more alarming is the fact that many of these agents are invisible to the eye and don't manifest themselves for days or even weeks. We have vaccines that can effectively counteract or prevent illness for some of these agents, but for others we do not.

The intent of this section is not to scare the public nor is it to instill an air of hopelessness. The fact remains, widespread chemical and biological warfare is a possibility, although a remote one. Better to be armed with knowledge than to be caught unaware and unable to process the threat. Weigh both the liability and probability of such a threat, and if you deem it a possible threat to your business operations, incorporate these events into your emergency planning process.

Case Study 1: Anthrax Letter Attacks, 2001

Never before in American history has the receipt of mail caused so much concern. In the 1990s, we were concerned over letter bomb packages sent by a mysterious person dubbed the "Unabomber." When the perpetrator—who killed three people and injured twenty-three—was finally discovered and captured, we learned about a domestic terrorist named Ted Kaczynski. We were concerned, but Kaczynski seemed to be targeting specific people, namely scientists and professors. If that didn't describe us, we were not overly concerned. Additionally, we became educated about the dangers of unknown packages, particularly those large in size. It was not until the anthrax letters immediately following the terrorist attacks of September 11, 2001, that we became really concerned about our mail delivery.

Anthrax spores formulated as a white powder were mailed to individuals in the government and major media from September 18 to October 9, 2001, in Florida, New York, New Jersey, and Washington, D.C. Postal sorting machines and the opening of these letters dispersed the spores as aerosols. As a consequence, twenty-two victims were infected (either through skin contact with the anthrax or through inhalation) and of those, five died. The effect was to disrupt mail services and to cause a widespread fear of handling delivered mail. Decontamination of the seventeen post office and public buildings where the letters were received took years at a cost of close to $1 billion.

*   *   *

Chemical warfare agents are poisonous vapors, aerosols, liquids, or solids that have toxic effects on people, animals, or plants. They can be released by bombs, sprayed from aircraft, boats, or vehicles, or used as a liquid to create a hazard to people and the environment. Some chemical agents may be odorless and tasteless. They can have an immediate effect (a few seconds to a few minutes) or a delayed effect (several hours to several days). While potentially lethal, chemical agents are difficult to deliver in lethal concentrations. Outdoors, the agents often dissipate rapidly. Chemical agents are also difficult to produce.

There are six types of agents:

1. Lung-damaging (pulmonary) agents, such as phosgene
2. Cyanide
3. Vesicants or blister agents, such as mustard
4. Nerve agents, such as GA (tabun), GB (sarin), GD (soman), GF, and VX
5. Incapacitating agents, such as BZ
6. Riot-control agents (similar to MACE)

Biological agents are organisms or toxins that can kill or incapacitate people, livestock, and crops. The three basic groups of biological agents that would likely be used as weapons are bacteria, viruses, and toxins.

1. **Bacteria**: Bacteria are small free-living organisms that reproduce by simple division and are easy to grow. The diseases they produce often respond to treatment with antibiotics.
2. **Viruses**: Viruses are organisms that require living cells in which to reproduce and are intimately dependent upon the body they infect. Viruses produce diseases that generally do not respond to antibiotics. However, antiviral drugs are sometimes effective.
3. **Toxins**: Toxins are poisonous substances found in, and extracted from, living plants, animals, or microorganisms; some toxins can be produced or altered by chemical means. Some toxins can be treated with specific antitoxins and selected drugs.

Most biological agents are difficult to grow and maintain. Many break down quickly when exposed to sunlight and other environmental factors, while others, such as anthrax spores are very long lived. They can be dispersed by being sprayed in the air or infecting animals that carry the disease to humans, as well as through food and water contamination.

Possible methods of dispersal:

- **Aerosols**: Biological agents are dispersed into the air, forming a fine mist that may drift for miles. Inhaling the agent may cause disease in people or animals.
- **Insects or Animals**: Some insects and animals, such as fleas, mice, flies, and mosquitoes, can be used to spread diseases. Deliberately spreading diseases through livestock is also referred to as agroterrorism.
- **Food and water contamination**: Some pathogenic organisms and toxins may persist in food and water supplies. Most microbes can be killed, and toxins deactivated, by cooking food and boiling water.
- **Person-to-person**: Person-to-person spread of a few infectious agents is also possible. Humans have been the source of infection for smallpox, plague, and the Lassa viruses.

HVAC System

One of the greatest concerns for building managers is the potential for biological agents to be spread via the HVAC system. To protect the HVAC system at its weakest point, pay particular attention to the fresh air intakes. If these are left unprotected, dangerous substances could be introduced into the HVAC system. From one location, an entire building can be infested with chemical or biological agents. Fresh air intakes can be protected in a number of ways. Simply installing security cameras at the intake location may be a good deterrent. A better way to protect the intake is to limit access to it. This can be achieved by installing fencing around the area where the intake is located.

When installing fencing remember that some chemicals such as pepper spray can be sprayed into air intakes from a distance. The installation of motion sensors within the parameters of the fence would serve as further protection. In a multistory environment experts suggest moving the air intake up from ground level, perhaps as high as four or five stories from the ground level.

Many building owners and managers have created a process that will allow them to shut down the entire HVAC system (including intakes, dampers, etc.) with one flip of a switch. In the past, shut down required many switches be turned off, was time consuming, and was not always completed correctly.

The Centers for Disease Control and Prevention (CDC) has created three categories for biological diseases and harmful agents based on the severity of impact and the ease with which they can be spread. The categories and examples of each include the following:

Category A

Public healthcare providers must be prepared to address a number of biological agents, including pathogens that are rarely seen in the United States. High-priority agents pose a serious risk to the national security because they can be readily produced and easily disseminated from person to person, resulting in deaths and the potential for a major public health impact. Additionally, occurrence of these agents might cause public panic and social disruption.

- Anthrax (*Bacillus anthracis*)
- Botulism (*Clostridium botulinum* toxin)
- Plague (*Yersinia pestis*)
- Smallpox
- Tularemia (*Francisella tularensis*)
- Viral hemorrhagic fevers (filoviruses such as Ebola or Marburg and arenaviruses)

Category B

These agents comprise a second tier of priority scale. Typically they are moderately easy to disseminate and result in moderate or low morbidity rates. Examples include:

- Food safety threats (e.g., *Salmonella, E. coli,* etc.)
- Water safety threats
- Brucellosis (*Brucella* species)
- Melioidosis (*Burkholderia pseudomallei*)
- Q fever (*Coxiella burnetii*)
- Ricin toxin (*Ricinus communis*)
- Staphylococcal enterotoxin B
- Typhus fever (*Rickettsia prowazekii*)
- Viral encephalitis

Category C

This third priority level includes emerging agents that could be engineered for mass dissemination in the future because of their easy availability or production and because of their potential for high casualties. With Category C diseases and agents, a major public health emergency could occur. Examples include infectious disease threats such as Nipah virus and hantavirus.

How to Prepare for a Chemical or Biological Attack

Assemble a disaster supply kit and be sure to include:

- Battery-powered commercial radio with extra batteries
- Nonperishable food and drinking water
- First-aid kit
- Sanitation supplies including soap, water, and bleach
- Roll of duct tape and scissors
- Plastic for doors, windows, and vents for the room in which you will shelter in place (this should be an internal room where you can block out air that may contain hazardous-chemical or biological agents. To save critical time during an emergency, sheeting should be pre-measured and cut for each opening.)

What to Do During a Chemical or Biological Attack

In case of a chemical or biological weapon attack near you, authorities will instruct you on the best course of action. This may be to evacuate the area immediately, to seek shelter at a designated location, or to take immediate shelter where you are and seal the premises.

Online and Digital Resources

For more comprehensive information on all types of chemical and biological information, visit the Centers for Disease Control and Prevention (CDC) bioterrorism Web site at emergency. cdc.gov/bioterrorism/index.asp. This is an excellent resource for bioterrorism preparedness and response and FAQs.

Other resources:

- ⋏   "Emergency Preparedness and You," also from the CDC: emergency.cdc.gov/ preparedness/
- ⋏   CDC on Twitter: @CDCemergency
- ⋏   "Biological Threats" from the Department of Homeland Security: www.ready. gov/biological-threats

To best protect yourself, take emergency preparedness measures ahead of time and to get medical attention as soon as possible, if needed.

1. Listen to your radio for instructions from authorities, such as whether to remain inside or to evacuate.
2. If you are instructed to remain in your home, the building where you are, or other shelter during a chemical or biological attack:

- ⋏   Turn off all ventilation, including furnaces, air conditioners, vents, and fans.
- ⋏   Seek shelter in an internal room, preferably one without windows. Seal the room with duct tape and plastic sheeting. Ten square feet of floor space per person will provide sufficient air to prevent carbon dioxide build-up for up to five hours.
- ⋏   Remain in protected areas where toxic vapors are reduced or eliminated, and be sure to take your battery-operated radio with you.

3. If you are caught in an unprotected area, you should:

- ⋏   Attempt to get up-wind of the contaminated area.
- ⋏   Attempt to find shelter as quickly as possible.

Sheltering in Place

Whether you are at home, work, or elsewhere, there may be situations when it's simply best to stay where you are and avoid any uncertainty outside. There are other circumstances when staying put and creating a barrier between yourself and potentially contaminated air outside, a process known as "sealing the room," is a matter of survival. Use available information to assess the situation. If you see large amounts of debris in the air, or if local authorities say the air is badly contaminated, you may want to take this kind of action.

The process used to seal the room is considered a temporary protective measure to create a barrier between you and potentially contaminated air outside. It is a type of sheltering in place that requires preplanning.

Sheltering in Place in an Office or Large Building

In normal operations, a building does little to protect occupants from airborne hazards outside the building because outdoor air must be continuously introduced to provide a comfortable, healthy indoor environment. However, a building can provide substantial protection against agents released outdoors if the flow of fresh air is filtered/cleaned, or temporarily interrupted or reduced. Interrupting the flow of fresh air is the principle applied in the protective action known as sheltering in place.

The advantage of sheltering in place is that it can be implemented rapidly. The disadvantage is that its protection is variable and diminishes with the duration of the hazard. Sheltering requires that two distinct actions be taken without delay to maximize the passive protection a building provides:

First, reduce the indoor-outdoor air exchange rate before the hazardous plume arrives. This is achieved by closing all windows and doors, and turning off all fans, air conditioners, and combustion heaters.

Second, increase the indoor-outdoor air exchange rate as soon as the hazardous plume has passed. This is achieved by opening all windows and doors, and turning on all fans to ventilate the building. The level of protection that can be attained by sheltering in place is substantial, but it is less than can be provided by high efficiency filtration of the fresh air introduced into the building. The amount of protection varies with:

- The building's air exchange rate. The tighter the building (i.e., the lower the air exchange rate), the greater the protection it provides. In most cases, air conditioners and combustion heaters cannot be operated while sheltering in place because operating them increases the indoor-outdoor exchange of air.
- The duration of exposure. Protection varies with time, diminishing as the time of exposure increases. Sheltering in place is, therefore, suitable only for exposures of short duration, roughly two hours or less, depending on conditions.
- Purging or period of occupancy. How long occupants remain in the building after the hazardous plume has passed also affects the level of protection. Because the building slowly purges contaminants that have entered it, at some point during plume passage, the concentration inside exceeds the concentration outside. Maximum protection is attained by increasing the air exchange rate after plume passage or by exiting the building into clean air.

▲ Natural filtering. Some filtering occurs when the agent is deposited in the building shell or upon interior surfaces as air passes into and out of the building. The tighter the building, the greater is the effect of this natural filtering. In a home, taking the actions required for sheltering (i.e., closing windows and doors, and turning off all air conditioners, fans, and combustion heaters) is relatively simple. Doing so in a commercial or apartment building may require more time and planning. All air handling units must be turned off and any dampers for outside air must be closed.

Procedures for a protective action plan, therefore, should include:

▲ Identifying all air handling units, fans, and the switches needed to deactivate them.

▲ Identifying cracks, seams, joints, and pores in the building envelope to be temporarily sealed to further reduce outside air infiltration.

▲ Keeping emergency supplies, such as duct tape and polyethylene sheeting, on hand.

▲ Identifying procedures for purging after an internal release (i.e., opening windows and doors, turning on smoke fans, air handlers, and fans that were turned off) to exhaust and purge the building.

▲ Identifying sheltering rooms (i.e., interior rooms having a lower air exchange rate) that may provide a higher level of passive protection.

It may be desirable to go to a predetermined sheltering room (or rooms) and:

▲ Shut and lock all windows and doors.

▲ Seal any windows and vents with plastic sheeting and duct tape.

▲ Seal the door(s) with duct tape around the top, bottom, and sides.

▲ Firmly pack dampened towels along the bottom of each door.

▲ Turn on a TV or radio that can be heard within the shelter and listen for further instructions.

▲ When the "all clear" is announced, open windows and doors.

Important considerations for use of sheltering in place are that stairwells must be isolated by closing fire doors, elevators must not be used, and clear evacuation routes must remain open if evacuation is required. Escape hoods may be needed if the only evacuation routes are through contaminated areas.

One final consideration for sheltering in place is that occupants cannot be forced to participate. It is important to develop a plan in cooperation with likely participants and awareness training programs that include discussions of sheltering in place and events (CBR attacks, hazardous material releases, or natural disasters) that might make sheltering preferable to evacuation. During an event, some building protective action plans call for making a concise information announcement, and then giving occupants three to five minutes to proceed to the sheltering area or evacuate the building before it is sealed. Training programs and information announcements during an event should be tailored to help occupants to make informed decisions.

Sheltering in Place at Home

- ⅄   Bring your family and pets **inside**.
- ⅄   **Lock** doors and **close** windows, air vents, and fireplace dampers.
- ⅄   **Turn off** fans, air conditioning, and forced air heating systems.
- ⅄   **Take your emergency supply kit** unless you have reason to believe it has been contaminated.
- ⅄   **Go into an interior room** with few windows, if possible.
- ⅄   **Seal** all windows, doors and air vents with plastic sheeting and duct tape. Consider measuring and cutting the sheeting in advance to save time.
- ⅄   Be prepared to **improvise** and use what you have on hand to **seal gaps** so that you create a barrier between yourself and any contamination.

Local authorities may not immediately be able to provide information on what is happening and what you should do. However, you should **watch TV, listen to the radio, or check the Internet often for official news** and instructions as they become available.

Indications of CBR Contamination

Researchers are working on a prototype device to automatically and continuously monitor the air for the presence of bacterial spores. The device would continuously sample the air and use microwaves to trigger a chemical reaction, the intensity of which would correspond to the concentration of bacterial spores in the sample. If an increase in spore concentration is detected, an alarm similar to a smoke detector would sound and a technician would respond and use traditional sampling and analysis to confirm the presence of anthrax spores. Researchers hope the device response time will be fast enough to help prevent widespread contamination.

In the absence of a warning, people can be alerted to some airborne hazards by observing symptoms or effects in others. This provides a practical means for initiating protective actions, because the susceptibility to hazardous materials varies from person to person. The concentrations of airborne materials may also vary substantially within a given building or room, producing a hazard that may be greater to some occupants than to others.

Other warning signs of a hazard may involve seeing and hearing something out of the ordinary, such as the hiss of a rapid release from a pressurized cylinder. Awareness to warning properties, signs, and symptoms in other people is the basis of a protective action plan. Such a plan should apply these possible protective actions: sheltering in place, using protective masks, and evacuating.

For protection against imperceptible agents, the only practical protective measures are those that are continuously in place, such as filtering all air brought into the building on a continuous basis and using automatic, real-time sensors that are capable of detecting the imperceptible agents.

Chemical, biological, and radiological materials, as well as industrial agents, may travel in the air as a gas or on surfaces we physically contact. Dispersion methods may be as simple as placing a container in a heavily used area, opening a container, or using conventional (garden)/commercial spray devices, or as elaborate as detonating an aerosol. Chemical incidents are characterized by the rapid onset (minutes to hours) of medical symptoms and easily observed indicators (e.g., colored residue, dead foliage, pungent odor, and dead animals, birds, fish, or insects.

Possible Signs of Chemical Threat

- Many sick or dead birds, fish ,or small animals are cause for suspicion—not just an occasional road kill, but numerous animals (wild and domestic, small and large), birds, and fish in the same area.
- Lack of insect life: if normal insect activity (ground, air, or water) is missing, check the ground/water surface/shore line for dead insects. If near water, check for dead fish/aquatic birds.
- Physical symptoms: numerous individuals experiencing unexplained water-like blisters, wheals (like bee stings), pinpointed pupils, choking, respiratory ailments, or rashes.
- Illness associated with confined geographic area: lower attack rates for people working indoors than those working outdoors and vice versa.
- Mass casualties: many individuals exhibiting unexplained serious health problems, ranging from nausea to disorientation to difficulty in breathing to convulsions to death.
- Unusual liquid droplets: numerous surfaces exhibit oily droplets/film; numerous water surfaces have an oily film. (Observed when there has been no recent rain.)
- Areas that look different—not just a patch of dead weeds, but trees, shrubs, bushes, food crops, or lawns that are dead, discolored, or withered (when there is no current drought).
- Unexplained odors: smells may range from fruity to flowery to sharp/pungent to garlic/horseradish-like to bitter almonds/peach to new mown hay. It is important to note that the particular odor is completely out of character with its surroundings.
- Low-lying clouds: a low-lying cloud/fog-like condition that is not explained by its surroundings.

▲   Unusual metal debris: an unexplained bomb/munitions-like material, especially if it contains a liquid. (No recent rain.)

If You See Signs of Chemical Attack: Find Clean Air Quickly

Quickly try to define the area or where the chemical is coming from, if possible, then take immediate action to get away.

If the chemical is inside a building where you are, get out of the building without passing through the contaminated area, if possible.

If you can't get out of the building or find clean air without passing through the area where you see signs of a chemical attack, it may be better to move as far away as possible and shelter in place (see previous section).

If you are outside, quickly decide what is the fastest way to find clean air. Consider if you can get out of the area or if you should go inside the closest building and shelter in place.

If You Think You Have Been Exposed to a Chemical

If your eyes are watering, your skin is stinging, and you are having trouble breathing, you may have been exposed to a chemical.

If you think you may have been **exposed to a chemical, strip immediately** and **wash**. Look for a hose, fountain, or any source of water, and wash with soap if possible, being sure not to scrub the chemical into your skin. Flush eyes with lots of water.

Remove eyeglasses or contact lenses. Put glasses in a pan of household bleach to decontaminate.

Put the contaminated clothing into a plastic bag if possible.

Seek emergency medical attention.

What to Do after a Chemical Attack

Immediate symptoms of exposure to chemical agents may include blurred vision, eye irritation, difficulty breathing, and nausea. A person affected by a chemical or biological agent requires immediate attention by professional medical personnel. If medical help is not immediately available, decontaminate yourself and assist in decontaminating others. Decontamination is needed within minutes of exposure to minimize health consequences. However, you should not leave the safety of a shelter to go outdoors to help others until authorities announce it is safe to do so.

1. Use extreme caution when helping others who have been exposed to chemical agents: Remove all clothing and other items in contact with the body. Con-

taminated clothing normally removed over the head should be cut off to avoid contact with the eyes, nose, and mouth. Put into a plastic bag if possible. Decontaminate hands using soap and water.

2. Flush eyes with lots of water.
3. Gently wash face and hair with soap and water; then thoroughly rinse with water.
4. Decontaminate other body areas likely to have been contaminated. Blot—do not swab or scrape—with a cloth soaked in soapy water and rinse with clear water.
5. Change into uncontaminated clothes. Clothing stored in drawers or closets is likely to be uncontaminated.
6. If possible, proceed to a medical facility for screening.

What to Do after a Biological Attack

In many biological attacks, people will not know they have been exposed to an agent. In such situations, the first evidence of an attack may be when you notice symptoms of the disease caused by an agent exposure, and you should seek immediate medical attention for treatment.

In some situations, such as the anthrax letters sent in 2001, people may be alerted to a potential exposure. If this is the case, pay close attention to all official warnings and instructions on how to proceed. The delivery of medical services for a biological event may be handled differently to respond to increased demand. Again, it will be important for you to pay attention to official instructions via radio, television, and emergency alert systems.

If your skin or clothing comes in contact with a visible, potentially infectious substance, you should remove and bag your clothes and personal items and wash yourself with warm soapy water immediately. Put on clean clothes and seek medical assistance. For more information, visit the Web site for the Centers for Disease Control and Prevention at www.cdc.gov.

About Specific Chemical and Biological Threats

Anthrax

Anthrax is an acute infectious disease caused by the spore-forming bacterium *Bacillus anthracis*. Anthrax most commonly occurs in hoofed mammals and can also infect humans. Symptoms of disease vary depending on how the disease was contracted, but usually occur within seven days after exposure.

The serious forms of human anthrax are inhalation anthrax, cutaneous anthrax, and intestinal anthrax. The death rate for anthrax from inhaled sources is very high, approaching 100 percent. Death rates are lower for anthrax that enters your body through food or a wound. Anthrax is easy to produce, and it's readily available around the world.

The spores don't require special handling procedures, so terrorists could take anthrax to many points for distribution. Unlike many disease-causing bacteria, spores can survive severe heat and cold.

Initial symptoms of inhalation anthrax infection may resemble a common cold. After several days, the symptoms may progress to severe breathing problems and shock.

The intestinal disease form of anthrax may follow the consumption of contaminated food and is characterized by an acute inflammation of the intestinal tract. Initial signs of nausea, loss of appetite, vomiting, and fever are followed by abdominal pain, vomiting of blood, and severe diarrhea.

Direct person-to-person spread of anthrax is extremely unlikely, if it occurs at all. Therefore, there is no need to immunize or treat contacts of persons ill with anthrax, such as household contacts, friends, or coworkers, unless they also were also exposed to the same source of infection.

In persons exposed to anthrax, infection can be prevented with antibiotic treatment. Early antibiotic treatment of anthrax infection is essential; delay lessens chances for survival. Anthrax usually is susceptible to penicillin, doxycycline, and fluoroquinolones. An anthrax vaccine also can prevent infection. Vaccination against anthrax is not recommended for the general public to prevent disease and is not available.

Smallpox

Smallpox is caused by the *variola* virus that emerged in human populations thousands of years ago. This disease is universally feared as the most destructive of infectious diseases. Smallpox was eradicated from humans in the 1970s, although both the United States and Russia store the virus in laboratories. There is some concern over the security of such labs, especially those in Russia. It is thought that other countries may also have small samples of the smallpox virus.

In the aftermath of the events of September and October, 2001, there is heightened concern that the *variola* virus might be used as an agent of bioterrorism. For this reason, the U.S. government is taking precautions for dealing with a smallpox outbreak.

About 30 percent of those infected with smallpox die of it. Many people have never been vaccinated for smallpox, and no one knows whether those who received vaccinations twenty-five or more years ago are still protected. Smallpox is harder to propagate than anthrax and less tolerant of severe conditions. However, it can spread very rapidly from person to person.

There is no proven treatment for smallpox although vaccination within four days of exposure can lessen the effects. Within two weeks after a smallpox exposure, high fever and headache give way to more visible symptoms including a rash on the mouth and hands.

Nerve Agents

In the late 1930s, a German chemist named Gerhard Schrader was working toward developing chemical pesticides for crops. He accidentally produced what is now called the nerve agent Tabun. Schrader later produced the nerve agents Sarin and Soman. Sarin is odorless and colorless in its pure form and thus a very dangerous and imperceptible agent.

Noteworthy events involving nerve agents have occurred in recent times. During the Iran-Iraq war (1980–1988), Iraq used Sarin, other nerve agents, mustard gas, and a mixture of other agents both in battle and against civilians, with deaths suspected to be 65,000 or more. In 1988, Iraq used nerve agents and mustard gas against Kurdish civilians at Halabja, causing 5,000 deaths. In 1994, the Aum Shinrikyo, a religious cult, released Sarin in Matsumoto, Japan, killing seven people and injuring 500. In 1995, Aum Shinrikyo again released Sarin, but this time in the Tokyo subway. This act of domestic terrorism killed twelve people and injured more than 1,000, some of whom were temporarily blinded. Two years ago, police in London foiled a plot to release Sarin among the spectators of a major soccer game.

Nerve agents such as Sarin can affect all parts of the central nervous system. Symptoms include eye pain, blurred vision, tightness in chest, nausea, vomiting, tearing, muscle weakness, convulsions, loss of consciousness, and coma. Long-term effects include anxiety, insomnia, depression, headaches, slurred speech, and difficulty concentrating. Atropine is a common drug used to treat nerve agent exposure. It has proven successful in treating many of the symptoms of nerve agent exposure. Other treatments exist, but they have limitations.

Mustard Gas

In World War I, the German army first used "mustard gas" (sulfur mustard) in 1917. It incapacitated the opposition through inhalation or skin contact. After dispersal, it could remain effective for a long time.

Although not normally deadly, mustard gas typically produces blisters and irritates the eyes and respiratory system. Large doses can cause burns and lung damage, can damage the immune system, and can be life threatening if the exposure is great. Unfortunately, there is no known antidote for mustard gas exposure. Decontamination must be completed within two minutes after exposure to limit damage. If exposed to mustard gas, the victim should immediately remove all clothing and begin the decontamination process. Decontamination includes washing with baking soda or Fuller's earth powder. If these products are unavailable, use water and soap. Be sure to irrigate eyes with saline solution, if available. If saline solution is not available, use clear water.

Other Threats

Other infectious diseases that pose a threat include plague, tularemia, botulism, viral hemorrhagic fever, and tuberculosis. But experts believe these organisms and diseases are unlikely to cause widespread illness because they're difficult to manufacture and distribute. These organisms are also less hardy than anthrax is. Alternatively, biological toxins derived from living organisms, such as the botulinum toxin derived from the bacterium *Clostridium botulinum*, or toxins derived from plants, such as ricin from castor beans, could be used in terrorist attacks.

Botulism

Botulism is a muscle-paralyzing disease caused by a toxin made by a bacterium called *Clostridium botulinum*. There are three main kinds of botulism:

Foodborne botulism occurs when a person ingests preformed toxin that leads to illness within a few hours to days. Foodborne botulism is a public health emergency because the contaminated food may still be available to other persons besides the patient.

Infant botulism occurs in a small number of susceptible infants each year who harbor *C. botulinum* in their intestinal tract.

Wound botulism occurs when wounds are infected with *C. botulinum* that secretes the toxin.

With foodborne botulism, symptoms begin within six hours to two weeks (most commonly between twelve and thirty-six hours) after eating toxin-containing food. Symptoms of botulism include double vision, blurred vision, drooping eyelids, slurred speech, difficulty swallowing, dry mouth, muscle weakness that always descends through the body: first shoulders are affected, then upper arms, lower arms, thighs, calves, and so on. Paralysis of breathing muscles can cause a person to stop breathing and die, unless assistance with breathing (mechanical ventilation) is provided.

Botulism is not spread from one person to another. Foodborne botulism can occur in all age groups. A supply of antitoxin against botulism is maintained by CDC. The antitoxin is effective in reducing the severity of symptoms if administered early in the course of the disease. Most patients eventually recover after weeks to months of supportive care.

6

Chemical Spills, Contamination, and Household Emergencies

There are thousands of chemicals in our homes and places of work. Some are dangerous and even more so when they get into the wrong hands. Most hazardous chemicals have warning properties that provide a practical means for detecting a hazard and initiating protective actions. Such warning properties make chemicals perceptible; for example, vapors or gases can be perceived by the human senses (i.e., smell, sight, taste, or irritation of the eyes, skin, or respiratory tract) before serious effects occur. The distinction between perceptible and imperceptible agents is not an exact one. The concentrations at which one can detect an odor vary from person to person, and these thresholds also vary relative to the concentration that can produce immediate, injurious effects.

Most industrial chemicals and chemical-warfare agents are readily detectable by smell. Soldiers in World Wars I and II were taught to identify, by smell, such agents as mustard, phosgene, and chlorine, and this detection method proved effective for determining when to put on a gas mask. An exception is the chemical-warfare agent Sarin, which is odorless and colorless in its pure form and, therefore, imperceptible.

Among the most common toxic industrial chemicals, carbon monoxide is one of the few that is imperceptible. Because it is odorless and colorless, it causes many deaths in buildings each year.

Chemical Incidents

Chemical incidents are characterized by the rapid onset (minutes to hours) of medical symptoms and easily observed indicators (e.g., colored residue, dead foliage, pungent odor, and dead animals, birds, fish, or insects).

Business owners and management should be prepared for the potential of a spill. Not only is this smart business, it is also required by law.

According to the Environmental Protection Agency (EPA), at least 123 plants across the country keep amounts of toxic chemicals that, if released, could form deadly vapor clouds that would endanger over 1 million people. Additionally, at least 700 plants store chemicals that, if released, could endanger over 100,000 people. The number of persons who will be injured following the release of chemicals and the extent of the damage will depend on numerous factors. Some factors are the properties of the substance, the size of the discharge, the period during which people are exposed, and the length of time that passes between exposure and treatment.

During the night of December 2 to 3, 1984, workers at the Union Carbide factory in Bhopal, India, reported to their supervisors that their eyes were burning and tearing. The cause of the discomfort was a dangerous chemical reaction that occurred when a large amount of water got into a methyl isocyanate (MIC) storage tank. For nearly an hour, thirty metric tons of methyl isocyanate poured out of the tank and escaped into the air, creating a cloud of poisonous gas over the city of nearly 1 million people. Because the accident occurred in the middle of the night, many of the city's inhabitants died in their sleep. All told, estimated deaths reached upwards of 4,000 people, and close to 500,000 people were sickened. Many of the victims were people living in poor shantytowns surrounding the Union Carbide plant. Many of the people affected in 1984 are still feeling the effects of the poisonous gas today.

A 1990 study commissioned by the EPA found that since 1980 there were at least fifteen accidents in the United States that exceeded the Bhopal, India, release in volume and toxicity of chemicals released. Only circumstances such as wind conditions, containment measures, rapid evacuations, and facility location prevented disastrous consequences from taking place.

There are on average 60,000 industrial chemical accidents every year and more than 250 people die each year as a result. These incidents include a range of events, not all of which necessarily resulted in consequences like injuries, deaths, or evacuations. More than 4,800 facilities in the United States each store at least 100,000 pounds of an extremely hazardous substances, which is more than the amount of volatile toxic chemicals released at Bhopal (some 90,000 pounds).

In 1990 as a part of the Clean Air Act Amendments Section 112(r), the U.S. Congress required industrial sites that use extremely hazardous substances to disclose Risk Management Plans (RMPs). The RMPs have three parts: first, a hazard assessment describes release scenarios, potential off-site consequences, and a five-year accident history; second, a prevention program addresses basic safety procedures such as training, maintenance, and safety audits; and third, an emergency response program covers response plans, drills, and coordination with local planners.

Case Study 1: The Love Canal, 1976

The infamous Love Canal Treatment Facility in Niagara Falls, New York, is perhaps the best (or worst) example of man's lack of concern for the earth's environment. During the

1940s, Hooker Chemical Company used the landfill—originally a shipping canal that was abandoned—extensively to dispose of a variety of chemical wastes. When the site reached its maximum capacity, Hooker Chemical covered the landfill with dirt. They sold the site in 1953 to the Niagara Falls Board of Education for one dollar. Eventually a public school was built on the site in addition to hundreds of single-family homes. As early as 1976, residents began to question the unknown substances seeping into their basements and storm sewers. Eventually, the school was closed and over 800 families were relocated.

Nearly 21,000 tons of toxic chemicals were dumped at the fifteen-acre Love Canal landfill. More than 200 different chemical compounds are identified as being buried there. In August 1978, President Carter declared a federal emergency at the Love Canal. In 1979 a federal report estimated the odds of Love Canal residents contracting cancer to be as high as one in ten. In 1980 the EPA discovered that chromosome damage was found in eleven out of thirty-six residents tested from the Love Canal area.

Case Study 2: General Chemical, 1993

On July 26, 1993, a leak of oleum (concentrated sulfuric acid and sulfuric trioxide) from a railroad tank car at a manufacturing plant operated by the General Chemical Corporation exposed 63,000 people to harmful fumes and sent approximately 24,000 people who had inhaled the acid mist to the hospital. Following the release of more than twelve tons of acid mist, a poisonous plume developed and drifted over fifteen miles from the General Chemical site at Richmond, California. Interestingly, prior to this event, General Chemical conducted a worst-case analysis and estimated a chemical release would produce a toxic cloud that would not travel more than one-half mile from the site. Most of the people who visited the hospital complained of skin rashes and breathing problems, although some people experienced more serious difficulties. As a result of this event, General Chemical was responsible for almost $200 million in legal actions, and public concern over the dangers of chemical plants across the nation became common.

What to Do Before a Hazardous-materials Incident

Many communities have Local Emergency Planning Committees (LEPCs) that identify industrial hazardous materials and keep the community informed of the potential risk. All companies that have hazardous chemicals must report annually to the LEPC. The public is encouraged to participate in the process. Contact your local emergency management office to find out if your community has an LEPC and how you can participate.

1. Ask your fire or police department about warning procedures. These could include:

   - Outdoor warning sirens or horns
   - Emergency Alert System (EAS)—Information provided via radio and television

A   "All-Call" telephoning: An automated system for sending recorded messages

A   News media—Internet, radio, television, cable, and digital

A   Residential route alerting—Messages announced to neighborhoods from vehicles equipped with public-address systems

2. Ask your LEPC or emergency management office about community plans for responding to a hazardous-materials accident at a plant or other facility, or a transportation accident involving hazardous materials.

3. Ask your LEPC about storage and usage of hazardous chemicals in your local area.

4. Use the information gathered from LEPC and local emergency management offices to evaluate your risks. Determine how close you are to factories, freeways, or railroads that may produce or transport toxic waste.

5. Be prepared to evacuate. An evacuation could last for a few hours or several days.

6. Be prepared to shelter in place; that is, to seek safety in your home or any other building you might be in at the time of a chemical release. At home you should select a room to be used as a shelter. The shelter room for use in case of a hazardous-material incident should be above ground, large enough to accommodate all household members and pets, and should have the fewest possible exterior doors and windows. You should also assemble a shelter kit to be used to seal the shelter room during a chemical release. The kit should include plastic sheeting, duct tape, scissors, a towel, and modeling clay or other material to stuff into cracks. (See chapter 5.)

If you are a business owner or manager, you should be concerned not only with the potential chemical spill within the confines of your business operations, but also with off-site spills at nearby businesses that could affect you as well. A natural gas plant across the street from your facility could experience problems that would directly affect your business, for example.

The obvious starting point is to identify hazardous chemicals kept on site. This requires an audit of janitorial closets, shop areas, mechanical rooms, production floors, and other related areas. While listing the chemicals present, look for properly labeled containers that identify the chemical and the hazards. This is important, especially in secondary containers (small containers and spray bottles). Next, each chemical should have a Material Safety Data Sheet (MSDS) that describes its hazards. By law, this MSDS must be provided to you by the manufacturer or the distributor of the chemical. MSDSs are created for all chemicals, even those that do not present a great danger (i.e., Windex).

> To report a hazardous substance release, oil spills, or radiation threats, contact the EPA's National Response Center at (800) 424-8802. The National Response Center is staffed twenty-four hours a day and will monitor the cleanup activities and assist in the cleanup as warranted.

Finally, you should identify other facilities in your area that use, transport, or produce hazardous chemicals. Determine whether chemical spills at their locations could affect your facility, and if it could, address how you would handle that emergency. Think about power plants, refineries, mills, highways, waterways, and railroads. Think worst-case scenario.

> For information on EPA's oil spill program, see their dedicated Web pages at the rather bulky url www2.epa.gov/oil-spills-prevention-and-preparedness-regulations#_ga=1 .105319361.350642967.1444688828. Or search for "Oil Spills" on the EPA's A–Z Index at www.epa.gov.

Household Chemical Emergencies

Nearly every household uses products containing hazardous materials. Although the risk of a chemical accident is slight, knowing how to handle these products and how to react during an emergency can reduce the risk of injury.

How to Prepare for Household Chemical Emergencies

1. Contact agencies with expertise on hazardous household materials, such as your local public health department or the Environmental Protection Agency, for information about potentially dangerous household products and their antidotes. Ask about the advisability of maintaining antidotes in your home for: cleaners and germicides, deodorizers, detergents, drain and bowl cleaners, gases, home medications, laundry bleaches, liquid fuels, paint removers, and thinners.

2. Follow instructions on the product label for proper disposal of chemicals. Proper disposal will ensure environmental and public health, as well as household well-being. If you have additional questions on chemical disposal, call your local environmental or recycling agency.

   - Small amounts of the following products can be safely poured down the drain with plenty of water: bathroom and glass cleaner, bleach, drain cleaner, household disinfectant, laundry and dishwashing detergent, rubbing alcohol, rug and upholstery cleaner, and toilet bowl cleaner.
   - Small amounts of the following products should be disposed by wrapping the container in newspaper and plastic and placing it in the trash: brake fluid, car wax or polish, dish and laundry soap, fertilizer, furniture and floor polish, insect repellent, nail polish, oven cleaner, paint thinners and strippers, pesticides, powder cleansers, water-based paint, and wood preservatives.
   - Dispose of the following products at a recycling center or a collection site: kerosene; motor or fuel oil; car battery or battery acid; diesel

fuel; transmission fluid; large amounts of paint, thinner or stripper; power-steering fluid; turpentine; gun cleaning solvents; and tires.

⚒ Empty spray cans completely before placing in the trash. Do not place spray cans into a burning barrel, incinerator, or trash compactor because they may explode.

⚒ Outdated medications can cause ill effects. Ask your pharmacist how to dispose of outdated and unused medicines—some may be flushed down the toilet. Flushing eliminates the risk of people or animals picking them out of the trash. Some police departments have drop boxes for unused medication. The U.S. Food and Drug Administration has more helpful hints at www.fda.gov in their consumer section.

3. Read directions before using a new chemical product, and be sure to store household chemicals according to the instructions on the label.

4. Store chemicals in a safe, secure location, preferably up high and always out of the reach of children.

5. Avoid mixing household chemical products. Deadly toxic fumes can result from the mixture of chemicals, such as chlorine bleach and ammonia.

6. Never smoke while using household chemicals. Avoid using hair spray, cleaning solutions, paint products, or pesticides near an open flame, pilot light, lighted candle, fireplace, wood burning stove, and so forth. Although you may not be able to see or smell them, vapor particles in the air could catch fire or explode.

7. If you spill a chemical, clean it up immediately with rags. Be careful to protect your eyes and skin, wear gloves and eye protection. Allow the fumes in the rags to evaporate outdoors, and then dispose of the rags by wrapping them in a newspaper and placing them in a sealed plastic bag in your trashcan.

8. Buy only as much of a chemical as you think you will use. If you have product left over, try to give it to someone who will use it. Storing hazardous chemicals increases the risk of chemical emergencies.

9. Keep an A-B-C rated fire extinguisher in the home and car, and get training from your local fire department on how to use it.

10. Post the number of the nearest poison control center by all telephones. In an emergency situation you may not have time to look up critical phone numbers. For pesticide poisoning, the toll-free phone number for the EPA's Poison Control is (800) 222-1222.

11. Learn to detect hazardous materials. Many hazardous materials do not have a taste or an odor, and some can be detected because they cause physical reactions, such as watering eyes or nausea. Other hazardous materials exist beneath the ground and can be recognized by an oil or foam-like appearance.

12. Learn to recognize the symptoms of toxic poisoning:

- Difficulty breathing
- Irritation of the eyes, skin, throat, or respiratory tract
- Changes in skin color
- Headache or blurred vision
- Dizziness
- Clumsiness or lack of coordination
- Cramps or diarrhea

What to Do During a Household Chemical Emergency

1. If your child should eat or drink a nonfood substance, find any containers immediately and take them to the phone. Medical professionals may need specific information from the container to give you the best emergency advice.
2. Call the poison control center, emergency medical services (EMS), 911, hospital emergency room, county health department, fire department, or your local pharmacy. They will give you emergency advice while you wait for professional help. You should have such numbers on hand for easy access and use.
3. Follow the emergency operator or dispatcher's instructions carefully. The first-aid advice found on containers may not be appropriate. Do not give anything by mouth until medical professionals have advised you.
4. Take immediate action if the chemical gets into the eyes. Delaying first aid can greatly increase the likelihood of injury. Flush the eye with clear water for a minimum of fifteen minutes, unless authorities instruct you not to use water on the particular chemical involved. Continue the cleansing process even if the victim indicates he or she is no longer feeling any pain, and then seek medical attention.
5. Get out of the residence immediately if there is danger of a fire or explosion. Do not waste time collecting items or calling the fire department when you are in danger.
6. If there is a fire or explosion, call the fire department from outside (a cellular phone or a neighbor's phone) once you are safely away from danger.
7. Stay upwind and away from the residence to avoid breathing toxic fumes.
8. Wash hands, arms, or other body parts that may have been exposed to the chemical. Chemicals may continue to irritate the skin until they are washed off.
9. Discard clothing that may have been contaminated. Some chemicals may not wash out completely. Discarding clothes will prevent potential future exposure.
10. Administer first-aid treatment to victims of chemical burns:

- Call 911 for emergency help.
- Remove clothing and jewelry from around the injury.
- Pour clean, cool water over the burn for fifteen to thirty minutes.
- Loosely cover the burn with a sterile or clean dressing. Be sure that the dressing will not stick to the burn.
- Refer the victim to a medical professional for further treatment.

7

Nuclear Threat and Exposure

Nuclear power plants operate in most states in the country and produce about 20 percent of the nation's power. Nearly 3 million Americans live within ten miles of an operating nuclear power plant.

Fortunately, the odds of being exposed to nuclear energy are not as great as the odds of other types of emergencies. Basically, two distinct nuclear exposures could affect us—nuclear warfare and nuclear exposure from a nuclear power plant accident. Although most people cringe when you mention a nuclear power plant, these plants are actually quite safe. Nuclear power plants are closely monitored and regulated by the Nuclear Regulatory Commission (NRC), which requires each utility that operates a nuclear plant to have both an on-site and off-site emergency response plan. The on-site plans are approved by the NRC, and the off-site plans are evaluated by the Federal Emergency Management Agency (FEMA). These agencies do a very thorough job, and the likelihood of an accident is small. If an accident were to occur and radiation were released, its impact would be determined by the amount of radiation released, the weather conditions, the wind direction, and speed. Radiation cannot be detected by the senses. It does not have a smell or a color. It can be detected and measured by sensors.

Local and state governments, federal agencies, and the electric utilities have emergency response plans in the event of a nuclear power plant incident. The plans define two "emergency planning zones." One covers an area within a ten-mile radius of the plant where it is possible that people could be harmed by direct radiation exposure. The second zone covers a broader area, usually up to a fifty-mile radius from the plant, where radioactive materials could contaminate water supplies, food crops, and livestock.

Even with all the safety measures built into the nuclear power plant, people with evil intentions could make the seemingly impossible become reality. Given recent world events, we've come to realize that an airplane can be hijacked and flown into a building causing mass destruction. We've heard threats of planes possibly being hijacked and flown into nuclear power plants. And we have the threat of nuclear weapons. Obviously, when considering nuclear weapons, one must understand that guidelines on their use and licensing just don't exist. A rogue nation could, without any warning, detonate a weapon that releases nuclear energy.

And the March 2011 earthquake and tsunami that devastated Japan also caused a nuclear accident at the Fukushima I Nuclear Power Plant: three meltdowns and the release of radiation. 300,000 people were evacuated. It was determined that the facility was not built to withstand such a powerful natural disaster. For these reasons, it is imperative that we include nuclear threat and exposure in our emergency planning efforts, no matter how remote we may believe the threat to be.

Case Study 1: Three Mile Island, 1979

Historically, the United States nuclear power industry has been a model of safety and efficiency. That perception was seriously and perhaps permanently damaged when the Three Mile Island Unit 2 Nuclear Generating Station in Harrisburg, Pennsylvania, was damaged. This event led to the most serious and infamous commercial accident in U.S. history. The nuclear industry would never be the same. Changes to standard operating procedures, safety contingencies, and regulations have been introduced, yet we all know the seriousness of the threat of a nuclear accident.

On March 28, 1979, at 4:00 a.m., the system that fed water to cool the steam generators malfunctioned. Emergency systems began operation, but a valve failed to completely close resulting in a small loss of coolant. This event was further compounded by operators who misinterpreted the developing problem. The minor mishap progressed into a full-blown accident that caused substantial damage to the reactor and associated components. All of the fuel cells and more than 90 percent of the reactor core were damaged. The containment building in which the reactor was located as well as several other locations around the plant were contaminated. Despite the severity of the damage, no injuries from radiation occurred. The resulting contamination led to the development of a ten-year cleanup and scientific study, and today the reactor is inactive.

Understanding Radiation

Radioactive materials are composed of atoms that are unstable. An unstable atom gives off its excess energy until it becomes stable. The energy emitted is radiation. Each of us is exposed to radiation daily from natural sources, including from the sun and Earth. Small traces of radiation are present in food and water. Radiation also is released from manmade sources such as X-ray machines, television sets, and microwave ovens. Nuclear power plants use the heat generated from nuclear fission in a contained environment to convert water to steam, which powers generators to produce electricity.

Radiation has a cumulative effect. The longer a person is exposed to radiation, the greater the risk. A high exposure to radiation can cause serious illness or death. The potential danger from an accident at a nuclear power plant is exposure to radiation. This exposure could come from the release of radioactive material from the plant into the environment, usually characterized by a plume (cloud-like) formation of radioactive gases and particles. The area that the radioactive release may affect is determined by the amount released from the plant, wind direction and speed, and weather conditions. The major hazards to people in the vicinity of the plume are radiation exposure to the body from the cloud and particles deposited on the ground, inhalation of radioactive materials, and ingestion of radioactive materials.

The three ways to minimize radiation exposure are distance, shielding, and time:

- **Distance**. The more distance between you and the source of the radiation the better. In a serious nuclear power plant accident, local authorities will call for an evacuation to increase the distance between you and the radiation.
- **Shielding**. Human skin is very sensitive and does little to insulate the internal organs from the effects of radiation. The more heavy, dense material between you and the source of the radiation the better. Other materials such as concrete and steel in buildings, for instance, may provide some shield from radiation for short durations. This is why local authorities could advise you to remain indoors if an accident occurs at a nearby nuclear power plant. In some cases, the walls in your home would be sufficient shielding to protect you.
- **Time**. Usually, radioactivity loses its strength fairly quickly. In a nuclear power-plant accident, local authorities will monitor any release of radiation and determine when the threat has passed.

What to Do Before a Nuclear Power Plant Emergency

1. Learn your community's warning system. Nuclear power plants are required to install sirens and other warning systems (i.e., flashing warning lights) to cover a ten-mile area around the plant. Find out when the warning systems will be tested next. When tested in your area, determine whether you can hear or see sirens and flashing warning lights from your home.
2. Obtain public emergency information materials from the power company that operates your local nuclear power plant or your local emergency services office. If you live within ten miles of the power plant, you should receive these materials yearly from the power company or your state or local government.
3. Learn the emergency plans for schools, day-care centers, nursing homes, and other places that members of your household frequent. Learn where people would go in case of evacuation.

Know the Terminology

Know the terms used to describe a nuclear emergency:

Notification of Unusual Event—A small problem has occurred at the plant. No radiation leak is expected. Federal, state, and county officials will be told right away. No action on your part will be necessary.

Alert—A small problem has occurred and small amounts of radiation could leak inside the plant. This will not affect you. You should not have to do anything.

Site Area Emergency—A more serious problem. Small amounts of radiation could leak from the plant. If necessary, state and county officials will act to ensure public safety. Area sirens may be sounded. Refer to your radio or television for safety information.

General Emergency—The most serious problem. Radiation could leak outside the plant and off the plant site. The sirens will sound. Tune to your local radio or television station for reports. State and county officials will act to protect the public. Be prepared to follow instructions promptly.

4. Prepare an emergency evacuation supply kit.
5. Be prepared to evacuate. (See chapter 12 for more information on evacuations.)
6. Consider your transportation options. If you do not own or drive a car, ask your local emergency manager about plans for people without private vehicles.

Fallout Shelters

Find out what public buildings in your community may have been designated as fallout shelters. It may have been years ago, but start there, and learn which buildings are still in use and could be designated as shelters again.

If no noticeable or official designations have been made, make your own list of potential shelters near your home, workplace, and school: basements or the windowless center area of middle floors in high-rise buildings, as well as subways and tunnels.

Give your household clear instructions about where fallout shelters are located and what actions to take in case of attack.

If you live in an apartment building or high-rise, talk to the manager about the safest place in the building for sheltering, and about providing for building occupants until it is safe to go out.

There are few public shelters in many suburban and rural areas. If you are considering building a fallout shelter at home, keep the following in mind:

➤ A basement, or any underground area, is the best place to shelter from fallout. Often, few major changes are needed, especially if the structure has two or more stories and its basement, or one corner of it, is below ground.

⋏ Fallout shelters can be used for storage during non-emergency periods, but only store things there that can be very quickly removed. (When they are removed, dense, heavy items may be used to add to the shielding.)

⋏ All the items you will need for your stay need not be stocked inside the shelter itself but can be stored elsewhere, as long as you can move them quickly to the shelter.

What to Do During a Nuclear Power Plant Emergency

If an accident at a nuclear power plant were to release radiation in your area, local authorities would activate warning sirens or another approved alerting method. They would also instruct you through the Emergency Alert System (EAS) on local television and radio stations on how to protect yourself.

1. Listen to the warning. Not all incidents result in the release of radiation. The incident could be contained inside the plant and pose no danger to the public.

2. Stay tuned to local radio or television. Local authorities will provide specific instructions and information:

   ⋏ The advice given will depend on the nature of the emergency, how quickly it is evolving and how much radiation, if any, is likely to be released.

   ⋏ Local instructions should take precedence over any advice given in this book.

   ⋏ Review the public information materials you received from the power company or government officials.

3. Evacuate if you are advised to do so:

   ⋏ Close and lock doors and windows.

   ⋏ Keep car windows and vents closed; use re-circulating air.

   ⋏ Listen to radio for evacuation routes and other instructions.

4. If you are not advised to evacuate, remain indoors:

   ⋏ Close doors and windows.

   ⋏ Turn off the air conditioner, ventilation fans, furnace, and other air intakes.

   ⋏ Go to a basement or other underground area, if possible.

   ⋏ Keep a battery-powered radio with you at all times.

5. Shelter livestock and give them stored feed, if time permits.

6. Do not use the telephone unless absolutely necessary. Lines will be needed for emergency calls.

7. If you suspect exposure to radiation, take a thorough shower:

- Change clothes and shoes.
- Put exposed clothing in a plastic bag.
- Seal the bag and place it out of the way.

8. Put food in covered containers or in the refrigerator. Food not previously covered should be washed before being put in containers.

   If you receive an alert, remember the following:

   - A siren or tone alert does not necessarily mean you should evacuate. Listen to the television or radio for further instructions.
   - Do not call 911. If this is a true alert, a special rumor-control phone number will be provided.
   - If you are instructed to shelter in place, be sure to close all doors, windows, and chimney dampers, and turn off all HVAC equipment.

If you receive a warning and you are instructed to go inside, it is advisable to shower and change clothes. After removing your clothes and shoes, place them in a plastic bag and seal the bag.

What to Do after a Nuclear Power Plant Emergency

1. If told to evacuate, do not return home until local authorities say it is safe.
2. If you were advised to stay in your home, do not go outside until local authorities indicate it is safe.
3. Seek medical treatment for any unusual symptoms, such as nausea, that may be related to radiation exposure.

8

Workplace Violence and Workplace Medical Emergencies

Workplace Violence

Workplace violence has unfortunately become all too common today. One in twenty private sector companies experiences an incident of workplace violence every year. State governments experience higher percentages of all types of workplace violence than local governments or private industry. Only one in five companies provides training on workplace violence.

According to OSHA there are generally four categories of workplace violence:

Criminal Intent: The perpetrator has no legitimate relationship to the business or its employee, and is usually committing a crime in conjunction with the violence. These crimes can include robbery, shoplifting, trespassing, and terrorism. The vast majority of workplace homicides (85 percent) fall into this category.

Customer/Client: The perpetrator has a legitimate relationship with the business and becomes violent while being served by the business. This category includes customers, clients, patients, students, inmates, and any other group for which the business provides services. It is believed that a large portion of customer/client incidents occur in the healthcare industry, in settings such as nursing homes or psychiatric facilities; the victims are often patient caregivers. Police officers, prison staff, flight attendants, and teachers are some other examples of workers who may be exposed to this kind of workplace violence, which accounts for approximately 3 percent of all workplace homicides.

Worker-on-worker: The perpetrator is an employee or past employee of the business who attacks or threatens another employee(s) or past employee(s) in the workplace. Worker-on-worker fatalities account for approximately 7 percent of all workplace homicides.

Personal relationship: The perpetrator usually does not have a relationship with the business, but has a personal relationship with the intended victim. This category includes victims of domestic violence assaulted or threatened while at work, and accounts for about 5 percent of all workplace homicides.

Certain industries are more susceptible to violence than others. Certain locations create a more dangerous and volatile atmosphere than other locations. But don't fall into the trap of believing your business is immune to workplace violence.

What is workplace violence? It can be offensive or threatening language. It may be a threatening note. It can be a push or a shove. It may be a mugging, rape, or robbery. In its most extreme form, it can be homicide. In fact, homicide is the third-leading cause of fatal occupational injury in the United States.

According to a Bureau of Labor Statistics census, from 2006 to 2010 there was on average 551 workplace homicides in the United States each year. These homicides accounted for 11 percent of all the fatal work injuries in the United States. Retail industry accounts for the greatest number of workplace homicides; in fact, retail typically accounts for half of the recorded workplace homicides each year. Not surprisingly, robbery is the leading motive for workplace violence. Those working in healthcare, government, and judicial fields are also especially susceptible to violence.

Factors which may increase a worker's risk for workplace assault might include the following:

- ⋏ Handling money
- ⋏ Serving alcohol
- ⋏ Working in high-crime areas
- ⋏ Driving delivery vehicles
- ⋏ Having a mobile workplace, such as cab drivers or meter readers
- ⋏ Working in law enforcement
- ⋏ Working with unstable or volatile persons in health care, social services, or criminal justice settings
- ⋏ Working alone
- ⋏ Working late at night or during early morning hours
- ⋏ Guarding valuable property

Case Study 1: Royal Oak Postal Facility, 1991

On November 8, 1991, letter carrier Thomas McIlvane lost his appeal for reinstatement to his job at the Royal Oak post office just outside of Detroit, Michigan. He had been fired for alleged insubordination stemming from false statements recorded on his timesheet. He vowed to "get back" at his supervisors. Just six days later he stormed through the loading dock area, passed through two large double doors, and immediately grabbed a woman and held his sawed-off .22-caliber Ruger rifle to her head. He let her go saying, "You're not the one I want." As McIlvane entered the office area of the postal facility, he searched for specific people. In six minutes, he shot and wounded six postal employees and killed three—including the former supervisor who turned down his appeal for reinstatement. Three other employees were injured as they jumped out of windows attempting to flee the shooting. After satisfying his anger, he turned his rifle on himself and pulled the trigger, instantly killing himself. McIlvane, a thirty-one-year old former Marine, was described by former co-workers as being a "waiting time bomb" and violent.

Case Study 2: Columbine High School, 1999

On April 20, 1999, the country watched in horror as the news report of yet another school shooting came across the wire. This particular event, though, proved to be especially tragic. At 11:19 a.m., two Columbine High School seniors, Eric Harris and Dylan Klebold, began a killing rampage that left thirteen people dead and injured twenty-one more.

The gunmen began their attack in the school parking lot and slowly made their way into the school's hallways, cafeteria, and finally the school library. By 11:35 a.m. the gunmen had wounded their last victims. By shortly after noon, they had committed suicide.

The attack was gruesome enough, but as the investigation ensued in the coming weeks and months, the public learned of the true intentions of these killers. Harris and Klebold had intended to kill far more people than they actually did. They had planted a pair of twenty-pound propane bombs in the school cafeteria. Had these bombs detonated they would have certainly killed the nearly 500 people in the cafeteria. Additionally, Harris and Klebold had planned to leave the school, hijack a plane, and fly it into a building. The public was shocked to learn of the depth of the anger of these two young men.

What to Do if Faced with Workplace Violence

OSHA requires that employers address workplace violence issues. Specific regulations have not been created, but OSHA's General Duty Clause covers all safety issues, such as ergonomics, indoor air quality, and workplace violence. OSHA requires that employers initiate a safe and healthy workplace and

- identify hazards in the workplace
- create a written safety plan
- perform regular safety inspections
- provide safety and health training
- record and report injury and illness
- commit to safety
- ensure employee participation
- evaluate the program periodically

OSHA believes that employers who enact the preceding requirements will proactively address the potential for workplace violence. First, employers must understand the seriousness of this problem. Management must take this problem seriously and must be

OSHA General Duty Clause

Section 5 (a)(1) of the William Steiger Occupational Safety and Health Act of 1970 is known as the "General Duty Clause." This section reads as follows:

5. Duties

(a) Each Employer

(1) Shall furnish to each of his employees employment and a place of employment which are free from recognized hazards that are causing or are likely to cause death or serious physical harm to his employees.

committed to a safe workplace, not just in word but also in deed. This may require new human resource policies such as "zero tolerance." Second, employers must examine both historical accounts of workplace violence and the future possibility of such actions. If trends are identified, employers must enact and enforce rules to mitigate these problems. Finally, employers must train their employees how to identify behavior that may indicate a tendency toward violence and how to handle a volatile situation. These three core responsibilities will provide a solid foundation for workplace violence mitigation.

Often behavior recognition and environmental controls are important factors to consider when attempting to reduce occurrences of workplace violence.

Behavior solutions might include

- Don't give orders.
- Remain calm.
- Show a caring attitude.
- Don't touch the other person.
- Don't raise your voice.
- Don't match the threats.
- Use calming language such as "I know you're frustrated. Let me try to help."

Environmental solutions might include

- Provide security (or better security).
- Install metal detectors, cameras, or security personnel.
- Restrict areas that the public can enter.
- Do not allow the public to enter the office area of the building.
- Provide alarms (verbal, mechanical, or visual) to warn of danger.
- Provide adequate illumination at entryways, parking lots, corridors, and other areas.
- Provide escorts to the parking lot at night.
- Ensure that employees are aware of the location of emergency exits.
- Install deep transaction counters to limit physical contact with the public.

In the event of a workplace emergency, first responders such as the police and emergency medical technicians need to know exactly where to go to assist the victims and apprehend the suspects. These responders are unlikely to be familiar with your building; therefore, you should assist them by having this information available prior to their entry into the building. In the Columbine High School emergency, floor plans were not available to the first responders. Students had to draw crude floor plans from memory so the responders could decide on the most appropriate action to take.

Workplace Medical Emergencies

Most people spend between eight and ten hours per day at their place of employment. Because of the amount of time spent at work, medical emergencies are a strong possibility. Each year about 1.25 million people experience a heart attack in the United States, and nearly 40 percent of those heart attacks result in death. Heart attacks don't just affect the elderly and retired. Of the 500,000 who die each year from heart attacks, more than 160,000 victims were younger than sixty-five. Imagine an organization that did not plan for a medical emergency such as a heart attack, and then an employee was stricken. Confusion would run rampant. Who would we call? Do we dial 911? How do we get an outside line? What is the address? How will the paramedics gain access to the building? Sadly, during the confusion, the employee might lose their life. But don't fall into the trap of planning only for heart attacks. That would be a serious oversight. Think about any emergency that might occur. Examples might include

- A diabetic experiences seizures
- A lab technician is overcome by toxic fumes
- A line worker's hand gets caught in machinery and he or she loses a large amount of blood
- An employee with high blood pressure experiences a stroke
- A daydreaming employee slips and falls down the stairs
- An employee is walking through the parking lot and trips, breaking a leg
- A nurse is stuck by a contaminated needle

What to Do if Faced with a Medical Emergency

If employees are expected to react properly during a medical emergency, employers must have a procedures manual in place. This manual will describe in detail what events should take place during a medical emergency. For instance:

- The names and phone numbers of employees who have emergency medical response training
- Location of the first aid kit or station
- First aid procedures
- Proper disease transmission avoidance

⋏   Injury and illness recordkeeping (OSHA) procedures
⋏   How to reach outside assistance (i.e., dial 911)
⋏   How to get an outside line

The last item is interesting. In many buildings, you must dial an "8" or a "9" to get an outside line. If a medical emergency occurs, confusion and chaos usually follow. We all know we need to dial 911, but in the confusion, we forget to dial the proper suffix for the outside line. And then again, in some telephone systems, the normal need to dial for an outside line is bypassed in the case of a 911 call. The time to settle the confusion is long before an emergency strikes.

Once we dial 911, the dispatcher will ask a number of questions concerning the nature of the emergency, your name, your phone number, and the address where the emergency has occurred. Often employees or visitors don't know the proper address of the building. Instead, they know a mailing address to a post office box, and the dispatcher will not be able to get emergency response personnel to the building.

Finally, give some consideration to how the paramedics will gain access to the building and to the injured. Will they know where to go? Will the receptionist require them to sign in, thus delaying their response? To solve these problems, it is advisable to assign somebody to wait at the building's entrance to escort the paramedics directly to the injured.

In the event of a medical emergency, employees must have an idea what to do. The procedure manual just discussed will provide employees with such a plan; however, the plan is useless if proper training is not provided. Many options exist, but some of the best training opportunities are delivered by the Red Cross (available at www.redcross.org) and the National Safety Council (available at www.nsc.org). These organizations offer local training covering a host of different first aid and medical emergency issues.

The Red Cross

The Red Cross is a leader in medical emergency training. Their classes include basic first aid; CPR; ergonomics; slips, trips, and falls; back injury prevention; workplace violence awareness; and managing stress. Typical classes last between one hour and six hours each. You can view course descriptions at www.redcross.org/take-a-class/Learn-About-Our-Programs.

Many people would like to help an injured person, but they are concerned that if they do lend assistance they could be sued by the injured party or their family. This creates an obvious dilemma for those normally willing to help. In most states, people who assist victims in medical emergencies are protected by Good Samaritan laws. It is advisable to check with your legal counsel or local Red Cross office prior to developing your procedures manual. According to the Red Cross, when citizens respond to an emergency and act in a reasonable and prudent way, they will be protected under the Good Samaritan laws. This will protect the rescuer from being sued by the injured person. One caveat does exist though:

if a rescuer does offer assistance but is negligent or not properly trained and they further harm the injured person, they could be held liable. Based on this fact, it makes sense to train certain employees in proper rescue techniques including first aid and CPR.

For those working in a health care environment, transmission of disease through needles and sharps are a reality that must be addressed. On November 6, 2000, the Needlestick Safety Prevention Act was signed into law. Two months later, on January 18, 2001, OSHA released the final version of the revised Bloodborne Pathogen Standard—29 CFR 1910.1030. Highlights include

- ▲ Employers must review the "Exposure Control Plan" annually
- ▲ Employers must select safer needle devices as they become available
- ▲ Employers must involve employees in the selection process
- ▲ Employers must maintain a "Sharps Injury Log." This log identifies which device was being used, the department in which it was used, and how the incident occurred

OSHA estimates that six million workers in the health care industry are at risk of occupational exposure to bloodborne pathogens. Bloodborne pathogens are pathogenic microorganisms that are present in human blood and can cause disease in humans. Possible diseases include Human Immunodeficiency Virus (HIV), Hepatitis B Virus (HBV), Hepatitis C Virus (HCV), and others. Each year, almost 800,000 needlestick injuries occur. Many of these injuries are the result of careless work habits such as using a two-handed method[1] to recap needles. In these scenarios, proper training is advised. OSHA also recommends the use of safer needles and sharps, including needleless systems and sharps with built-in safety features that reduce the risk of bloodborne pathogen exposure.

---

1. When recapping a needle is absolutely necessary, it should be performed using a mechanical device or forceps rather than using a two-handed approach. If a mechanical device or forceps is not available, a one-handed scoop method is advisable: holding the sharp or needle in one hand and then scooping up the cap from a flat surface without touching the cap.

9

More Non-natural Events

Civil Disturbances, Blackouts, Structural Collapse

Civil Disturbance and Demonstrations

Civil disturbances are part of the nation's landscape. In a land where freedoms abound, citizens have the right to demonstrate and voice their opinions. These demonstrations are usually peaceful. Occasionally they turn ugly and even violent; therefore, it would be prudent to incorporate planning for such possibilities. Civil disturbances encompass not only riots and demonstrations but also such problems as vandalism, looting, gangs, labor disputes, and robbery. In some scenarios, such as labor disputes, the demonstrators are protesting against a certain organization, and the threat to surrounding organizations is small. In other cases, such as rioting after a championship sporting event, all buildings and vehicles are exposed to damage and looting. For these reasons it is imperative that you have addressed the possibility of civil disturbance and demonstration.

Case Study 1: Los Angeles Riots, 1992

On April 29, 1992, jurors in Sylmar, California, reached final verdicts in the emotional case involving the 1991 beating of Rodney King by four Los Angeles Police Department officers. The entire nation had been able to see the beating, thanks to a citizen who had recorded the entire event on his personal video camera. Many citizens were upset about the brutality of the beating, but held back judgment until the case was heard in court. The verdicts were delivered on live television, and the decision surprised and infuriated many. Of the four police officers charged, three were cleared of all charges—the jury could not agree on a verdict for the excessive force charge for the fourth officer.

For many this was another example in a long line of examples of the unjust treatment the LAPD gave the African-American community. Some people demonstrated peacefully, while others began to riot and loot. During the next several days the rioting became particularly violent and innocent bystanders were beaten. One particular example caught on film was the beating of truck driver Reginald Denny.

On April 30, Mayor Tom Bradley imposed a curfew and many schools and businesses were closed. More than 800 buildings were burned and looting was widespread. Parts of Los Angeles resembled a war zone. Governor Pete Wilson called in more than 4,000 National Guard troops. Finally, on Monday, May 4, police and the National Guard began to regain control over the city. Schools and businesses reopened, but the scars remained. The entire nation had watched in horror as the events unfolded. The city of Los Angeles received a black eye, the LAPD lost credibility, fifty-three people were killed, 2,000 were injured, 11,00 were arrested, and $1 billion in property damaged was tallied.

Case Study 2: World Trade Organization Protests, Seattle 1999

The World Trade Organization held its annual conference in Seattle, Washington, from November 30 through December 4, 1999. What figured to be an event with just passing interest in the news became the story of the week. Tens of thousands of demonstrators showed up to protest globalization and unregulated growth they believed was encouraged by World Trade Organization activities. Despite their great number, the protestors were actually quite organized. A diverse group of social activists, environmental advocates, and trade and labor unionists targeted this event, and the number of protestors swelled past 45,000. The majority of these protestors was peaceful, but as often happens, a small contingent of troublemakers and vandals mixed in. The authorities had expected some demonstrations, but the sheer size of the group and the vandals left the authorities flat-footed. The Seattle police were unable to establish a safe corridor between the protestors and the WTO delegates, who couldn't reach the conference.

Mayor Paul Schell declared downtown Seattle a state of civil emergency on the scheduled first day of the conference. The crowds became restless and more vocal. Self-described anarchists stoned store windows and patrol cars and sprayed graffiti. The demonstration quickly grew out of control. As the Seattle police attempted to quell the troublemakers, they found the task of separating the peaceful protestors from the bad guys to be difficult. Earlier, the police had resorted to pepper spray as a means to scatter the crowd. But as reinforcements arrived, they donned riot gear and used rubber bullets to disperse the crowds. The officers also stopped using the less-effective pepper spray in favor of the more potent CS tear gas.

Schell called on Washington Governor Gary Locke for help. The governor called up the National Guard, and a twenty-four-hour curfew was put into effect covering a forty-six-block area surrounding the WTO conference. Protesting would only be allowed in certain areas away from the conference, and all protestors were required to obtain a permit. As the WTO conference ended and the protestors began to disperse, the city began to calculate the costs. The city's projected cost of $6 million for hosting the conference swelled beyond $9 million, with overtime for police officers and damages. The city paid out $1 million in a settlement to protesters for violating their due process rights during the police crackdown (and police chief Norm Stamper resigned). The city's businesses faced $20 million in property damage. Indirect costs such as lost sales and bad publicity certainly cost the city and its businesses millions of dollars more.

What to Do if Faced with a Riot or Civil Unrest

There are limitations on what can be done during a riot or civil unrest. Taking the law into your own hands can be dangerous and have some very heavy legal ramifications. The best way to mitigate or discourage a riot or vandalism would be to take effective, proactive steps prior to the event. In many scenarios, with a little bit of foresight, trouble can be limited or avoided altogether.

First, be aware of events that may trigger demonstrations or unrest. These events might include

- Labor disputes
- Layoffs and downsizing
- Environmentally sensitive meetings or conferences
- Economic conferences
- Major sporting events
- Political rallies
- Judicial decisions
- Music concerts
- Religious gatherings
- Biased racial or cultural events

This list is, of course, just a sampling of events that could start out peacefully and turn destructive. Again, do not attempt to solve riot-related events without the assistance of proper law enforcement personnel. If an event is scheduled and you believe it may turn ugly, consult with your local police department. They will be able to advise you in the steps that should be taken. These steps might include

- Hiring temporary guard service
- Installing storm shutters
- Locking gates in the parking lot
- Lowering security grating
- Removing vehicles from the premises
- Removing trash containers or other items that could be thrown or set on fire

Obviously, it makes sense to distance demonstrators from the employees of an organization. This is especially important during labor disputes, because those working and those not working will be at odds with one another. It may be advisable to provide the protestors with a place to demonstrate. That may be an off-site area such as an easement or behind a fence or barricade. At Florida State University in Tallahassee, Florida, the university provided local tribal protestors with a fenced-in area in the parking lot. Their protests stemmed from the perceived disrespectful use of the name "Seminoles" and the war chant during sporting events. By providing a place to peacefully demonstrate, the university protected the tribe from harm from counter-demonstrators and protected the university from potential liability.

Another effective way to reduce the threat of civil disturbance involves the use of good public relations. Take, for example, a music and arts festival. Suppose this festival will attract large crowds of college students. Beer will be sold at this venue and the concerts will extend until 2:00 a.m. or 3:00 a.m. It should be easy to foresee a potential problem with an unruly crowd? Certainly, so it makes sense to proactively work with the police department. It might also make sense to contact the concert promoters and seek their assistance. It might even make sense to work with the local colleges and ask them to speak to the students about behavior off campus, reminding them of the police presence in the areas surrounding the festival. These may seem like simplistic ideas that don't really work, but they do.

Blackouts/Loss of Utility

Ordinarily, loss of utility might not be considered an emergency. It is an inconvenience, perhaps, but certainly not an emergency or disaster. Consider, however, the plight of a hospital. Loss of electrical utility could be deadly. Consider the call center that serves your local fire department. Without telephone service, they would be unable to respond to emergencies and lives could be lost. In your business, even if lives are not at stake, business continuity is compromised. For this reason you should make certain that your emergency planning addresses the loss of utility.

Case Study 1: New York Blackout, 1977

On July 13, 1977, at approximately 8:37 p.m. lightning knocked out two 345kV power lines. At approximately 8:55 p.m., lightning strikes caused the loss of two additional lines. By 9:30 p.m., New York City was without power.

Usually the loss of power can be solved by rerouting power from other nearby utilities; however, because of the loss of protective equipment, all of the nearby utilities quarantined themselves from the Consolidated Edison Electric Company, which served nearly 9 million customers in the New York area. The entire electrical system was down from Staten Island, Brooklyn, Queens, and areas north. Some of these customers were without power for twenty-five hours. It did not take long for some people to take advantage of this opportunity to riot, vandalize, and loot area businesses. More than 1,600 stores were damaged and looted. Neighborhoods were trashed. More than 500 police officers were wounded and thousands of arrests were made. Firefighters were busy as well. Approximately 1,040 fires were attributed to arson during this emergency. After the lights came back on, $300 million in damage had occurred.

Case Study 2: California Brownouts and Blackouts, 2000 and 2001

The most serious energy shortage since the 1970s struck California in 2000 and 2001. Unusual weather and problems with energy deregulation caused extreme power shortages. Mandatory load-shedding plans were activated. Nonessential equipment was required to be shut down. Thermostats were adjusted to 78 degrees Fahrenheit, instead of the normal 72 degrees. These steps helped but did not solve the energy crisis. Finally, a Stage-3 power alert necessitated rolling blackouts across the state on January 17 and 18, 2001. Many employees were forced to work by candlelight. People were stuck in elevators. According to the Electric Power Research Institute (EPRI), a three-day brownout in January cost businesses $1.9 billion in lost productivity.

Confidence in the electric utility industry was lost and the bad feelings expressed by the public increased with the downfall of Enron, one of the nation's top electricity and natural gas marketers. Additionally, people were angry to learn of utility companies' lack of planning by failing to keep up with the demand.

What to Do if Faced with Loss of Utility

The loss of utility is certain in most business operations. The first step in mitigating the damage is to identify utilities that may be affected. These critical operations may include

- Manufacturing equipment
- Computer equipment
- Telecommunications
- Security systems
- Water and sewer
- Gas
- Electric
- Life support systems
- HVAC

Next, determine the impact of service interruption. This impact may be measured in lost production, spoilage, comfort, accessibility, or any other measurable unit. The impact may change as the duration of the interruption increases. For instance, a two-minute power blip may not be cause for concern, whereas a sixty-minute interruption may cause great concern. Understand your businesses thresholds for utility interruption.

Finally, establish contacts and procedures for system restoration. This might include contacts with local utility providers, contractors, providers of generator backup, or other related services. In areas of a critical nature, redundancy and off-site/after-hours monitoring should be implemented.

Structural Collapse

Fortunately, the collapse of a building is a very rare occurrence. Credit agencies such as OSHA and the existence of building codes for ensuring safe construction practices and structural integrity. Unfortunately, when a structural collapse does occur, it is always costly, both in property damage and human life. Structural collapse is usually the result of an unusual external event such as bomb, fire, or—as we've witnessed—a fully fueled jumbo jet being flown into the building. The next two case studies concern faulty construction.

In the early 1980s, various municipalities created specialized urban search and rescue teams to assist with emergencies, especially those involving structural collapse. These teams gained popularity as their successes were documented. Their expertise has been called upon both domestically and internationally. In 1991, the Federal Emergency Management Agency (FEMA) incorporated search and rescue teams into the Federal Response Plan. Currently FEMA sponsors more than twenty-five national urban search-and-rescue task forces. These task forces are equipped to conduct search-and-rescue operations following earthquakes, tornadoes, floods, hurricanes, aircraft accidents, hazardous materials spills, and catastrophic structure collapses.

Case Study 1: Willow Island Cooling Tower Collapse, 1978

April 27, 1978, began like many other days at the Pleasants Power Station in Willow Island, West Virginia. That morning, workers were busy constructing one of the two 430-foot-tall cooling towers being erected on site, perched on scaffolding as a crane lifted concrete to create the next level. The height of tower two was at 166 feet. Suddenly and without warning, the crane began to fall and in a matter of seconds the tower collapsed—concrete peeling away and scaffolding with it—and fifty-one lives ended. Workers on the ground compared the helpless eventuality of the falling tower to dominos. Safety nets were placed in the mouth of the tower, but they proved useless.

OSHA arrived on the site and conducted investigations. Final results pointed to "green concrete" as a major cause of the collapse. As the tower was being erected, sections were formed up and concrete poured. While the concrete was still green, or not fully cured, the forms were stripped off and the next section was formed and readied for the next pour. Additional blame was directed at scaffolding that surrounded the structure. As the tower became taller, so did the scaffolding. The massive scaffolding system was held in place by bolting into the exterior wall of the cooling tower. When these reinforcing rods were placed in areas of concrete that were not fully cured, they put undue stress on the structure. In hindsight, this was an obvious recipe for disaster.

Since this failure, OSHA has created new concrete testing standards. OSHA calculates these new standards will cost contractors approximately $28 million per year. Although the expense is high, OSHA believes it will save an average of twenty-seven lives per year; a reward that we can all agree is worth the price.

Case Study 2: Hyatt Regency Walkway Collapse, 1981

On July 17, 1981, guests at the Hyatt Regency in Kansas City, Missouri, were victims of a very sad and deadly catastrophe. The newly built hotel was hosting a tea dance that attracted 1,600 people. Many of these guests were on the ground level of the hotel lobby while others were dancing on the hotel's suspended walkways. These walkways connected the hotel's conference room facilities on the

> Two organizations are leaders in structural collapse education and response. The National Association for Search and Rescue (available at www.nasar.org) and Federal Emergency Management Agency (www.fema.org) are excellent resources for the unique challenges facing a structural collapse.

second, third, and fourth floors. A design flaw caused the suspended walkways to collapse, and 114 people died while 216 more were seriously injured.

The collapse occurred because the walkways were not built to withstand the load. During the design stage a miscommunication occurred between the structural engineer and the company hired to fabricate and erect the structure. Upon completion of the investigation the engineering company's license was revoked and the engineers who had affixed their seals to the design drawings lost their licenses in the states of Missouri, Kansas, and Texas.

What to Do if Faced with a Structural Collapse

Because of the specialized nature of search and recovery and the danger inherent to that type of work, it is advisable to bring in professionals to coordinate rescue efforts when a building collapse has occurred. FEMA has developed and can deploy teams of trained response personnel to coordinate your activities.

If an emergency occurs and warrants search and rescue support, FEMA will deploy the three closest search and rescue teams within six hours of notification. If additional teams are necessary, FEMA will provide them as well. These teams serve to support state and local emergency responders.

There are sixty-two people, divided into two thirty-one-person task teams, in each FEMA task force. Each thirty-one-person task team includes four canines and 60,000 pounds of equipment valued at over $1.4 million. The task teams are totally self-sufficient for the first seventy-two hours of their deployment.

Task force members are highly trained and specialized professionals. They do much more than simply provide the labor for digging through the rubble of a collapsed building. Each task force member is a trained emergency medical technician and is required to complete hundreds of hours of specialized training. Typically, the task force team is divided into four unique areas of specialization:

- ▲   Search team—Finds victims trapped after a disaster
- ▲   Rescue team—Safely extricates victims from the rubble
- ▲   Technical team—Structural specialists who evaluate and stabilize the structure
- ▲   Medical team—Cares for the victims of the disaster

The FEMA urban search and rescue teams are not limited to building collapse. They can be deployed after mining accidents, transportation accidents, and natural emergencies such as hurricanes, tornadoes, earthquakes, floods, hazardous chemical releases, and terrorist activities. Additionally, FEMA provides training to first responders in search and rescue techniques and may be able to provide grants local communities.

II

PLANNING, PROCEDURES, MITIGATION, AND RECOVERY

10

The Emergency Action Plan, Part One
Laying the Groundwork

The Basic Stages of Planning: Where Do I Start?

Before you can create an emergency action plan (EAP) you have to know what you are protecting—all your critical assets, both tangible and intangible—and what you are protecting them from. That may seem obvious but it isn't always apparent.

If you manage a large office building you have to consider not only your own staff but tenants, visitors, and all the others who come and go. Hospital EAPs are even more onerous because you not only have medical, administrative, and other staff to consider but bedridden patients and visitors as well as hazardous materials, drugs, and even radioactive equipment.

You must be absolutely clear about the exact nature of your facility—what is its main mission or function, what are your critical assets, and what are those things that are absolutely essential for performing that mission. Critical assets can be people, equipment, systems, and processes or a combination of any or all of these.

For instance, a school's main function is to teach and its critical assets are the teachers and students. Also important are the computers and other teaching aids that are used as well as the ancillary staff—but these are not as important as the teachers themselves. So you have to not only identify your critical assets you have to prioritize them as well.

Whatever type of facility you have, you must identify the key functions and all subsidiary functions and then identify the critical assets that are essential for maintaining and sustaining those functions. How would your ability to stay in businesses be impacted if, in the event of an attack or a hurricane, your critical assets were damaged or destroyed? How readily could these assets be replaced? Could they be replaced?

Now you know what you are protecting, you must identify what threats you face and where these threats might come from. This means identifying all internal and external threats, hazards, and risks, and understanding how they might impact you. If you are in a high-profile industry, you could be a target for terrorism; if you handle sensitive data you could be the victim of a cyberattack, and if you sell jewelry or pharmaceuticals you might be burglarized. The threat could also come from inside—violence or sabotage by a disgruntled employee or theft. And, of course, it could come from a natural disaster such as a tornado or earthquake.

Next, you have to get "buy-in" from senior management that something needs to be done. Management has to be persuaded that the risks of not doing something far outweigh the time and cost of having an emergency action plan in hand. Once you have their permission you can start planning your EAP.

When planning, there are really two scenarios—if and when. The "if" scenario covers planning and procedures to prevent the likelihood of an incident and is concerned with deterrence, detection, and delay, response, recovery and reevaluation and how each of these impacts four key elements—people, operations, interdependency, and information. The "when" scenario covers planning and procedures both during and after an incident and is mainly concerned with mitigation.

Deterrence provides countermeasures such as policies, procedures, and technical devices and controls to defend the assets being protected.

Detection monitors for potential breakdowns in protective mechanisms that could result in security breaches or compromising security zones/layers.

Delay—If there is a breach, measures are needed to delay the intruders long enough to allow a security team to apprehend them before they achieve their objective.

Response, which requires human involvement, covers procedures and actions for assessing the situation and responding to a breach.

Recovery is your plan to continue business and operations as normally as possible following an incident.

Re-evaluation is critical. You must constantly keep your EAP under review and keep revisiting your original assessment and objectives. Has the situation changed, do you now face new threats and dangers, what must be done to ensure the EAP continues to meet your goals and objectives.

Breaking the Large Task into Bite-Sized Pieces

Any time projects of any size are undertaken, project managers must not let the magnitude of the projects freeze them. Do your research; think about the finished product, but at some point the pen must meet the paper. Failure to do so results in paralysis by analysis, and you're not likely to get acceptance from management if you find yourself caught in this web of indecision.

Always try to break the large, seemingly overwhelming project into bite-sized and workable pieces.

Determining Your Objectives and Scope

You don't normally start a journey until you have some idea where you'd like to end up. To identify where you hope to be, ask a few simple questions:

- ⋏ What do I want this plan to do?
- ⋏ Why do we need a plan?
- ⋏ Who will this plan have jurisdiction over?
- ⋏ What events present the greatest liability?

These questions form the basis for your emergency planning project. They identify both objective (specific event versus all emergencies) and scope (departmental plan versus company-wide plan). Until you ask these key questions, you really can't go to the next step. What is the next step? Now would be a great time to identify your resources, either members of your team or those business experts who can help you put the plan together.

Identifying Your Resources

A team of people is needed to adequately develop a plan. Even if you are a small organization, you'll need the expertise of a diverse group of people. Regardless of your title and position, you can't possibly know all of the aspects of your company in the detail required for a workable plan. Your knowledge base may be one of great breadth (and that's a great attribute for the emergency planner to have), but you'll need the assistance of people whose knowledge has real depth to it. Remember that some of the knowledge you need will likely be found outside the company—from police and fire departments and Red Cross to local and state emergency management and FEMA. Having a multidisciplined approach to the emergency plan is of utmost importance.

Understanding the Costs Involved

Depending on the scope of your emergency plan, costs can quickly escalate. You have an obligation to management to estimate the cost prior to commencement. It's not likely, nor is it advised, that you simply purchase a book (this one included) and copy the plan without adjusting it to your organization's specific needs and idiosyncrasies. If the development of a plan were that easy, the costs would be low, the process not labor intensive, and everybody would do it tomorrow. For most organizations, the cost need not be large. Here are some of the costs with which you are likely to be faced:

- ⋏ Non-billable time while producing the plan
- ⋏ Support from administration (producing, editing, copying/printing, distributing)

▲ Printing the emergency plan

▲ Distribution of the plan

▲ Training and drills

▲ Revisions to the plan

Again, this book is not a one-size fits all solution to emergency planning. Beware of software and other resources that over-promise and underperform. This book is a great vehicle for educating the average employee about the steps involved in developing a workable emergency action plan. In the appendices of this book, boilerplate audits, checklists, and even a sample emergency plan are included so you can edit and customize the documents for your own use.

Presenting Your Case to Management

One area of great concern is the role of management. Many a good planning team has been disbanded and told to "get back to work" because management failed to recognize the importance of the emergency planning task. Certainly in light of September 11, 2001, and Hurricane Katrina, emergency planning has gained greater acceptance, but what if events of that magnitude never occur again? It is not a question of *if* they will happen again, but *when* and you must be prepared for them.

Justifying the Cost

If management balks at the cost or the time required to effectively plan for emergencies, you must take a stand. In any task of this magnitude it is absolutely key that management be aware of and supportive of your vision. In fact, the vision must be a shared one. This may take a bit of convincing or at least a good dose of resource reality. You don't wake up one day and decide you want an emergency plan, go to the store, and buy one. It just doesn't work that way. Each organization is unique. The geographic location of your organization introduces unique challenges. The business you conduct presents its own special challenges.

Give management an idea of the resources (time, funding, and personnel) that you'll need to complete this task. Too often, the employees assigned the task of providing an emergency plan treat it as something other than a real project. Regardless of your profession, you have been assigned a very important and complex task. Treat it as such. Develop a scope. Create a schedule. Do a cost analysis. Write a mission statement. This is a real project with real objectives and milestones. By treating this project as any other important project that you undertake, you will instill an attitude of seriousness and professionalism in your planning team and among senior management who you are attempting to persuade.

Consequences versus Rewards

Typically there exist two avenues of thought on selling your ideas to another person.

One tactic is to stress the negative impact of not following a recommended course.

Negative selling points:

- Inability to quickly rebound after an emergency
- Financial loss
- Loss of market share
- Higher insurance premiums
- Bad press coverage
- Increased chance of legal liability

The consequences of not having an emergency plan are costly. Fear serves as a great motivator, so tactfully using fear and consequences are an effective way to highlight the importance of having an emergency and business continuity plan.

A second tactic is to stress the positives of following a recommended course. By appealing to management's sense of responsibility or greed (or both), you can present quite an effective case for your desired course of action. Everybody likes to be rewarded. If you can demonstrate effective ways to reduce risk and therefore protect the company assets, you increase your chances of persuading management to accept your proposal for emergency planning.

> In his excellent book *Artful Persuasion* (2000), Harry Mills explains "people are more motivated by the fear of losing something than by the reward of gaining something of equal value. Psychologically, it's much more painful to lose $100 than it is pleasurable to win $100."

Positive selling points:

- Moral responsibility to employees
- Better able to rebound financially
- Compliance with codes and regulations
- Business continuity
- Possible reduction in insurance premiums
- Reduces civil or criminal liability
- Environmentally responsible

When deciding upon the use of rewards or consequences, you should focus on one area. A person skilled in persuasion will use both tactics to influence their audience. If your corporate culture is such that management is particularly persuaded by rewards, then spend more time outlining the rewards. In doing so, you'll capture their attention, but don't forget to discuss the negative consequences of not having a plan as well. Another great selling point is that a workforce that knows there is an EAP in place, that appreciates the point for it and has rehearsed it in practice drills, tends to be a happier and more secure workforce and that generally translates into a more productive workforce.

The Mission Statement

Organizations both large and small have created mission statements to articulate who they are, what they do, and what they intend to do in the future. The mission statement has become the cornerstone of many good organizations. By the same token, for many, the mission statement has become an overused yet underutilized formality that holds little bearing on a company and its business.

Although some people may discount the importance of the mission statement, the mission statement does serve a worthwhile purpose, especially in the early stages of any large new venture, including emergency planning. In these formative stages, many people, especially management, will not fully understand the scope or even the purpose of emergency planning. Sure, it sounds important. We know it's the right thing to do, but what will it do for us? Who will be covered? The goal of the mission statement is to answer those questions in thirty seconds or less. Think of the mission statement as an executive summary of sorts.

Typically, the mission statement answers the following three questions:

- What will we do?
- Why are we doing it?
- How will we do it?

Emergency Management Team—Mission Statement

Our mission is to protect the employees, property, business, and the community in the event of an emergency.

We are committed to providing the company with effective and useful solutions that will reduce or eliminate emergencies and their negative impact.

We will accomplish this by conducting risk assessments, creating a written emergency action plan, and conducting employee training.

Additionally, we will create viable plans for restoration and recovery in the event of an emergency.

The mission statement actually serves three distinct purposes, each independent and each occurring at different stages on the timeline.

In its beginning stages, the mission statement serves as a home base for the emergency management team. If the team is ever unclear about its purpose or scope, they can go back to the mission statement and get back on track. Second, it serves as an effective marketing tool for the proposal to management. It tells them exactly what you plan to do and why you are doing it. It serves to justify the endeavor, which will require the support and resources of management. Lastly, the mission statement bestows legitimacy to your endeavor. This plan must be accepted and supported by all employees, from the CEO to the night janitor.

For obvious reasons, the mission statement is most effective when created by the emergency management team. However, at some point, ownership of the mission statement should be transferred to the organization's corporate executives. This must happen prior to the mission statement being distributed to the rest of the organization. A mission statement coming from the ranks of management carries much more weight than a mission statement created by a team consisting of various mid-level managers and frontline workers.

The emergency management team must have authority to make decisions and procure resources. Corporate management can facilitate those needs by heralding the mission statement as its own.

Establishing Authority and Chain of Command

An obvious area of concern and the cause of many planning failures stems from a lack of authority. The position of emergency planning director is a position that should not be granted without careful thought. The elected individual should be sensible, able to direct and delegate, able to communicate with all levels of the organization (not an easy task), and—most importantly—able to make decisions without fear of being vetoed by others.

As mentioned before, effective emergency planning requires the input of a very diverse group of people. The emergency planning director should have the ability and the courage to understand different points of view and make a decision that is best for the organization. Any time a group is formed, different views and ideas will materialize. The planning director needs to have the authority to make a competent decision based on all the data received.

Understanding Your Business

The Occupational Safety and Health Act (OSHA) requires employers to evaluate the hazards that exist at their workplace and create an emergency plan specific to their business. For instance, a healthcare facility worker will be exposed to hazards that an office worker would not be. Exposure to bloodborne pathogens, needlesticks, and sharps are very real concerns for healthcare workers and must be addressed in the corporate safety plan. Browse through a corporate safety plan for a retail store and it's unlikely that needle sticks will be addressed. It is not a concern; those hazards do not exist in that business. OSHA does not provide businesses with a "canned" safety plan because every business is unique and the exposure to hazards is different. OSHA requires that you evaluate your business and develop a customized plan to keep your employees safe.

Following this same line of reasoning, you need to evaluate your business and the hazards that are produced by your building use and develop an emergency plan that addresses those hazards. Where is the property located? In a flood zone, perhaps? Do you own the building or is it leased? What kind of business are you conducting? What functions of your organization are most critical to its survival? These are the types of questions that must be asked when developing your emergency action plan. To develop a useful emergency plan, you must understand every aspect of your business.

Identifying Core Business

In any business there exists core functions that define the organization. For instance, an electrical utility company has a core function to provide electricity to customers. You can break the customers into priorities as well. A utility company may decide to restore power to hospitals first, law enforcement agencies second, and eventually residential neighborhoods. Each organization is encouraged to identify their core business and then examine ways to protect that core business in the event of an emergency. In the event business is interrupted, you must have some idea of what aspects to restore first. If this important step is not completed, you risk spending valuable time restoring noncore business functions. All resources available must be used to restore business continuity.

Hospitals are an example of an organization expected to provide core functions during and after emergencies. To ensure that this happens, the Joint Commission on Accreditation of Healthcare Organizations (JCAHO) performs regular inspections of healthcare organizations. During these inspections, JCAHO reviews items such as the generator capacity, maintenance records, water storage, and bioterrorism plans. These inspections can be grueling and quite intensive, but they are also very necessary. We understand that hospitals serve a valuable and necessary function. We understand that without hospitals, recovery from an emergency would be difficult, maybe even impossible.

If your business is not part of the healthcare industry, you might not have an external agency watching your every move. If that is the case, don't feel like you can relax. You should create an audit process to ensure that your organization is prepared in the event of an emergency. This discussion should start with the identification of your core business and quickly move to the identification of the cost of business interruption.

Cost of Business Interruption

After many emergencies organizations have difficulty recovering. Any delay in production of a product or delivery of a service will have a negative effect on the cash flow of the business. Some companies have reserves or are able to conduct business in a remote area not affected by the emergency; however, many businesses large and small never recover and are forced to close their doors. After the 1993 World Trade Center bombing, nearly half of the businesses located in the towers went out of business as a result. Furthermore, a very small percentage of those organizations had a business continuity plan in place. For this reason, the cost of business continuity must be examined and addressed. Here are a few of the questions that need to be answered at a strategic level:

- What is the daily cost of unproductivity?
- How long can we absorb a business interruption?
- Will the inability to provide a product or service affect our future market share?
- Will the inability to provide a product or service affect our reputation in the industry?
- Does it make sense to acquire insurance to protect lost productivity?
- Does it make sense to create financial reserves for business continuity?
- Is the cost of flexible, contingent office space a viable option?
- If we are leasing the space, what assurances do we have that the property owner will move quickly to repair the property?

These questions must be answered at an executive level within the organization. Most managers, including those responsible for emergency planning, understand how their department supports the organization but are less likely to understand how other business units and departments support the organization. Emergency planning managers need to understand the organization from a point of view that extends beyond the specific area they control. An organization will often identify critical mission or business functions in a business plan. Even with a business plan in place, it is unlikely that all of the answers will be readily available; therefore, research must be done. Options must be examined against three factors—probability of the emergency, liability of the loss of productivity, and the cost. There must be a worthwhile return on investment.

Understanding Your Property

When creating an emergency action plan for your business, a number of issues play a critical role in the events you are likely to experience. While you can't account for every emergency event, you can address those that present the greatest risk. Later in this chapter we will explore the risk assessment matrix as a tool that can help us to identify the events that pose the greatest liability. Based on the results of the risk assessment, the emergency planner would begin to develop step-by-step procedures for the emergency events. Before we delve into the actual risk assessment we should spend some time examining the various factors that could increase our exposure to an emergency event.

Leased Versus Owned

The relationship between lessor and lessee can create a number of emergency management questions. The tenant may feel that total responsibility for emergency planning and recovery belongs to the landlord. In turn, the landlord may expect each tenant to be responsible for their own emergency planning. This disconnect is often not realized until it is too late. To prevent misunderstandings, at the time of lease signing and at least annually thereafter, the owner of the property should meet with representatives of the tenants to review the emergency plan.

This also would be a great time to schedule evacuation drills and elect floor captains. It is critical that a chain of command be established. One person should be elected as the emergency manager for the entire building with a nominated deputy as well. (Murphy's Law dictates that the day after the emergency manager has left the country on vacation the disaster will hit.) Usually this emergency manager is a member of the landlord's team because they will be making decisions that affect the whole building. This person should be assisted by a team of representatives from each tenant. Among the core functions of the emergency manager is the communication of proper evacuation procedures to the team members. These team members would be responsible for training their individual employees. Additionally, the team members would keep the emergency manager informed of changes that might affect the safety of the building. Examples of such changes include chemicals stored, employee count, and floor plan reconfigurations.

Additionally, here are additional questions that should be considered during a landlord/tenant meeting:

- Who is responsible for staging evacuation drills?
- Is each tenant responsible for their own emergency plan?
- Who makes the decision to return to the building after an evacuation?
- What happens to the lease if the property is uninhabitable for an extended period of time?
- What kinds of insurance policies are required and in what amounts?
- Are the landlord, tenant, or both parties required to acquire insurance?
- How much damage must be assessed before the property is considered uninhabitable by the insurance provider?

Geographic Location

The geographic location of your building is perhaps the greatest indicator of the types of emergencies that you must prepare for. Those businesses stationed on the eastern seaboard, particularly from the Carolinas south, understand the probability of a hurricane or a violent tropical storm. Based on their geographic location, organizations in Hawaii, Alaska, Washington, Oregon, and Northern California should understand the dangers of volcanoes. Companies in the Midwest realize the likelihood of a tornado. It seems that each area in the country is susceptible to its own unique emergency events; if we live in a certain area, we understand these hazards and prepare for them accordingly. This is where the real danger lies. If we are not careful, we will focus on the obvious events that could occur and overlook the unusual—but very possible—emergency events. For instance, it has snowed in Florida. Terrorist bombs have rocked the quiet Midwest. Floods have occurred in the desert and earthquakes can strike in Boston, Massachusetts.

When performing a risk analysis for a building based on its geographic location, we sometimes focus on the natural, weather-related events. True, these events are more common and the damage is often more costly, but do not forget to analyze *all* emergency events that could occur. For instance, is your building located near a nuclear power plant, refinery, or a chemical manufacturing plant? If it is, you should have a specific plan in place to deal with these potential liabilities. This isn't news to most of us. We realize the dangers that exist when located in close proximity to these types of businesses; but let's take this example a bit further. Is your building located near a highway, railway, or navigable waterway? Could this transportation route be used to transport hazardous chemicals? Suppose an accident occurred and hazardous chemicals were released. Suddenly, a cloud of poisonous gas drifts toward your property, located two miles away. Would your organization know how the handle the emergency? This example shows the importance of going beneath the surface, really digging down and finding the not-so-obvious dangers that are present. You have to consider every eventuality no matter how improbable.

When examining your business, you may feel insulated from many emergency events because you are a small, low-key organization. You don't produce hazardous chemicals, you believe in a safe workplace, and historically your city has not experienced many devastating emergency events. This may be true, but based on proximity to other businesses and events, dangerous situations can materialize. The risk factors outside of your immediate control might include:

- Sporting events
- Political rallies
- Flood zones
- Water dams
- Large metropolitan areas
- Airports

In a multi-tenant environment, the business being conducted by other tenants can have a negative impact on your organization and employees. In fact, in some scenarios your business continuity or even the lives of your employees are in danger. For example, abortion clinics are frequently the target of demonstrators. If your company shares space with an organization with a bad public image, you could have problems. Issues range from impeded access because of demonstrators, to verbal abuse, vandalism, and even injury or death. If this is a concern for your organization, you must address the problem. It will be necessary to distance your company from the target organization. Speak with the organizers of the demonstrations and express your concern as an uninvolved third party. If they are legally demonstrating, you have no recourse but to try to make the best of a bad situation. Perhaps, you can wear identification that would distance you from the target. Stress your organization's desire to remain neutral in such affairs.

The situation is much different if your organization is the target of such demonstrations. You must take a different approach. Reasoning with the demonstrators will probably not work. Fighting back will definitely not work. In many similar situations, the target company has hired security guards to protect those crossing a picket line or entering a clinic. These organizations have found that an unbiased third party with a badge and a gun can keep relative peace. The installation of security cameras may influence the crowd not to do anything radical. The installation of fences and gates are often used to keep a buffer between the demonstrators and the individual targets. Sometimes employees who cross a picket line are bused in with a police escort. Visitors to a company that is the target of protests may be required to use a back entrance that has restricted access. Regardless of the situation and the eventual solution, you must address these possibilities in your emergency action plan.

So where is your property located? Does that location introduce factors that could create an emergency? What are the obvious issues that endanger your business? Don't focus solely on the obvious, but explore all possibilities. Don't limit your exposure to weather-related or naturally occurring events. Understand that many emergencies can be the result of human error or deliberate acts.

Building Use

Consider the kind of property you are managing and the tasks that are performed there. Each property will have its own unique issues and concerns. An alert emergency planner would have a good understanding of these issues and would customize the emergency plan to address these issues. The planner would also consider the building occupants and their attitudes or physical and mental limitations. Based on the planner's observations, details would be added to the emergency plan that address these issues as well. A number of different building classifications exist, but let's examine just four types—the industrial, commercial, educational, and healthcare facilities.

Industrial Facility

Industrial facilities tend to house equipment and chemicals that could produce hazards if used improperly. Chemical spills and fires are not uncommon in such buildings and therefore must be addressed in the emergency plan. Questions to ask include:

▲   Is an industrial fire brigade necessary?

▲   Can we contain and clean up a chemical spill?

▲   Is the alarm audible over the machinery?

▲   Have all shifts been trained in emergency procedures?

▲   Have employees been trained in shut-down procedures in the event of an evacuation?

▲   Do we have a way to safely store flammable and toxic chemicals?

Commercial Property

Multistory, multi-tenant commercial buildings present a number of communication and logistical problems when emergency planning is concerned. Too often, commercial tenants view emergency procedures and evacuation drills as unnecessary and a waste of time. The emergency planner should be aware of these attitudes and work toward changing these perceptions. Questions to ask include:

▲   How would all occupants be notified?

▲   Has a chain of command been specified?

▲   Have all tenants been trained in emergency evacuation procedures?

▲   What kinds of flammable or toxic chemicals are the tenants storing?

▲   Do the chemicals all have current MSDS documentation?

▲   Have emergency responsibilities and expectations been added to the lease agreement?

▲   Who is responsible for testing alarms, fire extinguishers, and other related equipment?

▲   Does the emergency planner have after-hours phone numbers for the tenants?

▲   If tenants make changes to the building structure or floor space, have the changes been added to the as-built drawings?

Educational Facility

Educational facilities present a number of challenging issues, and each of those should be addressed in the emergency plan. Preschool and elementary schools are not likely to have many of the hazards that higher grade educational facilities might have, but the lower comprehension level of the students must be addressed. High schools, technical schools, and colleges will have labs that use chemicals and machinery that could malfunction and create an emergency event. Evaluation of facilities should take into account both the hazards that exist and the comprehension level of the students. Because of the young age of the majority of the occupants in an educational facility, the administration must provide an increased level of direction and hands-on assistance when evacuations are required. Questions to ask include:

⤳   Have we established specific staging areas for each classroom?

⤳   How will we handle bomb threats?

⤳   How will we handle false alarms?

⤳   How will we communicate with parents?

⤳   How will we account for students who are picked up by parents?

⤳   Can transportation be brought in to take students to a safe location?

⤳   Have we addressed the potential for violence?

⤳   Is the school facility near any hazardous sites that might force an evacuation?

Healthcare Facility

Although healthcare facilities can expose workers to some of the most dangerous hazards, the industry is also highly regulated. Agencies such as the Occupational Safety and Health Administration (OSHA) and the Joint Commission on Accreditation of Healthcare Organizations (JCAHO) speak directly to the unique hazards present in healthcare environments. These regulations will have bearing on your emergency planning and recovery activities. Questions to ask might include:

⤳   Would we be able to handle chemical or biological exposure?

⤳   Do we have procedures for bloodborne pathogen exposure?

⤳   How long can we operate without utilities?

⤳   How would we handle an evacuation?

⤳   How can we practice evacuations without impacting the patients?

⤳   Does the facility have safe "areas of refuge" to which patients can be moved?

Of course, these are not the only questions you would ask when developing an emergency action plan. These questions represent just a sampling of the issues that must be addressed. The emergency planner must play the role of detective, looking for weaknesses in the current plan or its processes. It's okay to play devil's advocate. It's important to role play emergency scenarios, and don't be afraid to ask the hard questions.

So far we've discussed the property, its geographic location, and the business it conducts. Usually these are issues that we can control. We should now change our focus to those external events that add to our risk.

Understanding Your Risk

The Risk Assessment Matrix

A logical starting point for determining risk would be to list any hazard that may occur. Upon completion of that list, you would then rank the hazards in order of probability. When completing this step of the process, it is advisable to consult with other sources that have already completed a risk assessment. For instance, many states and local agencies have already completed risk assessments and mitigation plans for your area. Public works departments, water management agencies, floodplain managers, and other agencies have done the legwork. Don't reinvent the wheel! In fact, many of the hazards that exist in your community may be "hidden" hazards which might be easily overlooked. To circumvent this possibility, consult with others.

Dams

One emergency planner was smart enough to realize that a dam some fifty miles upriver presented his facilities with additional risk. If you are not sure about the existence of dams in your area, contact the Association of State Dam Safety Officials (ASDSO). Their Web site is www. damsafety.org (click on "The States"). The majority of the dams in the United States have Emergency Actions Plans that identify areas that are likely to be flooded in the event of a breach.

Liability versus Probability versus Cost

After determining the probability of an event occurring, you should also determine the liability and the cost. A high-probability, low-liability event such as temporary loss of electrical utility may not warrant much consideration. However, a low-probability, high-liability event such as extended loss of utility must be planned for. A third component to consider is cost. Is the cost of the emergency event elimination or reduction worth the trouble? Is the return on investment worthwhile? For instance, you could construct a totally storm-proof, fireproof, and secure building, but at what cost? Is that cost too high based on the liability or probability of an emergency event? These are the factors that must be considered when performing a risk analysis.

The frequency and duration of emergency events will also play a role in your planning efforts. We will discuss these factors later in the chapter, but realize that your geographic location will play a big role in the frequency and even the duration of an emergency event. This information should be taken into consideration when developing an emergency action plan.

The Federal Emergency Management Agency (FEMA) has created an excellent matrix for performing a risk analysis. (See figure 10.1.) The matrix is effective because it allows you to assign a probability factor and human, property, and business impacts in addition to an internal and external resource scale. You would grade each of these components based on a scale of one to five. After grading out each emergency event, you simply add the number from left to right with the total tallied in the right-hand column. The higher the number, the greater the concern. This matrix forces you to evaluate potential emergency events against a consistent measuring stick. It focuses your attention on the greatest needs and concerns.

If you think it's expensive to do emergency planning, consider the alternative. It is always more expensive to address the effects of an emergency *after* the event has happened. It is a

Type of Emergency	Probability	Human Impact	Property Impact	Business Impact	Internal Resource	External Resource	Total
	Hi Lo 5 ←→1	Hi Lo 5←→1	Hi Lo 5 ←→1	Hi Lo 5 ←→1	Weak 5 ←	Strong →1	
Fires							
Severe weather							
Hazardous material spills							
Transportation accidents							
Earthquakes							
Terrorism							
Utility outages							
Other							

Figure 10.1. Risk Analysis Matrix.

fact: organizations that do not have an emergency action plan have a more difficult time recovering from an emergency event—and many do not.

Various reports have estimated that between 40 percent and 90 percent of businesses that experience disasters will go out of business within five years as a direct result of that disaster. Furthermore, 95 percent of those businesses were operating without the safety net that an emergency action plan provides.

Regarding liability, it would be a mistake to dwell too much on the "hundred year" flood and discount the less disastrous annual flood. In actuality, the annual flood may cause more damage over the long term because of its frequency. Take care not to focus too much on the "big" event at the expense of the "everyday" occurrences.

Online Hazard Maps and Databases

Wouldn't it be nice if you could retrieve historical information about natural hazard events in your area? You could review newspaper clippings and other announcements, but that process would be tedious and time consuming. You could ask people who have lived in the area for a long time, but memories fade and the details may be sketchy. Or you could simply visit a database that tracks hazards and allows visitors to perform a historical study of natural events and near misses. This database is a partnership between the Federal Emergency Management Agency (FEMA) and the Environmental Systems Research Institute (ESRI). Their goal is to provide multihazard maps and information to the public via the Internet. FEMA provides the historical hazard data and ESRI brings the information to life by providing GIS mapping and software. The end result is an invaluable tool for the emergency planner. See the ESRI Web site at www.esri.com/services/disaster-response/disaster-relief.

Understanding Your Responsibilities

OSHA Regulations

In addition to the moral responsibility you have to your employees and the fiscal responsibility you have to your employer, you have a distinct responsibility to OSHA. OSHA requires that employers protect employees from fire and other emergencies. Part 1910 of OSHA addresses general industry, which covers most operating facilities. Specifically 1910.38 (a) (1-5) requires the following components:

- ▲ Emergency escape procedures
- ▲ Emergency escape routes
- ▲ Procedures to be followed by employees who address critical functions prior to evacuation
- ▲ Procedures to account for employees after evacuation has been completed
- ▲ Rescue and medical duties for those employees authorized to perform them
- ▲ The preferred means of reporting fires and other emergencies
- ▲ Names of persons who can provide further information about the plan
- ▲ An alarm system that employees recognize for emergencies

In addition to these items, OSHA requires employers to train a sufficient number of people to assist in the safe and orderly emergency evacuation of employees. The employer is then required to review the plan with each employee covered by the plan at least once and then again whenever the employee's emergency evacuation duties are changed or when the plan itself is revised. The written plan must be available for all employees to review.

In addition to the emergency evacuation plan, OSHA requires a specific fire prevention plan. The requirements of the fire prevention plan are discussed in greater detail in chapter 12.

It's important to remember that OSHA standards are considered to be minimum safety standards. OSHA regulations would supersede less demanding local codes that may exist; however, the opposite is often the case. Local codes can be more rigorous than the OSHA requirements, and when this occurs, the stricter local codes supersede the less strict OSHA regulations.

> The OSHA regulations referenced in this book are federal OSHA standards. Twenty-six states, Puerto Rico, and the Virgin Islands have OSHA-approved state plans. OSHA requires state plans to be at least as stringent as the federal plan, and many are more demanding. To determine if your state has its own plan, visit the OSHA Web site at www.osha.gov and click on the link for state plans in the directory to go to www.osha.gov/dcsp/osp/index.html. If your state has its own plan, a link will be provided that will allow you to leave the federal site and go directly to your state OSHA Web site.

Signage

Safe exit from a building in the event of an emergency is not just a good idea, it's also the law. The Occupational Safety and Health Act, the National Electric Code, the National Fire Protection Association, and your local municipality all have specific requirements concerning building signage and emergency lighting. The purpose of these regulations is to ensure the safety of all building occupants as they exit your building. This includes not just employees but also visitors, vendors, clients, and anyone else who may be at your place of business. Many of these people are unfamiliar with your building and won't readily know the best route for evacuation.

OSHA has created a number of standards that address the need for proper signage. The OSHA regulations found at 29 CFR 1910.37(q)(1)–(8) include:

- Exits shall be marked by a readily visible sign.
- Any door or passage that is not an exit but could be mistaken for an exit shall be identified by a sign reading "Not an Exit."
- No decorations or furnishings shall hide or obstruct the sign.
- Every exit sign shall be in a distinctive color and contrast with the interior finish.
- Every exit sign shall be illuminated by a reliable light source giving a value of not less than five foot candles.
- Every exit sign shall have letters not less than six inches high and three-quarters of an inch wide.

Although not an OSHA requirement, the Americans with Disabilities Act (ADA) requires building signage in many areas to be both visual (capable of being visually read) and tactile (capable of being physically read). Raised and Braille characters are required on signs that designate permanent spaces such as restrooms, exits, and rooms and floors designated by numbers or letters. ADA law does not specify that informational and directional signage be tactile, but it does specify other aspects such as the height and width of the lettering. Likewise, OSHA specifies certain letter sizes on exit signs. Remember, both ADA and OSHA are federal agencies and your local municipality or code enforcement board can create regulations that supersede these federal regulations if they are stricter.

> In many municipalities, low-level signage or floor-proximity exit signs are now required. These illuminated exit signs are usually installed six to eight inches above the floor level and are visible when ordinary exit signs installed near the ceiling level are obscured by smoke.

Material Safety Data Sheets

Would you know what to do if you inhaled or ingested a strong chemical? What would happen if you attempted to wash an acid-based substance off with soap and water? Since a chemical spill or a release of hazardous gas might constitute an emergency, we'll spend some discussing hazard communication. The Occupational Safety and Health Agency has developed specific requirements concerning the chemicals you have in your buildings. OSHA's hazard communication standard, and specifically the "Right-to-Know" standard 1910.1200, requires that employers provide the following:

- ▲ Material Safety Data Sheets (MSDS)
- ▲ Chemical inventory list
- ▲ Written hazard communication plan
- ▲ Proper labeling on all containers
- ▲ Employee training

The first two items on the list, MSDS and chemical inventory list, play an important role in emergency planning and recovery and therefore should be addressed in the emergency action plan. The MSDS are the standardized documents that provide this type of information. Information found on an MSDS includes:

- ▲ Manufacturing company information
- ▲ Exposure limits
- ▲ Treatment if exposed to eyes
- ▲ Treatment if exposed to skin
- ▲ Treatment if inhaled
- ▲ Treatment if ingested
- ▲ First aid measures
- ▲ Storage requirements

The MSDS serves as a protection for employees who are overexposed to a chemical or are exposed without proper personal protective equipment. If a current MSDS logbook is kept by the employer, an assisting employee could access the exposure information and act accordingly. The MSDS information could be given to rescue personnel when they arrive. Because of the thousands of substances in existence, they may not be familiar with the chemical that caused the problem. The MSDS will assist the rescue personnel in prescribing the proper treatment.

Another reason to have MSDS documents available is to protect emergency rescue personnel as they enter your building. Imagine your building is on fire and somebody calls 911. The dispatcher sends the local fire department. As the firefighters arrive, they quickly survey the building and the fire. It's nearly midnight and there is no sign of employees in the building; however, there are a few automobiles in the parking lot. The fire doesn't appear to be too bad, so the firefighters enter the building to search for possibly trapped employees and to better extinguish the flames. Unbeknownst to the fire fighters, your company produces and stores large quantities of sulfuric acid and other hazardous chemicals. Additionally, a natural gas pipeline runs through the building. Just about the time the firefighters reach the core of your building, a series of large explosions occur creating a thick cloud of toxic gas. The lives of the firefighters were unnecessarily put at risk. Because detailed information was not available to the firefighters, they entered a building that contained multiple hazards. Many fire departments are requiring MSDS log books, floor plans, and other warning information to be present before they will enter a building.

MSDSs are available for all chemicals, even those not considered dangerous. By law, an MSDS must be provided to you by the manufacturer or the distributor of the chemical. Upon accepting delivery of a chemical, make sure the MSDS is included. If it is not, ask for it. When purchasing small quantities of a chemical from a retail store, ask a clerk for a copy. If they don't have a copy, there are online MSDS databases to find answers. Simply provide some basic information and you'll be able to print out the needed MSDS. (See also OSHA's chemical database at www.osha.gov/chemicaldata/.)

Another piece of important information is the chemical inventory list (figure 10.2). This document is required by OSHA and works in conjunction with MSDS information. The chemical inventory list identifies by name all the chemicals that are on site, the area in which they are stored, the date they were brought on site, and when they were removed (if applicable). The chemical inventory list would be especially useful for emergency rescue personnel because they could quickly glance at the chemical list and identify any concerns. Since the chemical inventory list identifies where the chemical is stored, the firefighter could cross reference this information against a floor plan and further gauge the risk of entry.

Chemical Name	Area Used	Date Introduced	Date Removed
Bleach	Janitor's closet	5/01/10	
Denatured Alcohol	Shop	11/15/13	11/20/14
Tile Mastic	Shop	11/15/13	
Shelia Shine	Janitor's closet	3/23/12	

Figure 10.2. Example of a Chemical Inventory List.

Americans with Disabilities Act

The Americans with Disabilities Act (ADA) offers many excellent suggestions for assisting those with disabilities during evacuation of a building. This issue is more difficult than most think. If handled improperly, the disabled can be hurt and the evacuation of other building occupants can be delayed. With this in mind, special consideration should be given to persons with disabilities. Hearing, vision, mental, and mobility issues need to be addressed prior to an emergency event, not during it.

In many cases, it is very easy to observe certain disabilities and make allowances for them. However, persons with disabilities, especially disabilities that are not readily visible, are often hesitant to reveal their disabilities. This presents the emergency planner with a very difficult task. How can the planner develop steps to protect the employee if the planner is not aware of a limitation? To bridge this gap, the planner should provide all employees the forum to privately reveal any limitations that may affect their ability to evacuate the

> The Americans with Disability Act defines a disabled person as anyone who has a physical or mental impairment that substantially limits one or more major life activities. This may include vision, hearing, mobility, mental, speech, or other serious health impairments including diabetes, heart disease, cancer, asthma, and alcoholism or drug use.

building. Employers do have the legal right to ask employees if they have a disability that would hinder them from evacuating the building. To avoid drawing attention to a disabled employee, all employees should be asked this question, not just employees who have an obvious disability. A great way to address these issues without making disabled employees feel uncomfortable is to get them involved in the evacuation planning effort. They will likely be able to add insight that most employees would have been unaware of.

Don't forget about temporary or nonprotected disabilities that may affect the employee's ability to safely evacuate the building. These issues may include pregnancy, knee or hip problems, broken bones, obesity, and asthma. Pregnancy is not a protected ADA classification, but a pregnant woman attempting to walk down seventy flights of stairs during an evacuation may have difficulties. The intelligent emergency planner understands that these temporary limitations must be addressed and will establish procedures to assist

> Prior to offering assistance to a disabled person, ask them how you can help them. Don't be pushy! Ask how they can best be assisted or moved and whether there are any special considerations you should know about. Also ask them if they have any items that need to come with them. Show this person respect and do not treat them like a child.

this person. Another example is the person with allergies or asthma. Under normal working circumstances, the symptoms are not revealed. Even if that person were required to evacuate the building and walk down seventy flights of stairs, the physical condition would not manifest itself. However, during the stress and excitement of an actual emergency coupled with the presence of smoke, the physical issue becomes a major liability. These are the types of nonprotected or temporary disabilities that need to be addressed.

Partner System

When evacuating a building there will inevitably be those people who require assistance. Many organizations have established partner systems (sometimes known as buddy systems) and have been successfully using them. Partner systems are not perfect, though. They work when both parties are aware of and respect the arrangement. Partner systems fail for a number of reasons including:

- The assisting partner is absent from the workplace
- The assisting partner is in the building but at a different location
- The disabled partner is absent from the building but the assisting partner does not realize it
- The disabled partner is in a different area of the building
- The assisting partner has not been trained on how to react and assist
- The assisting partner is not physically appropriate for the task
- The assisting partner or the disabled partner are not patient with one another
- The assisting partner becomes frightened and leaves without the disabled partner
- The disabled partner evacuates without the assisting partner or with the help of someone else

These examples may seem like non-issues. Certainly we wouldn't leave someone who was depending on us, right? In times of emergency, we sometimes do strange things. The partnership must be one that is mutually respected and understood. Training must be delivered to both parties on a regular basis and prior to an emergency event. Some of the possible solutions to the problems inherent to partner systems include:

- The disabled partner should play an active role in selecting their partner
- The assisting partner should understand the potential rigors of evacuating a disabled person
- A system should be established to communicate absences or "not founds" to floor captains
- A system should be established for disabled partners who do not use their assisting partners (and safely exit the building) to communicate their status to the exterior group leader
- A backup partner should be assigned and trained for each disabled partner
- The assisting partner should work near the disabled partner

Partner systems work. If both parties understand the assignment and take it seriously, lives can be saved and evacuations can be conducted more efficiently.

Visual Impairments

We sometimes fail to comprehend the importance of our senses, in particular our vision. Imagine performing basic life functions without sight. Imagine not knowing what obstacles are in your path. Imagine not knowing where the closest emergency exit is located. For obvious reasons, those with visual limitations require special attention during an evacuation. By using a partner system, the visually impaired can be led to safety. Because many of us are not accustomed to assisting the blind, here are a few reminders:

- Announce your presence as you enter the work area.
- Do not shout at them; they are blind, not deaf.
- Do not grasp a visually impaired person's arm.
- Ask if they would like to hold onto your arm as you exit.
- Ask them to explain what assistance they need.
- Before walking toward the exit, let them know that debris or crowds are present.
- Verbally provide warning of stairs, ramps, doorways, or other obstacles.

Once outside the building, do not abandon the visually impaired person. He or she will be in unfamiliar surroundings, in a crowd of moving people, and perhaps in the way of emergency rescue personnel. Bring this person to a staging area or other safe haven.

Hearing Impairments

The National Center for Health Statistics estimates that more than 37 million U.S. adults have hearing trouble, making this the largest class of people protected by ADA law. Given these large numbers, there is a good chance that you will have people in your building with hearing impairments. Again, we often take our senses for granted. Imagine an alarm being sounded and an evacuation being ordered over the loudspeaker. Without hesitation, we would make our way toward the exit routes and out of the building. Now think about people with hearing impairments. Let's assume they are working at their computer, fully engrossed in what they are doing. Based on their hearing limitation and their involvement in their work, they would be oblivious to the emergency event. Like those with visual limitations, those with hearing limitations also require special attention during an evacuation. The partner system is the best way to assist those with disabilities, but because many of us are not accustomed to assisting the hearing impaired, here are a few reminders:

- Speak directly to the individual, not to their interpreter.
- Get their attention by touching them and keep it through eye contact.
- When entering their office, flick the lights to get their attention.
- Clearly state the problem using gestures and pointing.
- Write a brief statement if the person does not seem to understand.
- Be patient, especially if they do not comprehend what you are saying.
- Give them a flashlight so they can read lips if the lights go out.

In many organizations, those with hearing disabilities are given a pager that vibrates in the event of an emergency. The alphanumeric pagers work best because a text message can be sent to give the employee an idea of what is going on and how they should proceed. Audible alarms should also be coupled with blinking strobes that would alert an employee who could not hear. In some hotels, persons with hearing disabilities are given rooms with beds that vibrate if the fire alarm is activated. The tools are out there. There is no good reason for not accounting for the unique needs of those with hearing disabilities.

*   *   *

For those organizations without an emergency action plan, the task of creating one can seem insurmountable. Like any large task, you must break the development of your plan into small manageable pieces. A good starting point is to perform a risk analysis. This analysis takes into consideration your geographic location, your resources, your core business functions, and the emergency events most likely to affect your business.

Of course, the development of a good emergency action plan doesn't happen without an investment of time and money. You may have to convince management of the importance of your endeavors. This should not be too difficult given the historical accounts of businesses that were unable to survive an emergency event. Much like an insurance policy, you hope you'll never need to use the emergency action plan, but that doesn't mean you can go without one.

The Emergency Action Plan, Part Two
Creating the Plan

The Emergency Action Plan

As we discussed in chapter 10, creating the emergency action plan is not a simple process. Risks must be evaluated. Critical business functions must be understood. The liability of an emergency must be compared to the probability of it happening. Contingency plans must be developed in any case. Assignments must be given and employees must be trained. At some point, all of this must be written down and the compilation of all this information becomes your plan. Unfortunately, the plan is often viewed as unnecessary and even unrealistic. Management needs proof that the investment they made in emergency planning was worth it. In an effort to satisfy their concerns, we often equate quantity with quality and produce a big thick emergency planning manual.

The manual may look impressive but a huge document is counter-productive. The emergency action plan must provide valuable, up-to-date information that can quickly be referenced during an emergency event. The manual must contain all actionable information without padding or irrelevant information that may confuse.

The emergency action plan is not static, it is a living document. It will change and evolve over time. The initial time spent developing the plan will not likely need to be repeated, but the document must be maintained and updated as times and circumstances change. The initial development of the document may be painful and time consuming, but it is project well worth the time and expense.

A benefit of developing the emergency action plan is that it forces you and your team to look at every aspect of your organization's operations. In the process you may find redundancies or better ways to doing things which can increase production or efficiency and may boost the bottom line.

This book was created to assist emergency planners with the development of such a plan. It's impossible to provide an emergency action plan that satisfies the needs of all organizations. A turnkey plan that can be purchased and simply placed on a shelf until an emergency occurs does not exist. Even with the help of this resource, you will be required to research and develop a plan that is specific to your business. With this in mind, let's discuss the plan, its purpose, and what it does in greater detail.

What Does It Do?

The emergency action plan exists to save lives and reduce injuries in the event of an emergency. It provides the means and methods to help you plan, survive, and recover from an emergency. Because lives, property, and business continuity are at stake, the emergency action plan must be considered an important part of your organization's business plan. It must be championed at the highest levels of the organization. It should educate employees and serve as a basis for ongoing employee training. Because people and processes do change, the emergency action plan must be reviewed on a regular basis and updated as required.

What Does It Contain?

Your emergency action plan should contain all pertinent information that will allow you to plan, survive, and recover from an emergency. This will require an evaluation of your building, type of business, and geographic location. The plan must contain names and phone numbers of employees who are able to offer assistance in the event of an emergency. In 29 CFR 1910.38(a)–(b), OSHA has developed regulations that identify the minimum requirements of an emergency action plan:

- Emergency escape procedures
- Description of potential hazards
- Emergency escape routes
- Procedures to be followed by employees who remain to operate or shut down critical building operations before they evacuate
- Procedures to account for all employees after evacuation has been completed
- Rescue and medical duties for those employees assigned to perform them
- The preferred means of reporting fires and other emergencies
- Names or job titles of employees who can further explain the emergency action plan

OSHA also requires that each facility have a fire prevention plan in place. This plan is specifically tailored for the threat of fire. The employer is required to train employees in aspects of the plan that pertain to their exposure. Components of the plan include:

- A list of fire hazards that exist in the workplace
- Names or titles of employees who are responsible for fire source hazards
- Names or titles of employees who are responsible for fire alarms and fire-fighting equipment

    ▲   Housekeeping procedures that limit fuel sources

    ▲   Employee training techniques and frequencies

In addition to these minimum OSHA requirements, a good emergency action plan would include the following items:

    ▲   Statement of policy, also known as a mission statement

    ▲   Floor plans with exits, fire extinguishers, pull stations, first aid stations, and other important features marked

    ▲   Location of MSDS information

    ▲   Names and numbers of external emergency service providers

    ▲   Inventory lists of emergency supplies

    ▲   Maintenance schedules for generators, fire sprinkler, alarm systems, and other related emergency equipment

    ▲   Chain of command established for emergency events

Who Gets a Copy?

That depends largely on your organization's preference. The actual emergency action plan can be quite large and detailed; if given in written format, most employees will not read it. OSHA does not require every employee to have a copy of the plan. Instead, OSHA requires that the plan be kept at the workplace and made available to all employees. A suggested best practice would be to provide all members of your emergency management team with a completed copy of the plan and simply make the plan available to all employees. Many organizations have done this by putting the plan on the company's intranet Web site. Other organizations have provided employees with a scaled-down version of the emergency action plan, usually during new employee orientation. A summary version explains proper evacuation procedures, alarms, staging areas, and other basic issues.

One important issue is the regular revision of the emergency action plan. You do not go through all the effort of creating a plan and then let it sit on a shelf. The plan should be reviewed at least annually and revised as needed. When changes are made to the plan, training should be provided to all employees affected by the changes.

In the event of an emergency, the action plan will be a vital reference. You will consult the plan on a regular basis, looking for names and number of key support personnel. You'll use the plan as a guide for making decisions. The plan will ensure that all the necessary actions are taken to promote business continuity during and after the emergency. Bottom line: the plan is of utmost importance! But think for a moment about the actual plan. Where do you keep it? Probably in your office. Would you be able to access the plan if the building burned down? What if an earthquake occurred and the building was unsafe to enter? What if everybody on the emergency management team kept their plans in their offices? Of course, you could go online to the company's intranet site and print it out. What if the electricity was out for an extended period of time? What if your computer was damaged during the emergency event? For these reasons, it is imperative that you keep a copy of the emergency plan at an offsite location such as your vehicle or home. It makes sense to keep a copy on your laptop or a thumb drive attached to your keychain as well. Don't be caught in a situation where the plan is not available!

The Emergency Management Team

Every good plan is supported by a team of dedicated people. The plan is just a reference manual. Decisions still need to be made. Direction must be given. Human interaction and leadership is a necessity. The plan comes to life when somebody picks it up and actually uses it. Furthermore, the emergency management function is not a one-person job. Instead, a team of people will be involved, each with a specific purpose.

Creation of an emergency management team is essential early in the planning process. Expertise will be needed from all areas of the organization. If the emergency management team consists of employees with similar backgrounds, education, responsibilities, and job titles, the plan will be written in a vacuum. Valuable expertise from outside your department will not be tapped into, so make sure you include a diverse group of employees on your team. This team will likely grow as the plan becomes a reality. Floor captains, runners, evacuation partners, and command post leaders will be need to be elected. For now, though, the team should be kept small but functional.

The length of time a member would sit on an emergency team is subjective. Some organizations like to rotate a percentage of team members on an annual basis. The belief is that by allowing a greater number of employees the chance to sit on the team, a greater number of employees will respect the plan and be able to react during crisis. This way, the bulk of the emergency team is left intact while employees with fresh ideas and viewpoints can be introduced. It is also believed that in the event a team member leaves the organization, the vacancy can be quickly filled by a past member.

After Hours

Because emergencies can happen anytime during the day or night, the emergency management team may need to respond after hours. A phone list of current members and responsibilities should be made available to each member of the team. For ease of use, print the information on a credit card–sized paper and laminate it. Team members will be able to keep this list in their purses or wallets and access it quickly in the event a response is needed.

If an emergency should happen at night make sure that your plan includes how to access the building after hours and deal with security systems and such.

Identifying Team Members and Responsibilities

When developing your emergency management team, be sure to include a diverse roster of employees. In addition to the obvious goal of saving lives and reducing injuries, your goal is to identify critical business functions that may be interrupted as a result of an emergency event. This is not usually accomplished through the eyes of a single individual. Once the diverse team of subject matter experts has been finalized, assignments and a hierarchy should be developed. During a crisis there must be a clear line of responsibility and command. Listed below are samples of some of the expertise needed on your team:

- Risk Management Specialist
- Logistics and Procurement Manager
- Media Relations Contact
- Human Resources Personnel
- Facilities Maintenance Manager
- Legal Counsel

Listed below are a few of the assignments that should be given:

- Emergency Director
- Business Continuity Manager
- Command Post Leader
- Group Leader
- Floor Captains
- Fire Brigade
- Evacuation Assistants
- Runners

Internal and External Support

The risk analysis matrix discussed in chapter 10 includes a column for internal support and a column for external support. Although you'll want to take advantage of your internal resources and employees that may not always be possible. Key to surviving any emergency event will be the support of external resources and vendors. Early identification of these resources is essential, as is involving them in the planning process.

When identifying internal and external resources, consider how quickly the resource will be available. This plays an important role when discussing internal resources. You may have an excellent staff of highly trained maintenance technicians who are skilled at solving building-related problems, but the emergency event may cause them to be unavailable. In the event of labor unrest, your internal resources may not be willing to cross a picket line. When an emergency event occurs, your employees and their families may be directly affected and, therefore, unavailable, so make plans for a backup.

Insurance providers play a critical role in your emergency planning and recovery efforts. Unfortunately, most people don't know in detail what coverage they have in place. The time to educate yourself on these important issues is prior to an emergency, not after it. Many organizations believed they were covered by their insurance policies, only to find later that an amendment to the policies excluded a specific event. Since coverage terms, property valuation, property size, and other issues change on a regular basis,

On October 30, 2000, President Bill Clinton signed the Disaster Mitigation Act of 2000 (Public Law 106-390). This law encourages and even rewards local and state (and tribal nation) disaster planning. It serves as a bridge between numerous local agencies and the state, thereby increasing timely communication between these groups. Those organizations that are not considered public entities are encouraged to contact their local and state agencies to ensure compatible planning.

you should meet annually with your insurance advisor to discuss your policy. Typical questions might include the following:

- ➤ How will the property be valued (replacement/actual/other)?
- ➤ Am I covered for spoilage of goods?
- ➤ Do I have all the policies needed (wind/flood/storm/contents/liability)?
- ➤ Do I have a policy protecting me in the event of lost income?
- ➤ If I do have a lost income policy, and what is the duration?
- ➤ In what way does the provider require proof of loss?
- ➤ What additional loss documentation is needed and is it stored in a safe place?
- ➤ Does it make sense to self-insure?
- ➤ What are my deductibles and are they at proper levels?

Identifying Vendors and Contractors

Contractors come and go; it is, therefore, imperative that you review your list of contractors with active purchase orders annually at a minimum. Be certain that you have updated office and cell phone numbers. In heavily populated metropolitan areas, area codes tend to change on a regular basis, so make sure you have the latest area code as well. An excellent form for tracking contractor availability is depicted in figure 2.3 in chapter 2.

Identifying a good contractor is just a starting point. A contractor may agree to offer assistance after the emergency event, but because of circumstances out of their control, may not be available. Access roads could be blocked, their office could be heavily damaged, or some other logistical problem might exist. For this reason, you need to have alternate contractors available. The "Contractor Availability Form" includes space to list alternate contractors.

Using the services of a contractor after an emergency event sounds like an easy process. Simply call the contractor, issue a work ticket, and tell them where to show up and what to do. In actuality, the process is not so simple. First, do you need permission from your insurance company before you can start clean-up and repairs? Following an emergency the insurance company will often tell you to proceed but to document in writing and pictures the position immediately following the emergency and then to continue to keep similar records as the repair work progresses. It could be many days before an insurance company claims adjustor arrives on the scene.

Often you know the contractor's services are needed, but you're not sure of the scope of work. For instance, after a tornado, you contact your landscaping contractor and dispatch them to your corporate headquarters. Based on the reports you've heard, trees are down and blocking access roads and parking lots. Other trees are not down but pose a danger and require removal. There will probably be some irrigation repairs as well. Because the scope is unclear, you simply instruct the contractor to get the property back in order. Ambiguous requests like this are likely to cause over-billing. To account for these issues, detailed records must be kept. Depending on the relationship you have with the contractor, you may require a field inspector from your organization to give approval prior to commencing work. This may keep costs under control, but it really slows down the recovery process.

A better way to handle large projects that are discovered by the contractor in the field is to require them to document the damage with a camera or video camera prior to commencing the cleanup efforts. If your relationship is good with the contractor, this process will protect you and keep the contractor busy. You may also elect to place a cap on cleanup efforts. For instance, any job that exceeds $2,500 must first be approved by the facilities department. By blending a quick efficient cleanup with cost protection measures, you'll get the job done without a financial hangover the next morning.

Prior to using the services of a contractor after an emergency event, you must iron out a few of the contractual details. The emergency creates unique circumstances. The contractor will bring in extra help. Many of the contractors will be providing assistance around the clock. Specialized equipment may need to be rented. When you consider the possible issues, you'll begin to realize the importance of creating contractor specifications for emergency events. Examples of these issues include:

- Overtime rates (time and a half, double time)
- Hotel reimbursement
- Mileage reimbursement
- Expense and receipt requirements
- Food reimbursement
- Laundry reimbursement
- Equipment rental responsibilities
- Personal protection equipment requirements
- Additional insurance requirements

Because much of the help you use will not be your primary contractors, you'll be tapping into companies that may not meet your usual company expectations. Specifically, insurance requirements come to mind. Do you feel comfortable contracting with companies that carry inferior amounts of liability insurance? It's a risk and you must weigh that risk against the restoration needs you face. Be very careful with this decision. Remember, after an emergency unusual and dangerous conditions will likely exist. If this contractor does not have adequate insurance for normal working conditions, how can you feel comfortable using them in a dangerous environment? Instead of lowering your standards, spend more time locating quality alternate contractors who already have the required coverage in place.

The indemnity agreement should be a standard document signed by all contractors, regardless of their insurance amounts. This document protects your company from lawsuits and judgments as a result of the contracted assignment. As a last resort, you may elect to use contractors with inferior coverage amounts if they agree to sign an indemnity agreement. This document does not provide total protection, but at least it is a start. Of course, when signing contracts, always consult with your legal counsel beforehand. An example of an indemnity agreement coupled with a safety clause may look like this:

> Contractor hereby agrees to indemnify and hold harmless [company name] its agents, officers, successors, and assigns against any and all claims, suits, judgments, and damages of any kind resulting from this contract or the work supplied by the contractor, its employees, or subcontractors.

> Furthermore, contractor shall be solely responsible for supervising its employees, providing personal protection equipment, training its employees, record keeping, and adhering to all federal Occupational Safety and Health Act regulations or state equivalent.

Stocking Emergency Supplies

Figure 11.1 identifies items that should be stored as soon as storm season begins. This storm preparation inventory list also has columns for multiple locations. Of course the actual inventory and the numbers needed depend on your individual location.

Items that have a limited shelf life such as food, batteries, and fuel need to be rotated out of storm inventory and into common inventory. This best occurs at the end of storm season. For instance, if you have stored three dozen AAA batteries for your radios and you have not used them at the end of storm season, use them elsewhere. Don't make the mistake of sitting on those batteries for five years and find that they have expired when you really need them. Don't make the inventory more complicated than it needs to be, but remember the golden rule of inventory management: First In = First Out.

STORM PREPARATIONS
Inventory of Materials

	Location A	Location B	Location C	Location D
TOOLS / EQUIPMENT				
Chain saws (18') with 1 gallon gas can	1	1	2	1
1 quart bar & chain oil	2	2	4	2
2-cycle engine oil	2	2	4	2
Shovels	4	4	4	4
Wet vacs (25 gallon)	2	2	2	2
Fire estinguisher	4	4	6	4
Axe	1	1	2	1
Crowbar	1	1	1	1
Push Brooms	2	2	2	2
Chains and locks	2	2	2	3
Extension cords	3	3	4	3
Circular Saw	1	1	1	1
Screw guns / drills	2	2	2	2
Duct Tape	3	3	3	3
60 mil plastic liner (roll)	2	2	2	2
Orange spray paint	1	1	1	1
Ladder	1	1	1	1
Fans	2	2	4	2
Barricades	4	4	8	4
Emergency caution tape	2	2	2	2
FUEL SUPPLIES				
Gas can (5 gallon)				
Propane gas (Bottles for lanterns)				
Propane - 20lb Bottle for gas grill				
LIGHTING				
Propane lanterns				
6-volt lanterns				
Flashlights				
Portable quartz lighting				
BEDDING				
Folding cots				
Wool blankets				
CLOTHING				
Rubber boots, Size 10				
Rubber boots, Size 11				
Rubber boots, Size 12				
Work gloves				
Rain jackets, large				
Rain hoods				
Rain pants				
Hard hats				
Dust masks				
Respirators				
Safety glasses/goggles				
Reflective vests				
ROPE/WIRE				
Tie wire (50' Roll)				
Rope, 1/2" (300' Roll)				
Rope, 3/8" (200' Roll)				
PUMPS				
Sump pump w/hose and discharge hose				
MEDICAL				
First Aid kits				
Aspirin				
Sunblock				
Insect repellent				
WATER HOSES				
2 1/2" 6' Hose pkgs.				
SAND SUPPLIES				
Burlap bags				
Sand delivered (by load)				
GENERATORS				
Portable generator				
Fuel (unleadead gasoline)				
Oil (for Diesel Generator)				

Figure 11.1. Storm Preparation Inventory List.

STORM PREPARATIONS
Inventory of Materials

	Location A	Location B	Location C	Location D
RADIOS / BATTERIES				
Radios, NOAA				
Radios, 2-Way				
Clock (battery operated)				
Batteries - (size AA to D and 6V lantern)				
Calculator				
WATER / ICE / FOOD				
Ice chests (50 qt)				
Ice				
Meals Ready To Eat (MRE's)				
Matches				
Utinsils				
Garbage bags				
Water purifying tablets				
Bottled water - 5 gal. bottles				
Can opener (manual)				
BUILDING MATERIALS				
Plywood (4' x 8' x 5/8" sheets)				
2"x4"x 8' studs				
Screws				
Nails				
RENTAL EQUIPMENT				
Port-O-Potties				
Boat w/oars and accessories				
PHOTO EQUIPMENT				
Digital camera				
Disposable camera (Waterproof)				
Video				
CASH				
Emergency cash				
OFFICE SUPPLIES				
Steno pads				
Highlighters				
Pens				
Pencils				
Clipboards				
Paper clips				
Staples				

Figure 11.1. Storm Preparation Inventory List, continued.

In preparation for emergency events, it may be necessary to store a limited amount of food supplies. This can present a problem because the shelf life of most foods is very limited. Other foods require preparation, including cooking. A popular solution to this dilemma is the use of MREs (Meals Ready to Eat). Originally developed for the military, MREs are fully cooked meals that, depending on storage temperatures, have shelf lives exceeding ten years without refrigeration. Each item is cooked and sealed in individual, high-strength pouches. A full-meal MRE typically includes a main entree, side dish, dessert, crackers and spread, beverage base, spoon, and accessory packet. Although cooking of MREs is not required, some foods taste better if heated. Chemical MRE heaters are available that will effectively heat your food in a matter of minutes using only a little water.

A number of organizations produce and package MREs. You do not need to be a member of the military or other government agency to purchase them; in fact, many personal households keep MREs in stock in the event of an emergency or for family camping trips. MRE packages can be purchased that also include lights, batteries, personal hygiene products, and first aid supplies.

Emergency Floor Plans

A number of tools can assist emergency teams during search and rescue missions after an emergency event. Most of these tools are readily available to the planner, such as floor plans annotated with exits, fire extinguishers, and first aid kits. Other tools, such as the Urban Search and Rescue Grid, are created by highly specialized professionals and are particularly important for use in multi-tenant high-rise buildings.

When creating your emergency plan, start by acquiring an updated copy of the building floor plan. In a leased building you will need to speak with the property owner or its agents. If the building is company owned, you should speak to the facility management department. Over the years buildings are renovated, so the floor plan that you have may not be an accurate representation of the building's configuration. Take time to ensure the accuracy of the floor plan. If you cannot locate any floor plan information, or if the plan is hopelessly outdated, it would be advisable to create a basic revised floor plan. And if you have the tools and expertise in-house, use them to create a basic floor plan.

It's not necessary to go to into great detail on your floor plans; remember, the purpose is not to build the structure. The purpose of this floor plan is to identify windows, doors, emergency exits, alarm panels, fire pull stations, and other emergency-related items. A basic single line floor plan minus the dimensions, details, and other non-essential items will be sufficient.

When developing an emergency floor plan, remember to include important details such as:

Egress Concerns

- Designated escape routes
- Stairways
- Windows
- Doors
- Emergency exits
- Evacuation staging areas

Fire Safety

- Fire alarm pull stations
- Fire extinguishers
- Smoke detectors
- Water sprinkler testing valves
- Alarm panels

First Aid

- First aid kits and stations
- Automated External Defibrillators (AED)
- Eye wash stations

Specialty Areas

- Mechanical rooms
- Telecommunications rooms
- HazMat storage locations
- MSDS locations
- Restricted areas

Utilities

- Gas mains and valves
- Utility shutoffs
- Water lines and valves
- Sewer lines

Power Systems

- Generator and switchgear locations
- Generator powered circuits
- Uninterruptible power system location

Drainage

- Storm drains
- Roof drains

> Take pictures or a video of the facility and its assets before and after an emergency event. This documentation will prove beneficial when dealing with insurance adjusters.

Critical Building Information

Critical building information must be made available during and after emergency situations. This is usually not a problem if company employees are available. Facility management or maintenance personnel are a ready source of critical building information, but what would happen if the emergency event occurred after business hours? For instance, what if a fire were to start in your building after hours? When the fire department arrives, will they have keys to your building? How will they locate a floor plan? Will they be able to locate your MSDS information? If the fire department does not have keys, they will enter your building forcefully, but considering the emergency that will be the least of your problems. The floor plan would be helpful but, again, not necessary. The MSDS information, however, is very important to the firefighters. Without an idea of what chemicals are being stored on the premises, the firefighters are putting themselves in a very dangerous situation. It would be unfair to ask any rescue personnel to enter your building without first identifying the hidden hazards.

The KNOX-BOX® Rapid Entry System provides a means for nondestructive emergency access to commercial and residential property. Key vaults are available in small sizes just large enough to hold a set of building keys. Larger vaults are available that can hold keys,

MSDSs, floor plans, and other critical building information. These vaults are specially keyed to the requirements of your local rescue personnel, much like an elevator key. Check with your local fire department to see if KNOX-BOX systems are used in your area.

Fire Extinguishers and Means of Egress

Portable fire extinguishers provide the first line of defense when fighting a small fire. In many cases, quick response to a fire coupled with the proper extinguisher can prevent loss of life, damage to property, and reduced productivity. In fact, if the fire is contained and extinguished, an evacuation of building's occupants may not be necessary. At worst, a partial evacuation of those areas nearest to the fire may be all that is required.

Portable fire extinguishers are critical for extinguishing small fires in their early stages. Prior to using a portable fire extinguisher, the operator should be properly trained. Three major of classes of fire exist, and if the emergency responder chooses the wrong fire extinguisher for a specific fire, he or she risks causing further harm. Proper training starts with identification of the fire source and proper selection of extinguisher. The three major classifications of fires are:

Class A Fires: Fueled by common combustible materials such as wood, cloth, paper, and many plastics. Use a water-based extinguisher with a green label and Class "A" identifier.

Class B Fires: Fueled by flammable liquids and gasses such as gasoline, kitchen grease, and paint. Use a carbon dioxide or aqueous film forming foam (AFFF) extinguisher with a red label and Class "B" identifier.

Class C Fires: Fueled by live electrical components or circuits including appliances, tools, and wires. Use an extinguisher with a blue label and Class "C" identifier.

Fire Suppression Systems

In the event of a fire, quick response from local firefighting professionals is critical. In reality, the response is often not quick enough. The firefighters often arrive in time to extinguish the fire, aid the victims, and ensure that the fire does not spread to adjacent properties. Unfortunately, the damage to the subject property is often great. A sensible solution, especially in buildings that are unoccupied during the evening, is the installation of fire sprinklers. In many areas, fire sprinkler systems are mandatory on new construction and renovations. In fact, the National Fire Protection Association (NFPA, www.nfpa.org) has been a leader in developing standards for the fire protection industry. The NFPA has determined that installation of a fire sprinkler system coupled with smoke detectors could reduce deaths attributed to fire by 82 percent. Armed with this information, we can appreciate the importance of functional fire suppression systems.

There are a number of fire sprinkler options:

- **Dry pipe systems** are used in areas where freezing conditions exist. Pressurized air is maintained in the sprinkler pipes. When a fire occurs, the heat ruptures a seal in the sprinkler head, the air escapes the pipes, and the water exits the sprinkler heads.
- **Wet pipe systems** do not use pressurized air. When a fire occurs, the heat ruptures a seal in the sprinkler head and the water exits the sprinkler heads.
- **Deluge systems** are similar to dry pipe systems in that they use pressurized air in the pipes. This system may be activated manually or automatically.

After the terrorist attacks of September 11, 2001, engineers determined that the World Trade Center towers collapsed due to weakened steel members and not due to the violent collision of the two aircraft into the buildings. The aircraft were fully loaded with fuel, and as the fuel burned inside of the towers, temperatures reached in excess of 2,000 degrees. The World Trade Center Towers contained fire sprinkler systems, but the impact of the aircraft ruptured the lines and rendered them useless. This should not lessen the credibility of fire sprinklers as an effective way to extinguish fires, especially considering the unusual nature of that particular emergency.

Testing Your Fire Sprinkler System

In the event of a fire, you would expect the fire sprinkler system to work properly, but will it? If you have not completed regular testing and maintenance on your system, you won't know if the system will work properly until a real fire tests it. That's not a good option! Regular testing of your fire sprinkler systems is critical to an effective emergency plan. The National Fire Protection Association has created standards that define testing requirements for fire sprinkler systems. The NFPA 25—Standard for the Inspection, Testing, and Maintenance of Water-Based Fire Protection Systems standard suggests opening the sprinkler systems test valve on a quarterly basis to simulate an actual fire event.

On that same day, another terrorist attack occurred at the Pentagon. An airplane taken over by terrorists slammed into wedge one and wedge two of the Pentagon, penetrating four out of the five rings that make up the structure. Engineers noted that damage to the newly renovated wedge one was minimized thanks to the fire sprinkler system. The fire did not extend to areas beyond where the fuel was spilled. At wedge two however, fire spread easily and rapidly because a fire sprinkler system had never been installed in this soon-to-be renovated area.

Pre-Planning and the Urban Search and Rescue Grid

When the fire department responds to a building after an emergency, critical building information is needed if they are to effectively and safely deploy their resources. Consider the fact that most rescue personnel will be unfamiliar with your building, its floor plan, its contents, and other important building issues.

To assist fire rescue personnel with this dilemma, former fire officer Curtis Massey founded Massey Enterprises, Inc., in 1986 (now Massey Disaster Planning). Since that time Massey Disaster Plans have become an industry standard. These plans are taught as part of the curriculum at the National Fire Academy, and are also the only preplanning system supported by every major fire department in North America. These plans address the emergency from the viewpoint of rescue personnel and include the not-so-obvious features that are critical to rescue personnel. Fire rescue, the Federal Emergency Management Agency, police departments, and other emergency personnel are assisted by Massey Disaster Plans. These plans are invaluable for all types of emergencies including fires, gas leaks, hazardous materials incidents, terrorism, biological/chemical attacks, mass shootings, hostage situations, technical rescues, and natural disasters.

Armed with the critical building information on the plans, fire rescue personnel can best utilize the building systems to their greatest advantage. Detailed, easy-to-read graphics complement the text. Floor plans, site plans, and riser diagrams show the fire department where everything is located—both horizontally and vertically.

The Massey Disaster Plans include two distinct features—the pre-plan and the urban search and rescue grid. The pre-plan features color-coded graphics that fire fighters understand and are able to quickly decipher. Items such as HVAC, shut-off valves, communications, alarms, and water supplies are noted on the pre-plan.

The second feature of the Massey Disaster Plan is the Urban Search and Rescue Grid. This document identifies support columns and other major features of the building that would enable firefighters to systematically search the building even if it experienced a collapse.

Because of the detailed nature of these plans, their completion may take months and cost thousands of dollars; however, the effort is well worth the expense, especially if you manage a high-rise building. Massey can be reached at:

Massey Disaster Planning
Southport Center
4525 South Boulevard, Suite 250
Virginia Beach, VA 23452
Phone: (757) 340-7800
Fax: (757) 340-4510
E-mail: massey@disasterplanning.com
Web: www.disasterplanning.com

Alarm Systems

OSHA requires employers to devise a method for notifying employees of an emergency. These emergencies might include fire, chemical spill, bomb threat, or other related events. The alarm must be able to be heard above the noise level in the workplace. In some areas—shop or manufacturing plants, for instance—this may be difficult to do. In these cases it is recommended that a secondary alarm warning system be used. For instance, an audible alarm coupled with a visual alarm such as a flashing strobe would provide much better protection. The employer must also explain to the employees the preferred means of reporting emergencies. Methods may include manual pull box, public address systems, radio, or telephone.

The Americans with Disabilities Accessibility Guidelines (ADAAG, 4.1.3 and 4.28) outline specifications for emergency alarms to ensure that they are accessible to persons with disabilities. ADAAG specifications for visual alarm devices specify intensity, flash rate, mounting location, and other characteristics. One major difference between the installation of audible alarms and visual alarms concerns location. It is always a requirement to install audible alarms less frequently than visual alarms. This requirement makes good sense because the reach of an audible alarm is much greater than a visual one. A visual alarm can be blocked by line of sight and unseen if the individual is in a room that does not have a visual alarm.

Understanding Your System

An alarm system is an integral part of your property's overall emergency management plan. The system must be operational and available during all hours of the day and night. It must be kept maintained, and you must test it on a regular basis. Of course, most organizations will contract this work out to others because they don't have the expertise in-house. If you elect to do that, it's not a problem; however, it would be advantageous to develop an in-depth understanding of your alarm system.

Although this book does not pretend to be a technical resource that provides an overview of alarm and fire suppression systems, we will discuss a few of the basic regulations and guidelines concerning your alarm systems.

First, familiarize yourself with the alarm system currently employed at your property. Start by identifying the systems in place. Reference your manufacture's literature including the technical information. If you are subcontracting maintenance or repairs to an alarm company, tap into their expertise. Ask them questions. Walk with them as they perform the regularly scheduled maintenance functions. In fact, invite them to a staff meeting and allow them the opportunity to conduct a training session on your alarm system. If you reach out and ask these contractors to assist you, you will begin to develop a partnership. They will gladly provide training because an informed consumer is better equipped to understand the contractor and their advice. As mutual respect is gained between consumer and contractor, a longer and more lucrative relationship is likely to develop. In today's ultra-competitive market, contractors are looking for ways to prove their worth, and you should take advantage of this.

Regular Testing

Even the most expensive and best designed alarm systems can be rendered useless if not properly maintained and tested. Time and time again, fire inspectors have discovered alarm systems that were adequate for the property at where they were installed, but because of improper maintenance, the alarm system did not operate properly and damage resulted. Businesses have been interrupted needlessly and in the worst scenarios, lives have been lost. The cost of maintenance is low, but the risk of not performing it is very high.

The problem with maintaining an alarm system usually stems from two areas. First, the building owners or managers don't understand the need for maintenance and testing, or the incremental cost to maintain the system is cut from the operating budgets. Those responsible for emergency planning must ensure that neither of these two scenarios takes place in your organization.

When evaluating your alarm system, it is important to know the age and condition of your system. A system that is more than five years old should be examined for potential component breakdown. Normal wear and tear set in around this time, especially if the system is exposed to voltage fluctuations, humidity, dust, and temperature fluctuation. Periodic testing by a NICET-certified contractor should identify these problems before they break down. NICET technicians are certified by the National Institute for the Certification of Engineering Technologies (NICET) and specialize in life safety issues. Technicians who hold NICET certification have a thorough knowledge of system installation and life cycle inspection, testing, and maintenance protocols.

If your system has not been inspected and maintained regularly, or if it has but only sporadically, beware. If the system is older than ten years, the equipment is susceptible to frequent and costly breakdown. Equipment installed more than twenty years ago should be evaluated and possibly scheduled for replacement. The technologies used in your system may be antiquated and many of the parts may be unavailable. Because the purchase of a new alarm system can be costly, evaluate the current system and develop a five-year plan for replacement if the condition warrants.

Most alarm system manufacturers recommend at least one full annual test and inspection; however, various agencies, organizations, and local authorities recommend—and in some cases mandate—more frequent testing intervals. Although not an all-inclusive list, the maintenance activities for fire alarm systems can be summed up in five basic areas:

1. **Test and calibrate**: Sensors such as smoke detectors must be tested and calibrated.

2. **Inputs and annunciators:** Place the system under test conditions and evaluate for problems.
3. **Set sensitivity:** Sensitivity must be adjusted based the system, location, and the potential emergencies. Specialized testing equipment is used for this task.
4. **Coordination:** Coordinate with the fire department and the monitoring company to test inputs to their system and communication.
5. **Battery:** The battery must be examined for corrosion and other visual indicators. Check expiration date and test the battery.

The National Fire Protection Association (NFPA) provides the National Fire Alarm Code (NFPA 72). This standard covers the application, installation, performance, and maintenance of protective signaling systems and their components. Included in this code is information devoted to inspection, testing, and maintenance. The National Fire Alarm Code does not address whether a fire alarm is required in a given building; it simply addresses the alarm post-installation.

In addition to NFPA standards, OSHA has developed minimum requirements that often mirror NFPA code. These OSHA regulations can be found in 29 CFR 1910.165. Furthermore, Appendix B to Subpart L of 1910 provides a cross-reference table that matches OSHA regulations to other applicable codes including NFPA and ANSI. An important point to remember is that in virtually all cases, these standards represent minimum requirements. These standards may be superseded by local jurisdictions and even manufacturers' recommendations. Even if you meet the strictest of standards, you may still not have adequate protection for your facility. Unique issues such as voltage fluctuations, weather, dust, humidity, salt water exposure, and other environmental concerns can shorten the life of your system or otherwise affect the system in a negative way.

> The National Fire Protection Association (NFPA) is an excellent resource for information about emergencies related to fires. The NFPA has developed a national fire alarm code (NFPA 72), and those responsible for emergency management should become familiar with that code. For detailed requirements of the code, visit the NFPA Web site at www.nfpa.org.

Hot Sites, Cold Sites, and Contingency Centers

Consider the aftermath of the September 11, 2001, terrorist attacks on the World Trade Center. From a real estate standpoint, nearly 30 million square feet of commercial space was destroyed or rendered unusable. Well over 1,000 businesses were affected, and four organizations lost over 1 million square feet of office space each, including Merrill Lynch (3.1 million square feet) and American Express (1.2 million square feet). Where did these organizations go? Unfortunately, many companies closed their doors for good. Others found it necessary to find space in New Jersey or other surrounding states. Imagine the mad rush for real estate. Imagine also the lost time as the office space had to be built to the specifications of the tenant. In many instances network cable, security, telecommunications, and office furniture had to be purchased and installed. Because of this dilemma, many organizations have turned to real estate companies that provide flexible office space.

These real estate providers offer both "cold" and "hot" contingency sites. The cold sites include little or nothing in terms of technology and furniture. A cold site can be made ready with a short notice, but it is not feasible to move into immediately. A hot site, however, can be moved into immediately. It is built to the tenant's specifications, including offices, cabling, computers, telecommunication, and furniture. In some cases the flexible office space is leased and used by temporary personnel or as swing space during renovations. If an emergency were to occur, the space could be quickly reconfigured and made available to core business units and functions. Other organizations simply lease the space and don't move in. It is used only if needed.

Management realizes that the expense is necessary, and even if underutilized, it is there if needed. They view the space in the same light as an insurance policy. This may be a solution worth exploring if your organization's real estate is in one location that, if a regional emergency occurred, would cause an interruption in business continuity. In its most effective (and expensive) variation, a hot site might be built to provide redundancy. A redundant site is a secondary site configured exactly like the primary site. This includes the same furniture, computers, telephone systems, and other equipment.

Another possible solution is to create reciprocal agreements with other organizations. In other words, your organization would promise to provide a predetermined amount of square footage to a partner organization, and they would promise to do the same. This agreement may be the least costly, but it is often the most difficult to make work. Even if an agreement is reached, parties may fail to live up to their end of the deal because of any number of extenuating circumstances.

The Command Center

In the event of a major emergency, especially during the recovery stage, a command center must be established. This command center may be on site or off site if the emergency location is dangerous or if multiple locations are involved. Based on the emergency event and the location, the command center should be easily set up and transferred. For example, let's assume you manage twenty buildings in a three-county area. Prior to an approaching hurricane you decide to create a command center to serve as home base. It would be wise to have multiple potential command center locations so that if the hurricane hits your north county property, the command center can be moved to the south county property. This would serve to keep the command center from being damaged and would preserve utility of the center.

Off-site Data Storage

Now more than ever before, data security is paramount. Given the role it plays in business continuity, companies can ill afford to be without it. In many cases, off-site storage of data is a necessity. To understand this, think about a disaster event like the World Trade Center attacks. Because the buildings were leveled, any data stored on site was lost.

When considering backup options, solutions such as cloud storage, magnetic tape, CD-ROM, microfiche, and digital formats exist. These decisions should not be made without fully understanding the strengths and weaknesses of each. Those issues cannot be adequately covered in this book, so consult with information technology professionals who can evaluate your needs and your unique situation. One final word about electronic data: consider the possibility of data corruption due to virus infection, sabotage, and other problems.

Data Security

Data security is a science unto itself, and certainly the pages of this book are unable to do the topic justice. This is not a book on disaster planning in a digital environment; however, a few words are in order.

- How often is the server backed up?
- Are employees saving documents to the central server or local hard drive?
- How long is the back-up data kept?
- Is off-site storage used?
- What physical security precautions are implemented at the server rooms?
- What would happen if the server rooms were damaged?
- Is a fully operational hot site necessary?
- Are we protected from viruses?
- Are we protected from hackers?
- If data were lost, how quickly can it be restored?
- Are we compliant with all laws and regulations covering protection and storage of corporate documents and e-mails and personal information.

In a world so driven by digital technology, loss of computer functions can be devastating. Contingency strategies must be developed and implemented to protect the digital integrity of your business. Typically, businesses protect themselves by performing regular data backup and securing off-site storage, but is this sufficient? In the wake of the 2001 terrorist attacks, we've had to rethink our contingency efforts. We've always planned for every possible contingency including terrorism and airplane crashes, but we've never planned for the scope of disaster that occurred on 9/11.

After the World Trade Center collapse, the New York financial district was in shambles. Thanks to aggressive preplanning and sheer determination, the New York Stock Exchange was back online in just four days. The NYSE had spent more than $20 million on a contingency site complete with an alternate trading floor in the event the New York location was damaged. Trading firms also had contingency sites in place, some of them outside of the state. One of the greatest concerns for any contingency site is the need for seamless communications. What systems are in place to ensure telecommunications will be available? Will computers operate as planned? Can backed up data be loaded on the hot site computers in a quick fashion? How quickly? If business continuity is critical to your organization, consult with your information technology employees and discuss available contingencies. It will likely be necessary to bring in specialized assistance that can match your needs with the proper contingency strategy.

Lack of Electricity Doesn't Mean "Go Home"

Loss of utility is an ever-increasing concern. Although rarely considered a disaster (or even an emergency), loss of utility can negatively impact an organization's productivity. Even momentary blips in electrical service can result in loss of digital data and disconnection of telecommunications. A number of solutions exist and can be realistically implemented to solve the problem of loss of electricity. There are pros and cons, of course, that must be addressed prior to making the investment. A good starting point is to identify the areas of your business that can least afford to be without electricity. These functions can be identified as "mission critical" functions.

Identifying Mission Critical Functions

Suppose your organization produces widgets. Your factory has an assembly line that produces 100 widgets per hour. Often, your line workers find themselves up against critical deadlines. For each hour that the assembly line is unable to produce widgets, your organization loses $10,000. It's very easy to identify the production floor as a mission critical function. Other times, it is not so easy to identify the mission critical functions of an organization. The problem usually occurs when every business unit believes it is equally important.

When an organization cannot prioritize the critical nature of its business, problems will exist. For this reason the emergency planning effort needs to include members of executive management. They will be able to provide direction and clarification concerning the strategic direction of the organization. Too often, if the task is left to mid-level managers, critical functions become synonymous with whatever those managers are in charge of. We tend to place more importance on our jobs, perhaps not understanding what other departments do and how that affects the organization's business plan. In our example of the widget factory, peripheral tasks such as human resources and marketing would not be considered mission critical tasks. This is not to say these tasks are not important. We are saying you should *prioritize* which business functions need to be restored first; human resources and marketing would come after production.

When evaluating business continuity and mission critical functions, some thought should be given to options that are available in the event of loss of utility. For example, based on your organization's business, is it too expensive to purchase and maintain an emergency generator? Is the probability of loss of utility a small one? In the event of prolonged loss of utility, would it make better sense to move processing to an alternate site? Are the consequences of a loss of information technology resources sufficiently high to justify the cost of various recovery options? Performing a risk assessment will allow you to focus on areas in which it is not clear which strategy is the best.

Uninterruptible Power Supply

When loss of electrical utility is experienced, the event usually lasts for a very short duration, just minutes or often seconds. However, the impact of the momentary loss of electricity can sting for a long time. If a computer server goes down, even for a minute, it will affect everybody routed through that server. Because of the lost productivity and the associated costs, information technology professionals view uninterruptible power supplies (UPS) as a necessity. The UPS system could be an inexpensive localized unit that supports the single computer plugged into it, or the UPS system could be a highly advanced and expensive unit that supports a full room of computers and equipment.

When considering a UPS system you must first understand what they can do and what they cannot. UPS systems perform two main functions. They supply short-term power to equipment during a loss of utility, and they compensate for electrical surges and sags that could damage hardware and corrupt data. Most UPS systems provide less than fifteen minutes of power, mostly via a battery power source. If a power outage extends beyond the backup capacity of your UPS system, you will have had time to save your work and properly shut down the computer equipment.

If you have the need and the budget, you can purchase UPS systems that provide power to a room full of computer equipment for an hour or longer. It is important to realize that UPS systems are not the best solution for powering up an entire building during an extended power outage. If you have a need for high-load, long-term power provision, emergency power generators should be considered.

Emergency Generators

An emergency power generator has the ability to provide electrical power over an extended period of time—hours and even days. When power into a building is lost and a generator senses the loss and transfers the power source from the utility feed to the generator. Modern, expensive generators kick in almost immediately while with less expensive models there may be a small time lag before they are fully operational. A good emergency power plan usually includes both a UPS system for short-term power loss and surges and a generator system that picks up where the UPS system leaves off.

The first step when considering the purchase of an emergency generator involves the sizing of the unit. Building occupants often mistakenly believe that the generator will supply power to the entire building. They falsely believe that all building systems—including heating, cooling, and lighting—will be operational. That is just not the case. To purchase a generator that would power an entire building during those rare moments of loss of utility would not likely be cost effective. Because of this, a risk analysis should be conducted prior to specifying and purchasing an emergency generator.

Begin by walking the building and taking into account the type of equipment present. Speak to building occupants to gain a thorough understanding of their business. Work with these employees to whittle down the list of mission critical equipment. Each employee will want their desktop printers and fax machines to be operational during a power interruption. They will insist upon properly working heating and cooling equipment. They will want the copy machine to be operational. And don't forget about the refrigerator and microwave in the break room. You will need to use your power of persuasion and reasoning, along with a good dose of political tap dancing, to help these employees understand the purpose and limitations of the emergency power generator.

You can approach the generator load factor in two ways. The first and perhaps most realistic option is to identify a budget for your generator purchase. Based on this budget, you will be able to afford an "X" kW generator size. Let's assume your budget will allow the purchase of a 100 kW generator. You now have a limited bucket of power available to your building occupants. You would work with them, getting their suggestions and support when deciding what equipment will be placed on the generator. The second option is to first work with your employees in deciding which equipment must be on the generator. Once this list has been compiled, you would then identify the size generator needed and budget accordingly. As you might imagine, option two will always be the more expensive option.

When evaluating generator options, you will be faced with several engine and fuel options. The most common options are diesel, gasoline, and natural gas. Each of these options has advantages and disadvantages, and you must take these into consideration. Most of the differences revolve around cost, fuel, and size.

Diesel

Positives:

- Excellent reliability
- Typically available in larger sizes than gasoline or natural gas
- Diesel fuel has a long tank life (if tested and treated properly)

Negatives:

- Can be more expensive than gasoline or natural gas
- May be difficult to start in cold weather

⋏   Cold weather units require oil heaters and engine block warmers

⋏   Diesel fuel must be tested and treated for water absorption

Gasoline

Positives:

⋏   Lowest initial price

⋏   Easy to start and run, particularly in cold environments

⋏   Available in a range of sizes up to 100kW

Negatives:

⋏   Gasoline has a relatively short tank life; gas must be treated

Natural Gas

Positives:

⋏   These generators are less expensive than diesel (slightly more than gasoline)

⋏   Fuel has a long tank life

⋏   Available in a range of sizes up to 100kW

Negatives:

⋏   Cost and availability of fuel could be an issue

The installation of an emergency power generator is no small project. In addition to the expense, you must have adequate space to place the unit. In addition to the generator, space will be required if you plan to install an automatic transfer switch. Because of the size, noise, and vibration that are inherent with an emergency power generator, an exterior installation usually makes the most sense. One of the common mistakes made when locating a generator is placing the generator and its exhaust near fresh air intakes or windows and doors. The exhaust generated can seep into your building and create a serious indoor air quality problem. You won't realize you have a problem until the generator is running. If your building is in a flood zone, consider placing the generator on the roof.

> There is a big difference between price and cost. Price describes the initial investment required to acquire something. Cost is used to describe the initial investment plus the cost of maintaining the equipment over its useful life. Often the lower priced option is the higher cost option over a period of years. For this reason, understand the value of the entire investment, not just the initial purchase price.

In some scenarios local utility providers will advise its customers to limit electricity usage. This is called "load shedding." In a practical sense, load shedding occurs when people raise their thermostats and turn off unnecessary items such as escalators and some lights. The load shedding process is usually a precursor to emergency power generator usage. If you have an emergency power generator, you should also develop emergency power procedures. These procedures will become part of your emergency plan. In addition to load shedding procedures you may include these issues in your emergency plan:

- If your generator does not include an automatic transfer switch, who will be responsible for switching generator power on?
- Who will confirm that generator power has transferred properly?
- Who will building occupants call in the event power does not transfer properly or the generator does not start?
- Who will provide regularly scheduled maintenance on the generator?
- What will the cost of regularly scheduled maintenance be?
- Who will be responsible for checking and ordering fuel for the generator?
- Has a purchase order and contract been initiated for fuel delivery?
- What additives must be used for the preservation of fuel?

After the initial investment in an emergency power generator, you must spend time and money maintaining the generator. Much like an automobile that requires an oil change every 3,000 miles, your generator requires regularly scheduled preventative maintenance. In fact, a generator engine is very similar to your automobile's engine. The generator has a battery, cooling system, belts, hoses, oil, plugs, and so on. Each of these items has a useful lifespan and must be maintained. Given these facts, you must initiate a preventative maintenance plan. Since most generators are installed outside and exposed to the elements, make sure that vegetation is trimmed back from the generator and leaves and other debris are not blocking the airflow to the generator's radiator. One good way to test the generator is to have it programed to come on for a few minutes once a month.

> Having a generator is great! Having a generator that actually starts up when you need it to is essential. Unfortunately, many generators don't start when we need them the most. What is the most common cause of generator failure? Believe it or not, most generators don't start because of a dead battery! The second most common reason generators don't start—lack of fuel or poor fuel quality! These problems can be easily solved if you have a regularly scheduled maintenance plan in place. It is essential.

A less expensive generator option might be to have a portable generator delivered to your location. These portable generators are not the micro-sized units available at the hardware store. These units can be as large as any permanent generator, except they are mounted on a flatbed truck or semi and delivered to your location when needed. Perhaps after performing a risk analysis you decide the price of the generator is not worth the investment, considering the occasional loss of utility. You would, however, like to protect your business continuity in the event of a major, long-term loss of utility such as that brought about by a hurricane or earthquake. If you elect to use this option you should consult with a generator vendor and ensure that a portable trailer-mounted generator will be available. This will often necessitate you purchasing an option on the generator. Don't take the vendor's word that they will have a generator for you! You must take steps to ensure the vendor will guarantee delivery. The contract must clarify issues such as:

- ▲ What size generator is needed?
- ▲ Who will wire the generator to the building?
- ▲ Is this building able to accept the generator?
- ▲ Who will be responsible for initial fueling and refueling?

This agreement will require that the generator provider visit your building and understand your needs. Just as if you were purchasing a generator, you must properly size it up. You must determine which circuits will be powered by the generator. This may require an electrician to rewire or add electrical circuits. Typically, receptacles that are plugged into generators are identified with a unique color, usually orange. These issues must be addressed prior to the delivery of the generator. If an event warrants the generator delivery, it will be too late to resolve these critical issues.

As a last option, depending on your recovery and continuity needs, the micro-sized portable generators may be an option. These units can provide small amounts of electricity in an emergency, but don't count on these units to power up your building. They may be sufficient to provide limited lighting at night or cool a refrigerator to prevent spoilage. Understand their limitations and prioritize your needs.

As a safety reminder, never plug the generator into the wiring at your circuit breaker. This can cause a backward flow of electricity, which could endanger utility personnel working on the power lines. Also, keep the generator in a well-ventilated area outside of the building. Exhaust fumes can be deadly, especially in gasoline-fueled generators.

Eight Steps to Creating the Finished Emergency Action Plan

Finally, in the development of your emergency action plan and collecting information, you need to actually create it. Here are eight suggested steps in plan development.

1. First draft
2. Review
3. Second draft
4. Tabletop exercises
5. Final draft
6. Print and distribute
7. Employee training
8. Annual review and revisions

The first three steps are often the most difficult. When developing the plan, understand that the first draft is not an exercise in perfection. It's a starting point, a launching point, if you will. It allows you to look at your business under a microscope and to identify all at-risk areas.

When working on the plan you may well discover actions that can be taken immediately that could improve efficiency, cut costs, or reduce vulnerabilities. You might identify areas in the building where access should be restricted but isn't—the computer server room, for instance—and you can take steps to ensure that from now on only authorized personnel have access to those areas. You may discover that the route taken each day to deliver the mail is not the most efficient and that orders going to the fulfilment department are delivered last rather than first so that they can be processed immediately. You may discover vulnerabilities in your chemical storage area or find that your HVAC system could be tampered with outside the building—again remedial steps can be taken immediately.

The second step is the review process. This step can be discouraging because you'll be poking holes in step one. When conducting the review, ask participants to "bring me solutions, not problems." This encourages constructive ideas instead of just random complaining. It's okay to play devil's advocate. Ask tough questions. If you don't understand a process, say so.

The second draft will be a better representation of the finished plan. It's not perfect, but it's getting close. The second draft is tested for validity through tabletop exercises. This is often known as the fire testing stage. It's like the beta launch of a software program—you want as many people as possible testing it to find all the problems so that they can be fixed. In tabletop exercises, scenarios are drawn randomly from a hat and the emergency management team walks through them using the plan as a guide. It is essential that these exercises are as spontaneous as possible. The team needs to get used to transitioning at a moment's notice from normal routine to full emergency management mode. Any conflicts or gaps discovered during the exercises would be corrected in the final draft.

At this point the plan has been battle tested and is ready to go. Printing and distributing the plan is a precursor to the most critical stage in this eight-step model—employee training. Employee training may consist of such diverse activities as electing floor captains, performing evacuation drills, and attaining CPR certification. A great emergency plan is worthless without employee involvement. Conversely, a good emergency plan supported by employee participation is worth its weight in gold.

Of course, writing the plan is an ongoing process. The emergency plan should be considered a living document, subject to growing pains and multiple revisions. A minimum annual review of the plan is a necessity and it should be looked at more often if your business is subject to frequent changes or other circumstances dictate review and revision.

Reviewing the Emergency Action Plan Annually

The emergency action plan should be evaluated on an annual basis at a minimum. No plan is ever perfect. Even if it were, people and processes change. A plan that sits on a shelf until an emergency occurs will be an outdated plan.

The responsibility of auditing the emergency action plan should be assigned to a specific employee. Usually, this will be a member of the emergency management team. That's not wrong, but consider assigning the audit to an employee who is knowledgeable about safety and emergency planning, but who did *not* have a role in developing the emergency action plan. They will often bring a fresh insight and new ideas to the table.

One of the areas that frequently becomes outdated in most emergency action plans is important support personnel data including names and phone numbers. This may include employees within the organization and contractors or governmental agencies outside of the organization. The auditor could confirm that individuals listed are still in the organization and still have the responsibilities that caused them to be included in the plan. Home, cellular, and work telephone numbers should be verified.

In addition to names and phone numbers of support personnel, an auditor should be able to answer the following questions:

- Does the organization have a formal plan for training its employees in emergency procedures?
- Is training being completed?
- Has the organization met with local community and government agencies and briefed them on its plan?
- Is the organization's insurance coverage adequate?
- Are there current photos or video of the facility and its assets?
- Does the plan reflect changes in the building layout?
- Does the plan reflect changes in policies and procedures?
- Does the plan reflect lessons learned from the drills and actual emergency events?

12

Training, Drills, and Evacuations

Congratulations! You've finally created the perfect emergency action plan. A lot of hard work went into the design of this plan, but a good plan is only half of the equation.

Rolling Out the Emergency Action Plan

Once the plan is finalized and all revisions have been made, the plan should be distributed to those playing a support role. These people might include emergency team members, floor captains, fire brigade members, evacuation assistants, runners, command post leaders, and anyone else who may be asked to play a key role in the emergency recovery efforts of the company. A good time to distribute the plan is at a training workshop for those employees who fill these support roles.

To add credibility to the initial training workshops, open the meeting with a word from the company president or some other high-ranking management member or better still, get them to attend. This will impress upon those in attendance the importance of the roles they play. Lives are at stake. Business continuity and therefore jobs are at stake. The organization's reputation and productivity can be affected in a good or bad way. If this is true, back it up by a quick word of thanks and encouragement from management. It really does set a positive tone for the planning and recovery team.

The second reason for the training meeting is the opportunity for key support members to meet one another. Since the group will be a diverse one, many of the members may not know each other. Your goal should be to cultivate an atmosphere of trust and reliance. This only comes when the members of the support team know and believe in one another. One of the best ways to cultivate this atmosphere is to conduct team exercises. There is no need to resort to corny team-building exercises, just have the members of the support group work on "what if" scenarios with members of their team. Of course, growth will not be experienced if everybody pairs off with people they already know, so suggest that they join a group of employees they don't know very well.

Finally, make the training enjoyable. By providing giveaways such as movie tickets and lunch certificates you'll gently nudge participation. To highlight the importance of this training and the supporting employees, consider awarding everyone present with a special golf shirt or coffee mug identifying the bearer as a member of the team. Each of these ideas will help foster credibility and stress the importance of the roles being filled by the members. Consider giving everyone a thumb drive containing the plan so that they can carry it at all times on their keychains.

Training the Emergency Action Team

Because the emergency action team will be taking the lead in the event of an emergency, team members must be familiar with the plan and the subject property. Both considerations will take time and training. The training will not be a one-time event. It will be an ongoing event with a goal of preparing those taking the lead. Specific training formats include the following:

- **Orientation training** should be delivered to new members of the emergency action team. Each member should understand not only their responsibilities, but also the responsibilities of the other team members. At the orientation, team members should be assigned a copy of the emergency action plan book. The book will be their personal property, and if they leave the team or the company, they must return the emergency action plan. The team member will be responsible for updating the plan as revisions are distributed.

- **Tabletop exercises** are an excellent way to train members of the emergency action team without disrupting the normal day-to-day activities of the organization. In a typical tabletop training exercise, members of the team sit in a conference room and pull emergency scenarios from a hat. Circling around the conference room table, each member would then explain their responsibilities to the group. A second pass around the table would allow team members to ask questions of other team members. If a weakness is discovered or an opportunity to improve is noticed, the entire team would work together to improve the emergency plan.

- **Walk-through drills** allow the emergency action team to perform their emergency responsibilities more accurately. During a walk-through drill, members of the emergency action team visit areas that are crucial to a successful plan implementation. Such areas might include shut-off valves, alarm panels, automated external defibrillators (AEDs), first aid stations, safe rooms, and exterior employee staging areas. The walk-through drills are essential for building familiarity and can be performed without impacting normal business productivity.

➤ **Pre-evacuation drills** are an extension of the walk-through drills. Involvement in this drill is limited to members of the emergency action team. Participants are instructed to evacuate the building, paying particular attention to the signage, exit routes, doorways, and staging areas. This is a perfect opportunity to evaluate the evacuation process without impacting the entire workforce. Participants should quickly evacuate as if an emergency is present. During the evacuation, notes should be taken, but that may force the participants to stop and write down their observations. A solution to this problem would be to provide participants with small tape recorders. As they evacuate the building they would simply record their observations into the tape recorder without even stopping. Most smart phones also have voice recording apps. After the exercise is completed, the participants would play back their recorded observations and make adjustments to the plan as necessary.

➤ **Full-scale exercises** are useful in many organizations. The purpose of a full-scale exercise is to closely simulate an actual emergency event as possible. This necessitates the involvement of emergency response personnel, employees, and community response organizations. Because of the involved nature of the full-scale exercise, this option may not be easily implemented. You'll need the cooperation of a number of different agencies, and they are not usually able to fulfill all requests. As an option, you may wish to have your emergency management team participate in another organization's full-scale exercise. This option won't address your organization's specific needs, but it will allow you to "go live" and experience a staged emergency event. The experience gained can be of tremendous value and should not be overlooked.

The orientation training should be delivered to new team members at the time of their assignment. Thereafter, training should be provided to all team members at least annually. Other occasions when training, or at least an update, would be required include:

➤ When a process or responsibility is revised
➤ When policies affecting emergency planning and recovery change

Revising the Emergency Action Plan

Revisions to the emergency action plan will occur. It is critical that you track these changes and ensure that all owners of the plan have the correct and latest information. You can accomplish this by inserting the page number, document title, and the revision date at the bottom of the page. This will allow you to quickly look at the emergency plan and determine if the information is up to date. As information is revised, simply print the newly revised pages and distribute them to your team. Be sure to leave three or four pages intentionally blank at the end of each section, so you don't have to reprint the entire manual.

- ⋏ When a change to the layout of the physical building occurs
- ⋏ When new equipment is introduced that may affect emergency planning (i.e., a generator or chemical storage)
- ⋏ When key personnel changes
- ⋏ When external circumstances change
- ⋏ After each emergency

Training the Employees

Training is particularly important for effective employee response during emergencies. There will be no time to check a manual to determine correct procedures if there is a fire. Depending on the nature of the emergency, there may or may not be time to protect equipment and other assets. Practice is necessary in order to react correctly, especially when human safety is involved. Although most employees will not receive the depth of training that the emergency action team members receive, they still need some training including new employee orientation, tabletop exercises, announced evacuations, and unannounced evacuations.

When training adult learners, three factors are required:

Awareness
Education
Involvement

The program starts with awareness. Next, formal education must take place. Finally, if any of this information is going to be retained, you must get involvement. It's really that simple!

Emergency orientation training should be delivered to new employees as they accept assignments with your organization. This may include contractors such as janitorial personnel who spend substantial time on your property. Realistically, when a new employee starts work at your organization, they spend the first day or two filling out paperwork, reading through the company policies, asking questions about health insurance, and other related activities. The emergency action policies that you provide them will be their first exposure to the safety culture your organization deems important. You have the opportunity to help them realize the importance placed on employee safety and business continuity. Don't miss this opportunity! It is likely that you will need to work with your human resources department to ensure that your emergency policies become part of the standard new employee orientation process.

In most organizations, especially mid-sized to large companies, a complete copy of the emergency action plan will not be given to employees. The plan contains information that is not relevant to most employees, and if you overburden these employees with information, they will not look at it. Instead, provide employees with a scaled-down version of the plan, perhaps an executive summary with important phone numbers and a simplified floor plan.

Tabletop exercises are an excellent way to train the general employee population without disrupting the normal day-to-day activities of the organization. In these tabletop exercises, many excellent ideas and improvements have come from the employees. Typically the employees will challenge the members of the emergency action team with questions and issues that were not discussed previously.

Announced evacuations are a great way for the employees and the emergency management team to gain confidence in one another. The problem with most evacuation drills is the timing. People are busy and the evacuation is rarely considered a priority. When the evacuation drill does occur, people are confused, meetings are interrupted, deadlines may be impacted, and more time is spent performing the evacuation because of the unfamiliarity with the procedures. By announcing the evacuation, you allow the employees to prepare for the event. You also allow the employees to find the emergency exits prior to being evacuated. You have a chance to explain the evacuation routes, staging areas, and other related procedures. Eventually, as the employees become more familiar with the evacuation procedures, they will be ready for the unannounced evacuation.

Unannounced evacuations more accurately simulate an actual emergency event. When faced with an emergency we often forget the obvious. Where do we go? Where is the closest emergency exit? Where is the secondary exit? Who needs assistance in evacuation? Where is our staging area? Who performs the employee's roll call? Questions like these are easy to answer during a tabletop exercise, but when the unannounced evacuation occurs, we often get rattled. By conducting unannounced evacuations you provide employees with the opportunity to work out the kinks. The unannounced evacuation should not be conducted until your employees are comfortable with the announced evacuations.

Fostering Employee Support and Enthusiasm

Some organizational programs are easy to sell to the employees. If a new and improved benefits package is being unveiled, employees are eager to listen. They can see the tangible benefits of this new package. As the package is being explained, employees will be on the edge of their seats, paying rapt attention, even asking thoughtful questions. Now take a less popular subject and see what kind of response you'll receive. Traditionally, emergency planning and recovery has been one of those less-than-glamorous topics that send people scurrying for the doors. This is a real problem because a great plan without employee support has little value.

Given today's realities, fostering employee support (and even enthusiasm) for emergency planning and recovery should be easier than in years past. It will still require effort. Excitement must be generated and nurtured; but how do you do that? When unveiling the emergency plan, start by letting the employees know that one exists! That's a logical starting point, but how do you make it happen? Management, at its highest levels, should take the lead in trumpeting the emergency plan. This announcement can be delivered via e-mail or text, posters, newsletters, or any other medium that employees are likely to listen to. The e-mail or text example is a good one for a few reasons. It's inexpensive to send. One e-mail or text message can be sent to thousands of employees. Think of the impact of receiving an e-mail or text "From the desk of R. A. Smith—President, Acme Industries." Would you read it? Of course.

The next logical step is to provide employees with training classes. Until you educate them about the plan, how can you expect them to get excited? Don't overwhelm them. Don't attempt to teach them everything you know about emergency planning and recovery in two hours or less. Provide the training in small increments. Keep the information specific to what they need to know, taking into account that not everybody needs to understand all of the details. For those volunteering for additional responsibilities such as fire brigade or floor captain, you'll provide them with additional training pursuant to their responsibilities.

Keep the training light, informative, and fun. You don't have to play silly games to get their attention, just keep them involved. Role playing emergency scenarios is a good way to keep employees interested. People like to get rewards, so why not bribe them? Inexpensive trinkets such as golf balls, lunch certificates, or movie passes can be awarded to participants who answer questions correctly. With a little preparation you'll be able to roll out the emergency plan with excitement and anticipation. If you have a company newsletter use it to focus in on a particular element of the emergency plan or to mention upcoming plan changes that impact them.

Getting Everybody Out Safely: Evacuations

Make no mistake about it; evacuations are performed to preserve the organization's greatest assets: its people. We don't evacuate computers or furniture, only people. Wouldn't it be tragic if, in an attempt to keep our employees from harm, we evacuated them from the building, but they were injured during the process? To protect our employees from injury, we need to establish a logical means of egress from the building. Evacuations are not an easy task. Sure, we exit the building each day, but we do so without duress. We follow the same predictable routines. The elevator quickly moves us to the lobby. We exit and make our way to our automobile. An evacuation forces the building occupants to do something entirely different. Because the elevators will be off limits, where will they find the emergency exits? What about employees with physical limitations? Is the exit route so intuitive that visitors will be able to exit? Is there a danger of too many people being funneled into a narrow hallway? Where do they go once they are outside? These are the types of questions we will begin to answer.

When developing evacuation plans for any building, especially high-rise buildings, you must take time to consider the results of any decisions made by the emergency management team. One of the best ways make this happen is to follow this simple advice:

Before you conduct an evacuation drill, do a walk-through. Before you have a walk-through, have a talk-through.

Evacuation Routes and Drills

Regular evacuation drills are a critical component of a successful emergency action plan, but who can afford the impact of evacuating an entire building during a single drill? Here's the good news: a total evacuation is not necessary, nor is it recommended. Smaller drills have proven to be quite effective, and they provide the training necessary for the employees to gain confidence in the event of an actual emergency.

A full evacuation of high-rise building is difficult thanks to a number of different factors. First, it's very time consuming. A large building typically contains thousands of people and it may take hours to get them out safely. This is especially important to note because most fires are localized to a floor or two. The NFPA has embraced an evacuation model that conducts a partial evacuation of the affected floors and the floors immediately above and below the affected floors. For most fires in most buildings, this course of action is sufficient. Of course, some extreme emergency events such as the 9/11 attacks warrant a full evacuation, but that is the exception to the rule.

Consider also the problems of reentering a large building after a total evacuation. It typically takes even longer to reenter a building. It is one thing to instruct employees to walk *down* seventy flight of stairs and quite another to ask employees to walk *up* seventy flights of stairs. Because of this, most employees will wait for the elevators to take them to their assigned floors. Buildings were not designed to accept an entire occupancy in a short period of time. Organizations within a large building usually stagger the arrival and departure times of their employees so as not to overburden the building's elevators and common areas. A mass reentry into the building works against this plan and creates a large problem.

A final reason to avoid the entire building evacuation approach is the negative impact on business continuity. This is a secondary consideration, but a consideration nonetheless. When a small fire directly affects two or three floors, does it make sense to evacuate seventy floors? Doing the latter would affect all of the building's occupants, resulting in a tremendous loss in worker productivity.

Helicopters and High-Rise Rescues

A common misconception when dealing with fires in a high-rise building is that it is safe to travel up toward the roof and await a dramatic helicopter rescue. True, this feat has been accomplished, but it is very dangerous and not recommended. Performing this type of rescue puts the helicopter pilot, building occupants, and fire fighters at risk. If the fire is severe enough, large thermal currents will rise from the burning building making the helicopter hard to control and the downward thrust from the helicopter's rotors can force smoke and hot air back down onto the fire rescue personnel who may be close by. Because of the danger involved, many pilots will not even attempt this sort of rescue. Even if they did, a helicopter is only able to evacuate a handful of people at a time. Individuals who wait at the rooftop are often left behind.

Chicago and High-Rise Safety

In light of perceived susceptibility of high-rise buildings in an emergency event, many local municipalities have developed additional safety requirements. The city of Chicago has enacted such rules and is recognized as being at the forefront of high-rise safety.

Some of the requirements of Chicago's emergency procedures (Title 13 of the Municipal Code of Chicago: Chapter 13–78) for high-rise buildings include issuance of an "emergency preparedness certificate" by the fire department upon receipt of adequate proof that the applicant is able and qualified to assume the duties required.

High-rise buildings are grouped into four categories based on height above grade. For instance, Category 1 structures are over 780 feet while Category 4 structures are 80 feet and over, up to and including 275 feet. Some of the categories of buildings are required to file a copy of the safety plan with the city's office of emergency communications.

Each emergency plan for Category 1 buildings must include the following required designated personnel:

- The Plan must designate a Fire Safety Director (FSD). The FSD must be an employee of that building. The FSD shall obtain and maintain an emergency preparedness certificate. A deputy Fire Safety Director may also be required.
- The Plan must designate a Building Evacuation Supervisor.
- The Plan must designate an Emergency Evacuation Team. Emergency Evacuation Team members shall know the location of all exits and lead emergency evacuations and drills as directed by a Fire Warden.
- The Plan must designate Fire Wardens in sufficient number to carry out their duties. The wardens must know the locations of all exits and direct emergency evacuations and drills from their assigned floor in accordance with the Plan.

In the event of an actual fire or emergency, the Fire Safety Director and Deputy Fire Safety Director must occupy the building's fire command station, conduct emergency operations, direct evacuations, and report conditions to first-arriving fire companies. Regular duties include:

- Conduct monthly building safety inspections
- Develop procedures for emergency evacuations and drills
- Direct emergency evacuations and drills
- Assign Fire Wardens and assign Emergency Evacuation Team(s), if required

As part of the minimum requirements of the plan, the actions all occupants should take in an emergency evacuation or drill should be described. In accordance with commonly accepted fire evacuation methodology, each plan shall set out a procedure for an evacuation of five floors below and two floors above any emergency resulting from a fire on a certain floor. Additionally, the plan must specify procedure for a full evacuation of the building. On certain occupancy classifications of Category 1 high-rise buildings, safety drills must be carried out under the direction of the FSD not less frequently than twice a year. Furthermore, on an annual basis the owner shall file an affidavit with the Fire Commissioner certifying that at least two safety drills have taken place on all occupied floors during the past year.

Each plan must list the name and location of each occupant who has voluntarily self-identified that they need assistance and the type of assistance required to swiftly exit the high-rise building in case of an emergency. This emergency plan must be kept in the office of the high-rise building, at the security desk, and in the vicinity of the fireman's elevator recall key or life safety panel. The development of specific emergency planning regulations for high-rise buildings is quickly becoming the norm throughout the country. The forced awareness of emergency events and how they should be handled can only serve to save lives in the future.

> Always be aware of local agencies that promulgate evacuation protocol and codes. The best way to learn about these issues and expectations is to invite your local fire marshal to visit your building and offer suggestions.

Disaster Simulations

Organizations may also arrange for on-site disaster simulations. These simulations are acted out with the utmost detail, including fake blood and wounds. Local emergency response teams are called in to participate. These simulations provide valuable information about flaws in the contingency plan and provide practice for a real emergency. While they can be expensive and time consuming, these tests can also provide critical information and expose weaknesses in a plan. The simulations are not suggested for every organization, but the more critical the functions of your business and the resources addressed in the contingency plan, the more cost-beneficial it is to perform a disaster simulation. These simulations are often performed at healthcare organizations and state or local government agencies.

Minimizing Interruptions and Down Time in Evacuation Drills

One of the problems with building evacuation drills is the loss of productivity. Businesses have deadlines to meet and an evacuation drill can impact those deadlines. If the evacuation, staging, roll call, and re-entry take an hour and one hundred employees are evacuated, the organization has lost one hundred hours of productivity. A further case against evacuation drills can be made if you attach a dollar amount to that lost productivity. For instance, assume the average billable dollar amount per employee is $25. Multiply that billing rate by the 100 employees and the cost to conduct that drill is $2,500. These are realistic concerns, but they should not prohibit you from conducting evacuation drills. The first question to ask is "What is the value of a human life?" Is it $2,500? Is it $25,000? Is it greater than that? It's impossible to realistically place a value on a human life, but I think we can agree $2,500 does not come close.

The emergency manager is not oblivious to the loss of productivity. The emergency manager will take steps to impact the employees as little as possible. Providing management with an idea of when the drills will take place gives them an opportunity inform you of conflicts. If a major corporate deadline is looming and employees are working overtime, perhaps the emergency evacuation drill can be deferred until next quarter. By training employees prior to the evacuation drill, you'll not only conduct a more efficient drill, you'll also finish it quicker, thus impacting the employees' productivity less.

So a full-scale evacuation of a building, especially a large building, is often difficult and time consuming. Many organizations have successfully devised a method to conduct emergency evacuations on a much smaller scale. Instead of setting the fire alarm throughout the building, an emergency manager may elect to enter a specific department and, using a whistle or megaphone, announce the fire drill. Only the building occupants in that work area would respond to the alarm. If the building occupants are likely to head for the obvious and closest fire exit, try adding a new component. Place an easel at the closest fire exit with the words "Do Not Enter—Fire Burning Here!" written on flip chart paper. Observe how the building occupants respond when they see the sign. Do they know where the next emergency exit is located? Regardless of how the drill is handled, this will provide the emergency planner with an excellent evacuation topic to address.

Healthcare facilities present unique but not impossible evacuation challenges. It's not likely the emergency planner will walk to a fire alarm pull station, trigger the alarm, and expect to evacuate the building occupants. Given the sensitive nature of the work being conducted in a healthcare environment, it is impossible to conduct evacuation drills. How can healthcare employees be trained in proper evacuation techniques in the event of an actual emergency?

In the healthcare industry, tabletop exercises have largely taken the place of full-scale evacuations. Employees gather in a conference room and are given emergency scenarios. The employees must discuss the sequence of events following the emergency. Which sections of the building should be evacuated? What alternate sources of power are available? How will employees communicate if phone and electric service is lost? Where can we safely move patients in the event of a fire in the east wing? These types of questions will provide mission critical employees the training they need without negatively impacting the safety or quality of their work. These same tabletop exercises can be used in a number of different scenarios, including tall buildings in which it would be impractical to evacuate employees from the seventy-sixth floor.

Alerting Building Occupants in an Emergency

OSHA requires employers to devise a method for notifying employees of an emergency.

In most scenarios this is accomplished via an audible alarm that can be triggered manually or automatically. But think for a moment about the problems with an audible alarm. Those with hearing disabilities may not hear them. In a loud shop area, the alarm may not be heard over the noise level of the equipment. When evaluating your alarm system, make sure you take these issues into consideration. If excessive noise or persons with hearing limitations are present, you should devise a secondary alarm warning system. For instance, an audible alarm coupled with a visual alarm such as a flashing strobe would provide much better protection. Also consider areas in your building that may not be covered by the audible alarm. These areas might include basements, restrooms, and nonrenovated portions of the building.

> Many hotels offer their visitors the option of a room with an audible alarm and a visual strobe. Hotels with a comprehensive evacuation plan have realized the importance of keeping a list of visitors with hearing impairments, and, in the event of an emergency, would take special steps to ensure they are aware of the alarm.
>
> In some government buildings, persons with hearing impairments are given a pager that vibrates when an alarm has been activated.

OSHA also suggests that distinctive alarm tones may be helpful. For instance, if your building has an organized fire brigade, they will need to know if the alarm is for a fire or if it is for another emergency that does not require them to assist. For a fire, the alarm may be a siren while an alarm for an approaching tornado might be a series of horn blasts. It is not recommended, however, that you have a distinct alarm tone for each type of emergency. Given the number of different types of emergencies, it would become difficult to remember what each alarm means.

In most cases, building occupants will discover the emergency. For this reason, the employer must explain to the employees the preferred means of reporting emergencies. Methods may include manual pull box, public address systems, radio, or telephone. If any method beyond a manual pull box is required, the employer should train the employees in proper procedures. Who should they call? What radio frequency should be used? How does the public address system work? What areas does it cover?

If a public address system is used to notify building occupants of an emergency, you should have a prewritten script ready to read. This script would explain the actions necessary. It should be kept short and without detail. Don't work the group into a frenzy. The language that you use can be calming and helpful, or it can be confusing and frightening. The latter (not recommended) is usually the result of not having a prepared script. A sample script might look like this:

(READ, REPEAT, WAIT 90 SECONDS, AND REPEAT AGAIN)

"We have received an alarm in _____ building. As a precaution, we are requiring evacuation of all employees in _____. Please immediately proceed in an orderly fashion to your assigned exterior staging areas."

In this hypothetical situation, it has been decided that a partial evacuation is all that is necessary, so we would fill in the blanks with the pertinent information and read it over the public address system:

"We have received an alarm in <u>the north wing of the</u> building. As a precaution, we are requiring evacuation of all employees in <u>the north and west wings</u>. Please immediately proceed in an orderly fashion to your assigned exterior staging areas."

Notice that this script does not provide space to discuss the details of the alarm. Does it matter if the emergency is a fire, bomb threat, or chemical spill? They are all emergencies, and the evacuation should occur immediately and in an orderly fashion. By providing details, you risk frightening the building occupants. When this happens, people get careless, run for the exits, and those with disabilities are left behind. If you've conducted evacuation drills in the past, the occupants will know exactly what to do; there is no need to scare them into leaving the building.

Notice also the language used in this announcement. The second sentence begins, "As a precaution. . . ." This is calming language meant to reassure the building occupants and remind them of their safety. However, at the risk of this alarm sounding unimportant and perhaps voluntary, we follow up with "we are *requiring* evacuation of. . . ." The last sentence encourages the building occupants to "immediately" and "in an orderly fashion" leave the building. Finally, a reminder is given to go to "your assigned exterior staging areas."

This is a good all-purpose script that can be adapted as you see necessary. A variation of the above script is to change the last sentence to read:

> "Please take your personnel belongings and immediately proceed in an orderly fashion to your assigned exterior staging areas."

This change is recommended in bomb threat scenarios. By reminding the building occupants to take personal belongings such as purses, briefcases, duffel bags, jackets, and lunch boxes, you remove many of the items that would have to be searched during the bomb sweep. This facilitates the bomb search and solves the problem of possible liability when searching personal items.

The verbal instructions given should be understood by all building occupants. This becomes a challenge when some building occupants don't understand English. In some areas of the county, Spanish, Polish, or some other language is spoken by many workers. You should make arrangements for non-English speakers by having someone who speaks the foreign language available to make the announcement. Another idea is to make a recording of the generic announcement in the foreign language and play the recording during an evacuation. As a final suggestion, the floor captains should be aware that non-English speakers may not understand the evacuation notice and may need to be directed out of the building.

For those rare buildings that do not have an audible alarm or a public address system, the building occupants can be notified of an emergency via a "telephone tree." The telephone tree works when one person is assigned a list of three people to call and provide the emergency warning or update. Each of those three people has a list of three people to call as well. Basically, it's the "friend told a friend, who told a friend" scenario.

The telephone tree system works well when a public address system is not available and the event does not warrant the setting of the audible alarm. For example, let's imagine a shopping mall setting and a severe weather advisory has been issued by the National Weather Service. You wouldn't go to a pull station and set the alarm; in fact, because of the severe weather, you certainly don't want people evacuating the building. You may elect to make an announcement via the public address system, but that may cause unnecessary concern as well. The telephone tree is an effective mechanism to warn shopkeepers, who could in turn warn the store patrons without raising undue concern.

Floor Captains and Fire Brigades

Floor captains can be very beneficial in the event of an emergency. Their purpose is to assist the employees and visitors to safely and efficiently evacuate the building. They may be trained in first aid and basic fire extinguishing techniques. Floor captains provide special attention to those with disabilities, and they ensure that everybody has left the building.

In some businesses, both floor captains and a fire brigade may be established. The responsibilities of a fire brigade are greater and require more advanced training.

OSHA defines a **fire brigade** as "an organized group of employees who are knowledgeable, trained, and skilled in at least basic firefighting operations." Fire brigades are used when the nature of a business exposes its employees to unusual danger and the delay in response from the local fire department would cause further risk. For example, a nuclear power plant may find it prudent to establish a fire brigade to commence the firefighting process prior to the fire department's arrival.

Fire brigades are not required by OSHA, but if you do elect to create a fire brigade, a few regulations do exist. In addition to the many regulations, OSHA suggests that pre-fire training should be conducted by the local fire department so the fire brigade will be familiar with the workplace and potential hazards. This meeting and training also fosters cooperation between the local fire department and the fire brigade so they will be able to work together in the event of an emergency. If you wish to create a fire brigade, consult with your local fire department and review OSHA's regulations at CFR 29 1910.156.

Shut Down Procedures in an Evacuation

When evacuating a building, it's usually not a good idea for everybody to just leave. Certain equipment and supply lines could present a major problem if left operational. For instance, suppose you have a natural gas service line entering your building. This line fuels four pieces of equipment. If these lines are left open during an evacuation for a fire, the risk of the fire being further fueled by the natural gas exists. A small fire could quickly get out of control and endanger the lives of the firefighters and other rescue personnel. To solve this problem, assign knowledgeable personnel the responsibility to shut down lines and equipment that might interfere with recovery efforts prior to evacuating the building. This will requires identification of potentially dangerous equipment, storage tanks, containers, supply lines, and valves.

Don't fall into the trap of identifying only lines that carry flammable or combustible substances. Flooding due to a broken water service line could hamper business operations and therefore create an emergency event. Remember to locate *all* supply lines and valves, whether they are gas, diesel, propane, chemical, water, or other.

The location of storage tanks and containers used to hold flammable or toxic chemicals must be communicated to the fire chief. This information will play a definite role in how the fire department uses its personnel and how it will fight the fire. Attempting to explain the hazards and their locations without a floor plan is folly. To make the floor plan user-friendly, the following information should be prominently identified:

- ▲   Shut off valves
- ▲   Shut off switches
- ▲   Storage tanks and containers
- ▲   Supply lines
- ▲   Breaker panels

Even when a floor plan is available, in the haste and confusion of the emergency, important features could be difficult to locate. To solve this problem, the visual floor plan must be cross-referenced with a written location system. The **location key** (see figure 12.1) is a good way to accomplish that. The location key is created in a table format. The critical points are identified in the leftmost column. The middle column identifies the location of the items. The location is derived from an easy-to-implement grid system. The grid system can be superimposed over the electronic version of the floor plan in a CAD system, or you can simply draw a grid over a hard copy of the floor plan. The grid system works on an x and y axis. The horizontal axis (x) would be divided into segments and labeled with ascending letters of the alphabet. The vertical axis (y) would also be divided into segments and labeled with ascending numbers. Much like a map, you can use this grid system to quickly locate important items.

The location key is most helpful when the items are arranged alphabetically. The final column includes a space for comments. This location grid should be attached, manually or electronically, to the actual hard copy of the floor plan.

Item	Location	Comment
Breaker panel	A-4	
Chemical storage	K-2 / P-17	See MSDS / Inventory log
Natural gas shut off valve	H-12	
Water shut off valve	H-13	Valve key above valve

Figure 12.1. Location Key.

At the actual shut-off locations, make certain the valve is clearly identified. A sign with letters no less than two inches in height should identify the type of shut off. Have you ever been confused by how to turn a valve off? Do you turn the valve clockwise, or is it counter-clockwise? It's not always apparent, so be sure to label (at the valve location) the correct directional rotation for on and off. It may be advantageous to color code the sign depending on its use. For instance, a red sign with white letters may be used for all flammable and combustible valve locations. A blue sign with white letters may represent water shut off valves, and so on. Finally, always be aware of special keys or wrenches that may be required to turn the valve. Valuable time will be wasted if you don't know where the key is located.

Because of the increase in chemical and biological threats, many building owners and managers have realized a need to shut down the building's heating, ventilating, and air conditioning system in the event of an emergency. Chemical or biological agents can be quickly distributed throughout the building via the HVAC system; therefore, it makes sense to create a single shut-off switch for the HVAC system. This is critical if for example, you have a large mail room and someone inadvertently opens a package containing a powder that is immediately blasted throughout the building.

Assisting Those with Special Needs in an Evacuation

The orderly evacuation of all occupants, including those with disabilities, can be a challenge. The Americans with Disabilities Act (ADA) offers many excellent suggestions for assisting those with disabilities during evacuation of a building. Those with hearing, vision, mental, or mobility issues need to be identified and their egress from the building must be addressed prior to an emergency event, not during it.

When considering specific evacuation procedures for those with special needs, you will see that typically two types of solutions are available—engineering and procedure-driven. Engineering solutions might include slings or controlled descent devices that allow the disabled person to exit via the emergency egress stairwell. Procedure-driven solutions might include the development of a partner system or the creation of areas of refuge for those with disabilities to wait for assistance. Often a mixture of both solutions will provide the best protection.

Even though you attempt to cover all of the possibilities, you cannot fully protect your employees unless you are aware of their limitations. People with permanent or long-term disabilities are relatively easy to identify and assist. The challenge occurs when dealing with people with temporary limitations such as pregnancy or those aided by crutches. Think also about the individual with asthma, who might be able to easily evacuate the building under normal circumstances but, because of the stress and presence of smoke, may have difficulty breathing. When developing your emergency plan and building evacuation procedures, give consideration to these situations.

Use of Elevators for Exit

During an emergency, elevators are not considered a permissible means of egress from the building. In most buildings, the elevator has been programmed to immediately descend to the bottom floor (unless a fire is present at the bottom floor) upon being triggered by the alarm. At this point, the elevator is rendered inoperable unless emergency response personnel activate it using a special key. Many people have wondered why elevators cannot be used. Some studies have shown that if elevators were used during evacuations, building occupants could leave the building up to 50 percent more quickly. In particular, those with disabilities could safely and efficiently evacuate, without impeding the progress of others.

Using elevators during an evacuation sounds like a good idea until you understand why they are off limits. Firefighters must have a way to get to the fire. Since building occupants are exiting the building and fire rescue personnel are entering, there exists an opportunity for interference. Use of the elevator by fire rescue personnel allows them to get to where the emergency is in a quick fashion. Imagine if the firefighters, with their heavy rescue gear, had to climb seventy flights of stairs! It is much easier for building occupants to walk down seventy flights of stairs than it is for fire rescue to walk up seventy flights of stairs.

Another problem with elevators is the increased potential for smoke inhalation. Elevators cars are not very airtight. Doorways at each floor allow smoke to enter the elevator shaft. Smoke inhalation is not as likely for fire rescue personnel because they carry self-contained breathing apparatuses (SCBA). Building occupants attempting to use an elevator during evacuation might not make it out alive.

The fact remains though, that elevators could speed the evacuation, especially for those with disabilities. The National Institute of Standards and Technology (NIST) has studied the feasibility of elevator use during an evacuation, and they have developed a series of recommendations. First, the enclosed lobby area at each floor and the elevator shaft would need to be pressurized so that both remain smoke free. Second, dual power systems would need to be installed for reliability. Lastly, elevator components would need to be sufficiently waterproof to prevent failure due to flooding of the shaft during firefighting operations. Given these requirements, there has not been a strong movement to build elevators that can be used by building occupants during an evacuation. It's also safe to imagine that if such elevators did exist, their use would not be limited to those with disabilities. A bottleneck could occur as occupants wait for the elevator to arrive.

Evacuation Assistance Devices

Those persons with mobility limitations will often find building evacuations to be a difficult and sometimes precarious event. Imagine someone attempting to navigate a wheelchair down a stairwell. Now, add hundreds of people to the scene and you can appreciate the difficulty with many evacuations. Even people with temporary disabilities will find evacuation difficult. To assist these individuals, a number of evacuation assistance devices have been developed. If your building is a multistory structure, you should seriously investigate the evacuation assistance devices that are on the market.

When considering different evacuation devices, consider the distance the person must travel, the person's confidence in the device, the impact on stairwell space, and cost. It would be advisable to ask wheelchair users for their advice and comfort level prior to equipment selection. If they are uncomfortable with the device or they do not know how to operate it properly, the device will likely go unused. When a decision is made on evacuation devices, be sure to train disabled persons and others how to use it properly.

Among the evacuation devices available are mechanical devices that allow a controlled descent in the stairwell. One such device allows the wheelchair user to roll onto a platform, secure himself or herself to the platform, and then descend to safety. The advantage of this device is the wheelchair user never has to be removed from the wheelchair. Other devices require the disabled person to be separated from the chair. This introduces an opportunity for injuries and may create an uncomfortable emotional separation for the person with mobility limitations. Another device requires the wheelchair-user to transfer from their wheelchair to a transportation platform which travels on specially installed tracks down the stairs. The descent speed can be controlled by a braking mechanism. Other nonmechanical devices are available to assist disabled persons with an evacuation. Various straps and harnesses are available that assist in the evacuation.

If you do not have any of these types of evacuation assistance devices and you are faced with manually assisting someone in a wheelchair, at least use a safe technique. For instance, two people can efficiently guide a wheelchair and its occupant. Start by positioning one person behind the wheelchair grasping the pushing grips. Next, tilt the chair backwards until balance is achieved. While keeping the balance, move the wheelchair forward toward the steps. As the chair moves down the steps, always remain one step above the chair. Keep your center of gravity low and let the back wheels gradually lower to the next step. The wheelchair occupant should be leaning back. The occupant may try to resist this position by leaning forward, but remind him or her not to lean

If any evacuation devices are used, make sure that the location of the device is noted in the emergency plan and on the emergency action floor plan. When an evacuation drill is conducted, use the devices. The time to get comfortable with these devices is not during the excitement and confusion of a real emergency. The emergency action plan must also address training on proper evacuation device use, including safe lifting techniques.

forward. Kindly ask them to remain in the chair, lean back, and let assistants control the chair's descent. Be sure to have a second person assist by positioning themselves in front of the wheelchair to keep the wheelchair from gaining too much speed during the decent. Both assistants will attempt to keep the descent as smooth as possible, but they should not lift the chair off of the ground. The weight of the disabled person and the wheelchair could easily injure the assistants. A third assistant may be needed at the rear of the wheelchair to share control of the push grips.

Regardless of the techniques utilized, don't forget to use proper lifting techniques. In past evacuations, people have hurt backs, twisted knees, and pulled muscles because they did not use proper lifting techniques. Usually the people who are hurt during these evacuations are the big and strong men who believe they can lift someone on brute strength alone. Meanwhile the smaller person who uses good techniques will come out uninjured. Some of the basic lifting techniques include:

- ⮤ Bend your knees
- ⮤ Keep your back straight
- ⮤ Use your leg muscles to lift
- ⮤ Hold the person close before lifting
- ⮤ Don't lift from an awkward position
- ⮤ Ask for help if it is needed

Areas of Refuge

The Americans with Disabilities Act (ADA) outlines specific requirements for fire-resistant spaces where persons unable to use stairs can call for and wait for evacuation assistance from emergency personnel. These areas are commonly known as **areas of refuge** and are often located at egress stair landings, but other areas that meet specific fire rating and smoke protection can be used. ADA regulations require that two-way communication devices be installed in these areas of refuge so those awaiting assistance can be identified.

The refuge area should only be used when the disability seriously impedes the evacuation of the individual. For instance, a wheelchair may present problems because of its weight and size, and you may elect to bring that person to an area of refuge. On the other hand, a person with a hearing or visual disability should be evacuated with the other building occupants, using the stairwell and emergency exits. An area of refuge is not a place to bring all people with any disability.

The Job Accommodation Network

An excellent resource for ADA questions, ideas, and resources is the Job Accommodation Network (JAN). The Job Accommodation Network is a service of the Office of Disability Employment Policy of the U.S. Department of Labor. They have an excellent Web site at www.askjan. org, where you can submit an email, subscribe to newsletters, find out social media contacts, and get live help.

JAN can also be reached at the following numbers:

Voice: (800) 526-7234
TTY: (877) 781-9403

The Evacuation Staging Area

An orderly evacuation from a building during an emergency saves lives. Think for a moment about an evacuation. Upon notification, personnel will begin to file out of the building, following the appropriate exit signage and routes. Eventually, all of the building occupants, perhaps thousands of people, will be standing in the parking lot or some other location. Now imagine the fire truck or ambulance driving up to the building. Will they be able to access the site? Will people be endangered as they wander around the site? Will they interfere with the emergency responders? For these reasons and many more, **staging areas** outside of the building must be developed.

- Employees should be instructed to move away from the exit doors.
- Ample staging area space should be provided for employees.
- Have several numbered staging areas, if necessary, with people allocated to a specific area.
- Groups should be kept relatively small so everyone can be accounted for.
- Exit doors should not empty to parking spaces or streets.
- Inclement weather such as rain, snow, or heat should be considered.

Keeping groups small is important. A large congested group of people wandering the parking lot creates confusion, and it is difficult to account for who has exited the building and who remains. Small groups are easier to manage. So keep the groups in the staging area small, twenty people or less per group, if possible.

One concern that must be addressed when evacuating the building is safety. Is it safer to stay inside? Is the exterior staging area more dangerous than remaining indoors? Inclement weather, biological attack, or nuclear accidents are examples that may make an evacuation dangerous. The decision is probably not one to make internally. Guidance from law enforcement agencies or rescue personnel should be sought. If you do elect to evacuate during inclement weather, is an alternate staging area available? If an earthquake or fire has occurred, is the staging area far enough from the building to keep the evacuees safe? These are the types of role-play questions you'll need to address in your safety plan. It is important to account for everyone during an evacuation because for instance, in the event of a biological or chemical attack you need to make sure that no one leaves the scene and possibly spreads contamination.

Accounting for Employees and Visitors

When evacuating a building, employees should have a specific area that they go to and remain at until the decision is made to go back into the building or to leave the premises. This staging area serves several purposes. First, the staging area keeps the crowd of building occupants away from the building and out of the way of emergency responders such as police, paramedics, and firefighters. It should be sufficiently far from the building so there is no danger from falling debris or glass if windows blow out. Second, the staging area provides emergency team members with an organized way to account for employees and visitors. This directive is so important that the Occupational Safety and Health Act requires it. OSHA 29 CFR 1910.38(a)(2)(iii) states procedures must be in place to account for all employees after an emergency evacuation has been completed.

Think about the process. Where will employees gather? Who will perform the roll call? If somebody is unaccounted for, do you have their cell phone or pager numbers? If somebody is missing, how will this information be related to the emergency rescue personnel? Who will give the "all clear" order? These are the types of questions that must be answered if you hope to conduct an orderly and safe evacuation.

It's important, too, that employees understand the reasons for having staging areas. If the building occupants simply exit the building and mingle in the parking lot, it becomes difficult to perform a roll call. When this happens, emergency rescue personnel are placed in harm's way because they are searching the building unnecessarily for people who are already outside of the building. Someone should be assigned the group leader whose primary responsibilities would include keeping the group together, performing roll call, and serving as spokesperson to the emergency command post.

> In the event of an actual emergency, who will give the command to evacuate? What type of emergency warrants an evacuation? Is a partial evacuation sufficient, or should the entire building be evacuated? These are the types of questions that must be considered when developing your emergency action plan. A chain of command must be established and an individual must take the lead. Time is precious and bad decisions can cost lives.

The Chain of Command in an Evacuation

During an evacuation, order must be kept. If not done in an orderly fashion, building occupants can be injured, time can be wasted, emergency response personnel can be injured, and company liability will be increased. It's critical that a clear chain of command be established prior to any evacuations whether they be training drills or actual emergencies. Here are a few of the important roles that make up the chain of command and which must be filled if an effective evacuation is to be conducted:

Fire Brigade

The fire brigade will perform basic first aid and extinguish small fires in the event of an actual emergency. In an industrial environment they may fight more advanced fires if properly trained and supplied. They may also assist the floor captains by directed building occupants to the available evacuation routes, but this is not their primary responsibility.

Floor Captains

The floor captains ensure that all building occupants have recognized the alarm and quickly head for the evacuation routes. Floor captains may also assist those with disabilities or those who do not speak English. Floor captains may be placed at stairway and elevator locations to monitor their use. They will also check restrooms, loud locations, and private offices for persons who may not have heard the alarm or chose to ignore it.

Group Leader

The group leader will gather employees in the pre-assigned location in the parking lot. They will take roll call and will call missing employees or visitors on cell phones or pagers. If contact cannot be made, they will relay this information to the runner.

Runner

The runner will serve as a liaison between the group leader and the command post leader. During the evacuation the runner (or runners if there is a large workforce) visits each individual group and gets a status report from the group leader. The runner will then relay this information to the command post leader.

Command Post Leader

The command post leader collects employee status from each of the groups and compiles a list of unaccounted personnel. The command post leader would pass this information on to emergency response personnel. If the evacuation is a drill, the command post leader would announce the "all clear" and direct all employees back into the building in an orderly fashion—for instance, staff could be allowed back in groups at five minute intervals based on their staging area number. If an actual emergency occurred, the command post leader would consult emergency response personnel to make the decision to reenter or leave the premises.

*   *   *

Because the group leader will be conducting a roll call, they must have a current list of employees and visitors. The list of employees is easy to compile. If the group is kept small, the list will be easy to keep current. It should include the employees' names and cell phone, pager, and home phone numbers. The list should be kept on a small wallet-sized laminated card. If your group includes fire brigade members, floor captains, or employees responsible for equipment shut down, they likely will not be exiting the building until they have completed their assigned responsibilities and may not be in the staging area when the roll call is conducted.

One of the most difficult aspects of the roll call is accounting for visitors such as vendors and customers. Most of the time these visitors will be in the presence of an employee. If an evacuation occurs, the visitor should follow the employee out of the building. The employee should instruct visitors to follow them. If the employee and their visitor are separated during the evacuation, make this known to the group leader as they are taking roll call. The names of visitors who are unaccounted for will be passed on to the command post leader. Any group that finds an unknown visitor in its midst should verify the person's name and the name of the person they were visiting. You should also instruct that person to stay put. It may be helpful to retrieve visitor logs from the reception area and use those for accounting for non-employees.

If you plan to conduct an evacuation drill, someone should be assigned as the drill co-ordinator prior to the drill. This person plans, conducts, and evaluates the drill. A best practice is to rotate this assignment so various members of the emergency action team will understand the position. It is always advisable to have trained alternates, and this is a great way to ensure that will happen.

Those Who Refuse to Participate in Evacuation Drills

There is no question about it; evacuation drills take time. Since time is valuable and we have so little of it to spare, some employees may resist taking part in the emergency evacuation drills. How will you handle this difficult situation? After all, you can't physically remove someone from the building, especially during a drill. This issue must be resolved and resolved quickly. If certain employees are allowed to sit out the drill because they are too busy, soon other employees will do the same. Before long you'll lose control of the drill.

The best way to ensure a well-participated evacuation drill starts with the organization's leadership. Management should clearly state their endorsement of the evacuation drills and make it clear that all employees are expected to participate. Of course, this includes executive management. They must be visibly participating as well! Management should put some bite into this requirement as well. For instance, a process could be established whereby the name of any employee not participating in the drill will be forwarded to the vice president of human resources. When the organization's leadership takes a leadership role in emergency planning, the employees will follow their example.

Employers also have the right to require nonparticipating employees to sign a waiver, releasing the company from liability if they fail to evacuate. The legal credibility of such a waiver may not be ironclad, but at least the employee will understand the importance placed upon the drill. Additionally, the burden of the added paperwork may be more painful than participation in the drill. Some organizations have made the required paperwork for nonparticipation so long and involved that the employees spend less time in an evacuation than they would filling out the paperwork!

If you have employees who refuse to evacuate or if they just grumble about it, they likely don't realize the importance of the drills. This is where training and education can help. The employee may feel burdened by meetings or important conference calls. Explain to them that it's permissible to end a meeting because of the drill. Teach them to tactfully excuse themselves from conference calls. Train them how to halt a meeting with a client and help them evacuate. Sometimes they just need permission to do these things. Give them the permission they are looking for.

The Reentry Process after an Evacuation

After an evacuation drill has been completed, the building occupants will be required to reenter the building in an orderly fashion. This may seem like an obvious and simple process, but it may not be as easy as you'd think. If your building is a large multistory structure, the reentry process can be especially difficult and frustrating. Most large buildings are not equipped to handle the entry of all occupants at the same time. For instance, the thousands of tenants in a large building such as the John Hancock Center in Chicago realize that if everybody started work at 8:00 a.m., it could take an hour or longer to get to your office. The lines at the elevator would be so long you would need to show up at the building's lobby at 7:00 a.m. just to get to work on time. To compensate for the rush of workers starting each day, most tenants stagger their arrival times. This serves to alleviate the crowds. By requiring some employees to start work at 8:00 a.m., others at 8:15 a.m., yet others at 8:30 a.m., you effectively lessen the impact of the mass of people entering the building.

The same concept applies to building entry after an evacuation drill. When the drill is completed, employees will break from their staging areas and walk directly to the elevators. Imagine the long lines, the chaos, and the frustration. The next time you attempt to practice an evacuation drill, you'll find many people unwilling to participate because of the time consumed in reentry and loss of productivity. To solve this problem, two good options exist. First, you may elect to conduct an evacuation drill in smaller groups, perhaps two or three floors at a time. This makes the management of the groups and reentry into the building much easier. You'll need to devise a way to alert the occupants of those floors being evacuated, without tripping the alarm and triggering an entire building evacuation. If your alarm system does not allow for a selective siren or message, you may decide to use your floor captains and a bullhorn. If you use this option, try to simulate the actual sound of the regular building alarm. A simple tape recording of the alarm played over the bullhorn may suffice. Another option is to purchase a small alarm horn or siren at an electronic store. Your desire is to condition the building occupants to recognize the alarm and immediately begin evacuation.

The second option is to conduct a complete building evacuation, but instead of allowing the building occupants to reenter the building all at once, you will release them in small groups. This is best done by releasing various staging areas in a staggered fashion. Groups would be released based on their location in the building and which elevator banks were available. All elevators, including cargo elevators should be utilized during the drill. If an elevator or escalator is out of service, you might be better served by postponing the evacuation drill until you have all systems operational. Evacuation captains and assistants will need to have communication via two-way radio to ensure a smooth release of building occupants. Some additional planning will be necessary, but this option more closely represents an actual emergency situation.

When an actual emergency occurs that requires an evacuation, law enforcement personnel may want to interview some of the building occupants. Employees who were in the area of concern or who witnessed a problem should be identified and made available to the investigating agencies. A simple process can be created to ensure that this happens. For instance, the involved employees should have evacuated the building and assembled at their assigned staging area. Involved employees should check in with their staging area group leader and inform them of what they witnessed. The group leader would share this information with the runner, who would in turn deliver the information to the command post leader. This structure will allow important information to be relayed to a central location in a quick and efficient manner.

Evacuation and Educational Facilities

Evacuation of educational facilities should take into account the hazards that exist and the comprehension level of the students. Because of the young age of the majority of the occupants in an educational facility, the administration must provide an increased level of direction and hands-on assistance when evacuations are required. Questions to ask include:

> How will we communicate with parents?
> How will we account for students who are picked up by parents?
> Can transportation be brought in to take students to a safe location?

After the Drill: Evaluating Performance

It is crucial to review the evacuation procedures after a drill is performed. If the emergency evacuation was a drill, let the group know how they did. Was the clocked evacuation time within the established benchmarks? Did they do better or worse than the last time the drill was practiced? If it was better, share that success with the employees. They need to know that the effort they have expended has been worthwhile. If the timing was substantially worse, ask the group why they think the performance was poor. They may be able to provide valuable insight into problems and the corrective measures that should be taken.

If you keep your building occupants apprised of the evacuation results, they will take an interest. They will want to improve their evacuation time the next time the drill is conducted. Most importantly, in the event of an actual emergency, the building occupants will have the confidence to evacuate without resorting to pushing, running, or other inconsiderate and dangerous behavior.

13

Basic First Aid and Medical Care in the Workplace or Anyplace

Often during an emergency situation—in the workplace, in a public place, at a school, at home, or anyplace—emergency responders will be delayed and critical first aid will not be readily available unless you—a bystander, a teacher, an employer, anyone—are able to provide it yourself. In this scenario, the first aid responder will provide the initial assistance that may help the victim survive until trained emergency medical technicians arrive. History has shown us that many of the people who are injured in a workplace emergency can be assisted with basic first aid.

In a workplace, providing first aid need not be an expensive proposition. You are not required to hire licensed physicians or nurses. Thanks to "Good Samaritan" laws enacted in most states, you need not be overly concerned with the added liability of providing first aid. Basic first aid, cardiopulmonary resuscitation (CPR), automated external defibrillator use, and emergency oxygen administration are some of the first procedures that are available to most organizations. It is good practice for management to pay the modest cost for designated employees to receive this training from the American Red Cross or other similar organizations.

The First Aid Kit

A first aid kit is an essential element of emergency medical response. The contents of your first aid kit should treat the types of injuries that might occur in your workplace and suit the expertise of the first responders providing initial care and relief. Cuts and burns often represent the greatest exposure in the workplace, so ointments and bandages are a minimum requirement. Other suggestions for the first aid kit include:

- Antiseptic ointment or wipes
- Antiseptic hand cleaner
- Ammonia inhalants
- Antacid tablets
- Pain-relief tablets such as aspirin, Ibuprofen, or non-aspirin

Training for First Aid Responders

The American Heart Association recommends these specific areas of training that should be required for first aid responders:

⋏   **Cardiopulmonary Resuscitation (CPR)**
    CPR in conjunction with AED has proven to be an important step in treating a person who experiences sudden cardiac arrest. Not every emergency needs AED; sometimes only CPR is needed.

⋏   **Automated External Defibrillators (AED)**
    AEDs are used to restore a normal heartbeat in an individual who has experienced sudden cardiac arrest. Sudden cardiac arrest is usually caused by ventricular fibrillation (VR). When ventricular fibrillation occurs, the heart ceases to pump in a normal rhythmic fashion, thus preventing the heart from pumping blood properly.

⋏   **Emergency Oxygen Administration**
    A lack of oxygen in the victim's bloodstream can lessen the effects of an AED device, cause brain damage, and even cause death. Emergency oxygen can provide relief until emergency medical technicians arrive on the scene.

⋏   **Bloodborne Pathogens (BBP)**
    Certain diseases such as Hepatitis and AIDS are carried in the bloodstream and can be transmitted to others, including first aid responders. A first aid responder must understand how these diseases are transmitted and how they can protect themselves from these diseases. The Occupational Safety and Health Act requires BBP training for anyone providing first aid.

⋏   Cold pack
⋏   Eyewash
⋏   Adhesive tape and strips (3/4" by 3" and 1" by 3")
⋏   Fingertip bandages
⋏   Gauze pads and roller gauze (assorted sizes)
⋏   Knuckle bandages
⋏   Triangular bandage
⋏   Latex gloves
⋏   Notepad and pen (actions and inventory)
⋏   Plastic bags
⋏   Biohazard bags
⋏   Scissors and tweezers
⋏   Cotton tip applicators
⋏   Blanket
⋏   Small flashlight and extra batteries

Depending on the environmental exposure and the in-house expertise, consider including these additional first aid supplies:

- ⚐ Activated Charcoal (use only if instructed by Poison Control Center)
- ⚐ Syrup of Ipecac (use only if instructed by Poison Control Center)
- ⚐ Assorted splints
- ⚐ Blood pressure kit
- ⚐ Burn relief spray
- ⚐ CPR mask with oxygen port
- ⚐ Defibrillator
- ⚐ Insect bite relief spray
- ⚐ Insta-Glucose
- ⚐ Nitrile gloves
- ⚐ Stethoscope

When assembling a first aid kit, create a first aid station as well. This station might be located in the shop area or in a break room and would consist of the first aid kit, first aid posters, and a log of incidents and contents used. The station need not be expensive; it could be as simple as a plywood board painted and attached to the wall. The employees should be trained in locating the first aid station, administering proper first aid care, and reporting injuries. In a large

> Remember to include in your kit a log of incidents and a log of first aid contents used. These logs serve a two-fold purpose. First, they will ensure the contents are reordered as they become depleted. An empty first aid kit does not benefit anybody! Second, the logs will provide you with a process to spot trends and take proactive steps to protect employees and visitors while in your buildings.

building, multiple first aid stations are recommended. It would not make sense for an employee working on the second floor of the building to be required to travel to the fifth floor to receive assistance.

First Aid for Burn Victims

In the event of an emergency, especially one that involves burns, proper care must be taken so as not to harm the victim further. Burns can be extremely painful, causing shock, infection, and even death. Before administering the proper first aid, you must be able to recognize the type of burn to be treated.

There are four types of burns:

- ⚐ **Thermal**: These burns are caused by fire, hot objects or liquids, and gases, or by nuclear blast.
- ⚐ **Electrical:** These burns are caused by electrical current or lightning strikes.
- ⚐ **Chemical**: These burns are caused by contact with wet or dry chemicals.

- ▲ **Laser burns:** These burns are caused by the concentrated heat emanating from a laser device.

Depending on the severity of the burn, one of three classifications will be assigned:

- ▲ **First-degree burns:** These are relatively minor burns in which only the outer layer of skin is burned. The skin is usually red and some swelling and pain may occur. Usually can be treated by first aid.
- ▲ **Second-degree burns:** These are burns in which the first layer of skin has been burned through and the second layer of skin is also burned. In a second degree burn, the skin reddens and blisters develop. Severe pain and swelling also occur. This burn should be examined and treated by medical professionals.
- ▲ **Third-degree burns:** This is the most serious type of burn because it involves all layers of the skin. Fat, nerves, muscles, and even bones may be affected. These burns should receive prompt emergency medical attention. Delay in treatment may result in further damage, shock, and infection.

The scope of this book does not allow an in-depth discussion of the four types of burns or the three degrees of burns; however, a few points are worth making.

When treating a burn victim, first attempt to determine the cause of the burn. If the burn is the result of electrical contact, do not touch the victim until you are sure they have been removed from the electrical current. Failure to do so will result in you being shocked and burned as well.

When treating minor burns follow these steps:

- ▲ If the skin is not broken, run cool water over the burn for several minutes.
- ▲ Cover the burn with a sterile bandage.
- ▲ Administer acetaminophen to relieve any swelling or pain.

In the event of a major burn, seek emergency treatment immediately. Until the arrival of trained medical personnel, follow these preliminary steps:

- ▲ Remove the person from the source of the burn (i.e., fire, chemical, electrical current).
- ▲ Ensure that the person is breathing. If they are not, begin mouth-to-mouth resuscitation immediately.
- ▲ Remove all smoldering clothing to stop further burning.
- ▲ Do not apply any ointments, creams, or ice on the burned area or break blisters.
- ▲ Stay with the victim and reassure them that they will be okay and that help is on the way.

First Aid for Chemical Exposure

In the event of chemical exposure, immediately remove the victim from the area of exposure; however, you must do this without exposing yourself. Begin by contacting 911 or your local emergency management agency. When attempting to enter the exposure area, you may need gloves, a respirator, or even SCBA gear. Before entering the exposure area, determine what chemical has been released. You may be able to do this by observing opened canisters, ruptured hoses, or other telltale signs. When the chemical is identified, immediately retrieve the Material Safety Data Sheet (MSDS) for that chemical and find the suggested treatment and warnings.

If you do not have the MSDS information available, visit an onsite MSDS database and search for the chemical name. (There is also OSHA's chemical database at www.osha.gov/chemicaldata/.) Because of the lack of time or an Internet connection, be prepared to describe the chemical, its name, smell, color, and the effects it is having on the victim. Of course, with any chemical exposure or burn, time is of the essence and should not be wasted. Every second counts.

First Aid for Broken Bones

Broken bones are a common byproduct of emergency events. Broken bones include minor fractures or multiple breaks that encourage shock and nerve damage. When examining a victim for broken bones, look for the obvious signs such as deformity, protruding bones, or bleeding. Less obvious signs include swelling, tenderness, pain, and bruising at the location of injury. Do not ask the victim to move the injured limb because movement of the fractured bone could cut through muscle, blood vessels, and nerves, further complicating the situation.

Professional medical attention must be given to the victim of bone fractures; however, in some scenarios, medical attention may not be readily available. If this is the case, fashion a splint to immobilize the fracture. Again, don't move the limb unnecessarily, and if you are not sure if the injury is a fracture or a sprain, assume the worst-case scenario and proceed accordingly.

Unless the victim is in immediate and life-threatening danger, resist the temptation to move a victim with neck or back injuries because this could also cause further long-term damage.

Defibrillators

According to the U.S. Department of Labor, sudden cardiac arrest occurs at least 1,000 times a day and accounts for 75 percent of all workplace deaths. According to the American Heart Association, 326,000 people in the United States suffer out-of-hospital cardiac arrests annually. Advocates of Automated External Defibrillators (AEDs) claim that tens of thousands of lives can be saved each year by installing AEDs in public places such as airports, theaters, sporting arenas, shopping malls, and other places where people congregate.

AEDs are used to restore a normal heartbeat in an individual who has experienced ventricular fibrillation, more commonly known as sudden cardiac arrest. Cardiac arrest is brought about by sudden chaotic and abnormal electrical activity of the heart. Because the heart is able to pump based on electrical impulses, the abnormal electrical activity causes the heart to quiver in an uncontrollable fashion resulting in little or no blood being pumped from the heart. The victim of sudden cardiac arrest will quickly lose consciousness, and unless the condition is reversed, death follows in a matter of minutes. The AED provides a controlled electrical shock to the heart that helps to restore a normal rhythm.

When administering assistance using an AED, you'll also need to know CPR because these two methods usually go hand-in-hand. Prior to commencing the use of an AED unit, the administrator must evaluate the victim to determine need. The AED does not help someone who is choking and needs the Heimlich maneuver. For obvious reasons, the AED administrator must receive training. But using an AED device is not difficult: you do not need to be a licensed physician or paramedic. An in-depth knowledge of the medical field is not necessary; however, you can't expect an employee to arrive on the scene of an emergency and hook someone up to the device and save their life. How easy is an AED to use? If trained properly, even "sixth-grade school children have learned to use AEDs," reports the *Journal of the American Heart Association*.

Prior to deciding to install AEDs in your place of business, here are a few items you'll need to consider:

- Decide how many AEDs you will need.
- Research where they will be located.
- Research all federal, state, and local regulations regarding AED usage.
- Create a process to keep informed of changes to regulations involving AED usage.
- A prescription from a state-licensed physician is required for AED installation.
- Coordinate your AED program with your local emergency medical service.
- Develop training programs for those responsible for using AED.
- Develop a system to provide retraining and document compliance for "Good Samaritan" requirements.

When considering how many AED units to install and where to place them, consider this: the *New England Journal of Medicine* recommends that AEDs should be located within a three-minute "drop-to-shock" window. In other words, the shorter the timeframe between the "drop" (the heart attack) and the "shock" (the AED application), the better the chance for survival. For each minute after the heart attack, the chance of recovery is reduced by 10 percent. After ten minutes, the chance of survival, even with an AED shock, is extremely low.

Your emergency procedures manual should specifically address the AED device and its proper usage. Be sure to specify the names, locations, and phone numbers of those who have been trained in proper use of the AED device. Again, update your plan annually as these trained employees come or go.

CPR

Cardiopulmonary Resuscitation (CPR) is a manual technique that keeps oxygenated blood flowing to the brain and heart when a person is experiencing sudden cardiac arrest. CPR bridges the gap between cardiac arrest and the time when advanced treatment, such as defibrillation, can be administered. Studies have proven that the survival rate of sudden cardiac arrest victims improves dramatically the sooner they receive CPR after the onset of cardiac or respiratory arrest. Further studies have shown that CPR, which can be done quickly, bridges the gap before the use of automated external defibrillation, which usually is not readily available.

CPR is not difficult to perform, but proper training and certification should be completed before an attempt is made to administer it. Organizations such as the American Red Cross (www.redcross.org) and the American Heart Association (www.heart.org) provide regular local CPR classes. CPR training is not required in most businesses, but a few exceptions do exist. For instance the logging industry, commercial diving operations, and rescue personnel assigned to permit-required confined spaces all require CPR training and certification. However, it makes sense if you have a large work force to have a number of people trained in CPR and first aid.

The Chain of Survival

The American Heart Association has identified five links that make up the "Chain of Survival" that can "improve chances of survival and recovery for victims of heart attack, stroke, and other emergencies":

1. Immediate **recognition** of cardiac arrest and **activation** of the emergency response system
2. Early **cardiopulmonary resuscitation (CPR)** with an emphasis on chest compressions
3. Rapid **defibrillation**
4. Effective **advanced life support**
5. Integrated post-cardiac arrest care

Recently, partly to encourage more bystander first aid in cardiac arrest situations, the American Heart Association has promoted "Hands-Only CPR," a two-step process whereby the untrained bystander (1) dials 911 (and puts their phone on speaker mode if possible) and (2) provides hands-only CPR to the victim. In their 2015 guidelines, they state:

> Untrained bystanders should still call 911 and provide Hands-Only CPR, or CPR without breaths, pushing hard and fast in the center of the chest to the rate of 100–120 compressions per minute. However, if the bystander is trained in CPR and can perform breaths, he or she should add breaths in a 30:2 compressions-to-breaths ratio.

For more on the latest CPR guidelines, see the AHA Web site cpr.heart.org/, or call 1-877-AHA-4CPR (1-877-242-4277).

14

Post-event Restoration

After an emergency has occurred, successful restoration and recovery actions are crucial. For business owners, this restoration phase can be the difference between business continuation and bankruptcy. The employer will be faced with many difficult decisions, and how quickly these decisions are made becomes critical to survival. Confident and quick communication with the media, suppliers, clients, and other groups must not be overlooked.

During the restoration phase employee comfort and safety must not be minimized. Employees will be concerned about their jobs. Many employees will be affected by the emergency at home, and the stress of the events can be overwhelming. Employees involved in the restoration phase will likely be working long hours, and in their zeal for recovery, will not always take proper precautions or get proper sleep. These are some of the issues that must be addressed during the restoration phase.

Activating the Emergency Response Team

When members of your emergency response team are called to action, they must be prepared mentally and physically for what they may find. If your team is an early responder, a group that responds within an hour after the emergency event, it is unlikely that team members will be able to predict the severity of what lies ahead. Water service could be disrupted. Heating or cooling may be nonexistent. Floodwater may impact their efforts. Lack of electric service will hamper recovery efforts. If the area has been hit hard by the emergency, food and water will be scarce. Finally, transportation in and out of the area may be difficult. Many an emergency team member has found themselves stranded in an inhospitable environment without food, water, or a way to quickly get back to civilization.

The emotional and physical trauma can cause early responders to feel hopeless and powerless. In severe cases, the responders may even shutdown, physically and emotionally. This phenomenon is magnified with a lack of food, water, or sleep. Finally, the experience reaches a crescendo after the initial adrenaline rush has passed and the realities of restoration become evident. Understand the physical and emotional swings during a restoration effort and address them proactively.

A list of provisions must be provided to emergency team members and responders prior to an emergency. The list should be part of the emergency action plan, and friendly reminders should be given to team members on an annual basis at minimum.

Members of the emergency response team or employees asked to assist in the recovery effort should be accounted for and tracked on a frequent basis. Essential information such as telephone numbers, home addresses, vehicles, location assignments, skills, and tools should be recorded. A sample "Contractor Availability Form" can be found in the appendices. This form can be an invaluable tool when trying to locate key staff post-emergency. After an emergency, maintenance employees can be invaluable; however, they might not be members of your emergency response team.

> Be aware of subtle changes in your team members. If fatigue is setting in, make arrangements for rest and relief. Quite often more injuries occur during the grind of restoration than during the emergency event itself. If team members have experienced loss of a family member or personal property, they should be excused from the restoration efforts to care for the needs of their families.

You need a process to quickly see who is available and what tools or skills they possess. The emergency responder identification form can do that. Additionally, this form can help facilitate relief efforts and ensure that all facilities are visited and audited after an emergency.

Post-Event Access

Murphy's Law dictates that more often than not an emergency will occur after business hours or when emergency team members are otherwise away from the office. After the emergency, employees will have been evacuated, roads may be closed, and access to "ground zero" may be limited. If this occurs, how will you and other emergency team members be able to reach your buildings?

Law enforcement officers or even the National Guard will restrict all but the most critical traffic in and out of the area. This restriction serves a number of purposes. First and perhaps most importantly, many of the access roads will be unsafe. Downed trees may be blocking the road or an earthquake may have caused loss of pavement. In an effort to protect the public, road travel will be temporarily unavailable. Second, roads that are available must be reserved for emergency response personnel. Slow-moving, non-essential vehicular traffic may hinder emergency response personnel. A third reason access is limited is because of the increased possibility of looting and vandalism. After an emergency, offices and other premises that are normally locked and guarded are now unprotected. Doors and windows may have been broken and are open. Alarms are not functioning as a result of power loss. Police forces are spread thin. The opportunity for a thief to strike is at its highest. Many businesses have lost computers, furniture, files, food, tools, and other valuable assets to theft following an emergency.

Given these reasons, it is understandable why free access after an emergency will likely be unavailable or curtailed. Law enforcement and rescue personnel have a duty to protect citizens, and they take their job very seriously! Your emergency response team will only be allowed access if you communicate with these agencies prior to an emergency. Have you met with local law enforcement and rescue personnel? Have you introduced your emergency response team? Have you discussed your emergency action plan? If you take these actions and develop a relationship with the local agencies, they will be more apt to grant access to your emergency response team.

These agencies may permit entry to a limited access zone, based on the critical nature of your business. For instance, utility workers will usually be granted greater access rights than a shopkeeper. At the initial meeting with the local law enforcement agency, be prepared to make your case for immediate access to your site. You will need to convince these agencies of the importance of allowing you to respond to your site. This should not be based on a desire to get to your site; rather, it should be based on a need. Is your business critical to community-wide disaster recovery? Does your business play a support role? Are employees on site? Can your response efforts decrease the need for police protection and allow them to work in other areas? Whatever your reasons for needing site access, be prepared to share this with local law enforcement and rescue personnel prior to an emergency.

These agencies may propose that certain identification be carried by emergency response team members. Perhaps a magnetic sign attached to the vehicle or a window hanger identifying the occupant of the vehicle as an emergency response team member would be sufficient. One word of warning, though, magnetic signs and other temporary forms of identification can be stolen. The holder of such identification now has unlimited access into a controlled zone, so many agencies prefer other means of identification. In many areas, law enforcement officers will have a list of emergency responders, and if your name is not on the list, you're not getting in. Find out if such a list is used and what is required to have the names of your team members added. Remember, the list of emergency team members will change over time and you must contact these agencies to revise their list.

Assessing the Damage

Now that you have arrived on the scene, you should immediately take steps to assess the damage to your building and the surrounding property. Depending on the nature of the emergency and the resulting damage, you may elect to bring in specialized help for this assessment. If you have any doubts about the structural integrity of the building, do not enter it! "General Building Issues" in the appendices contains sample building assessments and can be used to assess the building's condition. Building audits provide an excellent starting point for post-emergency recovery; however, they should be revised to incorporate the specifics of your property and site.

Insurance and Salvage Decisions

As you walk through your property after an emergency event, you'll need to document any property damage that may have occurred. If you have an insurance policy on the building and its contents, this documentation will be essential if you hope to be reimbursed for your loss. If you are not familiar with the insurance coverage of your property, immediately contact your risk management department or insurance provider to make certain you are following correct procedures for documentation. If your organization is self-insured, you are not exempt from the documentation

> When entering a building for an assessment, make certain you have the proper personal protective equipment (PPE) available and in use. This might include hardhat, steel-toed shoes, long-sleeved shirt, nuisance dust mask, respirator, and safety glasses. Employees assigned PPE must be properly trained in its use, and with many items such as respirators, the gear must be fit tested.

process. You will still need to document the damage if you hope to take a tax write off or take advantage of federal or state aid that may be available.

Some type of visual recording device should be used when performing an assessment of your building and the associated property. If possible, a video camera should be used to record the damage. Continuous video gives a more accurate and complete description of what has occurred than photographs. Remember, insurance adjusters and government agencies providing aid—such as FEMA—will be reviewing this documentation. If a video camera is not available, a digital or film camera may be used or your smart phone. The date and time stamp should be included when filming or taking pictures. If you do use a digital camera or video recorder, remember the limitations: How much video can it record before

> Relying on the copy of the building assessment in your emergency action plan or on your computer's hard disk might be risky. If electrical service is compromised, you would be unable to use a photocopier or a printer. For this reason, you should have a number of preprinted assessment forms ready to go. A common practice is to covert these assessment forms to an electronic document accessible on a smartphone or thumb drive attached to your key chain. Back up battery chargers are also a good idea to keep your phone operational.

its memory is used up? How long will the battery last? Do you have a means to recharge the battery once it is depleted? In areas where loss of electrical power has occurred, many emergency responders prefer to use simple disposable cameras.

Keep salvageable property separated from "damaged-beyond-repair" property. The damaged property should be kept until an insurance adjuster has had the opportunity to evaluate it. If the damaged goods are a hindrance to recovery and exposure to the elements will not further harm them, establish a temporary staging area on site and move those items to that location. Prior to moving these items, document their condition and where they came from. If salvaged or damaged items are sold or otherwise removed from the property, be certain to collect a signed inventory list from the party removing the goods.

After a particularly devastating disaster, insurance response may not be immediate. When Hurricane Andrew struck south Florida, many people who were affected said that it took weeks, and in some cases months, for the insurance companies to meet with them. Some insurance adjusters were unable to find their clients because the buildings were no longer standing and they had no alternate means of communication due to the loss of telecommunications. If a major disaster occurs and your building no longer exists or is hard to identify, build a large sign out of plywood and paint the address where you can be located, the company name, and your insurance provider on the board.

The Restoration Phase

At some point after victims have been aided and the damage has been assessed the actual restoration phase must begin. During this time, if unprepared, confusion, exhaustion, and often depression can set in. Having a detailed plan of attack will decrease the downtime caused by the emergency event. A few words of warning are in order, though. The task of rebuilding often seems monumental, even impossible. If the emergency event was a regional one, the ability to get quick-responding local help may be impossible. The pressure of getting the business back on line may be stressful as well. The restoration phase may require long hours supplemented by little sleep and hard work rewarded with subpar food. You may have serious family concerns but little family interaction. These are the very real issues and emotions that are likely to be experienced by those supporting the restoration phase.

However, the restoration phase is not all pain and misery. A spirit of unity can overtake a previously apathetic community. You'll witness true human compassion being expressed on a regular basis. The ability to recover from adversity gracefully is uniquely human. It's a side we don't always see, or perhaps just don't notice. Sometimes the worst events bring out the best in people.

Logistics

One of the most difficult aspects of emergency recovery is logistics—the movement of equipment, supplies, and personnel to locations where they are needed most. This movement becomes difficult when the access roads have been damaged. It becomes complicated to achieve when telecommunications are down. It's nearly impossible when your employees and contractors are literally digging themselves out of the ruins. Even with all these issues satisfied, the rush to get back to business puts extra pressure on the restoration team.

Things can't happen quickly enough. The problem with logistics is made more difficult when you have multiple damaged properties in your portfolio. You find yourself juggling conflicting priorities, schedules, and demands.

Some of the logistical issues we will discuss in this chapter include:

- Communications
- Food provision
- Housing/sleeping accommodations
- Safety and security
- Emotional distress and fatigue

One of the best solutions for logistic difficulties is to have an inventory of the basic necessities waiting and ready to go prior to an emergency. Understanding that this inventory could become a casualty of the emergency (i.e., your inventory of food and water may be destroyed during an earthquake), it would be wise to spread your supplies over a few locations, if possible. If you are a member of the emergency response team or are counted upon as a first responder, you should be self-sufficient for at least twenty-four hours, preferably for seventy-two hours. Initially, the emergency responders have the responsibility to provide the basic necessities for their personal consumption. By having seventy-two hours' worth of supplies, they can survive and be modestly comfortable until formal provisions can be initiated. Such provisions might include:

Clothing

- Three changes of clothes
- Rain jacket
- Cold weather jacket
- Safety goggles
- Hard hat
- Sunglasses
- Two pairs of work shoes (steel toed preferred)
- Sturdy gloves
- Spare pair of glasses

Healthcare and toiletries

- Soap
- Shampoo
- Wash cloth and towel
- Razor and shaving cream
- Toothpaste and toothbrush
- Personal hygiene products
- Deodorant

- Toilet paper
- Sun block
- Insect repellant
- Contact lens solution and spare lenses

Miscellaneous

- NOAA weather radio
- Alarm clock
- Blankets
- Sleeping bag or cot
- Batteries
- Flashlight (self-powered flashlights that you crank are great)
- Pen or pencils
- Notepad and audit forms
- Camera (digital or film; including disposable)
- Video camera
- Cellphone with automobile battery charger or solar powered chargers.
- Driver's license
- Credit card
- Cash
- Plastic container(s) to keep items dry

Medicines

- Prescription medicines
- Antacids
- Athlete's foot spray
- Pain relief cream
- Aspirin and ibuprofen
- First aid kit

Food and Water

- Meals Ready to Eat (MRE)
- Snack bars
- Fruit
- Trail mix or nuts
- Bottled water (drinking and cleaning)
- Instant coffee
- Cooler with ice and ice pack
- Propane stove (optional)
- Propane fuel tank (extra)

This list is not all-inclusive and, depending on the emergency, not all items will be necessary. The list is just long enough to provide a level of comfort without burdening the emergency personnel with a tractor trailer full of supplies. Remember, this inventory is for their consumption only. Encouraging emergency team members and first responders to be responsible for their twenty-four to seventy-two hour inventory will allow them to be better able to respond prior to the restoration of the infrastructure.

> **John Lee, an emergency planning consultant based in North Carolina, provides the following recollection of events after Hurricane Andrew:**
>
> > During Hurricane Andrew in August of 1992, I was supporting a large corporate building that housed nearly 2,000 employees and the corporate computer mainframe. We felt comfortable that we had planned for all contingencies. We had generators and uninterruptible power supply for the computer mainframe system. We secured the air handler units on the roof. There was enough food and potable water to feed a skeleton staff for several days. We knew there would be 300 to 400 employees in the building for several days just to keep communications up. I felt comfortable that we were prepared for the storm. We had a good plan, and the employees were properly trained to provide support after the storm. The building faired the storm well—just a few minor roof leaks. All emergency power systems were working and the computer mainframe did not miss a beat. The one item we did not plan for turned into a major inconvenience. We were unable to flush the high-pressure flush valve commodes. Unlike the ones most of us have at home, a bucket of water doesn't work. The municipal water company lost power for a few days and was unable to pump. The moral of the story: No matter how much planning you do, something unexpected will always crop up and present problems. Learn from your past and make adjustments as necessary. I don't write a plan without identifying Port-o-Let vendors!

The Command Center

The command center is an integral component of any emergency recovery plan. There must be a central location where the management of the recovery efforts can be performed without interruption. Even in an evacuation drill, a command center should be established as the focal point of communication.

Whether you elect to locate the command center at the damaged property or off-site typically depends on a number of factors. For instance, after an actual emergency that requires restoration, the command center must be equipped with phones, fax machines, computers, and other communication resources. If electrical service has not been restored and emergency generator service is not available, the command center should be located elsewhere. Having said that, in most cases the command center would better be served at the location where restoration is being done. In scenarios where you have multiple properties that have been damaged, a central command center should be established and then backed up by individual on-site command centers.

What happens at a command center? Again, the key word is communication. The command center serves as the "brain center" of the recovery effort. Contractors, employees, media, government agencies, insurance providers, or anyone else with an interest in the property needs to have a place to go to ask questions and get answers. The command center must know everything that is going on to ensure that priorities are being met and that resources are not being wasted.

Because of the tremendous amount of coordination that a restoration effort requires, the command center is a must. In addition to communication, the command center may be responsible for:

- Personal protective equipment
- Meals and beverages
- Property security
- Accommodation arrangements
- Tool checkout
- Contractor sign-in
- Media relations
- Government agency liaison
- First-aid

Because the command center will become the focal point of communication, keeping up with the questions, answers, and promises made will become overwhelming if left to memory. All correspondence should be documented using a correspondence log (figure 14.1). The correspondence log works much like a telephone log, but it documents all conversation, whether by telephone, e-mail, verbal, or fax. The correspondence log tracks conversations with vendors, suppliers, emergency management teams, members of the media, or any other entity. Copies of press releases, contractor insurance certifications, PPE checkout, deliveries, and any other important issues can be documented in this book as well. So many things will be happening that it becomes very difficult to manage an organized emergency restoration effort without the log. The log is critical both during the restoration phase and in the post-emergency review and assessment. During the restoration phase the log provides continuity. If one member of the emergency management team has to leave for any reason, their replacement can get up to speed very quickly by reviewing the log. If there is a call from the media you can look at the log to see what the most recent press statement said so that everyone speaks with the same voice.

Corresponence Log

Date: _____   Time: _____

Caller	Issue	Name	Office Phone	Cell Phone	Action Required
Vendor					
Contractor					Yes
Employee					No
Police					
Fire / Paramedic					
Insurance Agent					
Other _____					

Date: _____   Time: _____

Caller	Issue	Name	Office Phone	Cell Phone	Action Required
Vendor					
Contractor					Yes
Employee					No
Police					
Fire / Paramedic					
Insurance Agent					
Other _____					

Date: _____   Time: _____

Caller	Issue	Name	Office Phone	Cell Phone	Action Required
Vendor					
Contractor					Yes
Employee					No
Police					
Fire / Paramedic					
Insurance Agent					
Other _____					

Assigned To

Assigned To

Assigned To

Figure 14.1.
Correspondance Log.

The Emergency Account Number

We've all witnessed the devastating results of emergency events. Whether the emergency is manmade or natural, the results can be very costly. Most organizations understand the potential costs associated with these events and they attempt to share this risk by purchasing property insurance. In addition to insurance providers, certain governmental agencies may be able to provide financial relief after an emergency.

The insurance providers and government agencies may provide financial relief, but they do have rules. They will require certain documentation to prove that expenses were used for emergency recovery efforts. You must ensure that recovery costs are not commingled with standard operating expenses. The funds must be used to repair damage as a result of the emergency, and not to buy new artwork for the corporate office. Each expense will be examined by auditors and tested for validity. Additionally, the recovery expense documentation must satisfy your internal auditors. Speaking with your internal auditors and allowing them to review your current accounting procedures would be a good starting point. They can serve as a liaison between your organization and the insurance provider. Additionally, in the event of an emergency the auditors should be relied upon to provide specific guidelines for what can be charged to the emergency account number and what cannot. In the event of a major disaster, some initial funds may be made available to assist restoration but it could be weeks, months, or even years before full payment is made.

It is one thing to provide an emergency account number; it is quite another to get employees to use it. If the paperwork is too complicated, employees will not fill it out and the company runs the risk of not being compensated for its restoration-related expenses. All employees need to understand the importance of properly categorizing restoration expenses. The paperwork may seem tedious and unnecessary until they understand the purpose.

One of the problems with emergency account numbers is the potential for abuse. A small stain in a carpet may result in total replacement. A couple of downed trees could be twisted into a complete landscaping overhaul. You have a responsibility to take necessary actions to ensure this doesn't happen. Corporations are under scrutiny because of creative accounting procedures. Insurance fraud is serious business and it's not worth the bad press and possible jail time. To ensure that the emergency account number is not abused, specific instructions concerning its use must be given. Start by providing employees with detailed guidelines about what can and cannot be categorized as a restoration expense. Don't forget to explain the consequences if they elect to abuse the emergency account number.

In the rare event of two different emergencies occurring within a short period of time, you must assign two unique emergency account numbers for each event. The added paperwork may seem a waste of time, but it is a legal requirement. In a two-event scenario you might be responsible for two different deductibles. In an effort to limit financial responsibility, we may attempt to categorize all damage under a single event, but most insurance providers are aware of this possible loophole. This is a concern because most insurance policies contain "misrepresentation and concealment" clauses that void the policy if there is any misrepresentation, fraud, or concealment of material facts during application or future claims. Simply put, if you knowingly misrepresent a claim, your policy provider can cancel your policy and reject all claims without any responsibility. This is not just a threat; numerous cases have been brought to court across the country, and the courts have sided with the insurance provider and not the policyholder.

An interesting twist to this multi-event question was raised after 9/11. Silverstein Properties, the master leaseholder of the World Trade Center property, got into litigation with its insurance providers, which included Swiss Re. The debate revolved around Silverstein's belief that the terrorist activities constituted two separate events. Two airplanes were flown into two different buildings at two different times. Eventually both buildings collapsed, but at different times. Based on this belief, Silverstein Properties argued there were entitled to two separate claims. The insurance providers considered the terrorist attacks a singular event and because the policy had a cap of $3.55 billion, they argued that was the limit of their responsibility. Silverstein Properties countered that $3.55 billion would not be sufficient to rebuild both buildings. In 2007, a settlement was reached whereby the insurers paid out $4.55 billion in total.

At some point, you'll need to close the emergency account number down. When you do, provide employees with adequate notice, as some invoices may not have been processed yet. Your organization's accounting department should be prepared to distribute additional information to employees about the emergency account number and its eventual closing.

Catering

In the event of a major emergency, the likelihood of local restaurants being open for business will be minimal. Regarding food and water, emergency team members and employees assigned to assist should be self-sufficient for the first twenty-four hours at a minimum. For ease of use, food provisions might include "meals ready to eat" (MRE). These self-contained meal packages have a long shelf life and do not require heat or refrigeration. Since the employees are responsible for their own provisions during the first twenty-four hours, the company is able to focus its efforts on the need thereafter.

If the emergency event is major and the recovery effort is likely to last longer than a few days, outside assistance with meal preparation will be necessary. The caterer will need to provide meals for a predetermined amount of people. The vendor should also be responsible for the tents, chairs, utensils, ice, and transportation to the recovery site. It may be necessary to contract with a primary vendor and have an alternate available in the event the primary is unable to service your needs.

Providing Sleeping Accommodations

Everyone needs a good night's sleep, especially when working long hours during the restoration phase. If the emergency was regional in nature, it may be very difficult to find adequate sleeping accommodations for your employees and contractors. Hotels will fill up quick, so early after the emergency, start contacting hotels about availability. If necessary, reserve a block of rooms; it is better to be over-prepared than underprepared. Because of room availability, it may be necessary to have employees share rooms.

If rooms are scarce and your employees are working around the clock, perhaps you could stagger sleeping room usage. For instance, in a room with two double beds, you could comfortably sleep two people. The two people working during the day shift would arrive at the hotel around 7:00 p.m. and leave by 6:00 a.m. the next morning. At around 7:00 a.m. two employees working the night shift would arrive to catch up on showers and sleep. By 6:00 p.m. they would leave the hotel and report back to work. By staggering the use of the hotel room, more people can use a room than under normal circumstances. These accommodations should only be used if additional rooms are not available, and the hotel manager should be made aware of the situation. Logistics such as cleaning, towel replacement, and changing of the linens should be arranged with hotel management.

Some employees may have tents, campers, or other recreational vehicles that they are willing to use during the restoration phase. Will you allow those on site? Is their presence safe? Will they interfere with the ongoing work? Is room available in the building for employees to sleep? Will you be providing cots for workers wanting to take a quick nap? Some organizations have brought in a doublewide trailer and filled it with sleeping cots for workers hoping to catch up on sleep. This may be a good idea, but be sure to get temporary clearance from your local code enforcement body.

Regardless of the provisions you make, you'll want to reiterate company policy on such issues as sleeping room guidelines, shared rooms, per diems, mileage, compensation, and anything else that might come into question. Based on the emergency and the protracted restoration efforts, your organization may find it advantageous to temporarily change some of the guidelines. Publish these temporary changes and distribute to all employees as soon as possible.

Environmental Issues

When a large scale disaster strikes, the damage can be incredible. Buildings can be ripped apart. Rising floodwaters can introduce moisture into walls, resulting in mold and mildew growth. If not taken care of, the growth could become a real indoor air quality issue, causing health problems well after the floodwaters have subsided. Broken or backed up sewer lines create an obvious health issue. Extreme emergency events require much more than a thorough cleaning. The cleanup required after a disaster can be time consuming, expensive, and even dangerous.

If a building experiences even a small level of structural collapse, **asbestos contamination** could be an issue, especially if the building was built prior to 1980. Think for a moment about possible sources of asbestos in your building. In many old buildings the nine-inch vinyl flooring tiles contain asbestos. The mastic that was used to adhere the tiles to the slab also contained asbestos. Certain types of insulation commonly found in mechanical rooms contain asbestos materials. Ceiling tiles and plaster walls may also contain asbestos. Before becoming overly concerned with the presence of asbestos, understand that asbestos is not considered dangerous until the asbestos fibers are introduced into the surrounding environment. Let's use the example of asbestos floor tiles. Even if your building contains these asbestos tiles today, it is probably not an issue. The asbestos fibers are encapsulated within the tiles. There is no danger until the fibers are disturbed and escape into the surrounding environment. Regarding the mastic, the asbestos contained in it is also encapsulated. No danger exists until the tiles are lifted from the floor and the mastic is disturbed. At this point the asbestos fibers are friable and you now have a very real environment concern.

Know the Terminology: Important Asbestos Definitions

Asbestos Containing Material (ACM): A term used to describe any material containing more than 1 percent asbestos.

Presumed Asbestos Containing Material (PACM): A term used to describe thermal system insulation and surfacing material found in buildings built prior to 1980. Describes materials that may contain asbestos but testing has not been completed to verify its presence.

Surfacing Material: Material that is sprayed, troweled, or otherwise applied to surfaces. These surfaces might include acoustical plaster, fireproofing materials sprayed on structural members, or other materials applied on surfaces for the purpose of fireproofing or acoustical soundproofing.

Thermal System Insulation (TSI): Asbestos containing material that is applied to boilers, pipes, fittings, tanks, ducts, or other such components to prevent heat loss or gain.

Now let's think about what may happen to the building during a major disaster. Let's assume an earthquake strikes and we experience a partial building collapse. A large portion of the roof falls in, breaking the asbestos ceiling tiles. The building's foundation was disturbed by the shock waves, causing the asbestos floor tiles to pop up off the slab. Where the floor tiles remained, many were cracked or completely shattered. A few of the interior plaster walls were damaged as well. Based on this building assessment, you have a real problem. Any workers entering this building risk asbestos exposure. If we are not aware of the danger, we may send employees into the building to sweep up the broken tiles. We might instruct a contractor to remove and rebuild the nonload-bearing wall that has been damaged. You have exposed these workers to dangerous asbestos fibers. In our haste to get back to business, we forgot about the environmental concerns of a disaster.

If you have buildings built prior to 1980, and asbestos removal has not been conducted, you should create a written process for safe entry and repairs after an emergency that causes damage to the structure. This process would include establishing a contract with an industrial hygienist who could quickly evaluate a building and provide testing and recommendations. Additionally, employees should be trained to understand the dangers of accessing a damaged building without proper personal protective equipment (PPE) as specified by the industrial hygienist. If employees are allowed to enter the building with specified PPE, OSHA requires employers to provide training and fit testing for the employees. Don't fall for the false belief that a simple dust mask can protect employees from asbestos fibers. These masks are created for nuisance dusts and fall far short of protecting workers from asbestos fibers. Donning inferior personal protective equipment may be the equivalent of fighting a forest fire with a garden hose.

> Regarding personal protective equipment (PPE), OSHA specifies the required respirators for different asbestos concentrations at CFR 29 1910.1001(g)(3) Table 1. Because of the technical nature of these standards, most employers will not be able to interpret the requirements and supply the appropriate respirator equipment. The testing and specification of personal protective equipment should be performed by an approved industrial hygienist.

For some organizations, an emergency event could result in a loss of stored hazardous materials. A storage tank could be ruptured and release its contents into the environment. The contents might be toxic gasses, diesel fuel, oil, or anything in between.

Organizations that have storage tanks should take precautions so the contents will not be easily released. Consider engineering solutions such as containment walls and slabs, alarm systems, and fencing to limit access to these tanks. These precautions should be followed up by procedures to be used in the event of a spill. These corrective procedures might specify the use of absorbent pads, booms, or skimmers. Additionally, contractors specializing in testing, containment, cleanup, abatement, and soil remediation should be identified and included as part of your emergency action plan. By having these contracts in place prior to an emergency event, you ensure quick response to the problem, possibly limiting the impact of the spill.

Assisting Affected Employees

When an emergency has passed and an organization begins its restoration phase, it will often turn to its employees. The best employees have a sense of ownership and they take the rebuilding of the business personally. They can be an excellent source of leadership through the difficult times. They band together and accomplish the unimaginable. But sometimes they get burned out. Sometimes the prolonged stress is too much. Sometimes they don't know how or when to stop and rest. The emotional trauma of a major disaster can cause depression and physical illness. Employers have a responsibility to be aware of the physical and emotional well-being of their employees after an emergency event. At a minimum, employers should observe their employees who are involved in the restoration phase. If they notice irritability, withdrawal, or some other behavior out of the ordinary, they must ask the employee to take time off and rest.

If the emergency event is severe, employers have a responsibility to offer crisis counseling to their employees. If the employees do not get well, how can the employee be of value to the company? That may sound inconsiderate, but think about it for a moment. If an employee is physically ill, they stay home from work and recuperate. During their recuperation period, they are not productive. Employers understand that; in fact, they give sick days for just this reason. It stands to reason that when exposed to emotional trauma, we can become emotionally ill as well. We need time to recuperate. We are not productive when in this state. When the trauma is great, crisis counseling may be necessary. An organization that is truly concerned about business continuity and the well-being of their employees will ensure that the employees are physically and emotionally well.

If an emergency is regional in nature, the damage will not be limited to your organization's business or property. Neighboring business will also be affected. The homes of employees may be damaged. Employees or their family members could be injured or even killed as a result of the emergency event. Family concerns should always take precedence over business. Realizing this, a caring organization would not expect employees personally affected by the emergency to be available for the restoration phase. They will have their hands full dealing with their own loss. In these cases, it makes sense to bring employees in from different locations that were not affected as deeply by the emergency.

In the worst disasters, some employees may be rendered homeless. As an organization, you'll want to assist, but realistically what can you do? This is not an issue that can be answered for you. It is unlikely that your organization will be able to purchase new homes for employees and that would not be expected. However, can your organization assist employees with temporary housing? Perhaps your organization can guide employees to federal or state assistance. FEMA spent $2.7 billion to provide 145,000 mobile homes and caravans after Hurricane Katrina.

The assistance is out there, but many people don't know how to access it. Can your company organize federal assistance workshops for displaced employees? Can your organization help employees with the mounds of paperwork required by insurance providers? Again, the level of service you provide will be a corporate decision, but remember, business can't get back to normal until the employees get back to normal. Employees are an organization's greatest investment and should be treated as such.

Don't Forget about Safety

Most employers are required to adhere to OSHA regulations, including specific recording and reporting responsibilities. The possibility of a workplace injury is increased while recovering from an emergency event, and for this reason particular attention must be given to employee and contractor safety.

In the event of an accident that results in any injury, even a minor one, a post-accident report should be completed. The purpose of the post-accident report is to identify all injuries, even those that do not trigger an OSHA recordable. Ultimately, the post-accident report form will serve as tool for trending analysis. If employees keep getting injured while moving sandbags, a proactive manager would look for ways to eliminate or reduce the risk involved. If the injury falls into OSHA's recording regulations, the injury and associated information must be transferred to the appropriate OSHA record keeping.

The post-accident report typically includes the following information:

- ▲ What happened?
- ▲ What activity were the employees engaged in?
- ▲ When did it happen (date and time)?
- ▲ Who witnessed the event?
- ▲ What were the weather conditions?
- ▲ Was the accident due to an unsafe condition or unsafe act?
- ▲ What preventative steps will be taken?

Although not required by OSHA, the post-accident report shows your organization's desire to proactively reduce workplace injuries. OSHA has created three specific forms that must be completed by employers when specific injuries or illnesses occur. Some industries and organizations employing ten people or fewer are exempt for OSHA's record keeping requirements unless selected by the Bureau of Labor Statistics to participate in an annual survey. The required OSHA forms include:

OSHA Form 300 (Log of Work-related Injuries and Illnesses)
OSHA's Form 300 is used to record information on all illnesses and injuries that require medical attention beyond basic first aid. The OSHA Form 300 is used to record information such as the employee's name, job title, date of injury, description of injury, and the location where the event occurred. The OSHA Form 300 replaced the old OSHA 200 form in 2002 and must be kept for five years.

OSHA Form 301 (Injury and Illness Incident Report)
The OSHA Form 301 is the individual record of each work-related injury or illness recorded on the 300 Form. It includes additional data about how the injury or illness occurred. The 301 Form replaces the former OSHA 101 Form.

OSHA Form 300A (Summary of Work-related Injuries and Illnesses)
The OSHA 300A replaces the summary portion of the former OSHA 200 Log and is now a separate form, updated to make it easier to calculate incidence rates. It must be signed by a company executive. Even if your organization does not have any recordable injuries, the OSHA Form 300A must be completed. Fill in all the blanks and add zeros in spaces that ask for total injuries and illnesses.

Regardless of the severity, all occupational illnesses must be recorded on the OSHA Form 300. An illness is defined as an abnormal condition resulting from something other than an occupational injury, caused by an exposure to environmental factor at the workplace. These factors include illness caused from inhalation, ingestion, and direct contact. Examples of illnesses can be categorized into four groups:

Don't Forget: OSHA Form 300A (Summary of Work-related Injuries And Illnesses) must be completed and be displayed next to the OSHA safety poster (Form 3165 or state equivalent) from February 1 through April 30 each year.

Skin disorders:

- Dermatitis
- Rash caused by poisonous plants
- Inflammation of the skin

Respiratory conditions:

- Silicosis
- Asbestosis
- Tuberculosis

Poisoning:

- Lead
- Mercury
- Carbon monoxide
- Insecticide

Other:

- Heatstroke/Sunstroke/Heat exhaustion
- Frostbite
- Anthrax
- AIDS/HIV
- Hepatitis B
- Mold

Most injuries and illnesses are simply recorded on the appropriate OSHA logs and made available for display during the months of February, March, and April. You are not required to contact OSHA by telephone unless a death or the in-patient hospitalization of three or more employees as a result of a work-related incident occurs.

Reporting Requirement

Within eight (8) hours after the death of any employee from a work-related incident or the in-patient hospitalization of three or more employees as a result of a work-related incident, you must orally report the fatality/multiple hospitalization by telephone or in person to the Area Office of the Occupational Safety and Health Administration (OSHA), U.S. Department of Labor, that is nearest to the site of the incident.

You may also use the OSHA toll-free central numbers:

(800) 321-OSHA (6742)
TTY (877) 889-5627

Do not send an e-mail.

When you contact OSHA to report an employee death or in-patient hospitalization of three or more employees as a result of a work-related incident, OSHA will ask the following questions:

- The establishment name
- The location of the incident
- The time of the incident
- The number of fatalities or hospitalized employees
- The names of any injured employees
- The name and phone number of a contact person
- A brief description of the incident

When evaluating an injury for OSHA record keeping purposes, always ask yourself, "Does this injury require medical treatment beyond basic first aid?" If the answer is yes, you must record the injury in the OSHA Form 300. For those areas considered questionable, the following list of medical treatments may be helpful:

- Treatment of infection
- Application of antiseptics during second or subsequent visit to medical personnel
- Treatment of second- or third-degree burn(s)
- Application of sutures (stitches)
- Application of butterfly adhesive dressing(s) or steri strip(s) in lieu of sutures
- Removal of foreign bodies embedded in eye

▲   Removal of foreign bodies from wound; if procedure is complicated because of depth of embedment, size, or location

▲   Use of prescription medications (except a single dose administered on first visit for minor injury or discomfort). Use of hot or cold soaking therapy during second or subsequent visit to medical personnel

▲   Application of hot or cold compress(es) during second or subsequent visit to medical personnel

▲   Cutting away dead skin (surgical debridement)

▲   Application of heat therapy during second or subsequent visit to medical personnel

▲   Use of whirlpool bath therapy during second or subsequent visit to medical personnel

▲   Positive X-ray diagnosis (fractures, broken bones, etc.)

▲   Admission to a hospital or equivalent medical facility for treatment.

Additionally, these incidents are *always* recordable:

▲   Loss of consciousness

▲   Restriction of work or motion

▲   Transfer to another job

▲   Death

If one or more of these events have occurred, you must record the injury. On the other hand, administration of simple first aid does not trigger an OSHA recordable. Events that would be considered first aid treatment would include:

▲   Application of antiseptics during first visit to medical personnel

▲   Treatment of first degree burn(s)

▲   Application of bandage(s) during any visit to medical personnel

▲   Use of elastic bandage(s) during first visit to medical personnel

▲   Removal of foreign bodies not embedded in eye if only irrigation is required

▲   Removal of foreign bodies from wound; if procedure is uncomplicated and is, for example, by tweezers or other simple technique

▲   Use of nonprescription medications and administration of single dose of prescription medication on first visit for minor injury or discomfort

▲   Soaking therapy on initial visit to medical personnel or removal of bandages by soaking

▲   Application of hot or cold compress(es) during first visit to medical personnel

▲   Application of ointments to abrasions to prevent drying or cracking

▲   Application of heat therapy during first visit to medical personnel

▲   Use of whirlpool bath therapy during first visit to medical personnel

▲   Negative X-ray diagnosis

▲   Observation of injury during visit to medical personnel

Again, keep in mind that the loss of consciousness, restriction of work or motion, or transfer to another job, even if the employee did not receive medical attention *does* trigger an OSHA recordable.

Now Is Not the Time to Let Your Guard Down: Security

Immediately following an emergency event, most people will be totally consumed with finding victims, mending their own wounds, making repairs to their buildings, or restoring business continuity. When we become so involved in these important matters, we sometimes miss the obvious around us. We may not be as perceptive as usual, overlooking the person with bad intentions. In life, and especially after an emergency, some people will prey on the misfortunes of others. We assume that after an emergency everybody wants to pitch in and help, but this is not always true. Even those who might not normally be inclined to dishonesty, in a moment of weakness and under the guise of providing for their family, may view your misfortune as an opportunity to get something for nothing.

In one example, a delivery of fifteen portable generators was sent to a power plant immediately following a hurricane. The generators were left in a semi-secure area, but within four hours they had disappeared. The employees of the power company were unable to watch the generators and the security guards who were called to duty were delayed in reaching the plant. In another example, immediately following the final game of an NBA championship series, fans of the winning team began to celebrate. Most of the celebration was harmless fun, but a few of the revelers had bad intentions. These people smashed shop windows and began looting stores. Liquor, furniture, and electronics were taken. Because of situations like these, you cannot take security for granted.

Because we never know when an emergency will occur, security contracts must be in place continuously. Writing a good contract will require you to ask yourself and the security provider a number of questions:

- What background checks will be done on the guards?
- How quickly will the guards respond?
- Can guards be brought in from another area not affected by the emergency?
- Will you need security around the clock or just during evening hours?
- Do you require the guards to be armed?
- Is there any other specialized training that is needed?
- Who will the guards report to?
- Where will they be stationed?

One of the key issues will be availability of guards immediately following the emergency. If the emergency event was regional in nature, an earthquake for instance, the usual guards may be unable to respond because phone service is out or they are assisting their own families. Can the security company you are contracting obtain additional guards from a nearby area not affected? If so, how long will it take them to arrive? It's often advantageous to have an alternate security company available in the event the primary company is unable to respond to your needs.

Monitoring Restoration Progress

Because of the psychological trauma a major emergency event causes, the restoration progress can be drawn out. Often the work seems overwhelming. There appears to be no end in sight. If you speak with people who have witnessed great destruction they will tell you that the damage is so great you sometimes don't even know where to start. After Hurricane Andrew struck south Florida, people were wandering around in a daze, unable to take care of (or unaware of) their injuries. People were without homes. They spent their day scavenging for food. They spent their evening sleeping in piles of rubble.

When this level of loss is experienced, work and the restoration phase are secondary. You may find that members of your emergency management team, restoration contractors, and employees have experienced great personal loss as a result of the emergency. They may not be able to focus on the large restoration task at hand. They may be easily distracted or they may be concerned with the welfare of their families. For this reason, be very selective about who you choose to monitor your restoration progress. You'll need to have a leader on board who can remove himself or herself from the emotional trauma of the event. This person may be an employee from a non-affected area or it may be an outside contractor. Regardless, make sure the person is emotionally able to handle the task.

Like any large project, the restoration phase must be kept on track as much as possible. If not managed, tasks will be overlooked and valuable time lost without significant progress being made. This is especially critical in cases in which business continuity is at stake. If your organization is unable to conduct business, and for every day it is unable to do so, the company loses $250,000, the impact is significant. After the emergency, building assessments must be performed. Based on your findings, you may decide to bring in an architect or structural engineer. At some point a scope of work should be decided upon and timelines should be developed. A project manager is critical if the required restoration is substantial. In fact, you may elect to bring in a project manager who specializes in recovery from disaster events. They have unique experiences dealing with restoration projects, and they can be instrumental in locating federal assistance that may be available to your organization.

Because of the stress of the restoration phase, people don't always act in ways that are normal. The slightest problem could blow up to be a major event. Disagreements will occur on any jobsite and usually the problems are worked out without a major conflict. But think for a moment about the restoration phase. A major disaster has just occurred. People are stressed. They haven't eaten or slept properly in days, perhaps weeks. They are working long hours, sometimes twenty hours a day, for seven days each week. They have been displaced and they haven't seen their families for weeks. Would you be a little edgy? Could you, in a moment of weakness, snap at somebody if you felt they weren't working as hard as you? We're all human and we should be aware of the negative emotional effects following a major disaster.

Safety is another concern after an emergency event. Many people have been unnecessarily injured or even killed during the restoration phase because of a lack of safety measures. In our zeal to get back to a sense of normalcy, we take shortcuts and practice unsafe work habits. Our property may not be structurally sound, but we enter it. Floodwater may create a breeding ground for mold and other indoor air quality issues, but we breathe the air without a respirator. Employees are eager to help out, but are not properly trained or clothed. Broken glass is strewn about the floor, yet we walk on it without proper work shoes. Do not minimize the risk associated with the recovery efforts. Insist that all workers—employees or contractors—don the required safety gear. Make sure that all workers are properly hydrated, fed, and protected from the elements. Conduct regular safety reminder meetings and stop those workers who might be working in an unsafe manner. It would be sad if an employee survived the emergency (over which they had no control) yet lost his or her life during the recovery stage (when he or she did have control over the situation).

Since we mentioned the negative aspects of emergency restoration, we should also give equal time to the positives, and there are many. The human spirit can accomplish wonderful things. When morale seems to be at its lowest, when the day is darkest, heroes are born. Normal everyday people stand up and do miraculous things. Take for example the World Trade Center attacks on September 11, 2001. Nearly 3,000 people lost their lives, shocking not just the country but the entire world. Immediately, trained rescue personnel from around the world flew in to join the search for victims. Eventually, search and rescue became search and recovery. The task of removing the rubble seemed impossible. Experts estimated the job would take over a year to complete. In just eight and one-half months, nearly 2 million tons of debris were moved to a Staten Island landfill. More than 3 million hours of labor were spent to conduct the clean-up of the World Trade Center site. The world watched with great interest as the community rose up and made unprecedented progress. The city could have thrown up its arms in despair. City leaders could have argued about the best way to perform the recovery. The world was watching, and what they witnessed was beyond belief. The compassion, industriousness, ingenuity, and resolve displayed by those working in the recovery phase will never be forgotten. Did the terrorists win? No.

Keeping the Lines of Communication Open

The flow of factual and comforting information is very important, especially following an emergency event. People are confused, even scared. Rumors run rampant. The emergency planner will play an important role in disseminating reliable information. Whether you are communicating with employees, the media, shareholders, or other interested stakeholders concise and truthful information must be shared.

A number of forums for communications exist:

- Radio or television advertising
- Written press releases
- Press conferences
- Interviews
- Site tours
- Telephone hotlines
- Corporate memos
- Web site updates
- Panel discussions
- Community meetings

These forums should be selected based on the severity of the emergency, the purpose, and the target audience.

Communication with the Media

The media will seek statements from your organization. Concerning the media, the worst action you could take is inaction. If you fail to return calls or respond to questions, you run the risk of the media consorting with other sources such as competitors, employees, or neighbors. These sources may be biased or uninformed, and false information could be delivered. So rule number one is: Don't avoid the media. Rule number two is: Don't say more than you should. No matter how articulate you might be, no matter how comfortable you might be in front of an audience, you absolutely must plan and practice the press conference. Practice in front of a "friendly" audience first. An audience of trusted employees in your organization would think of all the hard questions that could possibly be asked. Discuss what should and should not be said. Draft out responses to the questions you know will be asked. For instance, you can count on the following questions being asked:

- What happened?
- When did it happen?
- Were there any injuries?
- How many?
- Were there any deaths?
- How many?
- Why did the accident happen?
- Will neighboring areas be affected?
- When will the situation be back to normal?
- What assurances can you give us that this will not happen again?

It is important to remember that reporters have a job to do. Their timing might not be the best. They may come across as pushy or trouble-makers. You can turn a negative press conference into a positive event. Instead of viewing the conference as intrusive and a waste of time, think of it in terms of free advertising. You can advertise your organization in a positive light, one that is proactive and concerned with the safety of its employees and the community. Imagine if your organization purchased a thirty-second advertisement on radio or television. It would be expensive, no doubt about it. During a crisis, you can take advantage of the free advertising afforded to you because of the news coverage, but make sure it is good advertising! Following an emergency, many organizations were recognized and awarded for their resolve in the face of adverse conditions. They took advantage of media available to them, and so can you.

Will you allow the media onsite? That depends on the safety of the site and your personal comfort level. Realize, though, that keeping reporters off the site for reasons other than safety will raise a red flag. If you label the site unsafe, you'll likely be met with doubters. It may be advantageous to have a fire safety spokesperson or an engineer available to back up your claim. If the site is truly unsafe, make sure the affected areas are taped off and warning signage is visible. You may also elect to supply photographs or videos of the inaccessible areas. Samples of the damage will also provide the nontechnical reporter with a clear understanding of the problems and the efforts to repair the facility. If you elect to bring the media to your site, arrange for a media briefing area. Do not allow media representatives to walk unescorted through your site.

Because an extended emergency event may require multiple communications with the media, you must keep detailed records of information released. When communicating verbally with the news media, also provide them with a written press release when possible. In the spirit of speaking to your target audience, avoid the use of technical terminology. Use plain English. If you find it necessary to provide technical information, complement that information with a written press release that will be handed out at the press conference. To clarify technical points, consider using charts, graphs, pictures, and videos to get your point across.

Because of the delicate nature of corporate communications, a few words of warning are in order. First, do not ever speculate about the incident or its causes. If you don't know the answer to a question, promise to keep the media informed as more information becomes available. Do not attempt to place blame or cover up facts. You must develop a clear chain of command regarding corporate communications. This can be accomplished by limiting the individuals with responsibility as company spokesperson. Typically one person is assigned spokesperson duties and one or two others are assigned as alternates. Finally, remind employees to direct all questions from the public to the company media relations department. If such a department does not exist, create one on a temporary basis to accommodate the emergency event.

It is crucial that the company speaks with a common voice so that all media inquiries are responded to in the same way. That is why all media inquiries and responses to them should be entered into the command center log. It is not uncommon when covering a major disaster for more than one journalist from a news organization to contact the company affected. If two company spokespersons respond with two opposing answers the ensuing news story is unlikely to be favorable. Analysis of the media questions might also indicate the angle the journalists are pursuing and allow you to take preemptive action. For instance you may get a number of different media questions asking why your chemical plant had not taken more safety precautions prior to the incident. This should send up a red flag that perhaps someone outside had already spoken to the press and suggested the event might not have happened had you been more diligent. Forewarned you can then include in your press statements that the safety of the plant, its workers, and the local community had always been of paramount importance and that everything that could have been done had been done.

As part of your emergency planning you should devote a section of your plan to communications and develop a series of media holding statements covering many scenarios that could be issued almost immediately to keep the press informed until a more definitive press release can be issued.

Communication with Employees

Fear, anxiety, and, in some organizations, distrust are natural byproducts of an emergency event that requires extended recovery. Employers have a responsibility to communicate with employees when emergency-related events occur. Employees want to know when it is safe to return to work. They may need additional assistance if they were directly affected by the event. In the event of an accident, employees want to know what has been done to ensure that the accident is not repeated. Quick and helpful information is an effective way for organizations to show that management cares for the well-being of the employees. Consider setting up a telephone hot line, a special information page on your company's Web site or texting breaking news to employees.

After an emergency event, communication should not be limited to verbal announcements. Written communication should also be provided to the employees. Although not actually a press release, the formal communication is an invaluable tool for the employee/employer relationship. Without communication, employees will turn to rumors and innuendo. Issues such as work locations, return-to-work dates, and compensation during restoration should be addressed. Reminders on how to handle media inquiries and rumors should also be covered. Keep the communication positive and always thank the employees for their dedication.

Communication with Families

When emergency events occur and the ramifications are protracted, the families of employees can be affected. Anxiety and fear can paralyze those who do not know the condition or whereabouts of their family members. If the emergency event causes extended financial hardship on the organization, employees and their families may be concerned about job security. A delay in delivery of a paycheck could prove disastrous for many families. If layoffs are necessary, employees and their families will be interested in severance packages, health insurance continuation, and job placement assistance. These concerns must be addressed as soon as possible.

Communication with Insurance Providers

Although insurance providers will send a claims agent to review damages to your property, you may consider a proactive approach to communication to be wise. This is especially important when an emergency is regional in nature and the insurance provider is overburdened with claims. A formal communication describing the event and how you were affected is suggested. The correspondence should describe the damage incurred and identify the employer's contact information.

Communication with Government Agencies

An often overlooked target audience is government agencies. These agencies might include FEMA, Red Cross, police, National Guard, FBI, fire rescue, and even OSHA. Formal written communication may be recommended based on the nature and impact of the emergency event. For instance, an on-site oil spill would warrant formal communication with the Environmental Protection Agency. They will be interested in what happened, when it occurred, what is being done to address the spill, and what measures are being taken to ensure the incident is not repeated. In scenarios such as this, it is better (and often required) to contact them before they contact you.

Communication with Customers and Stakeholders

Contact with customers is often overlooked after an emergency event. If the emergency event is great and critical operations are impacted, customers and other stakeholders, such as shareholders, may be impacted as well. They will have concerns about your ability to provide services or products in a timely fashion. They may also be concerned with your organization's ability to pay for services rendered. Remember too, your customer may also be the shareholders in a corporation. They have some very real concerns about their investment that should be addressed. Because of these legitimate concerns, you must be proactive in communicating with them in a formal manner.

Sample Press Releases

The first example is a typical press release format. Simply fill in the appropriate information for the particular event.

For Immediate Release

From: [Your company name]
Address: [Your address here]
Date: [Today's date here]

Contact: [Name and phone number of company representative]

[Sample text]
On September 22, at approximately 2:30 a.m., a Category 3 hurricane swept across the southern Louisiana area including New Orleans.

Allied Industries has three properties in the affected areas, two of which were damaged. The affected properties are located at 123 South Street and 87 Canal Street.

The extent of the damage appears to be minimal. The properties are currently being assessed and further information will be made available as it arrives.

Restoration of the affected buildings will commence immediately after the assessments are completed.

There were no injuries and all employees have been accounted for.

END OF RELEASE

This next example is an internal memo from the president of a corporation. The target audience in this scenario is the company's employees; therefore, it warrants a different style. New information and reminders of company policy are addressed in this example.

Dear Fellow Employee,

Our business was built on hard work and dedication from our employees. That need for hard work and dedication has never been as evident as it is today. Your efforts are greatly appreciated and I have no doubt we will persevere. We are faced with an excellent opportunity to show our resolve and character, and I invite you to show your best.

When faced with unusual events such as what we have just experienced, a few reminders are in order. We will keep our employees updated via e-mail, the company Web site and texts. For those unable to access these mediums, we have established an emergency hotline (800-XXX-XXXX) with recorded updates and frequently asked questions. We realize that rumors and innuendo will abound but please do not help spread them. We will strive to keep you up to date and all official communication will be provided through the methods listed above.

For many of our employees, the media will be observing your work. Again, you have an opportunity to present the company in a positive way. Unfortunately, some media representatives may attempt to sensationalize disasters and how they are dealt with. If asked about your restoration efforts, you may briefly explain what you are doing, stressing the fact that your efforts are part of a larger restoration effort by all of the employees of the company.

We ask that you refer all questions involving detailed aspects of your work to our corporate communication department at (800-XXX-XXXX). Finally, if you don't know an answer to a reporter's question, don't speculate. It's okay to say, "I don't know." If you find yourself in an uncomfortable situation, thank the reporters for their time, and kindly remind them that you need to get back to work and that they need to talk to the company's press spokesperson.

I am very proud of the efforts of all our employees and I know that we can all count on each other to make a complete recovery a reality. Remember, we have an opportunity to make a difference and your efforts are greatly appreciated.

President, Acme Industries

15

Guidelines for Emergency Mitigation

Design Guidelines

As security and emergency concerns grow in importance, commercial real estate must adjust accordingly. What worked fifty years ago won't work today. For that matter, what worked ten or even five years ago may now be obsolete. The bad news is some emergency events will never be eliminated. The good news is that the negative effects of just about every emergency can be reduced. The reduction of these events or effects starts with proper planning. Most of this book discusses planning from a what-do-we-do-if-"X"-event-occurs frame of reference but planning in the design phase is an equally important mitigation factor. Proper design of the building structure and surrounding site is critical, especially in those buildings that are open to the public.

Before you can work on proper design, however, you need to know what you are protecting. Critical assets can generally be divided into the following groups:

- People
- Operations
- Information
- Interdependencies

People

What is the building use and mix? For example, a multistory building might consist of an underground car park, shops on the first floor, offices on the next few floors and apartments on the top floors. How do people access the building? How many people are employed and what do they do? How many visitors are there on a daily basis? Are staff background checks carried out? Do you have security staff, how are they trained, are security procedures updated and practiced at regular intervals? Has the staff bought into the need for the upgraded security?

Map what different people do, where they go inside the building and how they get there. This will identify main traffic flows and how close they get to sensitive areas and critical assets. Do measures need to be introduced to redirect this traffic flow or do the sensitive areas need greater protection? Are certain parts of the building off-limits to some people and, if so, how is access controlled and monitored? Are there different layers of security within the facility and, if so, how is the interface between the different levels (door, turnstile, etc.) controlled?

You must understand the traffic flow to, within, and around your facility. This flow includes both people and vehicles. How many people and vehicles access your site and where do they gain access? Who uses the site and how can they be categorized—staff, visitors, delivery people, contractors, and so on.

Do you provide parking facilities? Can vehicles park on the street outside close to the building? You need to have to have this information in order to work out flow charts. This will show you which access points and doors are most used, any critical areas that are close to vehicle or people traffic and so on.

Operations

This covers all operations within the facility including security and safety—the day-to-day running of the building, shifts and shift changes, operating and operational procedures, equipment, maintenance, parking, deliveries, and so on.

Information

Information covers internal matters such as in-house communications, protecting networks and sensitive documents, making sure that security staff and employees know what is happening, keeping documents and plans up-to-date. External issues include communications with all outside stakeholders (police, fire, local officials, etc.), defending against cyberattack and ensuring that the appropriate authorities have access to documents and plans of your facility in the event of a major incident.

Interdependencies

You cannot secure your building in isolation. You have to take into account upstream and downstream—what happens to shipments and materials before they enter your facility and after they have left, and what is happening around you. You must consider your relationship with your neighbors and other facilities that might affect you if they are attacked, with first responders and with the wider community. While often overlooked, your insurance company is a key player and may be willing to assist with the implementation of a physical security plan if it reduces its liability in the event of an incident. You must identify and assess all the risks, threats, and vulnerabilities associated with each element, prioritize them and then decide on the best method of reducing or eliminating those threats. You must also take into account the often complex relationship between the various elements.

Identify Building Infrastructure

After the core functions and processes are identified, an evaluation of building infrastructure is the next step. To help identify and value rank infrastructure, the following should be considered, keeping in mind that the most vital asset for every building is its people:

- Identify how many people may be injured or killed during an incident that directly affects the infrastructure.
- Identify what happens to building functions, services, or occupant satisfaction if a specific asset is lost or degraded. (Can primary services continue?)
- Determine the impact on other organizational assets if the component is lost or cannot function.
- Determine if critical or sensitive information is stored or handled at the building.
- Determine if backups exist for the building's assets.
- Determine the availability of replacements.
- Determine the potential for injuries or deaths from any catastrophic event at the building's assets.
- Identify any critical building personnel whose loss would degrade, or seriously complicate the safety of building occupants during an emergency.
- Determine if the building's assets can be replaced and identify replacement costs if the building is lost.
- Identify critical components/assets.
- Identify security systems.
- Identify the locations of key equipment.
- Identify life safety systems and safe haven areas.
- Determine the locations of personnel work areas and systems.
- Identify the locations of any personnel operating "outside" a building's controlled areas.
- Determine, in detail, the physical locations of critical support architectures:
  - Communications and information technology (IT—the flow of critical information and data)
  - Utilities (facility power, water, air conditioning, etc.)
  - Lines of communication that provide access to external resources and provide movement of people (road, rail, air transportation, etc.)
  - Determine the location, availability, and readiness condition of emergency response assets and the state of training of building staff in their use.

Identifying Threats

Before you can take mitigating action, you must identify what threats you face and where these threats might come from. This means identifying all internal and external threats and hazards and understanding why they might attack you. If you are in a high-profile industry, you could be a target for terrorism; if you handle sensitive data, you could be the victim of a cyberattack; and if you sell jewelry or pharmaceuticals, you might be burgled. The threat could also come from inside—theft, violence, or sabotage by a disgruntled employee.

You need to know who the bad guys are. This is done in a number of ways. You conduct a design basis threat assessment and consult with your local police, FBI, and security consultants to create "what if" scenario-based assessments to cover every conceivable eventuality. While the tragic events of 9/11 showed how vulnerable we were to attack—from either foreign or domestic terrorist groups—you will need to protect your facility from many other threats, both internal and external. These include everything from internal pilfering and violence from a disgruntled employee to external threats such as theft, trespass, industrial espionage, natural disasters, and terrorism. When you have identified your various adversaries, you can determine the probability of attack and the degree of threat that each one poses. Recent information gathered by intelligence and law enforcement agencies has led government officials to believe that both foreign and domestic terrorist groups continue to pose threats to the security of our nation's infrastructure, including our public buildings.

Your facility may not be a likely target for a terrorist attack, but it may be in a high-profile area where any attack will attract widespread publicity—a major aim of terrorism. Or you may be a soft target: while your facility may not carry out a critical function, it may be an easier hit than the hard target up the road which has state-of-the-art security in place.

Information you need to define threats:

- Type of adversary and tactics
- Potential actions of adversary
- Motivations of adversary
- Capabilities of adversary

One way to identify threats and where they could come from is to conduct a Design Basis Threat analysis.

Design Basis Threat (DBT)

Design Basis Threat (DBT) was originally developed to protect the nation's nuclear industry but the principles can be applied to any facility that needs to implement a physical security plan. Whether you are building a new facility or retrofitting an existing one, DBT helps you identify all your likely adversaries, lists their strengths and capabilities, what their targets might be, the likelihood of them attacking you and if so, how. When you have answered these questions and identified all threats, you are better able to design and incorporate safeguards to protect your facility and its critical assets. Consult local law enforcement, the FBI, Department of Homeland Security, and other government agencies to help develop your DBT.

As an example, the nuclear industry is charged with doing design basis threat assessments to mitigate against threats equivalent to:

- The events of September 11, 2001
- A physical, cyber, biochemical, or other terrorist threat
- An attack on a facility by multiple coordinated teams of a large number of individuals
- An attack assisted by several persons employed at the facility
- A suicide attack
- A water-based or air-based threat
- The use of explosive devices of considerable size and other modern weaponry
- An attack by persons with a sophisticated knowledge of the operations of a sensitive nuclear facility operations
- Fire—especially a fire of long duration
- Any other threat that the Nuclear Regulatory Commission determines should be included as an element of the design basis threat

Your facility may not be as high-risk as a nuclear power plant, but the methodology used to identify adversaries, their motivations, their strengths, their capabilities, and how they might attack you are just as applicable to your facility.

It is important to note that assessment is not a one-time process. It is an ongoing process that must be kept under constant review. New or changed circumstances mean different scenarios will have to be analyzed and this may lead to changes or refinements in your planning.

Vulnerability Assessment

Having identified your critical assets and who might attack them, you now have to determine how vulnerable those assets are to attack. How effective is your existing security? Do you have any physical security in place? Conduct a security inventory based on an assessment checklist.

- What is your current security situation?
- Are you at risk from your neighbors?
- How secure is your location?
- What is your current perimeter security?
- How structurally safe is your facility?

⅄   Are your utilities protected?

⅄   What communications/IT protection do you have?

⅄   Is your equipment protected?

⅄   What external security protection do you have?

⅄   What internal security protection do you have?

Remember the basic principles of physical security: deter, detect, delay, and response (DDDR). Does your current physical security help achieve effective DDDR?

Note: There are many methodologies for conducting risk assessment and they may use different criteria. Seek advice to decide which methodology is best for you. For instance, some funding sources may require that a particular methodology is used or some methodologies may be more appropriate for your type of enterprise.

Risk Assessment

The risk assessment uses the threat, asset value, and vulnerability assessments to determine the level of risk for each critical asset against each applicable threat. This takes into account the likelihood of the threat occurring (probability) and the effects (consequences) of the occurrence if the critical asset is damaged or destroyed. The risk assessment provides security consultants, engineers, designers, and architects with a relative risk profile that defines which assets are at the greatest risk against specific threats. Any threat subjects an organization to risk. Therefore, when a threat is exhibited a risk rating needs to be applied to understand how to manage the risk. A threat management team should have processes and procedures in place for measuring the probability and the severity of loss, in light of a threat. The following primary risk types should be considered in determining risk exposure:

⅄   Mission or function risks

⅄   Asset risks

⅄   Security risks

You have to decide what risk each critical asset faces. Is there a low, medium, or high risk of that asset being attacked, damaged, or destroyed? This analysis gives you your threat rating and will determine your priorities when it comes to mitigation.

Because it is not possible to completely eliminate risk, and every project has resource limitations, you must analyze how mitigation measures would affect risk and decide on the best and most cost-effective measures to achieve the desired level of protection (risk management).

When considering your options remember that the goal is to put in place procedures and systems that protect your critical assets and eliminate weak spots and vulnerabilities.

Building and Site Mitigation

Long before any emergency affects you, you can take steps to mitigate the effects. The following section discusses many of the measures that can be taken. These measures should also be taken into account if you have to repair or rebuild your building damaged during an emergency.

When discussing building and site mitigation, it makes sense to separate the space into six distinct areas, working from the inside outward:

- Interior—Limited access
- Interior—Public access
- Point of Entry
- Exterior—Building perimeter
- Exterior—Parking and other off-site areas
- Exterior—Neighbors

Interior—Limited Access

The interior limited access areas include spaces such as storage rooms, telecommunications areas, computer server rooms, and mechanical rooms. Because of the threat from suspicious packages, mail rooms should also be considered limited access areas. A building can have several different layers of restricted access depending on its function and each would need separate access controls.

These areas are off limits to most people, including visitors and employees. Access can be controlled through the use of keys, proximity cards, mag-lock, card swipe system, or any other feasible manner. Start by performing an analysis of your building's space and determine what spaces need to be off limits due to security and safety concerns.

Interior—Public Access

In most buildings, especially those that offer public access, the amount of limited access interior space will be minimal. Even if this is true in your building, care must be taken to secure areas open to the public. For instance, can visitors to the building gain access to the roof? Are they able to access HVAC systems including intakes and discharges? Could a visitor with bad intentions force his or her way into limited access areas? By performing an assessment of your building's public spaces, you'll be able to identify areas of concern.

You must know who uses the building and when, how they access and exit it, where they go when they are inside, and whether their movement is controlled. You must also know what procedures are in place to screen staff and to train them in the event of an emergency.

Point of Entry

Spending large amounts of money and time securing the inside of a building without addressing points of entry could be akin to changing the oil in an automobile after the engine has blown. It might be too little too late. What will you do to ensure that bad people and their tools of destruction don't gain access into your building in the first place? The obvious starting point is to have some way to police the entrances. This can be accomplished by employing security guards, card access, employee escorts, or a number of different solutions. For after business hours, an intrusion detection system should be installed. However, the danger lies in assessing your building's point of entry security from a doorway access point of view only. Think about other less obvious points of entry such as windows, loading docks, fresh air intakes, and other such penetrations. Have you identified and protected all utility inlets? Prepare a map showing all the different utilities used—water, gas, electricity, telecoms, and so on—how they come on to the property, their pipelines or cables while on property, and where they exit the property. It should show all manholes, inspection points, and sewer lines, and so on. It should also show where water is stored on property, the source of water for the fire suppression system, the location of all electric service points, and additional storage sites for other fuels.

Exterior—Building Perimeter

The immediate exterior building perimeter can also be an area of weakness. Perimeter protection is extremely important for urban buildings because in most cases the facility perimeter is defined by the external walls of the building. There is no buffer zone with wires, fences, and controlled access points to keep terrorists and others a safe distance away from your building.

Walk around your perimeter to ensure the immediate surroundings are secure. Planters, overhangs, and other building features could be the perfect place to hide an explosive device. When performing a security assessment take these areas into consideration. Is the immediate perimeter lighting adequate? Can visitors with bad intentions gain access to or sabotage utilities or the emergency generator? Could a toxic substance be introduced into your building via a fresh air intake? Does the perimeter landscaping create a possible hiding place for criminals or explosives?

Exterior—Parking and Other Off-site Areas

A person with bad intentions may not even need access inside of your building to do damage. In the case of the Alfred P. Murrah Federal Building in Oklahoma City, the terrorist was able to bring down most of the building and kill 168 people without ever entering the facility. By parking a van full of explosives near the building and detonating them from a distance, incredible damage was inflicted. Studies have been performed that suggest standoff distances of 100 feet or more will lessen the impact of a bomb. Since the

Oklahoma City bombing, we realize the importance of not allowing unattended vehicles to park in front of buildings.

Keeping this 100-foot standoff distance in mind, can you keep distance between your parking lot and the building? If you do, you may wish to make special arrangements for those with disabilities because the distance may create hardships. Parking garages create a dilemma. Since they are a building structure that could fail, an explosion could create tremendous damage. Consider limiting access to your parking garages and installing closed-circuit television to monitor movement. If you employ underground parking, it may be wise to limit it to registered vehicles, motorcycles, and perhaps small cars. Better yet, it may be prudent to eliminate that parking area altogether if feasible.

Place parking as far as practical from the building. Off-site parking is recommended for high-risk facilities vulnerable to terrorist attack. If onsite surface parking or underground parking is provided, take precautions such as limiting access to these areas only to the building occupants or having all vehicles inspected in areas near the building. If an underground area is used for a high-risk building, the garage should be placed adjacent to the building under a plaza area rather than directly underneath the building. To the extent practical, limit the size of vehicles able to enter the garage by imposing physical barriers on vehicle height.

Access control refers to points of controlled access to the facility through the perimeter line. The controlled access check or inspection points for vehicles require architectural features or barriers to maintain the defensible perimeter. Architects and engineers can accommodate these security functions by providing adequate design for these areas, which make it difficult for a vehicle to crash onto the site. Remember that you might have to implement different security layers at different points around or close to the perimeter and these will have to be planned into your physical protection system. Deterrence and delay are major attributes of the perimeter security design that should be consistent with the landscaping objectives, such as emphasizing the open nature characterizing high-population buildings. Because it is impossible to thwart all possible threats, the objective is to make it difficult to successfully execute the easiest attack scenarios, such as a car bomb detonated along the curb or a vehicle jumping the curb and crashing into the building prior to detonation.

Site design considerations for bomb resistance might include:

- Bollards or planters
- Elevation of building level
- Curbs
- Security lighting, sensors, and cameras
- Gates
- Limiting the number of access points
- Discuss with utility companies and local authorities about padlocking manholes.

The purpose of protective bollards, planters, or even large pieces of exterior artwork is to keep a vehicle from gaining close access to a building and detonating explosives. Although bollards and retaining walls are effective, they can be aesthetically unattractive if not designed properly. The use of natural barriers such as tress with thick trunks can prove to be an efficient barrier that is aesthetically pleasing as well.

When reviewing your building and the desired level of security, always remember ascetics and the role it plays in employee satisfaction and desirability of public interaction. You could build an intimidating fortress without windows which affords a great measure of security but is that really desirable? Would employees enjoy working there? Might their productivity be reduced in such an environment? Would the public be too intimidated to visit and do business there? On the other hand, you could design a high-tech, functionally proper, aesthetically pleasing masterpiece. But at what cost? Anything can be accomplished if the price is right, and when it comes to a totally secure and safe structure, the price will likely be too high. The trick is to find an acceptable balance of risk and cost. Performing a risk analysis would be a prudent starting point.

Consulting with a design specialist who understands security and safety would also make sense. The science of designing viable buildings that are safe and secure is known as "crime prevention through environmental design" (CPTED). Designers and consultants specializing in CPTED bring an added dimension to your building design. Their intimate knowledge of security and safety is integrated with an architecturally attractive and functional building. These consultants will identify opportunities based on your need and budget and typically are well worth the price.

To learn more about the science of CPTED, contact Atlas Safety & Security Design, Inc.

The Atlas Web site features some very interesting information on CPTED and how it can be integrated into both remodels and new buildings alike.

Atlas Safety & Security Design, Inc.
333 Las Olas Way #1605
Fort Lauderdale, FL 33301
www.cpted-security.com

Exterior—Neighbors

Review all the facilities in your neighborhood to see which, if any, pose a threat to you. Are there high-risk targets that might be attacked and, if so, what would the impact be on your facility and your ability to continue operating? Is there a distribution depot in the next street that houses toxic chemicals?

Are there roads or rail tracks running near the building? Could people in parked vehicles use electronic devices to eavesdrop on what is going on or use weapons to fire at us or launch a grenade attack? Use fences or walls to screen the building from these vantage points. Is the road or railroad used to transport hazardous or nuclear materials? What would happen if a tanker crashed on the road close to your facility or a train derailed and exploded?

Structures

Windows and Doors: The Weakest Link

The windows and doors of a building often present the path of least resistance during an emergency. Whether the event is terror related or weather related, windows in particular are usually the weakest link. Next to total building collapse, more people are injured from flying glass during an explosion in a building. In fact, most people who are injured by flying glass are within fifteen feet of the windows when the blast occurred. An example of this phenomenon is seen in the coordinated terrorist bombings of U.S. embassies in Nairobi, Kenya, and Dar es Salaam, Tanzania, on August 7, 1998. In the more lethal Nairobi attack, the first explosions were produced by grenades detonated outside of the embassy. The grenades did very little damage but startled the occupants of the embassy. As the occupants of the building began to walk toward the windows to investigate the loud noise, a much larger bomb planted in an automobile was detonated. The tremendous explosion shattered glass and turned the shards into razor sharp missiles, killing 224 people and wounding more than 4,000.

When examining the problems with windows, glass is just one of the issues. Many windows are not installed in a way that offers true blast protection. Often during an explosion or storm, the entire window becomes dislodged from its wall opening. A number of safety features are available that can mitigate the damage caused by windows and glass. In some areas, such as south Florida, window shutters are now required to protect people and buildings from the effects of storms. Protective window film applied over existing windows can also provide some protection from pressure experienced during a storm or explosion. The protection, however, is limited. The real purpose of window film is to keep glass from shattering and dangerous shards from becoming airborne. Protective film does resist impact. The glass will break; it just won't disperse as readily as it would if unprotected. If you are looking for protection from shards and impact resistance, then ballistic-grade glass would be an option worth exploring. The cost may be high, but the protection provided, especially in a high-risk building, may well be worth the investment.

When installing blast-resistant glass, it is important to understand construction methods for installing the windows. If installed improperly, the window may absorb an impact and the glass would remain unbroken, but the entire window frame would become dislodged from its opening. Installation of blast-resistant glass should include extra reinforcing around the window opening. Consult with the manufacturer and structural engineers when installing blast-resistant glass.

The Pentagon

The Pentagon is a good example of a properly con-structed, high-risk building. Because of the high profile of the Pentagon, the windows need to be blast resistant. Each window unit weighs about 1,600 pounds and the glass is 1.5 inches thick. The windows are bolted to mas-sive structural tubes that run the entire height of the building. At the bottom of each window, extra reinforce-ment is provided by a steel plate that is attached to the window and the steel tubes. This would likely be consid-ered overkill for most buildings; however, the Pentagon serves as a model for proper blast-resistant construction. The window components including the glass, window frame, and its installation are constructed in a manner that ensures proper blast resistance.

Permanent storm shutters offer the best protection from the high winds of a hurricane. If you live in an area that is susceptible to hurricanes, the investment in storm shutters is a good one. If you do not have permanent storm shut-ters, the next best option is to construct window coverings using 5/8-inch marine-grade plywood. Pre-drill holes every eighteen inches for screws and pre-install wall anchors. Don't forget to mark each piece of plywood so you'll know where it belongs on the building.

The General Services Administra-tion (GSA) is the agency that pro-vides and manages real estate for the federal government. Because of the likelihood of a federal building becoming a target for a terrorist, the GSA has created specific stan-dards for glazing installed in federal buildings. Level 1 is the highest category and specifies that "glaz-ing does not break." This would necessitate the installation of bal-listic glass. The lowest protection category is Level 5 and is defined as "windows fail catastrophically." When considering the purchase of blast-resistant windows or pro-tective film, speak to the window manufacturer about its ability to meet GSA level specifications.

Doors, louvers, and other openings in the exterior envelope should be designed so that the anchorage into the supporting structure has a lateral capacity greater than that of the element. There are two general recommendations for doors:

▲ Doors should open outward so that they bear against the jamb during the positive-pressure phase of the air-blast loading.
▲ Door jambs can be filled with concrete to improve their resistance.

For louvers that provide air to sensitive equipment, some recommendations are:

▲ Provide a baffle in front of the louver so that the air blast does not have direct line-of-sight access through the louver.
▲ Provide a grid of steel bars properly anchored into the structure behind the louver to catch any debris generated by the louver or other flying fragments.

Exterior Frame

There are two primary considerations for the exterior frame. The first is to design the exterior columns to resist the direct effects of the specified threats. The second is to ensure that the exterior frame has sufficient structural integrity to accept localized failure without initiating progressive collapse. Because columns do not have much surface area, air-blast loads on columns tend to be mitigated by "clear-time effects." This refers to the pressure wave washing around these slender tall members, and consequently the entire duration of the pressure wave does not act upon them. On the other hand, the critical threat is directly across from them, so they are loaded with the peak reflected pressure, which is typically several times larger than the incident or overpressure wave that is propagating through the air.

For columns subjected to a vehicle weapon threat on an adjacent street, buckling and shear are the primary effects to be considered in analysis. If a very large weapon is detonated close to a column, shattering of the concrete due to multiple tensile reflections within the concrete section can destroy its integrity. Buckling is a concern if lateral support is lost due to the failure of a supporting floor system. This is particularly important for buildings that are close to public streets. In this case, exterior columns should be capable of spanning two or more stories without buckling. Slender steel columns are at substantially greater risk than are concrete columns. Confinement of concrete using columns with closely spaced closed ties or spiral reinforcing will improve shear capacity, improve the performance of lap splices in the event of loss of concrete cover and greatly enhance column ductility. The potential benefit from providing closely spaced closed ties in exterior concrete columns is very high relative to the cost of the added reinforcement.

For steel columns, splices should be placed as far above grade level as practical. It is recommended that splices at exterior columns that are not specifically designed to resist air-blast loads employ complete penetration welded flanges. Welding details, materials, and procedures should be selected to ensure toughness.

For a package weapon, column breach is a major consideration. Some suggestions for mitigating this concern:

- Do not use exposed columns that are fully or partially accessible from the building exterior. Arcade columns should be avoided.
- Use an architectural covering that is at least six inches from the structural member. This will make it considerably more difficult to place a weapon directly against the structure. Because explosive pressures decay so rapidly, every inch of distance will help to protect the column.

Load-bearing reinforced concrete wall construction can provide a considerable level of protection if adequate reinforcement is provided to achieve ductile behavior. This may be an appropriate solution for the parts of the building that are closest to the secured perimeter line (within twenty feet). Masonry is a much more brittle material that is capable of generating highly hazardous flying debris in the event of an explosion. Its use is generally discouraged for new construction. Spandrel beams of limited depth generally do well when subjected to air blast. In general, edge beams are very strongly encouraged at the perimeter of concrete slab construction to afford frame action for redistribution of vertical loads and to enhance the shear connection of floors to columns.

Roof System

The primary loading on the roof is the downward air-blast pressure. The exterior bay roof system on the side(s) facing an exterior threat is the most critical. The air-blast pressure on the interior bays is less intense, so the roof there may require less hardening. Secondary loads include upward pressure due to the air blast penetrating through openings and upward suction during the negative loading phase. The upward pressure may have an increased duration due to multiple reflections of the internal air-blast wave. It is important to consider the downward and upward loads separately.

The preferred system is cast-in-place reinforced concrete with beams in two directions. If this system is used, beams should have continuous top and bottom reinforcement with tension lap splices. Stirrups to develop the bending capacity of the beams closely spaced along the entire span are recommended. Somewhat lower levels of protection are afforded by conventional steel beam construction with a steel deck and concrete fill slab. The performance of this system can be enhanced by use of normal-weight concrete fill instead of lightweight fill, increasing the gauge of welded wire fabric reinforcement and making the connection between the slab and beams with shear connector studs. Because it is anticipated that the slab capacity will exceed that of the supporting beams, beam end connections should be capable of developing the ultimate flexural capacity of the beams to avoid brittle failure. Beam-to-column connections should be capable of resisting upward as well as downward forces.

Precast and pre-/post-tensioned systems are generally considered less desirable, unless members and connections are capable of resisting upward forces generated by rebound from the direct pressure or the suction from the negative pressure phase of the air blast.

Concrete flat slab/plate systems are also less desirable because of the potential of shear failure at the columns. When flat slab/plate systems are used, they should include features to enhance their punching shear resistance. Continuous bottom reinforcement should be provided through columns in two directions to retain the slab in the event that punching shear failure occurs. Edge beams should be provided at the building exterior.

Lightweight systems, such as untopped steel deck or wood frame construction, are considered to afford minimal resistance to air-blast. These systems are prone to failure due to their low capacity for downward and uplift pressures.

Floor System

The floor system design should consider three possible scenarios: air-blast loading, redistributing load in the event of loss of a column or wall support below, and the ability to arrest debris falling from the floor or roof above.

For structures in which the interior is secured against bombs of moderate size by package inspection, the primary concern is the exterior bay framing. For buildings that are separated from a public street only by a sidewalk, the uplift pressures from a vehicle weapon may be significant enough to cause possible failure of the exterior bay floors for several levels above ground. Special concern exists in the case of vertical irregularities in the architectural system, either where the exterior wall is set back from the floor above or where the structure steps back to form terraces.

Structural hardening of floor systems above unsecured areas of the building such as lobbies, loading docks, garages, mailrooms, and retail spaces should be considered. In general, critical or heavily occupied areas should not be placed underneath unsecured areas, because it is virtually impossible to prevent against localized breach in conventional construction for package weapons placed on the floor. Precast panels are problematic because of their tendency to fail at the connections. Pre-/post-tensioned systems tend to fail in a brittle manner if stressed much beyond their elastic limit. These systems are also not able to accept upward loads without additional reinforcement. If pre-/post-tensioned systems are used, continuous mild steel needs to be added to the top and the bottom faces to provide the ductility needed to resist explosion loads.

Flat slab/plate systems are also less desirable because of limited two-way action and the potential for shear failure at the columns. When flat slab/plate systems are employed, they should include features to enhance their punching shear resistance, and continuous bottom reinforcement should be provided across columns to resist progressive collapse. Edge beams should be provided at the building exterior.

Interior Columns

Interior columns in unsecured areas are subject to many of the same issues as exterior columns. If possible, columns should not be accessible within these areas. If they are accessible, then obscure their location or impose a stand-off to the structural component through the use of cladding. Methods of hardening columns include using closely spaced ties, spiral reinforcement and architectural covering at least six inches from the structural elements. Composite steel and concrete sections or steel plating of concrete columns can provide higher levels of protection. Columns in unsecured areas should be designed to span two or three stories without buckling in the event that the floors below and possibly above the detonation area have failed, as previously discussed.

Interior Walls

Interior walls surrounding unsecured spaces are designed to contain the explosive effects within the unsecured areas. Ideally, unsecured areas are located adjacent to the building exterior so that the explosive pressure may be vented outward as well.

Fully grouted concrete masonry unit (CMU) block walls that are well-reinforced vertically and horizontally and adequately supported laterally are a common solution. Anchorage at the top and bottom of walls should be capable of developing the full flexural capacity of the wall.

Lateral support at the top of the walls may be achieved using steel angles anchored into the floor system above. Care should be taken to terminate bars at the top of the wall with hooks or heads and to ensure that the upper course of block is filled solid with grout. The base of the wall may be anchored by reinforcing bar dowels.

Interior walls can also be effective in resisting progressive collapse if they are designed properly with sufficient load-bearing capacity and are tied into the floor systems below and above.

This design for hardened interior wall construction is also recommended for primary exit routes to protect against explosions, fire and other hazards trapping occupants.

Structural

Consider these points:

- Incorporate measures to prevent progressive collapse.
- Design floor systems for uplift in unsecured areas and in exterior bays that may pose a hazard to occupants.
- Limit column spacing.
- Avoid transfer girders.
- Use two-way floor and roof systems.
- Use fully grouted, heavily reinforced CMU block walls that are properly anchored to separate unsecured areas from critical functions and occupied secured areas.
- Use dynamic nonlinear analysis methods for design of critical structural components.

Exterior Wall/Cladding Design

The exterior walls provide the first line of defense against the intrusion of the air-blast pressure and hazardous debris into the building. They are subject to direct reflected pressures from an explosive threat located directly across from the wall along the secured perimeter line. If the building is more than four stories high, it may be advantageous to consider the reduction in pressure with height due to the increased distance and angle of incidence. The objective of design at a minimum is to ensure that these members fail in a ductile mode, such as flexure, rather than a brittle mode, such as shear. The walls also need to be able to resist the loads transmitted by the windows and doors. It is not uncommon, for instance, for bullet-resistant windows to have a higher ultimate capacity than the walls to which they are attached. Beyond ensuring a ductile failure mode, the exterior wall may be designed to resist the actual or reduced pressure levels of the defined threat. Note that special reinforcing and anchors should be provided around blast resistant window and door frames.

Poured-in-place, reinforced concrete will provide the highest level of protection, but solutions like pre-cast concrete, CMU block, and metal stud systems may also be used to achieve lower levels of protection.

For pre-cast panels, consider a minimum thickness of five inches exclusive of reveals, with two-way, closely spaced reinforcing bars to increase ductility and reduce the chance of flying concrete fragments. The objective is to reduce the loads transmitted into the connections, which need to be designed to resist the ultimate flexural resistance of the panels.

Also, connections into the structure should provide as straight a line of load transmittal as practical.

For CMU block walls, use eight-inch block walls, fully grouted with vertically centered heavy reinforcing bars and horizontal reinforcement placed at each layer. Connections into the structure should be designed to resist the ultimate lateral capacity of the wall. For infill walls, avoid transferring loads into the columns if they are primary load-carrying elements.

The connection details may be very difficult to construct. It will be difficult to have all the blocks fit over the bars near the top, and it will be difficult to provide the required lateral restraint at the top connection. A preferred system is to have a continuous exterior CMU wall that laterally bears against the floor system. For increased protection, consider using twelve-inch blocks with two layers of vertical reinforcement. For metal stud systems, use metal studs back-to-back and mechanically attached to minimize lateral torsional effects. To catch exterior cladding fragments, attach a wire mesh or steel sheet to the exterior side of the metal stud system. The supports of the wall should be designed to resist the ultimate lateral out-of-plane bending capacity load of the system. Brick veneers and other nonstructural elements attached to the building exterior are to be avoided or have strengthened connections to limit flying debris and to improve emergency egress by ensuring that exits remain passable.

Mechanical and Electrical Systems

The key concepts for providing secure and effective mechanical and electrical systems in buildings are the same as for the other building systems: separation, hardening, and redundancy. Keeping critical mechanical and electrical functions as far from high-threat areas as possible (lobbies, loading docks, mail rooms, garages, and retail spaces) increases their ability to survive an event. Separation is perhaps the most cost-effective option.

Additionally, physical hardening or protection of these systems (including the conduits, pipes and ducts associated with life-safety systems) provides increased likelihood that they will be able to survive the direct effects of the event if they are close enough to be affected. Finally, by providing redundant emergency systems that are adequately separated, there is a greater likelihood that emergency systems will remain operational after the event to assist rescuers in the evacuation of the building.

Architecturally, enhancements to mechanical and electrical systems will require additional space to accommodate additional equipment. Fortunately, there are many incremental improvements that can be made that require only a small change to the design. Additional space can be provided for future enhancements as funds or the risk justify implementation. Structurally, the walls and floor systems adjacent to the areas where critical equipment is located need to be protected by means of hardening. Other areas where hardening is recommended include primary egress routes, feeders for emergency power distribution, sprinkler systems mains and risers, fire alarm system trunk wiring, and ducts used for smoke-control systems.

Emergency Egress Routes

To facilitate evacuation consider these measures:

- Provide positive pressurization of stairwells and vestibules.
- Provide battery packs for lighting fixtures and exit signs.
- Harden walls using reinforced CMU block properly anchored at supports.
- Use nonslip phosphorescent treads.
- Do not cluster egress routes in single shaft. Separate them as far as possible.
- Use double doors for mass evacuation.
- Do not use glass along primary egress routes or stairwells.

Emergency Power System

An emergency generator provides an alternate source of power should utility power become unavailable to critical life-safety systems such as alarm systems, egress lighting fixtures, exit signs, emergency communications systems, smoke-control equipment and fire pumps.

Emergency generators typically require large louvers to allow for ventilation of the generator while running. Care should be taken to locate the generator so that these louvers are not vulnerable to attack. A remote radiator system could be used to reduce the louver size.

Redundant emergency generator systems remotely located from each other enable the supply of emergency power from either of two locations. Consider locating emergency power-distribution feeders in hardened enclosures, or encased in concrete, and configured in redundant routing paths to enhance reliability. Emergency distribution panels and automatic transfer switches should be located in rooms separate from the normal power system (hardened rooms, where possible).

Emergency lighting fixtures and exit signs along the egress path could be provided with integral battery packs, which locate the power source directly at the load, to provide lighting instantly in the event of a utility power outage.

Fuel Storage

A non-explosive fuel source, such as diesel fuel, is acceptable for standby use for emergency generators and diesel fire pumps. Fuel tanks should be located away from building access points, in fire-rated, hardened enclosures. Fuel piping within the building should be located in hardened enclosures, and redundant piping systems could be provided to enhance the reliability of the fuel distribution system. Fuel filling stations should be located away from public access points and monitored by the CCTV system.

Transformers

Main power transformer(s) should be located in the interior of the building if possible, away from locations accessible to the public. For larger buildings, multiple transformers, located remotely from each other, could enhance reliability should one transformer be damaged by an explosion.

Ventilation Systems

Air-intake locations should be located as high up in the building as is practical to limit access to the general public. Systems that serve public access areas, such as mail receiving rooms, loading docks, lobbies and elevators, should be isolated and provided with dedicated air handling systems capable of 100 percent exhaust mode. Tie air intake locations and fan rooms into the security surveillance and alarm system.

Building HVAC systems are typically controlled by a building automation system, which allows for quick response to shut down or selectively control air conditioning systems. This system is coordinated with the smoke-control and fire-alarm systems.

Fire Control Center

A Fire Control Center should be provided to monitor alarms and life safety components, operate smoke-control systems, communicate with occupants and control the fire-fighting/evacuation process. Consider providing redundant Fire Control Centers remotely located from each other to allow system operation and control from alternate locations. The Fire Control Center should be located near the point of firefighter access to the building. If the control center is adjacent to the lobby, separate it from the lobby using a corridor or other buffer area. Provide hardened construction for the Fire Control Center.

Emergency Elevators

Elevators are not used as a means of egress from a building in the event of a life-safety emergency event, as conventional elevators are not suitably protected from the penetration of smoke into the elevator shaft. An unwitting passenger could be endangered if an elevator door opens onto a smoke filled lobby. Firefighters may elect to manually use an elevator for firefighting or rescue operation.

A dedicated elevator, within its own hardened, smoke-proof enclosure, could enhance the firefighting and rescue operation after a blast/fire event. The dedicated elevator should be supplied from the emergency generator, fed by conduit/wire that is protected in hardened enclosures. This shaft/lobby assembly should be sealed and positively pressurized to prevent the penetration of smoke into the protected area.

Smoke, Fire Detection, and Alarm Systems

A combination of early warning smoke detectors, sprinkler-flow switches, manual pull stations, and audible and visual alarms provide quick response and notification of an event. The activation of any device will automatically start the sequence of operation of smoke control, egress, and communication systems to allow occupants to quickly go to a safe area. System designs should include redundancy such as looped infrastructure wiring and distributed intelligence such that the severing of the loop will not disable the system. Install a fire-alarm system consisting of distributed, intelligent fire alarm panels connected in a peer-to-peer network, such that each panel can function independently and process alarms and initiate sequences within its respective zone.

Sprinkler/Standpipe System

Sprinklers will automatically suppress fire in the area upon sensing heat. Sprinkler activation will activate the fire alarm system. Standpipes have water available locally in large quantities for use by professional fire fighters. Multiple sprinkler and standpipe risers limit the possibility of an event severing all water supply available to fight a fire.

Redundant water services would increase the reliability of the source for sprinkler protection and fire suppression. Appropriate valving should be provided where services are combined. Redundant fire pumps could be provided in remote locations. These pumps could rely on different sources, for example one electric pump supplied from the utility or emergency generator and a second diesel fuel source fire pump. Diverse and separate routing of standpipe and sprinkler risers within hardened areas will enhance the system's reliability (such as reinforced masonry walls at stair shafts containing standpipes).

Smoke-Control Systems

Appropriate smoke-control systems maintain smoke-free paths of egress for building occupants through a series of fans, ductwork, and fire smoke dampers. Stair pressurization systems maintain a clear path of egress for occupants to safe areas or to evacuate the building. Smoke control fans should be located higher in a building rather than at lower floors to limit exposure/access to external vents. Vestibules at stairways with separate pressurization provide an additional layer of smoke control.

Communication System

A voice communication system facilitates the orderly control of occupants and evacuation of the danger area or the entire building. The system is typically zoned by floor, by stairwell, and by elevator bank for selective communication to building occupants. Emergency communication can be enhanced by providing:

- Extra emergency phones separate from the telephone system, connected directly to a constantly supervised central station.
- In-building repeater system for police, fire, and Emergency Medical Services (EMS) radios.
- Redundant or wireless firefighter's communications in building.

Protective Bollards, Planters, and Green Space

As experts study the destruction caused by explosions, they have unanimously agreed that "standoff distance" is the best solution for decreasing the impact of the explosion. Simply put, the more green space between the building and the bomb, the less of an effect the explosive will have on the structure. In a practical sense, standoff distances can be increased by installing protective bollards or planters around the building. The bollards are reinforced concrete posts, usually cylindrical, ranging from four inches in diameter to twelve inches diameter or greater. These bollards are very successful in keeping vehicular traffic from entering a restricted area. On the negative side, bollards tend to look unattractive. They look as if they were placed to keep people out.

> Because vehicles can be used to store and transport powerful bombs, you must take proactive steps to protect your building from these dangers. Begin by not permitting unoccupied vehicles to park in front of your building. Enforcing no parking zones is also suggested. In some scenarios parking permits are issued for employees and visitors must park in a special area that is located at a sufficient standoff distance from the building. It is imperative to contact your local police department if you find unidentified vehicles in your parking lot, and have the vehicle owner identified and the vehicle towed, if necessary.

Urban designers and architects agree that protective barriers should blend into the environment. They should not be readily noticeable to the average person. There are barriers cleverly disguised as decorative walls, planters, benches, or artwork. Landscaping and fencing can be used to keep vehicles at bay. Forcing points of entry into a building through a long corridor minimizes the effects of an explosion as well.

Virtual Reality Software and Related Technology

Scientists and engineers have realized the importance of recreating events with a goal of improving processes or finding out what went wrong. This study of events can be applied to building failure due to an emergency event. In particular, building simulation and the creation of virtual environments have assisted engineers in determining why a building structure failed. In true proactive fashion, engineers have used this data to better design buildings that can absorb emergency events including fire, earthquakes, terrorism, and other such events.

Typically, computer-aided design (CAD) software is used to create a three dimensional model of a building. This virtual building would then be placed in a digital environment that mirrors the subject property. At this point, programmers can subject the building to a host of virtual events while recording the outcomes of each. Modifications can be made to the 3-D building including ballistic glass, increased standoff distances, or other design features, and the effectiveness of each modification can be measured. This process allows the engineer to select the appropriate modifications for the safety level desired.

Although the availability of such software and expertise is currently limited to certain high-risk structures, the value of these studies is evident and growing in popularity. As technology evolves and expertise is developed, the cost of these studies will become more tolerable as well.

Post-failure Analysis

Immediately after a building collapse, specialized scientist and engineers will comb the premises to collect as much data as they can. To the untrained eye, the pile of rubble where the building once stood seems to contain very few clues of any value. To the highly trained eye, the site is a treasure trove of information. What caused the building failure? Where did the problem start? Could it have been prevented? Could better building materials have averted this disaster? Could better building techniques helped? These are the types of questions that can be answered by performing a post-failure analysis. The collapse of the World Trade Center Towers presented and necessitated a post-failure analysis at an unprecedented level. Well over a year after the World Trade Center collapse, engineers were still sifting through the rubble, searching for any clues that may shed more light on the event. We have learned from this disaster and our buildings, particularly high-rise buildings, are better protected.

Building Codes

Development and implementation of improved building codes has been instrumental in mitigating the impacts of various emergencies. Codes requiring tie down straps on rafters, fire sprinkler systems, storm shutters, or other proactive steps have saved lives and property. As we continue to better understand our exposure and we improve our building techniques, we can expect to minimize the effects of many emergencies.

Because codes are not uniform across the nation, this book will not attempt to examine the individual codes and provide endorsements. Instead, become familiar with the local codes that bind your building and renovation projects. Many of the existing structures across the country were built to inferior standards and therefore present a greater risk if faced with an emergency. When an emergency event, particularly a weather-related emergency, strikes a community, architects and engineers study the buildings that fared well and the buildings that did not fare so well. Time and time again, older buildings built prior to the stricter codes comprised the bulk of the damaged structures. Because of this fact, when considering the purchase or lease of a building, part of your due diligence auditing should be based on the construction techniques of that building.

Across the country, the National Fire Protection Association's codes are becoming standard: NFPA 1—Fire Prevention Code (2015 Edition) or the NFPA 101®—Life Safety Code® (2015 Edition). These resources contain specific requirements for fire drill frequencies in a number of different kinds of buildings. Many local jurisdictions will refer to the NFPA standards and adopt them "by reference." Even those jurisdictions that do not directly refer specifically to the NFPA requirements are using them as a model for their own codes. For these reasons, it is worth getting copies of the NFPA codes and becoming familiar with them. For more information, go to the NFPA site at www.nfpa.org/codes-and-standards/document-information-pages?mode=code&code=1 or www.nfpa.org/codes-and-standards/document-information-pages?mode=code&code=101.

Mitigation Assessment Team (MAT) Program

The Mitigation Assessment Team (MAT) Program is an updated and enhanced version of FEMA's Building Performance Assessment Team (BPAT) program. MAT—drawing on the resources of the public and private sectors—evaluates building and related infrastructure performance after natural and non-natural emergency events. The goal of the program is to better understand what makes a building survive emergencies and how the negative effects of emergencies can be mitigated.

After an emergency event, a Mitigation Assessment Team is dispatched to the emergency location to inspect the affected buildings. The assessment team will conduct engineering analysis to determine the cause of failure or the reasons for successful structural integrity. At the end of the team's analysis, they will recommend actions that could reduce future damages and protect lives during similar hazards. The positive results of the MAT program include improved disaster-resistant building codes, design methods, and material selection.

The Mitigation Assessment Team consists of FEMA representatives, state and local officials, and public and private sector technical experts. These technical experts include persons from the fields of:

- Structural and Civil Engineering
- Geotechnical Engineering
- Environmental Engineering
- Coastal Engineering
- Retrofitting
- Shoreline and Coastal Erosion
- Flood-Resistant Design and Construction
- Floodplain Management
- Wind-Resistant Design and Construction
- Historic Preservation
- Earthquake-Resistant Design and Construction
- Water Resources
- Hurricane-Resistant Design and Construction
- Building Code Analysis and Evaluation
- Forensic Engineering
- Architecture

For those interested in learning more about FEMA's MAT program, including how to volunteer and be included in the BPAT expert database, go to FEMA's Web site (www.fema.gov) at www.fema.gov/what-mitigation-assessment-team-program or www.fema.gov/you-can-become-part-mitigation-assessment-team-program.

Since the early 1990s, FEMA has deployed MATs in response to a wide variety of disasters including hurricanes, floods, and the bombing of the Alfred P. Murrah Federal Building in Oklahoma City. To appreciate the thoroughness of the MAT's work, you need look no farther than the World Trade Center Disaster on 9/11. The Mitigation Assessment Team conducted field observations at the World Trade Center site and steel salvage yards. They meticulously removed and tested samples of the collapsed buildings, looking for clues. They interviewed hundreds of witnesses and persons involved in the design of the towers. Team members culled through thousands of pictures and hours of video. They examined how the building was constructed and how it was maintained. The information gathered helps future design and construction of high-rise buildings.

Of course, the valuable information gathered from FEMA's research must be applied by state and local governments as well as private industry. This often happens when building codes are revised to reflect the findings of the research. In an effort to transfer this knowledge, FEMA distributes their findings via Web site, workshops, technical manuals, and training through the Emergency Management Institute (EMI) at National Training and Education (NTE)—see training.fema.gov/emi.aspx.

Over the years, MAT has experienced many success stories. One example of successful application of lessons learned is the Mobile, Alabama, Convention Center. Throughout history, Alabama has been susceptible to hurricanes and tropical storms. The city of Mobile desired to build a structure that would be hurricane resistant, yet aesthetically pleasing and cost effective. In addition to strong winds, hurricanes often bring floodwaters, so the convention center was built above the 100-year flood elevation.

In 1998, Hurricane Georges swept through the southern United States coastline, deluging Mobile with nearly fourteen inches of water. Large portions of the downtown Mobile area were flooded. The Convention Center only received minor damage from the hurricane, and most of it was water related. The lower level of the building, which was primarily used for parking, was covered with approximately four feet of water. Because of this, some electrical repairs were necessary in addition to repair of the fire control panel and electronic parking equipment. Minor drywall repair and general removal of mud and water was also necessary. Total costs for repairs were approximately $350,000—a very small percentage of the cost of the $52 million structure.

Thanks to a design that addressed the possibility of hurricane-induced floodwaters, the building's HVAC equipment was elevated and remained unharmed during the hurricane. If this one simple design had not been featured, the repairs to the Convention Center could have cost millions of dollars.

Because the damage to the Convention Center was minor, the center was able to remain in operation and no events were canceled. In fact, the Convention Center was able to book additional events from other local facilities that were affected by the hurricane. If the Convention Center were not available shortly after the storm, a major convention of the Southeast United States/Japan Trade Commission Conference would have been canceled, costing more than $1 million in revenue. It is estimated that the design and elevation of the building represented a major economic success that exceed $5 million dollars in terms of both damages avoided and lack of business interruption costs. This is the type of success for which FEMA's Mitigation Assessment Team program strives.

*   *   *

Although we cannot eliminate many emergencies, we can change how we prepare for them and how we react to them when they do occur. We can also go back after the emergency has occurred and examine the affected buildings. Did the building survive? If it did, why did it survive? By analyzing the affect the emergency event had on the building, we develop better building codes. We can specify better building materials. We can take the lessons that history has taught us and design better buildings. Doing so will advance business continuity, reduce insurance costs, and—most importantly—save lives.

16

Emergency Preparedness

Hospitals and Healthcare Facilities

Some facilities have specific needs when it comes to emergency preparedness and the special requirements of two of these—hospitals and schools—are discussed in the next two chapters.

Hospitals and nursing homes are required to have emergency plans in place to cope with manmade and natural disasters. The Centers for Medicare and Medicaid Services require hospitals and nursing homes that receive Medicare or Medicaid payments to maintain emergency plans. The Joint Commission on Accreditation of Healthcare Organizations requires that hospitals and nursing homes it accredits maintain emergency plans that include processes for evacuations. Hospital and nursing home administrators often have the responsibility for deciding whether to evacuate their patients or to shelter in place during a disaster.

State and local governments can order evacuations of the population or segments of the population during emergencies, but healthcare facilities may be exempt from these orders.

Hospital administrators usually evacuate only as a last resort and facilities' emergency plans are designed primarily to shelter in place.

Even when county or state officials recommend that hospitals and nursing homes evacuate their facilities, the final decision is made by the hospital or nursing home administrator.

Both options—shelter in place and evacuation—must be considered as part of emergency planning.

The facility must have adequate resources to shelter in place. Examples of resources include staff, supplies, food, water, and power. Without these resources, a facility may be unable to care for patients at the facility, and therefore may be more likely to evacuate.

Risks to patients must be considered in deciding when to evacuate—for instance when a hurricane threatens. Evacuating too soon may place patients needlessly at risk if the potential threat does not materialize. Evacuating at the same time as the general public may increase risk to patients' health if traffic congestion and other road complications increase travel time. Evacuating too late increases risk if patients do not arrive at their destination before a storm strikes.

Evacuating a hospital or nursing home requires a facility to secure transportation to move patients and a receiving facility to accept patients. Facilities are likely to have arrangements for these services locally, but they are less likely to have arrangements with organizations in other localities or states, as was necessary for an event such as Hurricane Katrina. Hospital and nursing homes also accept that their contracted transportation providers would be unlikely to support them during a major disaster because local demand for transportation would exceed supply.

The destruction of facility infrastructure due to a storm may force a facility administrator to decide to evacuate after the event due to building damage or a lack of utilities. For example, a nursing home in Florida evacuated after Hurricane Charley in 2004 because the facility's roof was destroyed and the facility lost power and water service.

The destruction of community infrastructure, such as the loss of communications systems and transportation routes, can further complicate the decision to evacuate. For example, during Hurricane Katrina, the destruction of communications systems left hospital and nursing home administrators unable to receive basic information, such as when assistance would arrive.

Nursing home administrators must also consider additional factors. Whereas hospital administrators may discharge as many patients as possible before a disaster to reduce the number of patients who need to be sheltered or evacuated, nursing home administrators may not have that option: nursing home administrators cannot reduce the number of residents because their patrons generally have no other home and cannot care for themselves. When a nursing home evacuates, the administrator must locate receiving facilities that can accommodate residents for a potentially long period. For example, a nursing home in Florida had to relocate residents for more than ten months because of damage to the facility.

Satellite Radiotelephone System

Consider adding a satellite radiotelephone system to your facility's emergency assets. A satellite radiotelephone offers very basic and limited telephone capability in the event of internal and external phone systems failure. The satellite radiotelephone must be able to make local, long distance, and international telephone calls directly over a satellite connection without using any land facilities.

Special Challenges

Most Americans are accustomed to receiving sophisticated and prompt medical attention after an injury or a medical problem occurs, anytime and anywhere in the country, without traveling great distances. Such expectations are even greater during mass emergencies that require immediate care for a large number of casualties. In circumstances in which hospital operations are disrupted or completely disabled, the adverse effects of such disasters can be quickly compounded, frequently with catastrophic results. A report from the Congressional Research Service (CRS), "Hurricane Katrina: The Public Health and Medical Response," examined the performance of the public health system during this devastating event.

According to the CRS report, Hurricane Katrina pushed some of the most critical healthcare delivery systems to their limits, for the first time in recent memory. Therefore, the importance of uninterrupted hospital operations and ready access to, and availability of, immediate medical care cannot be exaggerated. The situation is even more complex when hospitals and other healthcare facilities have to evacuate patients and staff for whatever reason.

Different natural and manmade phenomena present different challenges, and each hazard requires a different approach and a different set of actions. When communities face more than one hazard—that is, they are in an area prone to flooding and tornadoes—the planning team must select the mitigation measures most appropriate for achieving the desired performance level, regardless of the immediate cause for the potential losses.

For instance, flooding is a more site-specific hazard than others. Obviously, the preferred approach for new facilities is to select a site that is not subject to flooding. But when that is not feasible for existing facilities, site modifications or other site-specific building design features that mitigate anticipated flood hazard can be made that will reduce the potential for damage. In extreme circumstances, when the hazard becomes so great that the only course of action is to evacuate the facility, plans have to be in place to enable them to happen in an orderly and timely manner.

The orderly evacuation of a hospital is an entirely different process than is recommended for most other buildings and involves special considerations. Due to the fact that so many patients may be medically unstable and dependent on mechanical support equipment, complete evacuation of the facility is to be initiated only as a last resort, and must proceed in a planned and orderly manner.

Events most likely to trigger activation of an emergency/evacuation plan are:

- Severe weather
- Large external accident—commercial plane crash or similar
- Large internal accident—contamination, infectious outbreak
- Fire
- Loss of utilities
- Bomb threat
- Radiation leak or threat of (internal/external)
- Terrorism (hostage taking, chemical, biological)

An Evacuation Plan (EP) must be developed, constantly reviewed updated, and tested so that everyone knows the part they have to play. The plan should be maintained by the Emergency Management Department with the cooperation of all departments within the hospital. Every department within should be responsible for implementing the protocol and for maintaining up-to-date disaster procedures in their work area. Departments should notify the Emergency Management Department if significant changes or alterations transpire which could impact implementation or performance of the plan.

As we've noted in earlier chapters with regard to Emergency Plans, the Evacuation Plan should be reviewed and updated regularly or as major changes/events in the facility occur. The hospital should conduct a scheduled review of the plan and coordinate updates with hospital emergency programs. The purpose of the EP is to save lives. It is intended to provide for the safety of the staff as well as the patients during a response to an emergency where partial or full patient evacuation may be required.

Remember: When you activate an emergency response or evacuation plan, it has an impact far beyond your facility and involves maybe thousands of other people. Essential staff and patients all have families who are likely to be affected by the same emergency. Key staff cannot function well if they are concerned about loved ones elsewhere. It is important that they have their own personal evacuation plans in place—for themselves and any family pets—as well as essential supplies. The plan should include an agreed remote destination if there is to be a regional evacuation or a local address—for instance if mobile home owners are going to a public shelter ahead of a hurricane's landfall.

If the emergency calls for essential staff to remain at the facility for an extended period, arrangements should be made in advance for child care. The facility's emergency plan might have limited provisions for child care facilities but, depending on the nature of the event, these may not be available at all times.

Security Concerns

Hospitals pose particular security challenges because people are coming and going around the clock and visitors often have unfettered access to most parts of the facility. In addition, hospitals have pharmacies which can be a target for criminals and addicts, they have expensive equipment which can be stolen, and, above all, they have patients who are at their most vulnerable. Security is essential to protect both patients and visitors and to control those who would do harm. Obviously strangers should not have access to the nursery to prevent newborn babies being kidnapped, gifts shops and cafes handling money need to be protected, and sensitive personal data—both of the patients and the staff—must be safeguarded.

Some of these security needs are obvious and some are not. In order to determine what needs to be done you must first conduct a vulnerability assessment to identify all risks. Once you know what risks you face, you can take steps to eliminate or mitigate them.

Some of these risks can be tackled straight away so resolving the problem. The vulnerability assessment might flag inadequate lighting in the visitor car park or unprotected utility hatches. These issues can be addressed. Other threats might only arise as a result of a terrorist attack or severe weather. That is why you need a comprehensive emergency plan.

The plan sets out exactly what must be done in the event of all your identified "what if" scenarios.

The plan must cover what you do and who does it and must cover everything that could possible happen including a catastrophic event that would force the evacuation of the entire facility.

Potential Vulnerabilities

Hospitals usually have high levels of occupancy, with patients, staff, and many visitors present twenty-four hours a day. Many patients require constant attention, and in many cases continuous specialized care and the use of sophisticated medical instruments or other equipment. Hospital operations also depend on a steady supply of medical and other types of material, as well as public services or lifelines. In addition, hospital vulnerability is aggravated by the presence of hazardous substances that may be spilled or released in a hazard event.

Given the importance of hospital services for response and recovery following emergencies, and the need for uninterrupted operation of these facilities, hospital administrators and designers must consider all aspects of their vulnerability as they prepare emergency response/evacuation plans. Three main aspects of hospital vulnerability must be taken into account:

- Structural
- Nonstructural
- Organizational

Structural Vulnerability

Structural vulnerability is related to potential damage to structural components of a building. They include foundations, bearing walls, columns and beams, staircases, floors and roof decks, or other types of structural components that help support the building. The level of vulnerability of these components depends on the following factors:

- ▲ The level to which the design of the structural system has addressed the hazard forces
- ▲ The quality of building materials, construction, and maintenance
- ▲ The architectural and structural form or configuration of a building

The aspects of adequate design and construction in most hazard-prone areas are regulated by building codes and other regulations. The main purpose of these regulations is to protect the safety of occupants. They are usually prescriptive in nature, that is, they establish minimum requirements that are occasionally updated based on newly acquired knowledge.

The building regulations alone, however, cannot guarantee uninterrupted operation of a hospital, because a great many other factors affect hospital functions.

Nonstructural Vulnerability

The experience of hospital evacuations and other types of disruption during such emergencies as Hurricane Katrina (mentioned above) have shown that hospital functions could be seriously impaired or interrupted even when the facilities did *not* sustain significant structural damage. The effects of damage to nonstructural building components and equipment, as well as the effects of breakdowns in public services (lifelines), transportation, re-supply, or other organizational aspects of hospital operations, can be as disruptive, and as dangerous for the safety of patients, as any structural damage.

Nonstructural vulnerabilities that can affect hospital functions and the safety of occupants include the potential failures of architectural components, both on the exterior and the interior of buildings. Damage to roof coverings, facades, or windows can make way for water penetration that can damage sensitive equipment and shut down many hospital functions. When roofing material is disturbed by wind, the roof may start to leak and the moisture can knock out vital equipment, disrupt patient care, and penetrate walls and other concealed spaces, allowing mold to build up over time. Window breakage resulting from high winds, earthquakes, and even flooding frequently requires patient evacuation from affected areas. Patients in critical care and acute care units are particularly vulnerable because the move separates them from medical gas outlets, monitors, lighting, and other essential support services.

Nonload-bearing and partition walls and ceilings, for instance, are rarely designed and constructed to the same standards of hazard resistance as the structural elements. Collapse of these components has caused a number of evacuations and closures of hospitals following a hazard event.

Installations and Nonstructural Vulnerability

Hospitals are extremely complex building systems that depend on an extensive network of mechanical, electrical, and piping installations.

The air and ventilation system is one of the most important ones because it is responsible for maintaining an appropriate environment in different parts of the hospital. Isolation rooms usually have negative pressure so that harmful airborne organisms do not migrate outside the patient's room and infect others. Likewise, wards housing patients with immune system deficiencies require a positive pressure differential, so that harmful organisms do not enter the patient room and needlessly infect them. The malfunction in any one part of this ventilation system could create a risk of infection to patients and staff. This system is also extremely vulnerable to disruption as a result of indirect building damage. Winds habitually overturn improperly attached roof-mounted ventilation and air-conditioning equipment, while the ductwork is very susceptible to collapse in earthquakes. Additionally, strong winds may change the airflow from ventilation exhaust outlets, potentially causing harmful discharges from patient care areas and the clinical laboratory to be sucked back into the fresh air intakes. Airborne debris from windstorms could quickly clog the air filtration systems, making them inoperable or impaired.

Hospitals depend on several essential piping systems. Medical gasses are among the most important, along with water, steam, and fire sprinkler systems. Physicians and nurses depend on oxygen and other gasses required for patient care. Unless properly secured and braced, these installations can be easily dislodged or broken, causing dangerous leakage and potential additional damage.

In floods and earthquakes particularly, sewers are apt to overflow, back up, or break down. Waste disposal is essential for any hospital, because when the toilets back up, or sterilizers, dishwashers, and other automated cleaning equipment cannot be discharged, patient care is immediately affected. Retention ponds or holding tanks coupled with backflow and diversion valves can be employed to solve this problem.

Elevator service is vulnerable not only to power outage, but also to direct damage to elevator installations. Wind and windborne debris can damage elevator penthouses, opening a path for water penetration that can disable elevator motors and controls, as has happened in numerous hurricanes in recent years. In the event of an earthquake, elevator shafts and other equipment can be damaged or dislodged, effectively shutting down the building. Flooding of elevator pits was a common problem during Hurricane Katrina, and responsible for the loss of elevator service.

The emergency power supply system is probably the most critical element in this group. Together with fuel supply and storage facilities, this system enables all the other hospital installations and equipment that have not sustained direct physical damage to function normally in any disaster.

However, uninterrupted operation of a hospital during a power outage is possible only if adequate electrical wiring is installed in all the areas that require uninterrupted power supply. Since extra wiring and additional circuits for emergency power increase the initial construction costs of the building, the decision on the emergency power coverage requires a thorough evaluation of the relative vulnerability of various functions to power outage. As patients become more critically ill and the nature of diagnosis and treatment becomes more dependent on computers, monitors, and other electrical equipment, the need for emergency power will continue to grow.

The experience of Hurricane Katrina has demonstrated the need for emergency power coverage even for services that typically have not been regarded as critical, such as climate control and air-conditioning systems. Extreme heat caused a number of hospitals to evacuate their patients and staff when the conditions became unbearable.

There are many other types of internal hazards that might occur as the result of a disaster. For example, bottles in clinical laboratories have fallen and started fires. Earthquakes have catapulted filing cabinet drawers and ventilators across rooms at high speed, with the potential of causing considerable injury to personnel. Any wheeled equipment is vulnerable to displacement and has the potential to cause injury.

Hospitals use and depend on many types of communication systems. For communications with emergency vehicles or first response agencies, hospitals depend on radio equipment that is frequently mounted on roofs and exposed to high winds and windborne debris impact. Satellite dishes, communication masts, antennae, and other equipment can be blown off the roof or be severely damaged, leaving the hospital without this vital service at a critical time.

Organizational Vulnerability

Most hospitals have disaster mitigation or emergency operation plans, but not all of them provide organizational alternatives in the event of disruption of the normal movement of staff, patients, equipment, and supplies that characterizes everyday hospital operations. The critical nature and interdependence of these processes represent a separate category of vulnerabilities that need careful attention. Spatial distribution of hospital functions and their interrelationship determine the extent hospital operations are affected when normal movement and communication of people, materials, and waste are disrupted. The disruption by natural hazard events of administrative services such as contracting, procurement, maintenance, as well as allocation of resources, can impair hospital functions almost as much as any physical damage.

Just-in-time delivery: Many hospitals have currently eliminated, or greatly reduced, on-site storage for linen, supplies, food, and other materials essential to normal operations. Any prolonged isolation or blockage of streets serving the hospital could lead to a need to ration supplies and triage patients for treatment, due to the limited supplies stored on site. During Hurricane Katrina, many hospitals were isolated by floodwaters for five or more days and, in many cases, could not replenish critical supplies, which in some instances contributed to the decision to evacuate the facility.

Hazard Analysis

In addition to looking at hospital vulnerabilities, facilities should inspect their surrounding environments for hazards as they prepare emergency response/evacuation plans.

There are many methods for identifying, evaluating, and defining hazards that may affect a facility. Depending on facility location and size, hazards may require considerable expertise to identify properly. Hazards are not necessarily limited to natural events, but include technological risks ranging from chemical spills due to loss of utilities. Hazard analysis can be provided by knowledgeable staff, software programs, and guidance from governmental emergency planners and consultants.

An additional tool in assessment is the use of "lessons learned" from similar incidents. Events that led to evacuation or shelter-in-place decisions can be pinpointed through data from associations, insurance companies, and community emergency planners/responders. By evaluating information from sources like these, facilities are more likely to identify potential hazards.

Frequency

To effectively identify the most likely evacuation scenarios, facilities must first qualify hazards and how often they occur. Frequency is not a stand-alone indicator, since a least likely scenario may have the largest impact.

Duration of Incident

Each emergency/evacuation plan should consider how long a hazard would impact facility operations. An example is whether a chemical release will be of short or long duration.

Scope of Impact

Plans for evacuation will depend upon how much of the facility is affected, for how long, and to what degree.

Destructive Potential to Life and Property

To understand the type and length of evacuation, facility planners should know how much destruction is likely from the risk at hand. If a flood lasts for three weeks and covers the entire structure, patients may be transferred for months to other sites. A chemical release, however, may have little destructive impact on the facility structure, but result in severe risk to patients and staff.

Controllability

Facility planners cannot control hazards but may be able to decrease associated risks by adequate planning.

Predictability

Based on past history, some events may be predictable. The ability to reasonably predict events will assist in planning for evacuation. An example would include the building and grounds being routinely flooded during high-rainfall years.

Speed of Onset

Every facility should have a method to quickly identify events that will create an immediate threat. In some cases, staff may have many days for planning and decision-making or have very little time to react. Lack of time to prepare can have a substantial impact on the health of patients and staff. Facility planners should find methods to provide early warning to staff for those events that can require evacuations within two hours of occurrence (e.g., earthquake, wildfire, dam break, bomb threat, etc.).

Length of Forewarning

The longer you wait to take actions to respond to a disaster, the fewer options you will have to react successfully. Equipping facilities with appropriate warning systems will maximize the response time for evacuation or sheltering decisions. These may include weather radios that activate immediately upon a warning from the National Weather Service, an automated warning service provided by phone, or a warning siren from a nuclear power plant. Facility staff should also be trained to identify local sirens or messages provided on radio or television by the Emergency Alert System.

Sheltering in Place and Evacuation

As mentioned at the beginning of this chapter, hospital administrators usually evacuate only as a last resort and facilities' emergency plans are designed primarily to shelter in place. But if the event and situation necessitates, there are several strategies for evacuation:

- Sheltering in place without moving clients
- Sheltering in place to a safe area on the same level
- Sheltering in place vertically (up or down)
- Evacuating just outside the facility
- Evacuating to a nearby like facility
- Evacuating to a distant like facility
- Evacuating to a shelter designated as a medical treatment unit (and originating facility continues to provide all staff and support services)

➤   Evacuating to a shelter designated as a medical treatment unit (and local health officials provide all staff and support services)

➤   Evacuating to a general public shelter with a temporary infirmary

NOTE: When considering movement of patients, whether within or outside the facility, facility planners must consider the inherent risk that the travel will adversely impact the individual's health.

Sheltering in Place Without Moving Clients

Depending on the degree of risk, facility staff may decide to remain in place because the threat may have less impact on client health and safety than a voluntary evacuation.

Example: A facility becomes aware of a chemical release that will affect it within a short period of time and local government advises staying indoors or evacuating the area. Evacuation could expose patients/residents to greater risks than sheltering in place.

Sheltering in Place to a Safe Area or Refuge on the Same Level

An evacuation may be necessary from one side of a building to another based on an approaching or impending threat. Staff would be expected to identify the path and speed of the threat to ensure the timely movement of patients and critical equipment.

Sheltering in Place Vertically (Up or Down)

For fast-moving, short-duration events it may be necessary to move residents above or below the ground floor. This is usually done because time in which to respond to a serious hazard is extremely limited. Lower-level sheltering may be required for high wind scenarios or during threats from some man-made threat (e.g., a nearby impending explosion). Upper-level sheltering may be required for scenarios involving very fast-moving waters or during the release of ground-hugging chemicals in the immediate area.

Example: A two-story facility has a fallout shelter in the basement. The National Weather Service has announced a tornado warning in the area. A staff member's relative has already seen a funnel cloud touch down less than a mile from the facility. Staff should consider moving patients from the upper floor and those near windows to the security of the basement until the tornado warning has subsided.

Evacuating Just Outside the Facility

There may be an internal emergency, which will require staff to evacuate patients from the building. This could be for an immediate problem or a long duration event. The evacuation plan should include locations where facility staff can perform an inventory of those who have left the building. The plan should also include contingencies for this occurring during inclement weather and the possible need for further evacuation to nearby like facilities.

Example: Staff smells smoke in the facility and calls 911. They are directed to move patients out of the building. Upon authorization from the fire department, they return indoors.

Evacuating to a Nearby Like Facility

Facilities with medically fragile residents should consider movement of patients/residents and staff to a nearby facility, with like capacity for care of patients/residents. This evacuation type might be considered during a voluntary or precautionary evacuation, and would definitely be appropriate during a mandatory evacuation order. It is critical that facilities have agreements with nearby like facilities to take clients. More than one facility should be identified, usually in opposite directions from the affected facility, in case the primary site is impacted by the same threat. Facilities should identify whether other medical and residential care facilities are also planning to use the same location to receive clients. In addition, plans should address accessible evacuation routes (depending on risks) and transportation logistics.

Example: Local government authorities have warned a facility that flood controls may fail within six hours. The facility has a high risk of being flooded within the next two days. Staff have been given adequate time to secure bed space and care at one of the designated like facilities. They have also been given time to arrange for transportation and verify a safe route for evacuation.

Evacuating to a Distant Like Facility

Very serious conditions may require a facility to move all patients to a distant site. This can occur during regional events with massive impacts. Examples include widespread flooding, earthquake, epidemic, and civil unrest. This choice would be preferable to movement to a nearby medical shelter if the impact of the event will have a substantial duration (more than three or four days) or there are extensive equipment and personnel support needs for the care of the patients.

Example: A large earthquake has severely damaged a facility and staff determines that all like facilities with which they have agreements are also disabled and unable to receive additional patients.

Evacuating to a Shelter Designated as a Medical Treatment Unit (and Originating Facility Continues to Provide All Staff and Support Services)

A rapid onset of a disaster may severely limit evacuation and transfer options available to the local emergency authorities and facility. Under these conditions, the local disaster authority may instruct a facility to evacuate and transfer the entire operation to a temporary shelter (i.e., school gymnasium) and continue to provide all care and treatment. This option is desirable for short-term evacuations. However, depending on the duration of the event, this may be the first step before transferring patients to another like facility.

Example: A nearby river is at flood stage and threatens to break through containment levees. If this occurs, the nearby facility will be flooded. A lawful evacuation order has been issued and the facility has been directed to move all patients and staff to a school gymnasium on higher ground. Patients, staff, equipment, and supplies must be transferred with the patients and the facility must be capable of maintaining operations for a minimum of seventy-two hours.

Evacuating to a Shelter Designated as a Medical Treatment Unit (and Local Health Officials Provide All Staff and Support Services)

When the scope of the disaster conditions are severe, facility planners may need to consider moving patients to a medical shelter before they can be moved to like facilities. Since they will have to be moved twice, this choice can create increased stress on patients, and the quality of care in the shelters may not be equal to the care available to them in the facility from which they are evacuating.

Example: An urban firestorm has burned down the neighborhood where a facility was located. Staff was able to evacuate all patients to a local community shelter for the medically fragile, but it has limited capabilities. Facility planners must arrange for movement of patients to a city that is in another county, as soon as the roads are passable and the fire threat is controlled.

Evacuating to a General Public Shelter with a Temporary Infirmary

In worst-case scenarios, facilities may have little choice but to evacuate to the nearest available general population shelter. This decision is made only when there is no other option available and when there is an immediate peril to life and safety of clients if they are not immediately moved to the closest available shelter. The plan must recognize this as a temporary condition requiring immediate triage activities, in coordination with local government, to move the arriving patients to the closest like facility available, whether or not there exist any previous agreements.

Example: A massive earthquake has rendered a facility unsafe for occupation. Staff has used every method available to safely move the patients out of the building. The only available shelter is a school auditorium two miles away. There is a temporary infirmary as part of the general population shelter, with limited nursing staff, medical supplies, and support.

Facility staff will need to set up a working relationship with local government as soon as possible to arrange for the movement of the patients to a like facility.

Security during an Emergency

During an emergency, security has multiple roles to play from monitoring the facility, equipment and drugs, ensuring the safety of patients, staff, and visitors, and even providing crowd control. Emergency planning must include detailed security responses to cover all eventualities. If there is as outbreak of a highly contagious virus or multiple casualties from a terrorist bomb, the facility could quickly become inundated with people seeking treatment. Local law enforcement is likely to be stretched to the limit so the onus will fall on facility security to carry out this function.

During any emergency the following measures should be taken:

- Lock all non-essential entrances
- Station security personnel at all entrances (Emergency Department, Hospital Front, Clinic Front, Atrium Circle, Garage Lobby, Purchasing and Dietary Loading Docks, etc.)
- Allow access for authorized persons only and only after ID badges have been screened
- Assist law enforcement and emergency response agencies
- Secure primary treatment areas for authorized personnel only
- Maintain after hours key control of elevator operation
- Monitor and disseminate flow of information from outside sources (i.e., National Weather Service, State Department of Health).
- Vehicular traffic control

It may be necessary to restrict or close access to parking garages, and if restricted only authorized key personnel with parking passes should be allowed entry.

Crowd control may be necessary both within the facility—in the ER for instance—and outside. The emergency plan must cover procedures to be put in place if crowd control is necessary and all ensure that the necessary equipment is available to do this: ropes, barriers, and so on.

Emergency Plan Template

Here is a sample template/outline for a hospital or healthcare facility emergency response/ evacuation plan. As a minimum it should contain the following information:

I. DISASTER PREPAREDNESS PLAN FOR "Insert the Name of Your Facility", Street Address, phone, and fax number.

DATE THE PLAN WAS WRITTEN

II. After the Cover Page
(1) a general statement describing your facility's services to its residents/patients,
(2) number of beds or capacity,
(3) number of employees,
(4) is there only one facility or is your facility part of a corporation, etc.

III. Emergency Notifications List (suggested list follows; add to it as needed)

MEDICAL, FIRE AND POLICE EMERGENCIES—911

Fire (Non-Emergency) - _____

Emergency Medical Services (EMS) (Non-Emergency) - _____

Police Department (Non-Emergency) - _____

Sheriff's Department (Non-Emergency) - _____

Local Emergency Management Agency (Business Office) - _____

Local Emergency Operations Center (If Activated) - _____

Local Electrical Power Provider (Business Office) - _____

Local Electrical Power Provider (Emergency Reporting) - _____

Local Water Department (Business Office) - _____

Local Water Department (Emergency Reporting) - _____

Local Telephone Company (Business Office) - _____

Local Telephone Company (Emergency Reporting) - _____

Local Natural/Propane Gas Supplier (Business Office) - _____

Local Natural/Propane Gas Supplier (Emergency Reporting) - _____

(Review and up-date this list as necessary or at least once per year)

IV. Table of Contents Page should follow the Cover Page. A suggested Table Of Contents Page follows:

Purpose Page 1

Annex A—Fire Safety Procedures Page __

Annex B—Tornado/Severe Weather Procedures Page __

Annex C—Bomb Threat Procedures Page __

Annex D—Flood Procedures Page __

Annex E—Severe Hot and Cold Weather Procedures Page __

Annex F—Earthquake Procedures Page __

Annex G—Chemical Spills __   _____ Page __

V. On the next page write a Purpose Statement or insert the following Purpose Statement:

PURPOSE: To continue providing quality care to the residents of "Insert Name of Your Facility" during times of major emergencies and/or disasters or when such events are reasonably believed to be pending by maintaining close coordination and planning links with local emergency response organizations on an ongoing basis.

Building Name: Hospital Building #1

Floor	Service/Department/Unit	Horizontal Evacuation	Vertical Evacuation	Building Evacuation
Basement				
floor:				
floor:				
floor:				
floor:				
floor:				
floor:				
floor:				
floor:				

Figure 16.1. Building Directory Inventory for Evacuation.

Hospital:

Building: **Floor:**

Department/Unit/Service:

Unit/Floor Type:

____ **Critical Care (OR, ICU, Recovery, ED)**

____ **Patient Care specialty (Telemetry, Hemodialysis)**

____ **Patient Care General**

____ **Outpatient care**

____ **Support patient care (labs, x-ray, EEG, EKG)**

____ **Support non patient care (food, mat. Mgt, transport)**

____ **Administrative (office, Medical Records)**

____ **Research**

____ **Other (mechanical rooms, storage, engineering shops)**

Number of beds on unit _____

Specialized Medical Equipment present on unit:
☐ Infusion Pumps; ☐ Portable ventilators; ☐ Portable Oxygen;
☐ Portable Suction Unit; ☐ Ambu bag; ☐ Defibrillator; ☐ Monitors

Specialized Medications:

_____
_____
_____

Hazardous Chemicals present on unit:
☐ Yes   ☐ No; If yes identify chemical and quantity

_____
_____
_____

Is this a locked unit?

☐ Yes   ☐ No

Do you have medical gases?
☐ Yes   ☐ No; If yes:
☐ Piped   ☐ Cylinder

Location and Exits: Attach Floor plan that includes location of medical gas shut off valves; location of exits; pull stations, extinguishers, sprinkler systems, designated smoke and fire doors.

Evacuation Route:

Horizontal: To _____ via

_____
_____
_____

Vertical:

Down to:_____

Up to: _____

Staging Area for full building evacuation:_____

Figure 16.2. Departmental Evacuation Template.

HOSPITAL:_____

Unit Name: _____   Unit Location: Building_____   Floor _____

Total Number of Staff on Unit at Start time of Evacuation: [   ]

RNs: [   ]   LPN's [   ]   NA's/PCA's [   ]   US [   ]   MD [   ]   Other [   ]

A. PATIENT CENSUS ON UNIT AT START TIME OF EVACUATION: [   ]

B. TOTAL PATIENT CENSUS   [   ]

C. PATIENTS TO BE ACCOUNTED FOR A - B = [   ]

PATIENTS OFF UNIT FOR PROCEDURES/OR/RADIOLOGY/DIALYSIS AT TIME OF EVACUATION:

Patient Name	Room Number	Current Location

Total # of patients off unit in other areas = [   ]

SCHEDULED ADMISSIONS TO THE UNIT THAT HAVE NOT ARRIVED AT TIME OF EVACUATION:

Patient Name	Room Number	Admitted from (ED, clinic, Admitting, etc)

Total # of patients admitted to unit, not yet arrived = [   ]

PATIENTS AT RISK AT TIME OF EVACUATION: (i.e. Suicide precautions, patients in restraints, Bipap, Active labor, Temporary External Pacer)

Patient Name	Room Number	Risk Issue

UNIT WORKSHEET   Page ____ of _____

HOSPITAL: _____

Unit Name: _____   Unit Location: Building_____   Floor _____

PATIENTS (use Addressograph to imprint patient name or utilize patient labels)	Category	Equipment Needs	Mode of Transportation	Date and Time patient left unit	Destination: Accepting Facility for Patient Transfer	Arrival at Destination
	☐ Red (significant resources for transport) ☐ Yellow (moderate resources for transport) ☐ Green (minimal resources)	☐ Oxygen ☐ Monitor ☐ Ventilator ☐ Pump ☐ Other (indicate)	☐ Ambulatory ☐ Wheelchair ☐ Stretcher ☐ Bassinet ☐ Isolette ☐ Other (indicate)	Date: Time:	Indicate destination: Equipment leaving with pt:	☐ Yes ☐ No Time: Contact:
	☐ Red (significant resources for transport) ☐ Yellow (moderate resources for transport) ☐ Green (minimal resources)	☐ Oxygen ☐ Monitor ☐ Ventilator ☐ Pump ☐ Other (indicate)	☐ Ambulatory ☐ Wheelchair ☐ Stretcher ☐ Bassinet ☐ Isolette ☐ Other (indicate)	Date: Time:	Indicate destination: Equipment leaving with pt:	☐ Yes ☐ No Time: Contact:
	☐ Red (significant resources for transport) ☐ Yellow (moderate resources for transport) ☐ Green (minimal resources)	☐ Oxygen ☐ Monitor ☐ Ventilator ☐ Pump ☐ Other (indicate)	☐ Ambulatory ☐ Wheelchair ☐ Stretcher ☐ Bassinet ☐ Isolette ☐ Other (indicate)	Date: Time:	Indicate destination: Equipment leaving with pt:	☐ Yes ☐ No Time: Contact:

Figure 16.3. Patient Care Unit Evacuation Tools.

Unit Work Sheet   Page _____ of _____

HOSPITAL: _____

Unit Name: _____   Unit Location: Building_____   Floor _____

Name and Telephone Contact Number of Visitor	Name of Patient visiting	Time Left Unit	Destination	Arrival at Destination
				☐ Yes ☐ No Initials:_____
				☐ Yes ☐ No Initials:_____
				☐ Yes ☐ No Initials:_____
				☐ Yes ☐ No Initials:_____
				☐ Yes ☐ No Initials:_____
				☐ Yes ☐ No Initials:_____

Figure 16.4. Visitor Tracking Evacuation Template.

STAFF EVACUATION TEMPLATE

UNIT WORKSHEET   Page _____ of _____

HOSPITAL: _____

Unit Name: _____   Unit Location: Building_____   Floor _____

STAFF NAME	DEPARTMENT	Time Left Unit	Destination	Arrival at Destination
				☐ Yes ☐ No Initials:_____
				☐ Yes ☐ No Initials:_____
				☐ Yes ☐ No Initials:_____
				☐ Yes ☐ No Initials:_____
				☐ Yes ☐ No Initials:_____
				☐ Yes ☐ No Initials:_____

Figure 16.5. Staff Evacuation Template.

17

Emergency Preparedness
Schools

While our schools are generally safe, over the last fifteen years there have been a number of fatal shooting incidents at schools and universities, including the 2012 tragedy at Sandy Hook Elementary in Newtown, Connecticut; Columbine High School (1999); Virginia Tech (2007); and Umpqua Community College in Roseburg, Oregon (2015). While gun control may be one way of trying to tackle the problem it is not likely to deter an aggressor determined to inflict maximum damage on others. After all, someone who is sufficiently deranged to want to kill and injure children and students has many options other than guns and bullets—from homemade bombs to releasing toxic chemicals.

While the risks do remain small they cannot be overlooked. When it comes to our schools you have to ask yourself, "No matter how small the risk, what is the risk of doing nothing?"

Some of the solutions already put forward include having an armed deputy at every school in the country and to arm teachers and train them how to use firearms. Another is to have a national register of people with mental health disorders. Some or all of these might be helpful but the two most effective ways to protect our children at schools are (1) to have practiced emergency procedure plans in place that can be implemented at a second's notice and (2) to improve school design and layout.

For example, if a suspicious person is seen approaching a school's main entrance, the alarm can be raised and, hopefully, the suspect apprehended before gaining access. Or, in another example, using point of sight surveillance over all main campus areas together with closed circuit television to identify and delay an attacker. Bullet proof glass protecting the main point of entry, usually the administration building, is another solution. If the building is breached, building design can be used to delay the attacker's progress and to protect those children and staff still inside. This involves safe routes for evacuation, safe rooms, and comprehensive building monitoring by closed circuit television which can, when necessary, be relayed to law enforcement agencies.

Surveillance and building design are also critical in protecting students and staff from other violent crimes. Better lighting and alarm buttons are just two of the many design modifications that can be implemented to make people safe in vulnerable areas such as car parks parking lots on dark nights. These and many other design features are discussed in detail later in this chapter.

Beyond school shootings and violence, there are of course other emergencies that can impact a school. The massive and powerful tornado that struck Moore, Oklahoma, in May 2013, leveled two elementary schools. Although nine children were killed, school staff were lauded for emergency planning (extensive drills) that saved many more lives. After the March 22, 2014, mudslide that devastated Oso, Washington, and took forty-one lives, officials conducted an assessment showing that twenty-eight of the state's public schools were at high risk of being damaged in a landslide.

In addition to the natural and non-natural events outlined in part one of this book, there are issues particular to schools to consider as well:

- ⅄ Bus crashes
- ⅄ Outbreaks of disease or infections
- ⅄ Student or staff deaths (suicide, homicide, unintentional, or natural)

Although schools have no control over some of the hazards that may impact them, such as earthquakes or plane crashes, they can take actions to minimize or mitigate the impact of such incidents.

The Department of Education (DOE), Department of Homeland Security, and FEMA provide excellent emergency planning guidelines, which we can look to here. They identify four phases of an emergency: mitigation and prevention, preparedness, response, and recovery. Emergency action plans are different from facility plans in that they take into account actions and needs of students and teachers, whereas a facility plan focuses on restoring the physical plant to its pre-disaster condition and performance. Emergency planning allows school facilities to be prepared for all eventualities, have the appropriate contingencies in place for when they happen, and return to normal as soon as possible afterward.

As outlined by the agencies above, the suggested basic planning process is:

Mitigation/Prevention

- ⅄ Conduct an assessment of each school building. Identify those factors that put the building, students, faculty, and staff at greater risk, such as proximity to rail tracks that regularly transport hazardous materials or facilities that produce highly toxic material or propane gas tanks, and develop a plan for reducing the risk. This can include plans to evacuate students away from these areas in times of crisis and to reposition propane tanks or other hazardous materials away from school buildings.

- Work with businesses and factories in close proximity to the school to ensure that the school's crisis plan is coordinated with their crisis plans.
- Ensure that a process is in place for controlling access and egress to the school. Require all persons who do not have authority to be in the school to sign in.
- Review traffic patterns and, where possible, keep cars, buses, and trucks away from school buildings.
- Review landscaping, and ensure that buildings are not obscured by overgrowth of bushes or shrubs where contraband can be placed or persons can hide.

Preparedness

- Have site plans for each school building readily available and ensure they are shared with first responders and agencies responsible for emergency preparedness.
- Ensure there are multiple evacuation routes and rallying points. First or second evacuation site options may be blocked or unavailable at the time of the crisis.
- Practice responding to a crisis on a regular basis.
- Ensure a process is established for communicating during a crisis.
- Inspect equipment to ensure it operates during crisis situations.
- Have a plan for discharging students. Remember that during a crisis many parents and guardians may not be able to get to the school to pick up their child. Make sure every student has a secondary contact person and contact information readily available.
- Have a plan for communicating information to parents and for quelling rumors. Cultivate relationships with the media ahead of time, and identify a Public Information Officer (PIO) to communicate with the media and the community during a crisis.
- Work with law enforcement and fire department officials and emergency preparedness agencies on a strategy for sharing key parts of the school crisis plans.

Response

- Identify the type of crisis that is occurring and determine the appropriate response.
- Develop a command structure for responding to a crisis. The roles and responsibilities for educators, law enforcement, and fire officials, and other first responders in responding to different types of crisis need to be developed, coordinated, reviewed, and approved.
- Maintain communications among all relevant staff.

Recovery

- Return to the business of teaching and learning as soon as possible.
- Identify and approve a team of credentialed mental health workers to provide mental health services to faculty and students after a crisis. Understand that recovery takes place over time and that the services of this team may be needed over an extended time period. Ensure that the team is adequately trained.
- The plan needs to include notification of parents on actions that the school intends to take to help students recover from the crisis.

Prevention and Mitigation

As explained in "Practical Information on Crisis Planning" (U.S. Department of Education, Office of Safe and Drug-Free Schools), school safety and emergency management experts often use the terms *prevention* and *mitigation* differently. Crises experts encourage schools to consider the full range of what they can do to avoid crises (when possible) or lessen their impact. The Federal Emergency Management Agency (FEMA) has done considerable work to help states and communities in the area of mitigation planning. It notes that

> The goal of mitigation is to decrease the need for response as opposed to simply increasing response capability. Mitigation is any sustained action taken to reduce or eliminate long-term risk to life and property from a hazard event. Mitigation encourages long-term reduction of hazard vulnerability. (FEMA, 2002)

Assessing and addressing the safety and integrity of facilities (window seals, HVAC systems, building structure), security (functioning locks, controlled access to the school), and the culture and climate of schools through policy and curricula are all important for preventing and mitigating possible future crises.

Mitigation and prevention require taking inventory of the dangers in a school and community and identifying what to do to prevent and reduce injury and property damage. For example:

- Establishing access control procedures and providing IDs for students and staff might prevent a dangerous intruder from coming onto school grounds.
- Conducting regular evacuation drills can reduce injury to students and staff because they will know what to do and how to avoid harm.
- Planning responses to and training for incidents involving hazardous materials is important for schools near highways.

There are resources in every community that can help with this process. Firefighters, police, public works staff, facilities managers, and the district's insurance representative, for example, can help conduct a hazard assessment. That information will be very useful in identifying problems that need to be addressed in the preparedness process. Rely on emergency responders, public health agencies, and school nurses to develop plans for and provide training in medical triage and first aid.

Mitigating emergencies is also important from a legal standpoint. If a school, district, or state does not take all necessary actions in good faith to create safe schools, it could be vulnerable to a suit for negligence. It is important to make certain that the physical plant is up to local codes, as well as federal and state laws.

Mitigating or preventing a crisis involves both the district and the community. Contact the regional or state emergency management office to help get started and connect to efforts that are underway locally.

Prevention and Mitigation: Assessing Threats and Planning

Know the school building. Assess potential hazards on campus. Conduct regular safety audits of the physical plant. Be sure to include driveways, parking lots, playgrounds, outside structures, and fencing. A safety audit should be part of normal operations.

Know the community. Mitigation requires assessment of local threats. Work with the local emergency management director to assess surrounding hazards. This includes the identification and assessment of the probability of natural disasters (tornadoes, hurricanes, earthquakes) and industrial and chemical accidents (water contamination or fuel spills). Locate major transportation routes and installations. For example, is the school on a flight path or near an airport? Is it near a railroad track that trains use to transport hazardous materials? Also address the potential hazards related to terrorism. Schools and districts should be active partners in community-wide risk assessment and mitigation planning.

Bring together regional, local, and school leaders, among others. Given that mitigation/prevention are community activities, leadership, and support of mitigation and prevention activities are necessary to ensure that the right people are at the planning table. Again, leadership begins at the top. Schools and districts will face an uphill battle if state and local governments are not supportive of their mitigation efforts.

Make regular school safety and security efforts part of mitigation/prevention practices. Consult the comprehensive school safety plan and its needs assessment activities to identify what types of incidents are common in the school.

Establish clear lines of communication. Because mitigation and prevention planning requires agencies and organizations to work together and share information, communication among stakeholders is critical. In addition to communications within the planning team, outside communications with families and the larger community are important to convey a visible message that schools and local governments are working together to ensure public

Students as Threats

Identifying students who may pose a danger to themselves or to others is sometimes called "threat assessment." The U.S. Department of Education and U.S. Secret Service have released a guide, *Threat Assessments in Schools: A Guide to Managing Threatening Situations and to Creating Safe School Climates* that may be useful in working through the threat assessment process. The results of a threat assessment may guide prevention efforts, which may help avoid a crisis.

Many schools have curricula and programs aimed at preventing children and youth from initiating harmful behaviors. Social problem-solving or life-skills programs, antibullying programs, and school-wide discipline efforts are common across the nation as a means of helping reduce violent behavior.

safety. Press releases from the governor and chief state school officer, that discuss the importance of crisis planning, can help open the channels of communication with the public.

Creating an Emergency Plan

Most of the elements of effective emergency planning for schools follow the same precepts outlined in chapters 10 and 11, but tweaked for the school environment. The web of stakeholders is a little more complex, and the fact that a school is part of a larger community is key.

Determine what emergencies the plan will address. Before assigning roles and responsibilities or collecting the supplies that the school will need during an emergency, define what constitutes an emergency for your school based on vulnerabilities, needs, and assets.

Describe the types of emergencies the plan addresses, including local hazards and problems identified from safety audits, evaluations, and assessments conducted during the mitigation/prevention phase. Consider incidents that may occur during community use of the school facility and prepare for incidents that occur while students are offsite (e.g., during a field trip).

Effective Crisis Planning Begins with Leadership

Every governor, mayor, legislator, superintendent, and principal should work together to make school crisis planning a priority. Top leadership helps set the policy agenda, secures funds, and brings the necessary people together across agencies. Other leadership also needs to be identified—the teacher who is well-loved in her school, the county's favorite school resource officer, or the caring school nurse. Leaders at the grassroots level will help your school community accept and inform the planning process. An organized management structure will be needed to respond to any crisis, and this structure begins with strong leadership.

Districts should be at the forefront in the creation of crisis plans for all of their schools. Schools should then tailor plans to fit their needs. At the school level, the principal serves as a leader. He or she should do the following:

- Secure commitment to crisis planning within the school and the larger community.
- Identify stakeholders who need to be involved in crisis planning, such as community groups, emergency responders, families, and staff. Cultivate relationships with these groups.
- Establish a crisis planning team. The staff in charge of prevention in a school (counselors, teachers, health professionals, administrators) should be part of the crisis planning team.
- Create an incident management structure. The structure should provide a comprehensive organizational structure designed for all types of emergencies. It is based on the premise that every crisis has certain major elements requiring clear lines of command and control.
- Know available resources. This activity includes identifying and becoming familiar with resources in the school, such as staff members certified in cardio-pulmonary resuscitation (CPR); in the community, including everyone from emergency responders to counselors; and in organizations, such as the parent-teacher association.
- Set up time to train and practice with staff, students, and emergency responders. Training is multifaceted and can include drills, in-service events, tabletop exercises, and written materials.
- Also include time to review and evaluate the plan.

In times of crisis, the principal serves as the manager and a leader. This does not always equate with being the person in charge of the entire crisis response. During a crisis, a principal should perform the following tasks:

- Respond within seconds and lead with a serious, calm, confident style.
- Implement the crisis plan.
- Yield authority, when appropriate, to others in the plan's designated command structure.
- Facilitate collaboration among school staff and emergency responders.
- Remain open to suggestions and information that may be critical in adjusting the response.

Crisis Plans Should Not Be Developed in a Vacuum

Crisis plans are a natural extension of ongoing school and community efforts to create safe learning environments. Good planning can enhance all school functions.

School and districts should open the channels of communication well before a crisis. Relationships need to be built in advance so that emergency responders are familiar with your school. Crisis plans should be developed in partnership with other community groups, including law enforcement, fire safety officials, emergency medical services, as well as health and mental health professionals. These groups know what to do in an emergency and can be helpful in the development of the plan. Get their help to develop a coordinated plan of response. And do not overlook local media. It is important that they understand how the district and schools will respond in a crisis. And often the media can be very helpful in providing information to families and others in the community.

It is essential to work with city and county emergency planners. You need to know the kinds of support municipalities can provide during a crisis, as well as any plans the city has for schools during a crisis. For example, city and county planners may plan to use schools as an emergency shelter, a supply depot, or even a morgue.

Reviewing this information in advance will help you quickly integrate resources. Participating in local emergency planning gives school and district administrators' insight into all the problems they might face in the event of a community-wide crisis and will help school efforts.

Consider Existing Crisis Plans as Resources

Before jumping in to develop your emergency plan, investigate existing plans (such as those of the district and local government). How do other agencies' plans integrate with the school's plan? Are there conflicts? Does the comprehensive school safety plan include a crisis plan? What information from the district's emergency plan can be used in the school's plan?

If the school recently completed a plan, efforts may be limited to revising the plan in response to environmental, staff, and student changes:

- Has the building been renovated or is it currently under renovation?
- Is the list of staff current?
- Have there been changes in the student population?
- Have other hazards revealed themselves?

Define Roles and Responsibilities

How will the school operate during an emergency? Define what should happen, when, and at whose direction, that is, create an organizational system. This should involve many of the school staff—important tasks will be neglected if one person is responsible for more than one function.

School staff should be assigned to the following roles:

- School commander
- Liaison to emergency responders
- Student caregivers
- Security officers
- Medical staff
- Spokesperson

During the planning process, both individuals and backups should be assigned to fill these roles.

If the district has not already appointed a public information officer, or PIO, it should to do so right away. Some large school districts have staff dedicated solely to this function. Many smaller districts use the superintendent, school security officers, or a school principal as their PIO.

Work with law enforcement officers and emergency responders to identify crises that require an outside agency to manage the scene (fire, bomb threat, hostage situations). Learn what roles these outsiders will play, what responsibilities they will take on, and how they will interact with school staff. Especially important is determining who will communicate with families and the community during an emergency.

Many schools and emergency responders use the Incident Command System, or ICS, to manage incidents. ICS provides a structured way for delegating responsibilities among school officials and all emergency responders during crisis response. An ICS or other management plan needs to be created with all emergency responders and school officials before an emergency occurs.

Crisis Plans and Communication Needs

Develop methods for communicating with the staff, students, families, and the media. Address how the school will communicate with all of the individuals who are directly or indirectly involved in the emergency. One of the first steps in planning for communication is to develop a mechanism to notify students and staff that an incident is occurring and to instruct them on what to do.

It is critical that schools and emergency responders use the same definitions for the same terms. Don't create more confusion because terms do not mean the same to everyone involved in responding to an emergency. It is important to determine how to convey information to staff and students by using codes for evacuation and lockdown, or simply by stating the facts.

Work with emergency responders to develop a common vocabulary. The words used to give directions for evacuation, lockdown, and other actions should be clear and not hazard specific.

FEMA recommends that plain language versus codes be used during emergency communications. Still, some districts have found it useful to use, but streamline, codes. Rather than a code for each type of incident they use only one code for each type of response.

With either approach, it is critical that terms or codes are used consistently across the district.

If students are evacuated from the school building, will staff use cell phones, instant messaging, texts, radios, intercoms, or runners to get information to the staff supervising them? Be sure to discuss the safest means of communication with law enforcement and emergency responders. For example, some electronic devices can trigger bombs. And verify that school communication devices are compatible with emergency responder devices. A cell phone or two-way radio is of no use if it cannot be used with the emergency responder's phone or radio. Also, check to see that the school's communication devices do not interfere with the emergency responder's equipment.

Plain Language

The Federal Emergency Management Agency recommends using plain language to announce the need for action, for example, "evacuate" rather than "code blue." Many districts note that with plain language everyone in the school building including new staff, substitute teachers, and visitors will know what type of response is required.

Identify several modes of communication for both internal and external communication. Keep in mind that in times of crisis, computers, intercoms, telephones, and even cell phones may not work or may be dangerous to use. Plan for several methods of communication in a crisis.

Make sure that schools have adequate supplies of communication gear and that the appropriate individuals have access to it. One school's crisis plan, for example, calls for the principal to immediately grab a backpack containing a cell phone and a walkie-talkie. Communication gear is of no use if no one can access it.

Create communication plans to notify families that a crisis has occurred at their child's school. These pathways should include several modes of communication, including notices sent home and phone trees, so the pathways can be tailored to fit the needs of a particular crisis. For example, it may be appropriate in some crises to send a notice home, while other crises require immediate parental notification. Use these pathways throughout the planning process to encourage parental input and support. Be sure you have up-to-date contact information for families.

Establish communication pathways with the community. This may be in the form of a phone or e-mail tree, a community liaison, or media briefings. It is crucial to keep the community informed before, during, and after a crisis. Consider writing template letters and press releases in advance so staff will not have to compose them during the confusion and chaos of the event. It's easier to tweak smaller changes than to begin from scratch. It may be necessary to translate letters and other forms of communication into languages other than English depending on the composition of the communities feeding the affected school(s). Be sure to consider cultural differences when preparing these materials.

Local AM and FM radio stations can be helpful in communicating which schools are open after a storm or event. Schedule these announcements to be made at the same time each day. In crisis situations, school districts and community colleges have used local radio stations to get information to personnel, parents, students, and the community.

Good communication during a crisis is crucial. Below are some key points to keep in mind:

- Keep staff who are managing the students informed. Regardless of the amount of training staff members have received, there is going to be chaos and fear. Communication mitigates those reactions and helps regain a sense of calm and control.
- Understand that parents are going to want immediate access to their children. Safely begin reunification procedures as soon as possible. Keep families informed as much as possible, especially in the case of delayed reunification.
- Communication often stops after a crisis subsides. However, during the recovery phase, keeping staff and community informed remains critical.

Crisis Plans: One Size Does Not Fit All

Every school needs an emergency plan that is tailored to its unique characteristics. Within a school district, however, it is necessary for all plans to have certain commonalities. Still, it is impractical for all schools to work individually with emergency responders and other local agencies, although school staff should meet the people who will respond to a crisis before one happens. It is important to find the right balance and to assign district and school roles early.

A school emergency plan should not be one document. It should be a series of documents targeted to various audiences. For example, a school could use detailed response guides for planners, flipcharts for teachers, a crisis response toolbox for administrators, and wallet cards containing evacuation routes for bus drivers.

Plans should be age appropriate. Elementary school children will behave much differently in a crisis than high school students.

Set a Realistic Timetable for the Preparation Process

While it is reasonable to feel a sense of urgency about the need to be prepared for an emergency, a complete, comprehensive plan cannot be developed overnight. Take the time needed for collecting essential information, developing the plan, and involving the appropriate people.

Emergency management is a continuous process in which all phases of the plan are being reviewed and revised. Good plans are never finished. They can—and should—always be updated based on experience, research, and changing vulnerabilities.

Start by identifying who should be involved in developing the plan. Include training and drills. Delegating responsibilities and breaking the process down into manageable steps will help planners develop the plan.

Plan for the Diverse Needs of Children and Staff

Our review of crisis plans found that few schools addressed children or staff with physical, sensory, motor, developmental, or mental challenges. Special attention is also needed for children with limited English proficiency. Outreach documents for families may be needed in several languages.

Consider the following issues:

- In an evacuation, there may not be enough time to move mobility impaired students and staff to traditional shelters. It is important to identify alternative, accessible, safe shelter locations and to communicate these locations to emergency responders. Assign sufficient staff to assist these individuals during a crisis.
- Consider providing basic sign-language training to designated school staff: individuals with hearing disabilities may not be able to communicate verbally, to read lips, or to hear fire alarms or other emergency signals.
- Visual impairments might impede reading signs or traversing unfamiliar or altered terrain—consider whether debris might obstruct the evacuation of such staff and students and necessitate alternative shelter locations.
- Are staff trained to assist students with developmental disabilities? These students may become upset if routine patterns of activity are disrupted.
- Do any students or staff have special needs for medicines, power supplies, or medical devices that are not likely to be available in emergency shelters? Consider what alternative arrangements can be made to provide these necessities.
- In addition to addressing these concerns, find out whether specific crises will require additional considerations for hazards, such as fire, severe weather, or earthquake. For example, mobility impairments might prevent some staff or students from being able to bend over to assume the protective position recommended during tornadoes.

Ten Common Mistakes When Developing an Emergency Plan

- ▲ Not Consulting With Local Emergency Response Officials
- ▲ Not Customizing Prepackaged Plans
- ▲ Plan is Difficult to Read under Stress
- ▲ Plan Components Aren't Consistent
- ▲ Using Coded Announcements or Too Many of Them
- ▲ Not Conducting Drills of Plan
- ▲ Not Telling Parents about Plan
- ▲ Not Planning for Power Failure or Phone System/Communications Failure
- ▲ Not Training All Staff on Plan
- ▲ Not Giving Administrators Decision Making Authority

Implementation

Now that you have the plan, you must implement it, which includes testing it and fine-tuning it—and being sure of custodians, faculty, and other members of staff are familiar with it.

Provide teachers and staff with ready access to the plan so they can understand its components and act on them. People who have experienced a crisis often report that they go on "autopilot" during an incident. They need to know what to do in advance not only to get them through an incident but also to help alleviate panic and anxiety.

Training and practice are essential for the successful implementation of crisis plans. Most students and staff know what to do in case of a fire because the law requires them to participate in routine fire drills, but would they know what to do in a different crisis? Many districts now require evacuation and lockdown drills in addition to state-mandated fire drills. Drills also allow your school to evaluate what works and what needs to be improved.

Emergency Equipment and Supplies

Obtain necessary equipment and supplies. Provide staff with the necessary equipment to respond to an emergency. Consider whether there are enough master keys for emergency responders so that they have complete access to the school. Get the phones or radios necessary for communication, as mentioned above.

Maintain a secure cache of first aid supplies. What about food and water for students and staff during an incident?

Prepare response kits for secretaries, nurses, and teachers so they have easy access to the supplies. For example, a nurse's kit might include student and emergency medicines ("anaphylaxis kits," which may require physician's orders, for use in breathing emergencies, such as severe, sudden allergic reactions), as well as first aid supplies. A teacher's kit might include an emergency management reference guide, as well as an updated student roster.

Create maps and facilities information. In a crisis, emergency responders need to know the location of everything in a school. Create site maps that include information about classrooms, hallways, and stairwells, the location of utility shut-offs, and potential staging sites. Emergency responders need copies of this information in advance.

Crisis Boxes or Go Kits

The California Safe Schools Task Force developed a helpful template for a crisis response box—a portable box that contains important information for use in an emergency or a disaster. Go to the California Department of Education's Web site for a thorough explanation of the contents at www.cde.ca.gov/ls/ss/cp/documents/crisisrespbox.pdf. Contents include:

- Street maps of the area (laminated and in multiples)
- Campus layout, building plans, and blueprints
- Aerial maps of the campus (helpful for insurance purposes)
- Teacher and staff roster
- Master key and extra key sets
- Fire alarm/sprinkler system reset procedures
- Utility information

Evacuation

Evacuation requires all students and staff to leave the building. While evacuating to the school's field makes sense for a fire drill that only lasts a few minutes, it may not be an appropriate location for a longer period of time.

The evacuation plan should include backup buildings to serve as emergency shelters, such as nearby community centers, religious institutions, businesses, or other schools. Agreements for using these spaces should be negotiated or reconfirmed prior to the beginning of each school year. Evacuation plans should include contingencies for weather conditions, such as rain, snow, and extreme cold and heat. While most students will be able to walk to a nearby community center, students with disabilities may have more restricted mobility. Your plan should include transportation options for these students.

If an incident occurs while students are outside, you will need to return them to the building quickly. This is a **reverse evacuation**. Once staff and students are safely in the building, you may find the situation calls for a lockdown.

Lockdowns are called for when a crisis occurs outside of the school and an evacuation would be dangerous. A lockdown may also be called for when there is an emergency inside, and movement within the school will put students in jeopardy. All exterior doors are locked and students and staff stay in their classrooms. Windows may need to be covered.

Shelter-in-place is used when there is not time to evacuate or when it may be harmful to leave the building. Shelter-in-place is commonly used during hazardous material spills.

Students and staff are held in the building and windows and doors are sealed. There can be limited movement within the building. The introduction of outside air must be stopped, usually accomplished by shutting off power to create a negative pressure.

During an emergency designate locations—**staging sites**—for emergency responders to organize, for medical personnel to treat the injured, for the public information officer to brief the media, and for families to be reunited with their children. Student reunification sites should be as far away from the media staging area as possible. Law enforcement will help determine the plans needed to facilitate access of emergency responders and to restrict access of well-wishers and the curious.

Student Release Procedures

During an emergency, traditional student release procedures are frequently unsafe or otherwise inoperable. As soon as an emergency is recognized, account for all students, staff, and visitors. Emergency responders treat a situation very differently when people are missing. For example, when a bomb threat occurs, the stakes are substantially higher if firefighters do not know when they are trying to locate and disarm a bomb whether students are in the school.

Be sure to inform families of release procedures *before* an emergency occurs. In many crises, families have flocked to schools wanting to collect their children immediately. A method should be in place for tracking student release and ensuring that students are only released to authorized individuals.

Consider the following elements for emergency student release procedures:

- **Update student rosters.** Rosters should be updated at a minimum of twice a year; some recommend updating rosters weekly.
- **Distribute updated rosters.** All teachers need updated rosters of all their classes. This should be stored in their classroom so that a substitute teacher could easily find it. A copy of all rosters should also be placed in the emergency response box, as well as with the principal and any other stakeholder as advisable. It is critical to know which students are present during an emergency.
- **Create student emergency cards.** At the beginning of the school year, make sure the school has an emergency card for each student containing contact information on parents/guardians, as well as several other adults who can be contacted if the parent or guardian is not available. The card should also indicate whether the student is permitted to leave campus with any of the adults listed on the card, if necessary. Some districts recommend authorizing one or more parents of children at your child's school to pick up your child. The card should also include all pertinent medical information, such as allergies, medications, and doctor contact information. These cards should be stored in the front office, both in hard copy and electronically, if possible.

🠑   **Create student release forms to be used in times of an emergency and store them with emergency response materials.** Create a back-up plan if forms are not available.

🠑   **Designate student release areas, as well as back-up options.** These areas should be predetermined and communicated to families.

🠑   **Assign roles for staff.** For example, a staff member is needed to take the emergency cards from the office to the release area, while several staff members are needed to deal with families and sign out students.

🠑   **Create student release procedures.** These procedures should create a flexible, yet simple, system for the release of students. Families will want immediate access to their children; emotions will be running high. Create a system that considers this, and train staff to expect it. Procedures should require proof of identity; if necessary, wait until such proof can be ascertained. It is important not to release a student to a noncustodial guardian if custody is an issue for the family. Do not release students to people not listed on student emergency cards. A well-intentioned friend may offer to take a child home; however, school staff must be certain that students are only released to the appropriate people so students' families will know where they are.

🠑   **Arrange for transportation for students who are not taken home by a parent or guardian.** Also arrange for shelter and provisions, if necessary.

Practice

Preparedness includes emergency drills and emergency exercises for staff, students, and emergency responders. Many schools have found tabletop exercises very useful in practicing and testing the procedures specified in their emergency plan. Tabletop exercises involve school staff and emergency responders sitting around a table discussing the steps they would take to respond to an emergency. Often, training and drills identify issues that need to be addressed in the plan and problems with plans for communication and response. Teachers also need training in how to manage students during an emergency, especially those experiencing panic reactions.

Careful consideration of these issues will improve your plan and better prepare you to respond to an actual emergency.

Emergency Plan Checklist

To review the comprehensiveness of the emergency plan, consider the items on the checklist below.

_____ Determine what crisis plans exist in the district, school, and community.
_____ Identify all stakeholders involved in crisis planning.
_____ Develop procedures for communicating with staff, students, families, and the media.
_____ Establish procedures to account for students during a crisis.
_____ Gather information that exists about the school facility, such as maps and the location of utility shutoffs.
_____ Identify the necessary equipment that needs to be assembled to assist staff in a crisis.

Recovery

Recovery is the ability to recuperate from the loss or damage to a school facility, whether due to natural disaster or malicious intent. Disaster recovery strategies include rebuilding and implementing procedures to restore a system or community to its pre-disaster condition. Recovery planning includes consideration for assets and services following an emergency. The recovery period also allows for the identification of systems and buildings that performed well in the disaster and others that failed. Learning from the experience is an important part of the recovery process.

The goal of recovery is to return to learning and restore the infrastructure of the school as quickly as possible. Focus on students and the physical plant, and take as much time as needed for recovery.

School staff can be trained to deal with the emotional impact of the emergency, as well as to initially assess the emotional needs of students, staff, and responders. One of the major goals of recovery is to provide a caring and supportive school environment.

- **Plan for recovery in the preparedness phase**. Determine the roles and responsibilities of staff and others who will assist in recovery during the planning phase. District-level counselors may want to train school staff to assess the emotional needs of students and colleagues to determine intervention needs. Experience shows that after an emergency many unsolicited offers of assistance from outside the school community are made. During planning, you may want to review the credentials of service providers and certify those that will be used during recovery.

- **Assemble the Emergency Intervention Team**. An Emergency Intervention Team is composed of individuals at either the district or school level involved in recovery. Even when emergency intervention teams exist within individual schools, it may be necessary for the superintendent to allocate additional resources on an as-needed basis.

Service providers in the community may want to assist after an emergency. With prior planning, those with appropriate skills and certifications may be tapped to assist in recovery. This will help district and school personnel coordinate activities of the community service providers and see that district procedures and intervention goals are followed.

- ▲ **Return to the "business of learning" as quickly as possible.** Experts agree that the first order of business following an emergency is to return students to learning as quickly as possible. This may involve helping students and families cope with separations from one another with the reopening of school after an emergency.

- ▲ **Focus on the building, as well as people, during recovery.** Following an emergency, buildings and their grounds may need repairing or repainting/ re-landscaping. Conduct safety audits to determine the parts of the building that can be used, and plan for repairing those that are damaged.

- ▲ **Provide assessment of emotional needs of staff, students, families, and responders.** Assess the emotional needs of all students and staff, and determine those who need intervention by a school counselor, social worker, school psychologist, or other mental health professional. Arrange for appropriate interventions by school or community-based service providers.

- ▲ **Conduct daily debriefings for staff, responders, and others assisting in recovery.** Mental health workers who have provided services after emergencies stress the importance of ensuring that those who are providing "psychological first aid" are supported with daily critical incident stress debriefings. Debriefings help staff cope with their own feelings of vulnerability.

- ▲ **Take as much time as needed for recovery.** An individual recovers from an emergency at his or her own pace. Recovery is not linear. After an emergency, healing is a process filled with ups and downs. Depending on the traumatic event and the individual, recovery may take months or even years.

- ▲ **Remember anniversaries.** The anniversary of an emergency will stimulate memories and feelings about the incident. In addition, other occasions may remind the school community about the emergency, including holidays, returning to school after vacations and other breaks, as well as events or occasions that seemingly do not have a connection with the incident. This underscores the notion that recovery may take a longer time than anticipated.

Staff members need to be sensitive to their own, as well as the students' reactions, in such situations and provide support when necessary. School emergency planning guides suggest holding appropriate memorial services or other activities, such as planting a tree in memory of victims of the emergency. Trauma experts discourage memorials for suicide victims to avoid glorifying and sensationalizing these deaths.

Reactions of Staff

The trauma of a disaster can affect everyone. You do not have to be a primary victim to feel the impact or stress of an event. Possible behaviors after a disaster include:

- Increased irritability and impatience with students and staff. Decreased tolerance of minor student infractions.
- Decreased concentration.
- Worries and fears that answers or responses to students could make things worse for them.
- Worries about reoccurrence and repercussions.
- Increased concern or hypersensitivity about school violence.
- Feelings of discomfort, with intense emotions, such as anger and fear.
- Denial that the traumatic event may impact the students.

Evaluation and Closing the Loop

Evaluating recovery efforts will help prepare for the next emergency. Use several methods to evaluate recovery efforts. Conduct brief interviews with emergency responders, families, teachers, students, and staff. Focus groups may also be helpful in obtaining candid information about recovery efforts.

Recovery may seem like an end, but it is also the beginning. You must close the loop on the circle. A critical step in emergency preparedness planning is to evaluate each incident. What worked? What didn't? How could you improve operations? Take what you have learned and start at the beginning. Update and strengthen the plan so that in a crisis, no child is left behind.

Recovery Checklist

____ Strive to return to learning as quickly as possible.
____ Restore the physical plant, as well as the school community.
____ Monitor how staff are assessing students for the emotional impact of the crisis.
____ Identify what follow up interventions are available to students, staff, and first responders.
____ Conduct debriefings with staff and first responders.
____ Assess curricular activities that address the crisis.
____ Allocate appropriate time for recovery.
____ Plan how anniversaries of events will be commemorated.
____ Capture "lessons learned" and incorporate them into revisions and trainings.

Preparedness and the Educational Facility

Facility emergency preparedness focuses on protecting educational facilities so that they can be used for their intended purposes. Preparedness activities vary depending on the disaster and whether there is warning. A hurricane provides warning only as its approach path can be estimated. A bomb going off on the roof of a school gives little or no warning.

Identifying Hazards

Specific facility hazard preparedness activities include:

Potential Manmade Hazards

- Identify potential threats or targets near the school, along with their impact (e.g., chemical plants, gas lines, heavy truck traffic, and railroad tracks).
- Identify hidden areas adjacent to the school that might provide offenders with cover or provide students with a location for illicit activities.

Seismic and Wind Hazards

- Identify alternate routes into and out of the site to avoid potential fallen trees, buildings, utility lines, or other hazards.
- Ensure backup emergency power and communication sources have been incorporated into the design.
- Ensure building setbacks are adequate to prevent damage from falling trees.

Flood Hazard

- Is the site located in a floodplain or at high risk if nearby water sources flood?
- Can emergency vehicles access the site during high water conditions?

Storm Hazard

- If there is construction on the campus, contact the facilities project manager to implement contractor tiedown procedures.
- All objects that may be blown by the wind should be taken into the building (e.g., garbage cans). Anchor objects that cannot be brought inside. Also, check the roofs of buildings for loose objects.
- Clean out all gutters and roof drains. One gallon of water weighs 8.35 pounds; the weight from backed-up water adds up quickly and can easily cause a roof collapse.

∧   Remove and relocate all portable physical education equipment to the interior of the school.

∧   Lower and secure window storm awnings (if applicable).

∧   Close all windows.

∧   Pools:

- Lower the water level of swimming pools one foot to accommodate heavy rains, but do not drain them completely.
- Add extra chlorine to pools to prevent contamination.
- Turn off electricity to pool equipment.

∧   Check generator and emergency lights (if applicable).

∧   Media Area/Computer Labs: If possible, relocate all equipment to tabletops and cover with plastic to reduce water damage.

∧   Relocate any valuable books in the collection to the upper shelves.

School Building Security and Safety: Facility Design

Every building is unique and there is great variety in school design; however, the purpose of schools, their occupancy, their economic basis, and their role in the social scene mean that there are certain common features of schools that distinguish them from other building types. The estimated value of the national public school inventory is well over $361.6 billion. Of the almost 15,000 local education agencies found throughout the United States, 41.9 percent are in small towns and rural areas and enroll 30.4 percent of the students, 25.9 percent are in large towns and cities and enroll 30.7 percent of the students, and 32.2 percent of the education agencies are in suburban areas and enroll 39 percent of the students.

More than half of our school facilities are at least forty years old and, even with minor renovations, have passed their prime in terms of adaptability to modern teaching methods and tools (e.g., computers, in-class electronic information displays, and group learning activities). Almost all states require new construction once replacement costs reach a certain level (usually 60 percent). The most recent studies (completed at the close of the last decade) show a range of $100 billion to over $300 billion would be needed to bring our nation's schools into good teaching condition.

FEMA has extensive information on designing schools with security and mitigation in mind. FEMA's Risk Management Series includes such guides and manuals as "Primer to Design Safe School Projects in Case of Terrorist Attacks" (FEMA 428, 2013) or "Design Guide for Improving School Safety in Earthquakes, Floods, and High Winds" (FEMA 424, 2010). These can be found online at (respectively): www.fema.gov/media-library-data/20130726-1455-20490-1896/fema428.pdf and www.fema.gov/media-library/assets/documents/5264.

Some of the security design considerations that these manuals describe:

- ⅄ Creating a campus of dispersed versus clustered functions: dispersing key functions in one place means that in a crisis where an attack or event occurs in one place, the whole school is not necessarily destabilized.
- ⅄ Controlling vehicle and pedestrian circulation through site design: installing high curbs and bollards effect maximize stand-off distance, designing roads to limit speeds, putting visitor parking lots away from the school.
- ⅄ Using landscaping for added protection as soft barriers.
- ⅄ Allowing for enhanced security systems that include closed-circuit television (CCTV) and lighting systems.
- ⅄ Allowing for underground, concealed, and protected utilities.
- ⅄ Designing building exteriors with minimal ornamentation (that won't become airborne projectiles in high wind or explosion).
- ⅄ Designing walls and wall systems with crises in mind: for example, using reinforced concrete wall systems in lieu of masonry or curtain walls to minimize flying debris in a blast or reinforced wall panels that protect columns and assist in preventing progressive collapse.
- ⅄ Minimizing the number of windows and using better window system technology, such as thermally tempered glass with a security film; laminated thermally tempered glass; laminated heat strengthened, or laminated annealed glass; and blast curtains.
- ⅄ Looking at door systems. For example: having exterior doors into inhabited areas open outward. In addition to facilitating egress, by doing so, the doors will seat into the door frames in response to an explosive blast, increasing the likelihood that the doors will not enter the school building as hazardous debris.
- ⅄ Preventing external roof access.

Not every school system or organization will find themselves building new facilities. Even so, the ideas in these manuals can still be of value for existing facilities. Replacing windows with better glass is one example. It may not be possible to create a visitor parking area for an urban school, but it is possible to create barriers and work with local officials to prevent street parking in front of the building.

Crime Prevention through Environmental Design (CPTED)

CPTED (Crime Prevention through Environmental Design) is a crime reduction technique that is used by architects, city planners, landscape and interior designers, and law enforcement with the objective of creating a climate of safety in a community by designing a physical environment that positively influences human behavior.

CPTED concepts have been successfully applied in a wide variety of applications, including streets, parks, museums, government buildings, houses, and commercial complexes. The approach is particularly applicable to schools, where outdated facilities are common and building designs are not always compatible with today's more security-conscious environment.

CPTED analysis focuses on creating changes to the physical and social environment that will reinforce positive behavior. It builds on three strategies:

- **Territoriality** (using buildings, fences, pavement, sign, and landscaping to express ownership)
- **Natural surveillance** (placing physical features, activities, and people to maximize visibility)
- **Access control** (the judicial placement of entrances, exits, fencing, landscaping, and lighting)

A CPTED analysis of a school evaluates crime rates, office-referral data, and school cohesiveness and stability, as well as core design shortcomings of the physical environment (e.g., blind hallways, uncontrolled entries, or abandoned areas that attract problem behavior). The application of CPTED principles starts with a threat and vulnerability analysis to determine the potential for attack and what needs to be protected. Protecting a school from physical attack by criminal behavior or terrorist activity, in many cases, only reflects a change in the level and types of threats. The CPTED process provides direction to solve the challenges of crime and terrorism with organizational (people), mechanical (technology and hardware), and natural design (architecture and circulation flow) methods.

CPTED concepts can be integrated into expansion or reconstruction plans for existing buildings, as well as new buildings. Applying CPTED concepts from the beginning usually has minimal impact on costs, and the result is a safer school. Each school, district, and community should institute measures appropriate for their own circumstances because there is no a single solution that will fit all schools.

Facilities and Recovery: Site Inspection and Recording Impacts

After the emergency, be sure to take pictures and document damage BEFORE recovery efforts begin. As you document damage, think long-term. The immediate damage, such as damage to roofs and windows, is obvious. The long-term, less detectable damage, such as air quality issues, also needs to be included in your estimates and reimbursement requests.

Both insurers and FEMA will require well-documented evidence of damages claimed. Personnel responsible for taking pictures should be instructed on the type of photos required, the proper labeling of photos, and what to avoid. Several thousand pictures of wet, damaged ceiling tile are worthless unless care has been taken to identify the school, building, and room where the tiles are located.

There is no single assessment process followed by all school systems; each school system has its own particular method. The assessment process used will depend on the severity of the event, number of facilities, staff available to perform damage assessments, distance between the facilities, and the ability to travel between campuses. Assessments vary as to level of detail; some boards with widely disbursed campuses will perform an initial "drive-by" inspection, attempting to obtain cursory information as to the extent of exterior damage, and follow up with a more detailed inspection at a later time. Other schools will begin with a detailed assessment, performing interior and exterior inspections right away. Some school systems are able to complete detailed reviews for all their campuses quickly (i.e., in two days), while others may take several days or weeks.

The Palm Beach Community College (PBCC), Florida, has developed a comprehensive set of processes and procedures for taking pictures and documenting damage. The system also includes forms used to document damage. PBCC has used this system and has found it to be very effective when dealing with FEMA and insurance providers.

Areas that should be considered when taking photos include the following:

Interior Areas

- Main Office, Lobby, Reception
- Administrative Areas and Staff Offices
- Mailboxes
- Health Clinic
- Guidance Office
- Conference Rooms
- Corridors, Circulation, Lockers
- Stairs, Stairwells, Landings, Steps
- Ramps
- Restrooms
- Classrooms
- Art Rooms
- Music Rooms
- Labs, Shops, Computer Rooms
- Dance Classrooms
- Gymnasiums
- Locker Rooms

- Media Center
- Auditorium and Theaters
- Cafeterias and Student Commons
- Coolers, Freezers
- Vending Machines
- Storage Rooms
- Equipment Rooms
- Elevators
- Portable, Modular, or Temporary Classrooms
- Non-Structural Building Hazards
- Obvious Building Damage
- Entryways
- Interior Walls
- Interior Doors, Windows
- Ceilings
- General Fire Requirements for Existing Buildings
- Utilities
- Air Handling and Filtration
- Fresh Air Intakes
- Gas Tank/Piping
- Interior Water Pipes
- Interior Lighting
- Lighting Fixtures/Poles

- Building Access Control
- Building Notification Systems
- Closed Circuit Television (CCTV) Surveillance Systems
- Telephone Systems
- Public Telephones
- Radio/Wireless Communication Systems

Exterior Areas

- Site Access
- Fencing
- Landscaping, Trees and Shrubs, Land Washout
- School Sign
- Flagpoles
- Playground Equipment
- Walkways
- Canopies, Awnings, Breezeways, Covered Walkways
- Courtyards

- Building Access
- Exterior Walls
- Siding
- Exterior Doors
- Windows
- Skylights
- Roofs
- Exterior Roof Damage
- Rooftop Vents
- Gutters, Downspouts
- Rooftop HVAC Units
- Exterior Water Pipe
- Water Fountains
- Water Supply and Storage
- Sewage, Backup, Sewage
- Plants
- Exterior Wiring

Aerial photography works well to document before and after situations affecting both school grounds and structures, and is well received by FEMA and insurance companies. Infrared photography can also be used; it does an excellent job of identifying where water has penetrated the roof, as well as where it may be leaking down walls. Single ply and built-up roofing that has experienced broken seals can look solid on the exterior when, in fact, its integrity has been compromised.

APPENDICES

Emergency Action Plan

for

[Insert Your Organization Name Here]

[Insert Your Address Here]

[Insert Your Company Logo Here]

Date of Current Revision

[Insert Date Here]

Revision

[Insert Revision Number Here]

Next Review Date

[Insert Date Here]

Buildings Covered

[Insert Building Names / Addresses Here]

Copies of This Manual Assigned To:

[Insert Names / Titles Here]

The Mission Statement

[Add a copy of your emergency management team's

mission statement here]

For Example:

Emergency Management Team—Mission Statement

Our mission is to protect the employees, property, business, and community in the event of an emergency.

We are committed to providing the company with effective and useful solutions that will reduce or eliminate emergencies and their negative impact.

We will accomplish this by conducting risk assessments, creating a written emergency action plan, and conducting employee training.

Additionally, we will create viable plans for restoration and recovery in the event of an emergency.

The Emergency Management Team

[Add phone number, cell phone number, and work location]

Title	Phone	Cell	Work Location
Emergency Director			
Business Continuity Manager			
Risk Management Manager			
Logistics Manager			
Procurement Manager			
Media Relations			
Human Resources			
Facilities Manager			
Legal Counsel			
Command Post Leader			
Group Leader			
Floor Captains			
Fire Brigade			
Evacuation Assistants			
Runners			

Other Important Contacts

In-house medical contact (CPR, First Aid)
Police Department
Fire Department
Health Department
Poison Control Center
Hospital

Chain of Command

In the event of an emergency *[Insert your answer here]* will be in command. In the event this person is unavailable, *[Insert your answer here]* will take command.

Vendors and Contractors

During an actual emergency, we will likely need the resources of our vendors and contractors. In an effort to identify those vendors and contractors, we have created a database including the specialties of each vendor. That list can be found below.

Because this database can become outdated, we will review the list each year on *[insert your answer here]*.

Contractor Availability Form: First Alternate

Issue	Contractor	Contact	Office Phone	Cell Phone	AVAILABLE	NOT AVAILABLE	LEFT MESSAGE	Comments
Generator								
Landscaper								
Sign Maker								
Parking Lot Sweeper								
Barricade Supplier								
Tool Rental								
Security Guard Service								
Motorized Gate								
Fence Contractor								
Roofing Contractor								
Ice Machine								
Ice Supplier								
Dumpster Rental								
Refuse Company								
Trash Hauler								
Port-O-Pottie Supplier								
Computer Systems								
Computer Network Tech								
Phone Technician								
HVAC Contractor								
Electrical Contractor								
Engineering								
Architect								
Plumber								
Locksmith								
Glass Company								
Movers								
Carpet Cleaner								
Janitorial								
Laundry Services								
Elevator Service								
Fire Protection Vendor								
Security System								
Electric Utility								
Gas Utility								
Water Utility								
Phone Company								

Figure A.1. Contractor Availability Form.

Emergency Supplies

The stocking of emergency supplies is an integral part of our emergency planning responsibilities. We also realize that the rotation of many of these supplies is critical. Therefore, we will review our emergency stock of supplies on an annual basis. This review will occur each year on *[insert your answer here]*.

To better facilitate the emergency stock of supplies, we have created a database which identifies materials to be stocked, the quantity needed, and the location where stored.

STORM PREPARATIONS
Inventory of Materials

TOOLS / EQUIPMENT	Location A	Location B	Location C	Location D
Chain saws (18') with 1 gallon gas can	1	1	2	1
1 quart bar & chain oil	2	2	4	2
2-cycle engine oil	2	2	4	2
Shovels	4	4	4	4
Wet vacs (25 gallon)	2	2	2	2
Fire estinguisher	4	4	6	4
Axe	1	1	2	1
Crowbar	1	1	1	1
Push Brooms	2	2	2	2
Chains and locks	2	2	2	3
Extension cords	3	3	4	3
Circular Saw	1	1	1	1
Screw guns / drills	2	2	2	2
Duct Tape	3	3	3	3
60 mil plastic liner (roll)	2	2	2	2
Orange spray paint	1	1	1	1
Ladder	1	1	1	1
Fans	2	2	4	2
Barricades	4	4	8	4
Emergency caution tape	2	2	2	2
FUEL SUPPLIES				
Gas can (5 gallon)				
Propane gas (Bottles for lanterns)				
Propane - 20lb Bottle for gas grill				
LIGHTING				
Propane lanterns				
6-volt lanterns				
Flashlights				
Portable quartz lighting				
BEDDING				
Folding cots				
Wool blankets				
CLOTHING				
Rubber boots, Size 10				
Rubber boots, Size 11				
Rubber boots, Size 12				
Work gloves				
Rain jackets, large				
Rain hoods				
Rain pants				
Hard hats				
Dust masks				
Respirators				
Safety glasses/goggles				
Reflective vests				
ROPE/WIRE				
Tie wire (50' Roll)				
Rope, 1/2" (300' Roll)				
Rope, 3/8" (200' Roll)				
PUMPS				
Sump pump w/hose and discharge hose				
MEDICAL				
First Aid kits				
Aspirin				
Sunblock				
Insect repellent				
WATER HOSES				
2 1/2" 6' Hose pkgs.				
SAND SUPPLIES				
Burlap bags				
Sand delivered (by load)				
GENERATORS				
Portable generator				
Fuel (unleadead gasoline)				
Oil (for Diesel Generator)				

Figure A.2. Storm Preparations, Inventory of Materials.

STORM PREPARATIONS
Inventory of Materials

	Location A	Location B	Location C	Location D
RADIOS / BATTERIES				
Radios, NOAA				
Radios, 2-Way				
Clock (battery operated)				
Batteries - (size AA to D and 6V lantern)				
Calculator				
WATER / ICE / FOOD				
Ice chests (50 qt)				
Ice				
Meals Ready To Eat (MRE's)				
Matches				
Utinsils				
Garbage bags				
Water purifying tablets				
Bottled water - 5 gal. bottles				
Can opener (manual)				
BUILDING MATERIALS				
Plywood (4' x 8' x 5/8" sheets)				
2"x4"x 8' studs				
Screws				
Nails				
RENTAL EQUIPMENT				
Port-O-Potties				
Boat w/oars and accessories				
PHOTO EQUIPMENT				
Digital camera				
Disposable camera (Waterproof)				
Video				
CASH				
Emergency cash				
OFFICE SUPPLIES				
Steno pads				
Highlighters				
Pens				
Pencils				
Clipboards				
Paper clips				
Staples				

Figure A.2. Storm Preparations, Inventory of Materials, continued.

Blueprints and As-Builts

Quick access to current copies of the floorplans of our buildings is important to our emergency management goals. To achieve this goal we have included updated floorplans as part of this emergency action plan. We have identified the following import building features on the floorplans.

- Windows
- Doors
- Emergency exits
- Alarm panels
- Fire alarm pull stations
- First aid kits and stations
- Automated External Defibrillators (AED)
- Generator location

- Generator-powered circuits
- Uninterruptible power system location
- Evacuation staging areas
- Gas mains and valves
- Utility shutoffs
- Generator and switchgear locations
- Water lines and valves

Storm drains
Roof drains
Sewer lines
Floor plans
Alarm locations
Water sprinkler testing valves
Fire extinguishers
Fire pull stations
Smoke detectors
Designated escape routes
Exits doors
Stairways
Restricted areas
Mechanical Rooms
Telecommunications Rooms
Haz-Mat storage locations
[Choose an answer]
We have included copies of our current floorplans in this emergency action plan.
Or
We keep copies of current floorplans at *[Insert location here]*.

Insurance

We understand that proper insurance coverage is vital to our organization's survival in the event of an emergency. To ensure that we are properly insured, we conduct an annual review of our policies. This annual review was last conducted on *[Insert your answer here]*. Our next annual review will occur on *[Insert your answer here]*. The annual review will be conducted by *[Insert your answer here]*.

Drills, Table Top Exercises, and Inspections

Date of last evacuation drill *[Insert your answer here]*

    ? Partial   (Which areas) *[Insert your answer here]*

    ? Full

Scheduled frequency *[Insert your answer here]*

Next scheduled evacuation drill *[Insert your answer here]*

Date of last tabletop exercise *[Insert your answer here]*

Scheduled frequency *[Insert your answer here]*

Attended by *[Insert your answer here]*

Topics discussed *[Insert your answer here]*

Next scheduled table top exercise *[Insert your answer here]*

Date of last inspection by fire department *[Insert your answer here]*

Scheduled frequency *[Insert your answer here]*

Attended by *[Insert your answer here]*

Next scheduled fire department inspection *[Insert your answer here]*

Actual Evacuation

In the event of an emergency, it may be necessary to evacuate the building. If this happens, the evacuation command will be given by *[Insert your answer here]*. This evacuation command will be communicated via *[Insert your answer here]*.

The following employees are assigned as floor captains:

[Insert your answer here]

The following employees are assigned to assist those with disabilities:

[Insert your answer here]

The following employees are trained for fire extinguisher use:

[Insert your answer here]

The following employees are responsible for equipment shutdown:

[Insert your answer here]

The following employee is responsible for bringing the MSDS logbook and delivering it to fire rescue personnel:

[Insert your answer here]

Our procedures for accounting for employees after evacuation is *[Insert your answer here]*

In the event of the following emergency events, evacuation will not be initiated:

- Civil disorder
- Chemical spill outside of the facility
- Severe weather
- Earthquake
- Other *[Insert your answer here]*

Evacuation Script

"We have received an alarm in _____ building. As a precaution, we are requiring evacuation of all employees in _____. Please immediately take your personnel belongings and proceed in an orderly fashion to your assigned exterior staging areas."

The Staging Area

In the event of an evacuation, employees and visitors are instructed to gather in their pre-assigned staging areas. A site plan which identifies the various staging areas is included in this plan (see the following).

The following employee will be assigned as Command Post Leader:

[Insert your answer here]

In the event of the assigned Command Post Leader's unavailability, the following employee will be assigned as a backup Command Post Leader:

[Insert your answer here]

The following employees will be assigned as Group Leaders for the pre-assigned staging areas:

[Insert your answer here]

The following employees will be assigned as Runners between the pre-assigned staging areas and the Command Post leader:

[Insert your answer here]

[Insert copy of site plan with staging areas identified here]

Emergency First Aid Kit

We keep our first aid kits in the following location(s): *[Insert your answer here]*

The following employee is responsible for regular first aid kit evaluation and restocking: *[Insert your answer here]*

Review and restocking of first aid kits are performed *[how often—insert your answer here]*

The following employees have been trained in first aid administration:

[Insert your answer here]

The following employees have been trained in CPR:

[Insert your answer here]

The following employees have been trained in AED usage:

[Insert your answer here]

The first aid kit is an integral part of our emergency action plan. We have created a first aid inventory list.

[Add or delete contents per your requirements]

- Adhesive tape
- Adhesive strips (¾" x 3" and 1" x 3")
- Ammonia inhalants
- Antacid tablets
- Antiseptic ointment or wipes
- Aspirin tablets
- Blanket
- Biohazard bags
- Cold pack
- Cotton tip applicators
- Eyewash
- Fingertip bandages
- Gauze pads and roller gauze (assorted sizes)
- Hand cleaner
- Ibuprofen tablets
- Knuckle bandages
- Latex gloves
- Non-aspirin tablets
- Notepad and pen (actions and inventory)
- Plastic bags
- Scissors and tweezers
- Small flashlight and extra batteries

- Triangular bandage
- Activated Charcoal (use only if instructed by Poison Control Center)
- Assorted splints
- Blood pressure kit
- Burn relief spray
- CPR mask with oxygen port
- Defribulator
- Insect bite relief spray
- Insta-Glucose
- Nitrile gloves
- Stethoscope
- Syrup of Ipecac (use only if instructed by Poison Control Center)

Generator Maintenance

An emergency power generator is an important part of our emergency action plan. It must be properly maintained, tested, and fueled. To ensure this happens, the following procedures have been established:

[If your generator does not include an automatic transfer switch]

The following employee(s) will be responsible for switching generator power on:

[Insert your answer here]

The following employee(s) will confirm the generator power has transferred properly: *[Insert your answer here]*

In the event emergency generator power does not transfer properly or the generator does not start, *[Insert your answer here]*, would be notified.

[Insert your answer here] is the contractor assigned to provide regularly scheduled maintenance on the generator.

[Insert your answer here] is responsible for checking and ordering fuel for the generator.

[Insert your answer here] is the vendor that provides generator fuel delivery. Our generator(s) uses *[Insert your answer here—diesel, gasoline, etc.]* fuel.

Alarm Systems

Alarms are an important part of our emergency action plan. We have identified the following alarms in our buildings:

[Insert your answer here; location/type]

[Insert your answer here; location/type]

[Insert your answer here; location/type]

Regular inspections of these alarms are performed by *[Insert your answer here]*

The Command Center

In the event of a major emergency, we have established a central command center for our organization at *[Insert your answer here]*.

In the event of a small-scale emergency, we may elect to set up a command center onsite. The employee (and title) responsible for making this call is *[Insert your answer here]*. That employee can be reached at *[Insert your answer here]*.

Data Security

Data security and integrity is vital to the survivability of our organization.

Our organization's contact person for data security is *[Insert your answer here]*.

Procedures for data security include *[Insert your answer here]*.

We protect against virus infection by *[Insert your answer here]*.

We protect against hackers by *[Insert your answer here]*.

Off-site storage

Due to the critical nature of our organization's electronic and hard copy data, we have elected to use off-site storage of data. The company we have contracted with for off-site storage is *[Insert your answer here]*. Their address and contact information is *[Insert your answer here]*.

Our organization's contact person for off-site storage is *[Insert your answer here]*.

Procedures for off-site storage of data includes *[Insert your answer here]*.

Natural Events

As part of our organization's emergency action plan, we have developed certain procedures for a number of different natural and weather-related events. These procedures are noted below.

Blizzards and Avalanches

We have determined that severe winter weather could affect our organization; therefore, we have elected to include the procedures below.

During inclement winter weather, we keep a rotating schedule for maintenance employees to be on call after hours in the event of an emergency. This schedule and the direction of work is the responsibility of *[Insert your answer here]*.

Included in this schedule is:

- Snow removal and salting of walkways.
- Check roof drains, gutters, catch basins, and other areas that can freeze or get clogged and impede the flow of melted snow.
- *[Other—Insert your answer here]*.

Winterizing of HVAC, fire sprinkler, and irrigation systems will occur during the fall. The person responsible for scheduling and directing this task is *[Insert your answer here]*.

In the event of inclement weather that forces shut down of the building, the following people will remain on site:

[Insert your answer here].

[Insert your answer here].

The decision to have certain employees remain on-site is the responsibility of *[Insert your answer here]*.

Drought

We have identified a list of specific locations that are drought prone. These areas include properties that have areas of vegetation exist, border on wooded areas, are non-irrigated or high visibility areas. These locations include:

[Insert properties and addresses here]

[Insert properties and addresses here]

[Insert properties and addresses here]

We have established internal terms that identify the severity of the drought. These terms include Advisory, Alert, Emergency, and Ration.

The announcement of each of these conditions will result in the following actions:

Advisory—When an advisory notice is given we will make an announcement to employees. The condition may escalate within the next five days, so we will review our procedures for each condition. Other steps include *[Insert your answer here]*.

Alert—When an alert order is given we will announce a voluntary reduction of water usage to employees and perform visual inspections of the premises to identify fire hazards. Other steps include *[Insert your answer here]*.

Emergency—When an emergency order is given, we will cut back vegetation and release a memo to employees and contractors concerning potential fire hazards. Specific care will be taken when welding or roofing work is being performed. Other steps include *[Insert your answer here]*.

Ration—When a ration order is given, water usage will be decreased at the direction of the local authorities. All irrigation on automatic timers will be adjusted accordingly. Other steps include *[Insert your answer here]*.

Earthquakes

We have determined that earthquakes are a possibility in our area; therefore, we have developed a number of earthquake specific safety procedures:

- In the event of an earthquake we have identified the following safe locations in the buildings:

  [Insert your answer here].

  [Insert your answer here].

  [Insert your answer here—you may elect to insert of copy of your floorplan here].

- Conversely, we have identified a number of dangerous areas in our buildings during an earthquake:

  [Insert your answer here].

  [Insert your answer here].

  [Insert your answer here—you may elect to insert of copy of your floorplan here].

- In the event of an earthquake, we understand that it may be advisable to turn off certain utilities. The employee responsible for assessing the utilities and making a decision to shut down is *[Insert your answer here]*.

We have trained employees to take refuge beneath a desk or table. If that is not possible, employees should move toward an inside wall away from items that could fall and injure them such as bookcases, vending machines, lighting, and other fixtures.

If employees are outdoors, they should move away from buildings, radio towers, light poles and overhead utility lines. In a high-rise building, do not use elevators.

In the event of an earthquake that causes structural damages, partial structural collapse, or total collapse, care must be taken to ensure that employees, contractors, and other visitors to the site are safe.

If an earthquake occurs that causes structural damage or collapse to a portion of the building, the facility manager must perform a building assessment. If the facility manager does not have the expertise to perform this assessment or if the scope of the assessment exceeds the expertise of the facility manager, we will use an architectural (or engineering) firm to complete this assessment. Our approved contractor for this assessment is *[Insert your answer here]*.

If the earthquake causes damage to the building, care should be taken to ensure the safe operation of utilities. If utility lines have been compromised, they must be turned off. The employee(s) responsible for utility shut off include *[Insert your answer here]*.

When entering a building that has experienced any level of collapse or structural damage, personal protective equipment (PPE) must be issued to employees and worn by employees and contractors at all times. A PPE station shall be erected on-site and a list of required PPE for entry shall be posted. The employee responsible for this station and PPE distribution is *[Insert your answer here]*.

Fire

Fire could occur in any building or location; therefore, fire protection is an important part of our emergency action plan. We have developed a list of all the major workplace fire hazards and their proper handling and storage requirements. These hazards include:

[insert your answer here - i.e. welding, smoking]

[Insert your answer here].

Their safe handling and storage requirements include:

[Insert your answer here].

[Insert your answer here].

Housekeeping procedures are important to ensure that work areas are kept free from accumulations of flammable and combustible materials. Housekeeping procedures include:

[Insert your answer here].

[Insert your answer here].

We have identified the following types of fire protection available to control each hazard:

[Insert your answer here].

[Insert your answer here].

The names of personnel responsible for maintenance of equipment installed to prevent or control fires include:

[Insert your answer here].

[Insert your answer here].

We understand that maintenance of fire equipment or systems (i.e., inspections, certifications) is an integral part of our emergency action plan. Our maintenance is conducted by *[Insert your answer here]*. The frequency of such maintenance is *[Insert your answer here]*.

A water sprinkler system is the most effective method of controlling fires automatically. We use the following types of fire sprinkler systems: *[insert your answer here—i.e., Wet Pipe System, Dry Pipe System, or Deluge System]*

In the event of a fire that causes structural damages, partial structural collapse, or total collapse, care must be taken to ensure that employees, contractors, and other visitors to the site are safe.

If a fire occurs that causes structural damage or collapse to a portion of the building, the facility manager must perform a building assessment. If the facility manager does not have the expertise to perform this assessment or if the scope of the assessment exceeds the expertise of the facility manager, we will use an architectural (or engineering) firm to complete this assessment. Our approved contractor for this assessment is *[Insert your answer here]*.

If the fire causes damage to the building, care should be taken to ensure the safe operation of utilities. If utility lines have been compromised, they must be turned off. The employee(s) responsible for utility shut off include *[Insert your answer here]*.

When entering a building that has experienced any level of collapse or structural damage, personal protective equipment (PPE) must be issued to employees and worn by employees and contractors at all times. A PPE station shall be erected on site and a list of required PPE for entry shall be posted. The employee responsible for this station and PPE distribution is *[Insert your answer here]*.

Floods

We have determined that floods can occur in our area and could negatively affect our organization. We cannot always control floodwaters, but we can keep adequate flood insurance coverage. The employee responsible for insurance coverage is *[Insert your answer here]*. This employee will review our insurance coverage *[Frequency—Insert your answer here]*.

We also believe that a proactive approach to floods is important; therefore, we have developed the following procedures:

[Insert your answer here—i.e., disconnect appliances and equipment as water rises].

[Insert your answer here—i.e., keep a supply of sand, sandbags, lumber etc].

[Insert your answer here—i.e., move valuables to higher area].

[Insert your answer here—i.e., use water pumps to displace water].

[Insert your answer here—i.e., dehumidify the building after water has receded].

[If you are located near a river and within fifty miles of a dam, explain any special considerations or communication with the agency responsible for the dam operations.]

In the event of a flood that causes structural damage, care must be taken to ensure that employees, contractors, and other visitors to the site are safe.

If a flood occurs that causes structural or cosmetic damage to a portion of the building, the facility manager must perform a building assessment. If the facility manager does not have the expertise to perform this assessment or if the scope of the assessment exceeds the expertise of the facility manager, we will use an architectural (or engineering) firm to complete this assessment. Our approved contractor for this assessment is *[Insert your answer here]*.

If the flood causes damage to the building, care should be taken to ensure the safe operation of utilities. If utility lines have been compromised, they must be turned off. The employee(s) responsible for utility shut off include *[Insert your answer here]*.

Hurricanes

We have established specific procedures for arriving storms. These procedures address actions taken 72 hours prior to the storm's arrival, 36 hours prior to the storm's arrival, and 24 hours prior to the storm's arrival. These activities are identified on the Pre-storm List found below.

[Attach Pre-storm List here]

Additionally, specific procedures to be taken after the storm has passed are found on the attached Post-storm List.

[Attach Post-storm List here]

Tropical Storm Watch

Within the next 36 hours, tropical storm conditions (winds from 36 to 73 mph) are possible in the storm watch area.

Tropical Storm Warning

Within the next 24 hours, tropical storm conditions (winds from 36 to 73 mph) are expected in the storm warning area.

Hurricane Watch

Within the next 36 hours, hurricane conditions (sustained winds greater than 73 mph) are possible in the hurricane watch area.

Hurricane Warning

Within the next 24 hours, hurricane conditions (sustained winds greater than 73 mph) are expected in the hurricane warning area.

Additionally, the following related warning might be given:

Flood Watch

Floodwaters are possible in the given area of the watch and during the time identified in the flood watch. Flood watches are usually issued for flooding that is expected to occur at least six hours after heavy rains have ended.

Flood Warning

Flooding is actually occurring or is imminent in the warning area.

Flash Flood Watch

Flash Flooding is possible in the warning area. Flash flood watches are usually issued for flooding that is expected to occur within six hours after heavy rains have ended.

Flash Flood Warning

Flash flooding is actually occurring or is imminent in the warning area.

Tornado Watch

Tornados are possible in the given area of the watch.

Tornado Warning

A tornado has actually been sighted by a spotter or by radar and is occurring or is imminent in the warning area.

Saffir-Simpson Rating and Storm Categories:

1. **Minimal:** Winds of 74 to 95 mph. Damage is minimal, usually limited to trees and power lines.
2. **Moderate:** Winds of 96 to 110 mph. Some roof damage may occur. Trees can be uprooted and power poles can be downed. Windows and storefronts can be damaged.
3. **Extensive:** Winds of 111 to 130 mph. Roofs are badly damaged or lost, structural damage is common.
4. **Extreme:** Winds of 131 to 155 mph. Damage to most structures is severe. Extreme flooding can occur along and near the coast. Loss of life is common.
5. **Catastrophic:** Winds in excess of 155 mph. Damage is total in many places, and many structures are destroyed. Severe flooding is common several miles inland.

In the event of a hurricane that causes structural damage, partial structural collapse, or total collapse, care must be taken to ensure that employees, contractors, and other visitors to the site are safe.

If a hurricane occurs that causes structural damage or collapse to a portion of the building, the facility manager must perform a building assessment. If the facility manager does not have the expertise to perform this assessment or if the scope of the assessment exceeds the expertise of the facility manager, we will use an architectural (or engineering) firm to complete this assessment. Our approved contractor for this assessment is *[Insert your answer here]*.

If the hurricane causes damage to the building, care should be taken to ensure the safe operation of utilities. If utility lines have been compromised, they must be turned off. The employee(s) responsible for utility shut off include *[Insert your answer here]*.

When entering a building that has experienced any level of collapse or structural damage, personal protective equipment (PPE) must be issued to employees and worn by employees and contractors at all times. A PPE station shall be erected on-site and a list of required PPE for entry shall be posted. The employee responsible for this station and PPE distribution is *[Insert your answer here]*.

Tornadoes

We have determined that tornados could occur in locations that we have properties; therefore, we have established a number of tornado-specific emergency procedures.

If a tornado is spotted, we have trained our employees to immediately contact 911 to report it. We have also trained employees to contact *[Insert your answer here—internal company contact]*.

In the event of a tornado strike, employees have been instructed to stay away from windows and doors. *[Does your building have a basement?—If yes: Move to the basement. If a basement is not available, employees have been trained and will be instructed to go to a safe area of the building]*.

Know the Terminology

Tornado Watch: Tornados are possible in the given area of the watch.

Tornado Warning: A tornado has actually been sighted by a spotter or by radar and is occurring or is imminent in the warning area.

We have identified the following interior locations as safe areas:

[Insert your answer here]

Additionally, in the event of a tornado, all employees have been instructed to stay on the lowest level of the building.

We have a NOAA weather radio available and will stay tuned for further instructions.

In the event of a tornado that causes structural damage, partial structural collapse, or total collapse, care must be taken to ensure that employees, contractors, and other visitors to the site are safe.

If a tornado occurs that causes structural damage or collapse to a portion of the building, the facility manager must perform a building assessment. If the facility manager does not have the expertise to perform this assessment or if the scope of the assessment exceeds the expertise of the facility manager, we will use an architectural (or engineering) firm to complete this assessment. Our approved contractor for this assessment is *[Insert your answer here]*.

If the tornado causes damage to the building, care should be taken to ensure the safe operation of utilities. If utility lines have been compromised, they must be turned off. The employee(s) responsible for utility shut off include *[Insert your answer here]*.

When entering a building that has experienced any level of collapse or structural damage, personal protective equipment (PPE) must be issued to employees and worn by employees and contractors at all times. A PPE station shall be erected on site and a list of required PPE for entry shall be posted. The employee responsible for this station and PPE distribution is *[Insert your answer here]*.

Tsunamis

We have identified the threat of a tsunami as being a potential in our area. For this reason we have developed a number of procedures.

We have identified an elevated evacuation route. Our elevated area of refuge is at least 50 feet above sea level and one mile in from the coast. This area of refuge is *[Insert your answer here—location and directions]*

Because evacuation routes may be blocked or unavailable, we have identified a second route. This second area of refuge is *[Insert your answer here—location and directions]*

In the event of a tsunami that causes structural damage, partial structural collapse, or total collapse, care must be taken to ensure that employees, contractors, and other visitors to the site are safe.

If a tsunami occurs that causes structural damage or collapse to a portion of the building, the facility manager must perform a building assessment. If the facility manager does not have the expertise to perform this assessment or if the scope of the assessment exceeds the expertise of the facility manager, we will use an architectural (or engineering) firm to complete this assessment. Our approved contractor for this assessment is *[Insert your answer here]*.

If the tsunami causes damage to the building, care should be taken to ensure the safe operation of utilities. If utility lines have been compromised, they must be turned off. The employee(s) responsible for utility shut off include *[Insert your answer here]*.

When entering a building that has experienced any level of collapse or structural damage, personal protective equipment (PPE) must be issued to employees and worn by employees and contractors at all times. A PPE station shall be erected on site and a list of required PPE for entry shall be posted. The employee responsible for this station and PPE distribution is *[Insert your answer here]*.

Volcano

We have determined our organization has property in the vicinity of volcanoes. Those properties include:

[Insert your answer here]

In the event of a volcanic eruption we will immediately evacuate the area.

We have identified an elevated evacuation route. This area of refuge is *[Insert your answer here—location and directions]*

Because evacuation routes may be blocked or unavailable we have identified a second route. This second area of refuge is *[Insert your answer here—location and directions]*

In the event of a volcanic disturbance that causes structural damage, partial structural collapse, or total collapse, care must be taken to ensure that employees, contractors, and other visitors to the site are safe.

If a volcanic disturbance occurs that causes structural damage or collapse to a portion of the building, the facility manager must perform a building assessment. If the facility manager does not have the expertise to perform this assessment or if the scope of the assessment exceeds the expertise of the facility manager, we will use an architectural (or engineering) firm to complete this assessment. Our approved contractor for this assessment is *[Insert your answer here]*.

If the volcanic disturbance causes damage to the building, care should be taken to ensure the safe operation of utilities. If utility lines have been compromised, they must be turned off. The employee(s) responsible for utility shut off include *[Insert your answer here]*.

During initial return to the building, employees and contractors must be aware of the danger of soot, dust, and volcanic ash. When entering a building that has experienced any level of collapse or structural damage, personal protective equipment (PPE) must be issued to employees and worn by employees and contractors at all times. A PPE station shall be erected on site and a list of required PPE for entry shall be posted. The employee responsible for this station and PPE distribution is *[Insert your answer here]*.

Non-Natural Events

We understand that weather-related and other natural events are not the only events to be concerned with. A number of non-natural events could also occur, so we have elected to address them here.

We have identified the following potential hazards in the workplace:

[Insert your answers here—i.e., chemical spill]

[Insert your answers here—i.e., fire from welding]

[Insert your answers here—i.e., injury from machinery]

Bomb Threat

If faced with a bomb threat we have three basic options: Ignore the threat, evacuate immediately, or search for the bomb and evacuate if necessary. Our decision as to which option we select will depend on a number of factors including:

Ignore the threat—The threat lacks credibility. *[Insert your answer here; i.e., the threat lacks credibility]*

Evacuate immediately—The threat is very credible. A bomb or other device has been located. *[Insert your answer here; i.e., the threat is very credible]*

Search for the bomb and evacuate if necessary—The threat seems credible. *[Insert your answer here; i.e., the threat seems credible]*

[Insert your answer here] is the employee responsible for calling an evacuation if the local authorities elect not to get involved.

We have contacted local police and fire departments to determine if a bomb squad is available to assist us with search and removal of a bomb. Their process for assistance is *[Insert your answer here]*. The names and phone numbers of the local authorities are *[Insert your answer here]*.

We have designated search team members and they include:

[Insert your answers here].

Because of their familiarity with the area, a volunteer from each department or area being searched is also required. A set of floor plans will be available for the search team and authorities. This floorplan is kept at *[Insert your answer here]*

In the event of a bomb threat and evacuation we will establish a Command Center outside of the building. That exact location is *[Insert your answer here]*.

In the event a bomb or other suspicious device is found, *[Insert your answer here]* will be responsible for communicating our findings to the local authorities and asking for assistance.

Loss of Utility

An extended loss of utility could adversely affect our organization. Loss of utility might include electricity, water, or sewer. We have determined that loss of electricity could have the greatest impact on our business. This loss is especially critical following another emergency event because it would slow our ability to respond and recover.

We have identified the following critical areas of our business that would be most affected by loss of utility:

[Insert your answer here—i.e., production area]

[Insert your answer here—i.e., computer centers]

[Insert your answer here—i.e., call center]

To ensure business continuity we have identified the following critical components and their availability.

- Generator: *[Insert your answer here—i.e., on-site generator located at . . .]*
- *[Insert your answer here—i.e., flatbed generator to be shipped to . . .]*
- Port-O-Potties: *[Insert your answer here—i.e., available from . . .]*
- Bottled Water: *[Insert your answer here—i.e., available from . . .]*
- Other: *[Insert your answer here]*
- Other: *[Insert your answer here]*

Medical Emergencies

We have determined that a medical emergency could affect our organization and our employees in a negative way; therefore, we have elected to develop certain medical related procedures.

We have identified the following areas of concern that could cause a medical emergency:

[Insert your answer here—i.e., machinery]

[Insert your answer here—i.e., confined spaces]

[Insert your answer here—i.e., chemical usage area]

We have identified employees who have emergency medical response training:

[Insert your answer here—include name, work location, office phone, and cell]

[Insert your answer here—include name, work location, office phone, and cell]

[Insert your answer here—include name, work location, office phone and cell]

Because of the potential for disease transmission while administering first aid, our emergency response employees have been properly trained and outfitted with devices that limit the potential for disease transmission avoidance.

We have identified the closest hospital facility as *[Insert your answer here]* and emergency response time is estimated to be *[Insert your answer here—minutes]*.

In the event of a medical emergency we will call *[Insert your answer here]*. If an outside line is required we will *[Insert your answer here—i.e., if you dial 911, must you first dial "9" to get an outside line?]*

We have located a First Aid kit and AED's on our floorplan included in this emergency action plan.

Within eight hours after a medical emergency or illness, our organization will perform all required OSHA injury and illness recordkeeping. The person or department responsible for this is *[Insert your answer here]*.

Chemical and Biological Concerns

Although not likely, we feel that the threat of chemical or biological concerns must be addressed in our organization. This is especially true in the event we were to receive mail that was tainted with biological agents.

In the event of receipt of a suspicious package, the employee handling the package would immediately seal or cover the package.

Next, all employees would leave the room and if possible lock it. If locking the room is not possible, the employees will post a sign warning not to enter. The package and the area it is stored must be quarantined.

All employees that came in contact with the package or were in the general vicinity of the package must immediately wash their hands with soap and water.

A list of people who were in the area and possibly exposed will be developed and given to the authorities.

Next, the employees in the affected area would notify the building manager and call 911.

CDC Web site: emergency.cdc.gov/bioterrorism/index.asp

To report a hazardous substance release, oil spills, or radiation threats, contact the EPA's National Response Center at (800) 424-8802, which is staffed 24 hours a day.

For regional Poison Control Centers, call (800) 222-1222.

Other procedures would include: *[Insert your answer here]*

Chemical Spills and Contamination

There is a risk that a chemical spill could affect our organization. We have identified the following potential spill or contamination sources:

[Insert your answer here—external sources, i.e., highway, navigable waters, nearby plants]

[Insert your answer here—internal sources, i.e., chemical storage, manufacturing]

In the event of chemical spill, employees must take certain precautions such as building evacuation or instructions to shelter in place.

If a decision is made instructing employees to shelter in place, employees must not attempt to leave the building. It has been determined that the chemical has been released and exposure is likely to occur if you leave the protective confines of the building. Additionally, the following steps should be taken:

- Close and lock all doors and windows.
- Seal all openings around doors with wet towels.
- Close all fireplace chimney dampers.
- Turn off all HVAC equipment and close or seal all fresh air intakes.
- Seal off, using plastic visqueen and duct tape, all other openings such as vents and exhaust fans.
- Other steps: *[Insert your answer here]*

To reduce the possibility of an internal chemical spill or contamination, the following steps must be observed:

Ensure that all containers storing chemicals are properly labeled.

Verify that all chemicals are stored in their proper containers.

Ensure that chemicals with the potential of a negative reaction to another chemical are stored in separate areas.

Verify that all chemicals have a Material Safety Data Sheet (MSDS) available.

Keep the MSDS logbook in a central location available to all employees.

Train employees to properly handle and store chemicals. Furthermore, train employees to recognize and how to properly handle chemical spills. These training records are kept *[Insert your answer here]*.

In the event of a chemical spill, our procedures to communicate the spill to employees, management, and, if necessary, the proper local agencies are *[Insert your answer here]*.

Nuclear Threat and Exposure

The opportunity exists for nuclear exposure that will affect our organization. We have identified the following nuclear exposure sources:

[Insert your answer here]

In the event of nuclear exposure, a decision may be made to shelter in place. If a decision is made instructing employees to shelter in place, employees must not attempt to leave the building. It has been determined that nuclear energy has been released and exposure is likely to occur if you leave the protective confines of the building. Additionally, the following steps should be taken:

- Close and lock all doors and windows.
- Seal all openings around doors with wet towels.

- Close all fireplace chimney dampers.
- Turn off all HVAC equipment and close or seal all fresh air intakes.
- Seal off, using plastic visqueen and duct tape, all other openings such as vents and exhaust fans.
- Other steps: *[Insert your answer here]*

If instructions to leave the building and evacuate to a safe area have been given, follow the instructions given by the authorities.

[The following text applies to those near a nuclear plant]

The Nuclear Regulatory Commission requires that nuclear power plants have a system for notifying the public in the event of an emergency. There exist four standard classifications of emergencies, including:

- Notification of Unusual Event—This is a non-specific warning and is the least serious of the four categories. The event poses no danger to employees or the public and no action (i.e., evacuation) is required of the public.
- Alert—This classification is declared when an event has occurred that could jeopardize the plants safety, but backup systems are in place. Emergency agencies are notified, but no action is required from the public.
- Site Area Emergency—This classification, is declared when an event has caused a major problem with the plants safety system and has progressed to a point where a release of radiation into the air or water is possible but would not exceed regulations instituted by the Environmental Protection Agency. No action is required by the public.
- General Emergency—This classification is the most serious and comes when the plants safety systems have been lost. Radiation could be released beyond the boundaries of the plant. Emergency sirens will sound and some people will be evacuated or instructed to remain sheltered in place. Listen for more specific instructions.

If we receive an alert, remember the following:

- A siren or tone alert does not necessarily mean we should evacuate. Listen to the television or radio for further instructions.
- Do not call 911. If this is a true alert, a special rumor control phone number will be provided.
- If we are instructed to shelter in place, be sure to close all doors, windows, chimney dampers, and turn off all HVAC equipment.

If we receive a warning and you are instructed to go inside, it is advisable to shower and change clothes. After removing your clothes and shoes, place them in a plastic bag and seal the bag.

Civil Disturbance and Demonstrations

We have determined that, although unlikely, it would be prudent to include the possibility of civil disturbance in our emergency action plan. Events that may trigger civil disturbance and, therefore, should be carefully watched when occurring in the general proximity of our properties might include

- Labor disputes
- Layoffs and downsizing
- Environmentally sensitive meetings or conferences
- Sporting events
- Political rallies
- Economic conferences
- Judicial decisions
- Music concerts
- Religious gatherings
- Biased racial or cultural events

In the event of civil disturbance, we may elect to take the following actions:

- Hiring temporary guard service
- Installing storm shutters
- Locking gates in the parking lot
- Lowering of security grating
- Removal of vehicles from the premises
- Removal of trash containers or other items that could be thrown or set afire
- *[Other—Insert your answer here].*
- *[Other—Insert your answer here].*

The decision to take any of these actions is the responsibility of *[Insert your answer here].*

Structural Collapse

Although a structural collapse of one of our buildings is not likely, we feet it is prudent to include this potential event in our emergency action plan.

In the event of an event that causes structural damage, partial structural collapse, or total collapse, care must be taken to ensure that employees, contractors, and other visitors to the site are safe.

If an event occurs that causes structural damage or collapse to a portion of the building, the facility manager must perform a building assessment. If the facility manager does not have the expertise to perform this assessment or if the scope of the assessment exceeds the expertise of the facility manager, we will use an architectural (or engineering) firm to complete this assessment. Our approved contractor for this assessment is *[Insert your answer here].*

If the emergency event causes damage to the building, care should be taken to ensure the safe operation of utilities. If utility lines have been compromised, they must be turned off. The employee(s) responsible for utility shut off include *[Insert your answer here].*

When entering a building that has experienced any level of collapse, personal protective equipment (PPE) must be issued to employees and worn by employees and contractors at all times. A PPE station shall be erected on-site and a list of required PPE for entry shall be posted. The employee responsible for this station and PPE distribution is *[Insert your answer here].*

In the event of a partial or total collapse, we understand that asbestos fibers could be released; therefore, proper care must be taken. We have identified the following buildings that feature asbestos-containing materials:

[Insert your answer here]

[Insert your answer here]

[Insert your answer here]

Contractors and employees performing work at locations that could produce an asbestos exposure must be informed of the potential asbestos exposure and must take proper precautions when working in the area. These precautions include *[Insert your answer here]*. Our preferred vendor for asbestos testing and abatement is *[Insert your answer here]*.

In the event of a total collapse that has trapped people, we will immediately contact the Federal Emergency Management Agency (FEMA) at *[Insert your answer here]*.

Workplace Violence

Workplace violence is an unfortunate reality, and we believe our organization has a responsibility to protect our employees. To accomplish this, management is committed to providing a safe environment for employees to work.

As an organization we have identified certain prohibited behavior including:

[Insert your answer here—i.e., threatening language].

[Insert your answer here—i.e., damage to company property].

[Insert your answer here—i.e., physically assaulting another person].

[Insert your answer here—i.e., sexually harassing another person].

[Insert your answer here—i.e., bringing weapons on company property].

Because of the serious nature of workplace violence and the incidents that could lead to violence, we reserve the right to discipline employees. Such disciplinary actions might include verbal warning, written warning, suspension and termination of employment. The severity of the penalty will be based on the severity of the infraction. The procedures for investigating reported incidents might include *[Insert your answer here]*.

Post Event Restoration

As soon as it is safe to enter the property affected by an emergency event, the facility manager or those assigned by the facility manager will assess the damage to the property. Based on this assessment, the company will begin restoration procedures.

Insurance and salvage decisions will need to be made. Employees responsible for making these decisions include *[Insert your answer here]*.

Those employees expected to report to the affected location must be self-sufficient for the first 48 hours *[or insert your answer here]*. These first responder employees are responsible for providing the following items:

Clothing

- Three changes of clothes
- Rain jacket
- Cold weather jacket
- Safety goggles
- Hard hat
- Sun glasses
- Two pairs of work shoes (steel toe preferred)
- Spare pair of glasses
- *[Other—Insert your answer here]*.

Health and Toiletries

- Soap
- Shampoo
- Wash cloth and towel
- Razor and shaving cream
- Toothpaste and toothbrush
- Male or female personal hygiene products.
- Deodorant
- Toilet paper
- Sun block
- Insect repellant
- Contact lens solution and spare lenses
- *[Other—Insert your answer here]*.

Miscellaneous

- NOAA weather radio
- Alarm clock
- Blankets
- Sleeping bag or cot
- Batteries

- Flashlight
- Pen or pencils
- Notepad and audit forms
- Camera (digital or film)
- Video camera
- Cell phone with automobile battery charger
- Driver's license
- Credit card
- Cash
- Airtight plastic container to keep items dry
- *[Other—Insert your answer here].*

Medicines

- Prescription medicines
- Antacids
- Athletes' foot spray
- Pain relief cream
- Aspirin and ibuprofen
- First aid kit
- *[Other—Insert your answer here].*

Food and Water

- Meals Ready to Eat (MRE)
- Snack bars
- Fruit
- Trail mix or nuts
- Bottled water (drinking and cleaning)
- Instant coffee
- Cooler with ice and ice pack
- Propane stove (optional)
- Propane fuel tank (extra)
- *[Other—Insert your answer here].*

Sample Press Releases

[This is just an example. Insert samples of your press releases here]

Dear Fellow Employee,

Our business was built on hard work and dedication from our employees. That need for hard work and dedication has never been as evident as it is today. Your efforts are greatly appreciated and I have no doubt we will persevere. We are faced with an excellent opportunity to show our resolve and character, and I invite you to show your best.

When faced with unusual events such as what we have just experienced, a few reminders are in order. We will keep our employees updated via e-mail and fax service. For those unable to access these mediums, we have established an emergency hotline (800-123-1234) with recorded updates and frequently asked questions. We realize that rumors will surface. We ask that you do not perpetuate these comments. All official communication will be provided through the methods listed above.

For many of our employees, the media will be observing your work. Again, you have an opportunity to present the company in a positive way. Unfortunately, some media representatives may attempt to sensationalize disasters and how they are dealt with. If asked about your restoration efforts, you may briefly explain what you are doing, stressing the fact that your efforts are part of a larger restoration effort by all of the employees of the company.

We ask that you refer questions involving detailed aspects of your work to our corporate communication department at (800-555-1212). Finally, if you don't know an answer to a reporter's question, don't speculate! It's ok to say, "I don't know." If you find yourself in an uncomfortable situation, thank the reporter for their time, and kindly remind them that you need to get back to work.

I am very proud of the efforts of our employees and I know we can all count on each other to make a complete recovery a reality. Remember, we have an opportunity to make a difference and your efforts are greatly appreciated.

President—Acme Industries

OSHA Record Keeping

Our organization is committed to employee safety. We are also obligated to OSHA compliance. With this in mind, especially after an emergency event, we have developed the following OSHA recordkeeping procedures:

[Insert your answer here—i.e. who is responsible for OSHA recordkeeping?].

[Insert your answer here—i.e. where are the OSHA recordkeeping forms kept?].

[Insert your answer here—i.e. who is responsible for annual posting of OSHA Form 300A?].

Within eight (8) hours after the death of any employee from a work-related incident or the in-patient hospitalization of three or more employees as a result of a work-related incident, you must orally report the fatality/multiple hospitalization by telephone or in person to the Area Office of the Occupational Safety and Health Administration (OSHA), U.S. Department of Labor, that is nearest to the site of the incident. You may also use the OSHA toll-free central telephone number, 1-800-321-OSHA (1-800-321-6742).

Storm Activities	(72 Hours) Before	(36 Hours) Before	(24 Hours) Before	Responsible Employee	Contractor/Company	Office Phone	Cell Phone
Grounds							
Shrubs and hedges	Survey/Trim as needed		Bring all planters into the building				
Trees	Trim all broken/dead limbs						
Light and flag poles			Remove all flags				
Newspaper stands		Bring into building or call newspaper vendor					
Drainage		Clear all drains of debris					
Parking			Remove vechicles from areas near trees				
Access		Make sure manual overide on gates are funtional					
Vehicle Fuel Tanks			Top off fuel tanks				
Building Exterior							
Shutters	Inventory all detachable shutters to verify completeness.		Close and secure all shutters				
Window Leaks		If appropriate seal leak. Indicate location on building floor plan. Move any materials/equipment away from leak area.	Same as 36Hrs before				
Rain Gutters		Remove debris from gutter	Remove debris from gutter				
Sand Bags	Notify sand supplier for delivery	Fill and place sand bags in low lying areas (doorways)					
Water Pumps	Motify rental company of impending need	Request pump(s) delivered. (250' - 500' hose)					
Building Interior							
Water System	Notify bottled water contractor of impending need.	Place order for 25 5-gallon water bottles					
Sewer System	Notify Port-o-Pottie of impending need	Request Port-o-Potties. (Store or have delivered post storm)					
A/C System	Inventory portable fans on hand	Rent any additional portable fans necessary					
Generator System	Notify generator maintenance contractor and top off fuel	Contractor check all operations. (Test WITH Building Load)	Contractor MUST have completed all checks and have generator operational.				
UPS System	(Do preventative maintenance check prior to storm season)						
Telephone System	Notify all people on the storm call list. Verify all phone numbers on list	Make corrections to phone numbers when they are reported	Make corrections to phone numbers when they are reported				
Radio	Set up a radio distribution list. Test all radios and batteries. Repair/replace as needed.	Distribute all radios per distribution list	All radio operators check in				
Garbage Pickup/Removal	Call for a pickup for all Dumpsters						
Food Operations	Notify food service management. Inventory food stocks (for 2-day supply, 4 meals per day). Place order for shortages.	Notify food service staff	Food service manager contact departments to verify meal schedule				
Refrigerators			Set to a colder setting and limit access				
TV & Cable Systems	Check all monitors for proper channel and operations		If antennas used, take down				
Fire Alarm System	Update callout list with monitoring contractor		Remove locks on shur-off valves				
Security System	Check all electro/mechanical locks for proper function. Repair any problems. Notify security contractor to determine personnel status.	Meet with departments to determine the number of people that will be on site DURING storm	Security guards are briefed on their role and given specific instructions. Security contractor places all guards (including any additional				
Storm Supply Storage	Identify (on map) potential staging areas for supplies to be stored during the storm		Clear out staging area of any non-storm material				
Miscellaneous							
Critical documents	Identify critical documents		Pack documents and move 50 to 75 miles inland away from storm				
Insurance	Review policy. Take video of interior and exterior.						
Inventory List	Complete and replinish where necessary						
Contractor Avaliability	Call contractors to ensure avaliability		Call key contractors again				

Figure A.3. Pre-Storm Activities List

Storm Activities	After	Responsible Employee	Contractor Company	Office Phone	Cell Phone
Grounds					
Shrubs and hedges	Survey site. Indicate all damage on site map. Report to landscape contractor				
Trees	Survey site. Indicate all damage on site map. Report to landscape contractor				
Light Poles & Flag Poles	Survey site. Indicate all damage on site map. Report to electrical contractor				
Newspaper stands	Return to original location				
Drainage	Unclog all drains				
Parking	Remove all debris. Indicate helicopter landing areas				
Access	Check all gates for proper operation				
Vehicle Fuel Tanks	Order fuel, if needed				
Building Exterior					
Shutters	Open/Remove all shutters. Store removable shutters in designated area. Open windows to air				
Window Leaks	Report all damage to Window contractor				
Rain Gutters	Remove all debris from gutter				
Sand Bags	Remove sand bags after water has subsided				
Water Pumps	Set-up and run until water subsides				
Building Interior					
Water System	Repair all damages to water system. Disperse water bottles. Replenish water bottles until water system				
Sewer System	Schedule pickups of Port-o-Potties until sewer system is operational				
A/C System	Repair all damage. (Check roof top units visually)				
Generator System	If activated, monitor operations. Check usage and refuel if necessary				
UPS System	Report all irregularities to UPS maintenance contractor				
Telephone System	Inform telecommunications contractor of any irregularities.				
Radio	Radio operators check in per schedule or as needed to report any concerns.				
Garbage Pickup/Removal	Call for pickups as needed during restoration period.				
Food Operations	Feed employees per schedule for duration of restoration process. Restock supplies as needed.				
Refrigerator	If no electricity, open only when needed. When electricity restored, set controls to normal position				
TV and Cable Systems	Repair any damage				
Fire Alarm System	Repair all damage. Replace locks on shut-off valves. Notify monitoring contractor when repairs are complete.				
Security System	Guards monitor buildings and report any irregularities.				
Storm Supply Storage	Facilitate smooth transition of storm material from staging area to area where needed				
Miscellaneous					
Critical Documents	Bring back once building is dry and secure				
Insurance	Take video of interior and exterior				
Inventory List	Replinish used stock after hurricane.				
Contractor Avaliability Li	Call contractors to assign tasks				

Figure A.4. Insert Post-Storm Activities List

Administrative Issues – Annual Audit

Administrative Issues	YES	NO	N/A	Comments
Injury Recording				
Are we keeping accurate OSHA injury and illness records?				
Are we displaying the OSHA 300A summary from February through April?				
Are we reviewing our injury and illness log for trends on an annual basis?				
Insurance Issues				
Do we have all the policies needed (wind/flood/storm/contents/liability)?				
What are our deductibles and are they at proper levels?				
How will the property be valued (replacement/actual/other)?				
Are we familiar with the riders, addendums, and exclusions?				
Have we performed an annual policy review?				
Are we covered for spoilage, lost income, etc.?				
If we have a lost income policy, what is the duration?				
In what way does the provider require proof of loss?				
What additional loss documentation is needed, and is it stored in a safe place?				
Does it make sense to self-insure?				
Has the insurance coverage been updated to reflect changes in changes in use, building size, or value?				

Administrative Issues – Annual Audit

	YES	NO	NA	Comments
Labor Issues				
Have procedures been developed for tracking emergency-related expenses?				
Do employees know how to contact their families in the event of an emergency?				
Do employees know how to contact their supervisors in the event of an emergency?				
Tenant/Owner-Related Issues				
Who is responsible for staging evacuation drills?				
Is each tenant's business responsible for their own emergency plan?				
Who makes the decision to return to the building after an evacuation?				
What happens to the lease if the property is uninhabitable for an extended period of time?				
What kinds of insurance policies are required and in what amounts?				
Is the landlord, tenant, or both parties required to acquire insurance?				
How much damage must be assessed before the property is considered uninhabitable by the insurance provider?				
How would all occupants be notified?				
Has a chain of command been specified?				
Have all tenants been trained in emergency evacuation procedures?				
What kinds of flammable or toxic chemicals are the tenants storing?				
Do the tenants have all current MSDS documentation?				
Have emergency responsibilities and expectations been added to the lease agreement?				
Who is responsible for alarm testing, fire extinguishers, and other related equipment?				
Does the emergency planner have after-hours phone numbers for the tenants?				
If tenants make changes to the building structure or floor space, have the changes been added to the as-built drawings?				

Emergency Plan Issues – Annual Audit

Emergency Plan Issues	YES	NO	N/A	Comments
Business Continuity				
Have you performed a risk analysis of each of your buildings?				
Have you identified mission critical functions within your organization?				
Have you established a threshold for how many days or hours your business could be down before essential services must be outsourced or moved to a new location?				
Is current data storage process adequate?				
Is redundancy available for electronic data?				
Is off-site storage of vital information being used?				
Are copies of floorplan and emergency action plan available off site?				
Are alternative worksites available?				
Has a process been established for alternate worksite activation?				
Training				
Have members of the emergency action team and supporting employees been adequately trained for their duties?				
Have annual refresher training classes been conducted for emergency response team members?				
Have tabletop exercises been conducted in the last year? When?				
Are certain employees trained in CPR? Who?				
Are certain employees trained in AED usage? Who?				
Are certain employees trained in First aid? Who?				
Are certain employees trained in portable fire extinguisher use? Who?				
Have the employees been trained in adequate emergency evacuation procedures?				

Emergency Plan Issues – Annual Audit

Emergency Plan Questions	YES	NO	N/A	Comments
Does your emergency action plan address the following events:				
Fire				
Drought				
Earthquake				
Hurricane				
Tornado				
Tidal Wave				
Blizzard				
Avalanche				
Tsunami				
Volcano				
Loss of utility				
Loss of communication				
Arson				
Water leak				
Chemical spill				
Acts of war				
Riot or demonstration				
Bomb threat				
Medical emergency				
Workplace violence				
Nuclear accident				
Other				
Does the organization have a formal plan for training its employees in emergency procedures?				
Is training being completed?				
Has your organization met with local community and governmental agencies and briefed them on your plan?				
Do you have updated photos or videotape of the facility and its assets?				
Has the emergency plan been updated to reflect changes in use, building size, or value?				

Emergency Plan Issues – Annual Audit

	YES	NO	N/A	Comments
Does the plan reflect changes in the building layout?				
Does the plan reflect changes in policies and procedures?				
Does this plan identify the person responsible for annual plan update and review?				
Are internal (employees) contact phone numbers accurate?				
Are external (contractors/vendors) contact phone numbers accurate?				
Are suppliers' contact phone numbers accurate?				
Are insurance agents' phone numbers correct?				
Are public safety agencies' phone numbers correct?				
Does the plan reflect lessons learned from the drills and actual emergency events?				
Are problem areas being addressed?				
Are the responsibilities of the following emergency team members assigned:				
Floor captains?				
Fire Brigade?				
Evacuation assistants?				
Other				

Evacuation

	YES	NO	N/A	Comments
Are employees responsible for emergency shut down procedures assigned and capable?				
Who has been assigned to call an actual evacuation?				
What is the preferred means of reporting fires and other emergencies?				
Do you have immediately available emergency scripts that can be read during an emergency event?				

General Building Issues – Annual Audit

General Building Issues	YES	NO	N/A	Comments
Alarm				
What forms of communication are available during an emergency (i.e., radio, cell phone, public address system, etc.)				
Can audible alarms be heard over machinery?				
Can audible alarms been heard in all locations?				
Is a visual warning system provided for people with hearing disabilities?				
Do you use distinct audible alarms for different emergencies?				
If yes, have employees been trained and do they understand each audible alarm?				
Has the emergency notification system (i.e., alarm and siren) been tested? When?				
Are there an adequate number of alarm pull boxes?				
Are they properly identified and placed in strategic locations?				
Are the pull boxes accessible by all employees, including those with disabilities?				
In locations that feature raised flooring, are water and smoke detectors utilized?				
Is the type of fire extinguisher applicable to the type of fire likely to occur?				
Is the placement of portable fire extinguishers accessible to all employees including those with disabilities?				
Does this building include a fire sprinkler system?				
Has the fire sprinkler system been tested? When? How often?				
Building Issues				
Are mechanical rooms kept locked at all times?				
Are electrical rooms locked and accessible by authorized personnel only?				

General Building Issues – Annual Audit

	YES	NO	N/A	Comments
Are tel/com rooms locked and accessible by authorized personnel only?				
Are computer/server rooms locked and accessible by authorized personnel only?				
Is good housekeeping observed in these areas?				
Are computer server rooms segregated from water lines, condensate pans, valves, caps, or plugs?				
Is a moisture detection system used in critical areas?				
Is a swipe card and mag-lock system used to restrict and record entry?				
Do you have a readily available list of the physical addresses of your buildings?				
Do you have the GPS coordinates for your buildings?				
Can emergency response personnel access your building after hours?				
If an external key box exists, has its presence been communicated to emergency response personnel?				
Is a process in place for assigning keys to building occupants?				
Does a key box exist with spare keys?				
Is the key box access limited and safe?				
Are the keys in the key box accurate?				
Is a master key available? Who has it?				
Are shut-off valves properly identified?				
Are shut-off valves labeled for on/off directions?				
Do the shut-off valves require a special key or wrench?				
If yes, where is the key kept?				
Are fire extinguishers inspected and recharged annually or as frequently as required by your local jurisdiction?				

General Building Issues – Annual Audit

	YES	NO	N/A	Comments
If standpipes, fire sprinklers, and hoses exist, are they inspected at least annually?				
Do breaker panels have latching doors?				
Are all breaker panels properly labeled?				
Is adequate space cleared around breaker panel?				
Are you using extension cords rather than permanent wiring?				
Are receptacles and power strips overloaded?				
Are photographs and/or video of the property updated?				
Do the elevators have automatic first floor recall when the fire alarm is tripped?				
Is a process in place to check for and rescue passengers trapped in elevators?				
Is the building address clearly visible from the street?				
Is there sufficient clearance for emergency vehicles beneath overhangs, carports, and parking garages?				
Is the building located near navigable waters that could be used to transport hazardous chemicals?				
Is the building located near railways that could be used to transport hazardous chemicals?				
Is the building located near highways that could be used to transport hazardous chemicals?				
Is the building located near businesses or plants that could experience a release of hazardous chemicals?				
Is the building located within 50 miles of a water dam?				
Are aisles and exit routes of sufficient width for emergency evacuation, including the evacuation of people with disabilities?				

General Building Issues – Annual Audit

	YES	NO	N/A	Comments

Chemical Storage

Are hazardous chemicals stored properly?

Are all containers used to store chemicals properly labeled?

Is MSDS documentation available for all chemicals?

How often is the MSDS log book updated?

Are obsolete and superceded MSDS documents archived for 30 years?

Have employees been trained to properly handle and store chemicals?

Have employees been trained to recognize and properly handle chemical spills?

Are chemical spill kits available? If yes, where are they located?

Has a procedure been established to communicate a spill to employees, management and, if necessary, the proper local agencies?

Have safe evacuation procedures been established and communicated to employees?

Emergency Inventory

Has the emergency food inventory list been reviewed and is it accurate?

Is the stock of water and food adequate (three days minimum)?

Are water and food supplies stocked and rotated to ensure freshness?

Are other emergency supplies such as batteries, first aid, and weather radios stocked?

Has the emergency equipment inventory list been reviewed and is it accurate?

General Building Issues – Annual Audit

	YES	NO	N/A	Comments

Equipment Maintenance
Is regularly scheduled preventative maintenance being performed on the following equipment:

Emergency Generator?

HVAC?

Cooling Tower?

Uninterruptible Power Supply?

Other?

Equipment Maintenance: Generator Issues
If your generator does not include an automatic transfer switch, who will be responsible for switching generator power on?

Who will confirm the generator power has transferred properly?

Who will the building occupants call in the event power does not transfer properly or the generator does not start?

Who will provide regularly scheduled maintenance on the generator?

Is the generator exhaust near the building's fresh air intake?

Has the emergency generator been tested under full load? When?

Has the emergency generator been exercised recently? When? How often?

Are load shedding priorities established?

How long can the emergency generator supply power?

What type of fuel does the emergency generator use?

Has the generator fuel been treated to prevent spoilage or contamination?

Who is responsible for refueling the emergency generator?

General Building Issues – Annual Audit

	YES	NO	N/A	Comments
How will you know if the emergency generator is in need of fuel?				
Do you have a secondary source of fuel for the emergency generator?				
How often is preventative maintenance performed on the emergency generator?				
Are preventative maintenance records for the emergency generator available?				
What equipment is connected to the emergency generator circuit?				
Is the correct (most critical) equipment connected to the generator circuit?				
Is the generator under/over loaded?				
Equipment Maintenance: Other How long will the emergency UPS system provide backup power?				
What equipment is connected to the emergency UPS system?				
Can HVAC equipment be shut down from a single location?				
Where are the HVAC fresh air intakes located?				
Is access to HVAC fresh air intakes limited?				
Are they free from possible contamination?				
Are you able to close down the fresh air intakes in an emergency? How?				
Is the mechanical room free of all paper, debris, chemicals, and other storage?				
Are roof drains and gutters kept free of debris?				
Are parking lot drains kept free of debris and operational?				
Are French drains working properly?				
Are sump pumps available and operational?				
Are sand bags and sand available? Can they be quickly shipped?				

General Building Issues – Annual Audit

	YES	NO	N/A	Comments
Floor Plan Are the following items located on the floor plan:				
Windows and Doors				
Designated escape routes				
Emergency exits				
Evacuation staging areas				
Stairways				
Elevators				
Restricted areas				
Mechanical Rooms				
Telecommunications Rooms				
Haz-Mat storage locations				
Loading Dock				
MSDS Station				
Right-to-know station				
Alarm panels				
Fire alarm pull stations				
First aid kits and stations				
Automated External Defibrillators (AED)				
Fire Pumps				
Water sprinkler testing valves				
Fire extinguishers				
Smoke detectors				
Generator location				
Generator powered circuits				
Uninterruptible power system location				
Gas mains and valves				
Water lines and valves				
Utility shutoffs				
Storm drains				
Roof drains				
Sewer lines				

General Building Issues – Annual Audit

	YES	NO	N/A	Comments

General Inspection

Is there any evidence of water leakage or smoke?

Is there any evidence of tampering with access doors, windows, or gate operators?

Is there any evidence of tampering with the security fence?

Are employees at risk of violence or abduction?

Are heavy items placed lower on storage racks, especially in areas susceptible to earthquakes?

Means of Egress

Are all exits doors working properly?

Do all exit doors open outward?

Are exit doors self closing?

Do emergency exit doors have panic hardware installed?

Are all emergency exits doors properly labeled?

Are doors that appear to be exit doors but are not labeled "Not an Exit"?

Are all exit doors kept unlocked and free of obstruction?

If a fire exit door empties into a parking lot area, is the pavement area striped and labeled "No Parking"?

Does the stairwell used as means of egress have working emergency lighting? When was it last checked?

Is the stairwell clean and free of dust and water?

Are fire escape routes clearly identified so that even visitors could recognize and follow them?

General Building Issues – Annual Audit

	YES	NO	N/A	Comments
Are floorplans posted that identify current location and two exit routes?				
At elevators, are signs present that warn of the dangers of use during a fire?				
Are stairwell floors labeled with floor numbers?				
Are floor numbers displayed on the exterior of emergency exit doors in stairwells?				
Are alternate exit routes used during evacuation drills?				

Health Related Issues - Annual Audit

Health-related Issues	YES	NO	N/A	Comments
AED Issues				
How many AEDs do you have installed?				
Where are they located?				
How will our organization keep informed of changes to regulations involving AED usage?				
Where is the prescription from a state-licensed physician for AED installation kept?				
Who is trained in proper AED use?				
Bloodborne Pathogens				
Is the company's "Exposure Control Plan" reviewed and updated annually?				
Are employees involved in the selection process of needles and sharps?				
Is a "Sharps Injury Log" maintained?				

Specific Threats – Annual Audit

Specific Threats	YES	NO	N/A	Comments
Bomb Threat				
Are employees provided with a bomb threat checklist?				
Have employees been trained in how to evacuate the building in a calm and orderly fashion?				
Is a bomb squad available to assist and in what ways will they respond?				
Has a bomb search team been established and trained?				
Is a set of floor plans available for the search team and authorities?				
Has a procedure been established to allow employees back into the building?				
Civil Unrest				
Do we foresee any events that may cause civil unrest?				
Trigger events may include:				
• Labor disputes				
• Layoffs and downsizing				
• Environmentally sensitive meetings or conferences				
• Sporting events				
• Political rallies				
• Economic conferences				
• Judicial decisions				
• Music concerts				
• Religious gatherings				
• Biased racial or cultural events				
Fire				
Have we completed a list of all the major workplace fire hazards and their proper handling and storage requirements?				
Have we identified potential ignition sources (i.e., welding, smoking)?				
The names of personnel responsible for maintenance of equipment installed to prevent or control fires include:				

Specific Threats – Annual Audit

	YES	NO	N/A	Comments

Weather: Heat/Drought

Have employees been trained in recognizing the dangers of heat and techniques for coping with heat?

Are heat index warning announced to employees working in hot environments?

Are mandatory water restrictions in effect (i.e., irrigating landscape)?

If yes, have we changed automatic timer setting to comply with restrictions?

In times of drought, have we trimmed back vegetation that could catch fire?

Have proper precautions been taken when welding or roofing work is performed?

Weather: Winter Storm Issues

Are snow removal tools available (shovels, salt, etc.)?

Have we created a rotating schedule for maintenance employees to be on call after hours in the event of an emergency?

Do we winterize HVAC, fire sprinkler, and irrigation systems in the fall?

Have roof drains been checked for blockages that could impede water runoff?

Have roof gutter systems been checked for blockages that could impede water runoff?

In the event of a blizzard, do we have a process in place for allowing workers to leave early?

What will determine if we allow workers to leave early?

Who will stay behind to monitor the building and perform shutdown if necessary?

Resources

Helpful Web sites

American Red Cross	www.redcross.org
Avalanches (American Avalanche Association)	www.avalanche.org
Disaster Center	www.disastercenter.com
Drought	www.usgs.gov and http://droughtmonitor.unl.edu
Earthquakes	earthquake.usgs.gov/
Emergency Management Training	www.carlyleconsultants.com
Federal Emergency Management Agency (FEMA)	www.fema.gov
Landslide Risk Areas	landslides.usgs.gov/
National Hurricane Center	www.nhc.noaa.gov
National Oceanographic & Atmospheric Administration (NOAA)	www.noaa.gov
National Weather Service	www.weather.gov/
State Dam Safety Officials	www.damsafety.org>
Tornado Project Online	www.tornadoproject.com
Tsunami Warning Center	www.tsunami.gov
U.S. Army Corps of Engineers	www.usace.army.mil/
Volcano hazards	volcanoes.usgs.gov/
Wildfire Dangers	www.weather.gov/ctp/FireWeather and www.srh.noaa.gov/abq/?n=forecasts-fireweather-firedanger and www.wfas.net

Where Else Can I Find Assistance?

Creating an emergency action plan is quite an involved exercise. If you have never been through this exercise before, you may easily become confused or frustrated. Of course this book will help your planning efforts tremendously. Additionally, a number of other resources exist and you should take advantage of their expertise. Mid- to large-sized businesses should meet with local governmental agencies and community organizations. By simply informing them of your efforts to create an emergency plan and asking them for their assistance, you will tap into an incredible resource. Often, they will be willing to assist you by coordinating planning, training, or mitigation efforts. They may be willing to share their plan. Since they've been through the planning experience, they will be able to add valuable insight and information. Don't hesitate to contact these outside organizations.

Local Fire Department

Your local fire department is an excellent resource for assistance and training. Typically, your local fire department will work with you in planning and executing your emergency evacuation drills. They may be willing to review your emergency action plan and offer suggestions. Quite often they will provide specific safety-related training such as proper fire extinguisher use. Well versed in all aspects of emergency planning and recovery, fire departments are an excellent resource and should not be overlooked.

Utility Companies

Utility companies play a critical role during times of emergency. In scenarios in which electrical power is lost for an extended period of time, a utility company can play a role in the speed of your organization's recovery. Certain businesses such as hospitals, fire rescue, and telecommunications facilities are critical to the community and must be made operational as quickly as possible. If your business provides a critical service, it would be wise to contact the local utility company and identify your critical needs. They may have some flexibility with when they will restore electrical power to your business. Remember, however, restoration of service will not be accelerated based on your perceived need. Instead, any early restoration will be based on your organization's impact on the community's ability to quickly recover from the emergency event.

American Red Cross

The American Red Cross is a humanitarian organization led by volunteers. The Red Cross has been instrumental in providing relief to victims of all types of disasters. The Red Cross also assists people in preparing for, responding to, and preventing emergencies. The Red Cross has provided health- and safety-related training for over a century. These education programs include such diverse topics such as first aid, AED, CPR, HIV/AIDS, swimming, and life guarding programs. In the average year, nearly 12 million people take Red Cross health and safety courses.

Although not a government agency, the Red Cross works closely with various government agencies including the Federal Emergency Management Agency (FEMA) during times of major crises. To learn more about the Red Cross, including the training and education programs available in your area, visit their web site at www.redcross.org.

Safety Consultants

Many organizations do not have in-house expertise when it comes to emergency planning, training, and recovery. For those organizations, consultants specializing in emergency planning and recovery can be invaluable.

The Carlyle Consulting Group is a consulting firm specializing in the corporate and commercial real estate arena. The consulting service and training workshops focus on easy-to-implement and common sense solutions to today's complex business problems including OSHA compliance and emergency action planning, training, and development. For a complete listing of services provides, visit the Carlyle Consulting Group's Web site.

Carlyle Consulting Group
8350 McCoy Road
Fort Meade, Florida 33841
Phone: (866) 227-5953
www.carlyleconsultants.com

In 1862, American Bureau of Shipping (ABS) began its legacy of safety in the maritime industry. Today ABS Consulting, Inc., has broadened its focus far beyond the marine industry with services relevant to virtually every market segment today. ABS Consulting identifies hazards, analyzes risk, and provides mitigation services to leading organizations worldwide. From structural engineering to risk consulting to catastrophe management, ABS Consulting offers solutions tailored to meet the specific needs of its clients.

ABS Consulting Inc.
ABS Consulting Headquarters
16855 Northchase Drive
Houston, TX 77060
www.absconsulting.com

Federal Emergency Management Agency (FEMA)

The Federal Emergency Management Agency (FEMA) is a government agency within the Department of Homeland Security. FEMA's mission is to plan for, respond to, and prevent disasters across the country. FEMA employs over 2,500 emergency response personnel, supplemented by over 5,000 stand-by reservists.

The services of FEMA are very diverse and include emergency planning, training, and coordination of response and the administration of assistance to states, communities, businesses, and individuals. Furthermore, FEMA is instrumental in flood plain management and administering the national flood insurance programs.

FEMA
www.fema.gov

United States Fire Administration

The United States Fire Administration (USFA) is an entity of the Federal Emergency Management Agency (FEMA). Its mission is to save lives and reduce economic losses due to fire and fire-related emergencies. The United States Fire Administration provides training and education services to the emergency services community. They have been very influential in developing fire safety–related codes for states and municipalities.

USFA
16825 South Seton Avenue
Emmitsburg, MD 21727
Switchboard: (800) 238-3358 or (301) 447-1000

National Fire Incident Reporting System (NFIRS)
Help Desk: (888) 382-3827
www.usfa.fema.gov

National Emergency Management Association (NEMA)

The National Emergency Management Association (NEMA) is a professional association of emergency management directors committed to providing expertise and leadership in the field of emergency planning and management. NEMA also takes a leadership role in developing strategic partnerships that provide continuous improvements in emergency management functions. The NEMA Web site is an excellent resource for up-to-date information on topics such emergency preparedness, including homeland security and bioterrorism.

National Emergency Management Association
2760 Research Park Drive
Lexington, KY 40511
Phone: (859) 244-8000
E-mail: nemaadmin@csg.org
www.nemaweb.org

National Fire Prevention Association (NFPA)

The National Fire Prevention Association (NFPA) is recognized as the leading authority where fire safety–related education, training, and code development is concerned. Municipalities across the nation have adopted NFPA standards as a basis for their building codes. The NFPA is an international nonprofit organization whose mission is to reduce the burden of fire and other related hazards. Its goal is to increase quality of life for all by advocating scientifically sound codes and standards, research, training, and education.

The National Fire Prevention Association is comprised of more than eighty national trade and professional organizations with a membership exceeding 65,000 professionals worldwide.

NFPA
1 Batterymarch Park
Quincy, Massachusetts 02169-7471
Phone: (617) 770-3000
www.nfpa.org

Building Owners and Managers Association (BOMA)

The Building Owners and Managers Association (BOMA) was founded in 1907 under the National Association of Building Owners and Managers name. Today BOMA International offers education, benchmarking studies, building performance data, and related services to real estate professionals who manage over 10.4 billion square feet of office space in North America. BOMA International represents over 100 North American associations and nine international associations.

BOMA International works to increase professionalism through designation curriculum and continuing education programs including those issues dealing with OSHA compliance, emergency planning, and disaster recovery in a commercial real estate environment. To realize that mission, in 1970 the Building Owners and Managers Institute (BOMI) was established by BOMA to provide industry-related curriculum. BOMI has developed four distinct professional designations—the Real Property Administrator (RPA®), the Facilities Management Administrator (FMA®), the Systems Maintenance Administrator (SMA®), and the Systems Maintenance Technician (SMT®) designations. In addition to subjects such as building maintenance and financial management knowledge, the BOMI curriculum teaches real estate professionals about topics such as OSHA compliance and emergency planning and management.

BOMA
1101 15th Street, NW, Suite 800
Washington, DC 20005
Phone: (202) 408-2662
E-mail: info@boma.org
www.boma.org

International Facility Managers Association (IFMA)

The International Facility Management Association (IFMA) was established in 1980 as a nonprofit, worldwide professional association of facility managers. IFMA membership exceeds 24,000 professionals in 105 countries. IFMA members make up over 134 chapters worldwide.

IFMA is a leader in providing direct and timely real estate training, including topics on emergency planning in a built environment. In addition to IFMA's regional training programs, World Workplace is an annual professional conference featuring educational programs, extensive networking opportunities, and the largest exposition of products and services relevant to the built environment.

IFMA
800 Gessner Road, Suite 900
Houston, TX 77024-4257 USA
Phone: (713) 623-4362
E-mail: ifma@ifma.org
www.ifma.org

Institute of Real Estate Management (IREM)

The Institute of Real Estate Management (IREM) was founded in 1933 and today remains a leading organization of professional real managers and owners. IREM membership includes more than 18,000 individuals and 550 corporate members. IREM is an affiliate of the National Association of Realtors (NAR), and its mission is to educate real estate managers, certify their competence, and serve as an advocate on issues affecting the real estate management industry. These issues include emergency planning and management in the real estate sector.

Institute of Real Estate Management
430 North Michigan Avenue
Chicago, Illinois 60611
Phone: (800) 837-0706
E-mail: getinfo@irem.org
www.irem.org

American Institute of Architects (AIA)

The American Institute of Architects (AIA) serves the needs of registered architects across the nation. The AIA has been instrumental in educating architects in areas of as diverse as building design and building security. As the industry deals with new issues such as terrorism, security, and disabled employees, the AIA provides direction and influences design and code development across the nation.

The American Institute of Architects
1735 New York Avenue, NW
Washington, DC 20006-5292
Phone: (800) AIA-3837
E-mail: infocentral@aia.org
www.aia.org/

Occupational Safety and Health Administration (OSHA)

In 1970, the Occupational Safety and Health Act was created. The Act gave birth to the Occupational Safety and Health Administration (OSHA), a federal agency whose goal is to save lives, prevent injuries, and protect the health of over 100 million workers in the United States. OSHA employs approximately 2,100 inspectors in addition to engineers, physicians, educators, standards writers, and other technical and support personnel spread over more than 200 offices throughout the country. These OSHA representatives develop safety standards, enforces those standards, and proactively educate both employers and employees about safe work. In the three decades since the inception of OSHA, injuries, illnesses, and deaths related to the work environment have steadily declined.

OSHA is a federal agency that has jurisdiction over half of the states in the union. The remaining states have created their own state OSHA plans, which supersede Federal OSHA. The state plans must be as strict and all-encompassing as Federal OSHA, and in some cases the state plans are even more demanding. If you are unsure of your responsibilities, visit the OSHA Web site and search for "State Plans."

U.S. Department of Labor
Occupational Safety and Health Administration
200 Constitution Avenue, NW
Washington, D.C. 20210
Phone: (800) 321-OSHA (6742)
www.osha.gov/

Americans with Disabilities Act (ADA)

The Americans with Disabilities Act was created to provide protection from bias and ensure fair and equal treatment to persons with disabilities. This includes protection during times of emergency and building evacuation. The ADA is a federal act and covers all commercial buildings; however, local municipalities may enact codes that are stricter than the federal regulations. The ADA has been instrumental in developing standards for building ingress and egress, resulting in numerous life-saving and life-enhancing laws for the benefit of the disabled.

U.S. Department of Justice
950 Pennsylvania Avenue, NW
Civil Rights Division
Disability Rights Section—NYA
Washington, D.C. 20530
Phone: (800) 514-0301 (voice)
(800) 514-0383 (TTY)
www.ada.gov

Corporate Real Estate Network (CoreNet)

On May 1, 2002, International Development Research Council (IDRC) and the International Association of Corporate Real Estate Executives (NACORE International) joined forces. This merger of two leading and respected associations led to the creation of CoreNet Global.

CoreNet Global consists of fifty-eight chapters in five global regions including Asia, Australia, Europe, Latin America, and North America including Canada. The nearly 7,000 members of corporate real estate executive, service providers, and developers make CoreNet Global the voice of the industry. CoreNet Global has been instrumental in developing best practices for security and emergency planning in the corporate real estate industry.

CoreNet Global
133 Peachtree Street, NE, Suite 3000
Atlanta, GA 30303
Phone: (800) 726-8111 (US and Canada)
www.corenetglobal.org/

The Weather Channel

In 1982 the Weather Channel was born. Although many people found it difficult to believe a 24-hour weather channel could succeed, today, the Weather Channel is the leading weather provider on the Internet and on television. The Weather Channel's Web site averages more than 130 million page views each month. The Weather Channel provides viewers with up-to-date weather conditions, five-day forecasts, and severe weather alerts. Because weather plays such an important role in emergency events, the Weather Channel seeks to keep the public informed about developing weather related problems.

The Weather Channel
www.weather.com

National Oceanic and Atmospheric Administration (NOAA)

The National Oceanic and Atmospheric Administration (NOAA) was created in 1970 to serve a national need for better protection of life and property from natural hazards. NOAA conducts research and evaluates changes in the oceans, atmosphere, space, and sun. Based on the data collected, NOAA works to predict and mitigate the effects of these environmental changes.

The National Weather Service (NWS) is a member of the NOAA organization and provides weather-related forecasts for the United States. In addition to weather forecasts, the National Weather Service provides severe weather warnings. The National Weather Service the official voice for issuing warnings during life-threatening weather situations in the United States. Because the nation is affected by weather-related events outside of the United States, the National Weather Service tracks these events as well. Additionally, the NWS Web site is a great source for Doppler radar, satellite observations, and a detailed glossary of weather-related terms.

National Oceanic and Atmospheric Administration
1401 Constitution Avenue, NW, Room 5128
Washington, DC 20230
www.noaa.gov

National Weather Service
www.weather.gov

Glossary

A selection of terms related to emergencies, disasters, natural and non-natural events, preparedness, protocols, building protection measures, and more. Many of these are standard terms used by FEMA and the CIA. These terms are sorted in the following sections:

- ⅄ Chemical and Biological Terms
- ⅄ Radiological Terms
- ⅄ General Emergency and Building Protection Terms

Chemical and Biological Terms

A

Acetylcholinesterase. An enzyme that hydrolyzes the neurotransmitter acetylcholine. The action of this enzyme is inhibited by nerve agents.

Aerosol. Fine liquid or solid particles suspended in a gas (e.g., fog or smoke).

Airborne contamination. Chemical or biological agents introduced into and fouling the source of supply of breathing or conditioning air.

Antibiotic. A substance that inhibits the growth of or kills microorganisms.

Antisera. The liquid part of blood containing antibodies that react against disease-causing agents such as those used in biological warfare.

Atropine. A compound used as an antidote for nerve agents.

B

Bacteria. Single-celled organisms that multiply by cell division and that can cause disease in humans, plants, or animals.

Biochemicals. The chemicals that make up or are produced by living things.

Biological agents (biological warfare agents). Living organisms or the materials derived from them that cause disease in or harm to humans, animals, or plants or cause deterioration of material. Biological agents may be used as liquid droplets, aerosols, or dry powders.

Biological warfare. The intentional use of biological agents as weapons to kill or injure humans, animals, or plants, or to damage equipment.

Bioregulators. Biochemicals that regulate bodily functions. Bioregulators that are produced by the body are termed "endogenous." Some of these same bioregulators can be chemically synthesized.

Blister agents. A casualty/toxic agent. Substances that cause blistering of the skin. Exposure is through liquid or vapor contact with any exposed tissue (eyes, skin, lungs). Examples are distilled mustard (HD), nitrogen mustard (HN), lewisite (L), mustard/lewisite (HL), and phenodichloroarsine (PD).

Blood agents. A casualty/toxic agent. Substances that injure a person by interfering with cell respiration (the exchange of oxygen and carbon dioxide between blood and tissues). Examples are arsine (SA), cyanogen chloride (CK), hydrogen chloride (HCl), and hydrogen cyanide (AC).

C

Casualty (toxic) agents. Produce incapacitation, serious injury, or death, and can be used to incapacitate or kill victims. They are the blister, blood, choking, and nerve agents (see individual entries).

Causative agents. The organism or toxin that is responsible for causing a specific disease or harmful effect.

Central nervous system depressants. An incapacitating agent. Compounds that have the predominant effect of depressing or blocking the activity of the central nervous system. The primary mental effects include the disruption of the ability to think, sedation, and lack of motivation.

Central nervous system stimulants. An incapacitating agent. Compounds that have the predominant effect of flooding the brain with too much information. The primary mental effect is loss of concentration, causing indecisiveness and the inability to act in a sustained, purposeful manner. Examples of the depressants and stimulants include agent 15 (suspected Iraqi BZ), BZ (3-quinulidinyle benzilate), canniboids, fentanyls, LSD (lysergic acid diethylamide), and phenothiazines.

Chemical agents. Substances that are intended to kill, seriously injure, or incapacitate people through physiological effects. Generally separated by severity of effect (e.g., lethal, blister, and incapacitating). Excluded from consideration are riot control agents, and smoke and flame materials. The agent may appear as a vapor, aerosol, or liquid; it can be either a casualty/toxic agent or an incapacitating agent.

Choking/lung/pulmonary agents. A casualty/toxic agent. Substances that cause physical injury to the lungs. Exposure is through inhalation. In extreme cases, membranes swell and lungs become filled with liquid. Death results from lack of oxygen; hence, the victim is "choked." Examples are chlorine (CL), diphosgene (DP), cyanide (KCN), nitrogen oxide (NO), perfluororisobutylene (PHIB), phosgene (CG), red phosphorous

(RP), sulfur trioxide-chlorosulfonic acid (FS), Teflon and PHIB, titanium tetrachloride (FM), and zinc oxide (HC).

Contagious. Capable of being transmitted from one person to another.

Contamination. The undesirable deposition of a chemical, biological, or radiological material on the surface of structures, areas, objects, or people.

Culture. A population of microorganisms grown in a medium.

Cutaneous. Pertaining to the skin.

D

Decontamination. The process of making any person, object, or area safe by absorbing, destroying, neutralizing, making harmless, or removing the hazardous material.

F

Fungi. Any of a group of plants mainly characterized by the absence of chlorophyll, the green-colored compound found in other plants. Fungi range from microscopic single-celled plants (such as molds and mildews) to large plants (such as mushrooms).

G

G-series nerve agents. Chemical agents of moderate to high toxicity developed in the 1930s. Examples are tabun (GA), sarin (GB), soman (GD), phosphonofluoridic acid, ethyl-, 1-methylethyl ester (GE), and cyclohexyl sarin (GF).

H

Host. An animal or plant that harbors or nourishes another organism.

I

Incapacitating agents. Agents that produce physical or psychological effects, or both, that may persist for hours or days after exposure, rendering victims incapable of performing normal physical and mental tasks. These include vomiting agents, tear (riot control) agents, central nervous system depressants, and central nervous system stimulants (see individual entries for these four).

Industrial agents. Chemicals developed or manufactured for use in industrial operations or research by industry, government, or academia. These chemicals are not primarily manufactured for the specific purpose of producing human casualties or rendering equipment, facilities, or areas dangerous for use by man. Hydrogen cyanide, cyanogen chloride, phosgene, chloropicrin, and many herbicides and pesticides are industrial chemicals that also can be chemical agents.

Infectious agents. Biological agents capable of causing disease in a susceptible host.

Infectivity. (1) The ability of an organism to spread. (2) The number of organisms required to cause an infection to secondary hosts. (3) The capability of an organism to spread out from the site of infection and cause disease in the host organism. Infectivity also can be viewed as the number of organisms required to cause an infection.

L

Line-source delivery system. A delivery system in which the biological agent is dispersed from a moving ground or air vehicle in a line perpendicular to the direction of the prevailing wind. (See also "point-source delivery system.")

Liquid agents. Chemical agents that appear to be an oily film or droplets. The color ranges from clear to brownish amber.

M

Microorganism. Any organism, such as bacteria, viruses, and some fungi, that can be seen only with a microscope.

Mycotoxin. A toxin produced by fungi.

N

Nebulizer. A device for producing a fine spray or aerosol.

Nerve agents. A casualty/toxic agent. Substances that interfere with the central nervous system. Exposure is primarily through contact with the liquid (skin and eyes) and secondarily through inhalation of the vapor. Three distinct symptoms associated with nerve agents are: pinpoint pupils, an extreme headache, and severe tightness in the chest. See also G-series and V-series nerve agents.

Nonpersistent agents. Agents that, upon release, lose the ability to cause casualties after ten to fifteen minutes. They have a high evaporation rate and are lighter than air and will disperse rapidly. They are considered to be short-term hazards; however, in small unventilated areas, these agents will be more persistent.

O

Organism. Any individual living thing, whether animal or plant.

Organophosphorous compound. A compound containing the elements phosphorus and carbon, whose physiological effects include inhibition of acetylcholinesterase. Many pesticides (malathione and parathion) and virtually all nerve agents are organophosphorus compounds.

P

Parasite. Any organism that lives in or on another organism without providing benefit in return.

Pathogen. Any organism (usually living), such as bacteria, fungi, and viruses, capable of producing serious disease or death.

Pathogenic agents. Biological agents capable of causing serious disease.

Percutaneous agents. Agents that are able to be absorbed by the body through the skin.

Persistent agents. Agents that, upon release, retain their casualty-producing effects for an extended period of time, usually anywhere from thirty minutes to several days. A persistent agent usually has a low evaporation rate and its vapor is heavier than air. Therefore, its vapor cloud tends to hug the ground. They are considered to be long-term hazards. Although inhalation hazards are still a concern, extreme caution should be taken to avoid skin contact as well.

Point-source delivery system. A delivery system in which the biological agent is dispersed from a stationary position. This delivery method results in coverage over a smaller area than with the line-source system. See also line-source delivery system.

Protection. Any means by which an individual protects his or her body. Measures include masks, self-contained breathing apparatuses, clothing, structures such as buildings, and vehicles.

R

Route of exposure (entry). The path by which a person comes into contact with an agent or organism (e.g., through breathing, digestion, or skin contact).

S

Single-cell protein. Protein-rich material obtained from cultured algae, fungi, protein, and bacteria, and often used as food or animal feed.

Spore. A reproductive form some microorganisms can take to become resistant to environmental conditions, such as extreme heat or cold, while in a "resting stage."

T

Tear (riot control) agents. An incapacitating agent. Produce irritating or disabling effects that rapidly disappear within minutes after exposure ceases. Examples are bromobenzylcyanide (CA), chloroacetophenone (CN or commercially known as Mace), chloropicrin (PS), CNB (CN in benzene and carbon tetrachloride), CNC (CN in chloroform), CNS (CN and chloropicrin in chloroform, CR (dibenz-(b,f)-1,4-oxazepine, a tear gas), CS (tear gas), and Capsaicin (pepper spray).

Toxicity. A measure of the harmful effect produced by a given amount of a toxin on a living organism. The relative toxicity of an agent can be expressed in milligrams of toxin needed per kilogram of body weight to kill experimental animals.

Toxins. Poisonous substances produced by living organisms.

V

Vaccine. A preparation of killed or weakened microorganism products used to artificially induce immunity against a disease.

Vaccine. A preparation of killed or weakened microorganism products used to artificially induce immunity against a disease.

Vapor agents. A gaseous form of a chemical agent. If heavier than air, the cloud will be close to the ground. If lighter than air, the cloud will rise and disperse more quickly.

Vector. An agent, such as an insect or rat, capable of transferring a pathogen from one organism to another.

Venom. A poison produced in the glands of some animals (e.g., snakes, scorpions, or bees).

Virus. An infectious microorganism that exists as a particle rather than as a complete cell. Particle sizes range from 20 to 400 nanometers (one-billionth of a meter). Viruses are not capable of reproducing outside of a host cell.

Volatility. A measure of how readily a substance will vaporize.

Vomiting agents. An incapacitating agent. Produce nausea and vomiting effects; can also cause coughing, sneezing, pain in the nose and throat, nasal discharge, and tears. Examples are adamsite (DM), diphenylchloroarsine (DA), and diphenylcyanoarsine (DC).

V-series nerve agents. Chemical agents of moderate to high toxicity developed in the 1950s. They are generally persistent. Examples are VE (phosphonothioic acid, ethyl-, S-(diethylamino)ethyl] O-ethylester), VG (phosphorothioic acid, S-[2-(diethylamino)ethyl] O, O-diethyl ester), VM (phosphonothioic acid, methyl-, S-[2-(diethylamino) ethyl] O-ethyl ester), VS (phosphonothioic acid, ethyl, S-[2-[bis(1-methylethyl)amino] ethyl] O-ethyl ester), and VX (phosphonothioic acid, methyl-, S-[2-[bis(1-methylethyl)amino]ethyl] O-ethyl ester).

Radiological Terms

A

Acute radiation syndrome. Consists of three levels of effects: hernatopoletic (blood cells, most sensitive); gastrointestinal (GI cells, very sensitive); and central nervous system (brain/muscle cells, insensitive). The initial signs and symptoms are nausea, vomiting, fatigue, and loss of appetite. Below about 200 rems, these symptoms may be the only indication of radiation exposure.

Alpha particles Alpha particles have a very short range in air and a very low ability to penetrate other materials, but also have a strong ability to ionize materials. Alpha particles are unable to penetrate even the thin layer of dead cells of human skin and consequently are not an external radiation hazard. Alpha-emitting nuclides inside the body as a result of inhalation or ingestion are a considerable internal radiation hazard.

B

Beta particles. High-energy electrons emitted from the nucleus of an atom during radioactive decay. They normally can be stopped by the skin or a very thin sheet of metal.

C

Cesium-137 (Cs-137). A strong gamma ray source and can contaminate property, entailing extensive cleanup. It is commonly used in industrial measurement gauges and for irradiation of material. Its half-life is 30.2 years.

Cobalt-60 (Co-60). A strong gamma ray source, and is extensively used as a radiotherapeutic for treating cancer, food and material irradiation, gamma radiography, and industrial measurement gauges. Its half-life is 5.27 years.

Curie (Ci). A unit of radioactive decay rate defined as 3.7×10^{10} disintegrations per second.

D

Decay. The process by which an unstable element is changed to another isotope or another element by the spontaneous emission of radiation from its nucleus. This process can be measured by using radiation detectors such as Geiger counters.

Decontamination. The process of making people, objects, or areas safe by absorbing, destroying, neutralizing, making harmless, or removing the hazardous material.

Dose rate (radiation). A general term indicating the quantity (total or accumulated) of ionizing radiation or energy absorbed by a person or animal, per unit of time.

Dosimeter. An instrument for measuring and registering total accumulated exposure to ionizing radiation.

E

Electromagnetic pulse (EMP). A sharp pulse of energy radiated instantaneously by a nuclear detonation that may affect or damage electronic components and equipment. EMP can also be generated in lesser intensity by non-nuclear means in specific frequency ranges to perform the same disruptive function.

G

Gamma ray. A high-energy photon emitted from the nucleus of atoms; similar to an x-ray. It can penetrate deeply into body tissue and many materials. Cobalt-60 and Cesium-137 are both strong gamma-emitters. Shielding against gamma radiation requires thick layers of dense materials, such as lead. Gamma rays are potentially lethal to humans.

H

Half-life. The amount of time needed for half of the atoms of a radioactive material to decay.

Highly enriched uranium (HEU). Uranium that is enriched to above 20 percent. Uranium-235 (U-235). Weapons-grade HEU is enriched to above 90 percent in U-235.

I

Ionize. To split off one or more electrons from an atom, thus leaving it with a positive electric charge. The electrons usually attach to one of the atoms or molecules, giving them a negative charge.

Iridium-192. A gamma ray emitting radioisotope used for gamma radiography. Its half-life is 73.83 days.

Isotope. A specific element always has the same number of protons in the nucleus. That same element may, however, appear in forms that have different numbers of neutrons in the nucleus. These different forms are referred to as "isotopes" of the element; for example, deuterium (2H) and tritium (3H) are isotopes of ordinary hydrogen (H).

L

Lethal dose (50/30). The dose of radiation expected to cause death within 30 days to 50 percent of those exposed without medical treatment. The generally accepted range is from 400–500 rem received over a short period of time.

N

Nuclear reactor. A device in which a controlled, self-sustaining nuclear chain reaction can be maintained with the use of cooling to remove generated heat.

P

Plutonium-239 (Pu-239). A metallic element used for nuclear weapons. Its half-life is 24,110 years.

R

Rad. A unit of absorbed dose of radiation defined as deposition of 100 ergs of energy per gram of tissue. A rad amounts to approximately one ionization per cubic micron.

Radiation. High-energy particles or gamma rays that are emitted by an atom as the substance undergoes radioactive decay. Particles can be either charged alpha or beta particles or neutral neutron or gamma rays.

Radiation sickness. Symptoms resulting from excessive exposure to radiation of the body.

Radioactive waste. Disposable, radioactive materials resulting from nuclear operations. Wastes are generally classified into two categories, high-level and low-level.

Radiological Dispersal Device (RDD). A device (weapon or equipment), other than a nuclear explosive device, designed to disseminate radioactive material in order to cause destruction, damage, or injury by means of the radiation produced by the decay of such material.

Radioluminescence. The luminescence produced by particles emitted during radioactive decay.

Rem. A **R**oentgen **E**quivalent **M**an is a unit of absorbed dose that takes into account the relative effectiveness of radiation that harms human health.

Roentgen Equivalent Man (REM or rem). A unit of absorbed dose that takes into account the relative effectiveness of radiation that harms human health.

S

Shielding. Materials (lead, concrete, etc.) used to block or attenuate radiation for protection of equipment, materials, or people.

Special Nuclear Material (SNM). Plutonium and uranium enriched in the isotopes Uranium-233 or Uranium-235.

U

Uranium 235 (U-235). Naturally occurring U-235 is found at 0.72 percent enrichment. U-235 is used as a reactor fuel or for weapons; however, weapons typically use U-235 enriched to 90 percent. Its half-life is 7.04×108 years.

X

X-ray. An invisible, highly penetrating electromagnetic radiation of much shorter wavelength (higher frequency) than visible light. Very similar to gamma rays.

General Emergency and Building Protection Terms

A

Access control. Any combination of barriers, gates, electronic security equipment, or guards that can deny entry to unauthorized personnel or vehicles.

Access control point (ACP). A station at an entrance to a building or a portion of a building where identification is checked and people and hand-carried items are searched.

Access road. Any roadway such as a maintenance, delivery, service, emergency, or other special limited use road that is necessary for the operation of a building or structure.

Active vehicle barrier. An impediment placed at an access control point that may be manually or automatically deployed in response to detection of a threat.

Airlock. A building entry configuration with which airflow from the outside can be prevented from entering a toxic-free area. An airlock uses two doors, only one of which can be opened at a time, and a blower system to maintain positive air pressures and purge contaminated air from the airlock before the second door is opened.

Area Commander. A military commander with authority in a specific geographical area or military installation.

Areas of potential compromise. Categories where losses can occur that will impact either a department's or an agency's minimum essential infrastructure and its ability to conduct core functions and activities.

ASCE. American Society of Civil Engineers. Founded in 1852, the first and oldest engineering society in the United States.

ASCE 7. The standard by the American Society of Civil Engineers covering "Minimum Design Loads for Buildings and Other Structures."

Assessment. The evaluation and interpretation of measurements and other information to provide a basis for decision-making.

Asset. A resource of value requiring protection. An asset can be tangible (e.g., people, buildings, facilities, equipment, activities, operations, and information) or intangible (e.g., processes or a company's information and reputation).

Asset protection. Security program designed to protect personnel, facilities, and equipment, in all locations and situations, accomplished through planned and integrated application of combating terrorism, physical security, operations security, and personal protective services, and supported by intelligence, counterintelligence, and other security programs.

B

Ballistics attack. An attack in which small arms (e.g., pistols, submachine guns, shotguns, and rifles) are fired from a distance and rely on the flight of the projectile to damage the target.

Barbed tape or concertina. A coiled tape or coil of wires with wire barbs or blades deployed as an obstacle to human trespass or entry into an area.

Barbed wire. A double strand of wire with four-point barbs equally spaced along the wire deployed as an obstacle to human trespass or entry into an area.

Barcode. A black bar printed on white paper or tape that can be easily read with an optical scanner.

Biometrics. The use of physical characteristics of the human body as a unique identification method.

Blast curtains. Heavy curtains made of blast-resistant materials that could protect the occupants of a room from flying debris.

Blast-resistant glazing. Window opening glazing that is resistant to blast effects because of the interrelated function of the frame and glazing material properties frequently dependent upon tempered glass, polycarbonate, or laminated glazing.

Blast vulnerability envelope. The geographical area in which an explosive device will cause damage to assets.

Bollard. A vehicle barrier consisting of a cylinder, usually made of steel and sometimes filled with concrete, placed on end in the ground and spaced about three feet apart to prevent vehicles from passing, but allowing entrance of pedestrians and bicycles.

Boundary penetration sensor. An interior intrusion detection sensor that detects attempts by individuals to penetrate or enter a building.

Building hardening. Enhanced construction that reduces vulnerability to external blast and ballistic attacks.

Business Continuity Program (BCP). An ongoing process supported by senior management and funded to ensure that the necessary steps are taken to identify the impact of potential losses, maintain viable recovery strategies and recovery plans, and ensure continuity services through personnel training, plan testing, and maintenance.

C

Cable barrier. Cable or wire rope anchored to and suspended off the ground or attached to chain-link fence to act as a barrier to moving vehicles.

Capacitance sensor. A device that detects an intruder approaching or touching a metal object by sensing a change in capacitance between the object and the ground.

CCTV switcher. A piece of equipment capable of presenting multiple video images to various monitors, recorders, etc.

Chimney effect. Air movement in a building between floors caused by differential air temperature (differences in density), between the air inside and outside the building. It occurs in vertical shafts, such as elevators, stairwells, and conduit/wiring/piping chases. Hotter air inside the building will rise and be replaced by infiltration with colder outside air through the lower portions of the building. Conversely, reversing the temperature will reverse the flow (down the chimney). Also known as stack effect.

Clear zone. An area that is clear of visual obstructions and landscape materials that could conceal a threat or perpetrator.

Closed circuit television (CCTV). An electronic system of cameras, control equipment, recorders, and related apparatus used for surveillance or alarm assessment.

Collateral damage. Injury or damage to assets that are not the primary target of an attack.

Community. A political entity that has the authority to adopt and enforce laws and ordinances for the area under its jurisdiction. In most cases, the community is an incorporated town, city, township, village, or unincorporated area of a county; however, each state defines its own political subdivisions and forms of government.

Components and cladding. Elements of the building envelope that do not qualify as part of the main wind-force resisting system.

Continuity of services and operations. Controls to ensure that, when unexpected events occur, departmental/agency minimum essential infrastructure services and operations, including computer operations, continue without interruption or are promptly resumed, and that critical and sensitive data are protected through adequate contingency and business recovery plans and exercises.

Control center. A centrally located room or facility staffed by personnel charged with the oversight of specific situations or equipment.

Controlled area. An area into which access is controlled or limited. It is that portion of a restricted area usually near or surrounding a limited or exclusion area. Correlates with exclusion zone.

Controlled perimeter. A physical boundary at which vehicle and personnel access is controlled at the perimeter of a site. Access control at a controlled perimeter should demonstrate the capability to search individuals and vehicles.

Conventional construction. Building construction that is not specifically designed to resist weapons, explosives, or chemical, biological, and radiological effects. Conventional construction is designed only to resist common loadings and environmental effects such as wind, seismic, and snow loads.

Crash bar. A mechanical egress device located on the interior side of a door that unlocks the door when pressure is applied in the direction of egress.

Crime Prevention Through Environmental Design (CPTED). A crime prevention strategy based on evidence that the design and form of the built environment can influence human behavior. CPTED usually involves the use of three principles: natural surveillance (by placing physical features, activities, and people to maximize visibility); natural access control (through the judicial placement of entrances, exits, fencing, landscaping, and lighting); and territorial reinforcement (using buildings, fences, pavement, signs, and landscaping to express ownership).

Crisis Management (CM). The measures taken to identify, acquire, and plan the use of resources needed to anticipate, prevent, and/or resolve a threat or act of terrorism.

Critical assets. Those assets essential to the minimum operations of the organization, and to ensure the health and safety of the general public.

Critical infrastructure. Primary infrastructure systems (e.g., utilities, telecommunications, transportation, etc.) whose incapacity would have a debilitating impact on the organization's ability to function.

D

Damage assessment. The process used to appraise or determine the number of injuries and deaths, damage to public and private property, and the status of key facilities and services (e.g., hospitals and other health care facilities, fire and police stations, communications networks, water and sanitation systems, utilities, and transportation networks) resulting from a manmade or natural disaster.

Defense layer. Building design or exterior perimeter barriers intended to delay attempted forced entry.

Delay rating. A measure of the effectiveness of penetration protection of a defense layer.

Design Basis Threat (DBT). The threat (e.g., tactics and associated weapons, tools, or explosives) against which assets within a building must be protected and upon which the security engineering design of the building is based.

Detection layer. A ring of intrusion detection sensors located on or adjacent to a defensive layer or between two defensive layers.

Detection measures. Protective measures that detect intruders, weapons, or explosives; assist in assessing the validity of detection; control access to protected areas; and communicate the appropriate information to the response force. Detection measures include Detection Systems, Assessment Systems, and Access Control System elements.

Disaster. An occurrence of a natural catastrophe, technological accident, or human-caused event that has resulted in severe property damage, deaths, or multiple injuries.

Disaster Field Office (DFO). The office established in or near the designated area of a presidentially declared major disaster to support federal and state response and recovery operations.

Disaster Recovery Center (DRC). Places established in the area of a presidentially declared major disaster, as soon as practicable, to provide victims the opportunity to apply in person for assistance or obtain information relating to that assistance.

Domestic terrorism. The unlawful use, or threatened use, of force or violence by a group or individual based and operating entirely within the United States or Puerto Rico without foreign direction committed against persons or property to intimidate or coerce a government, the civilian population, or any segment thereof in furtherance of political or social objectives.

Duress alarm devices. Also known as panic buttons, these devices are designated specifically to initiate a panic alarm.

E

Effective stand-off distance. A stand-off distance at which the required level of protection can be shown to be achieved through analysis or can be achieved through building hardening or other mitigating construction or retrofit.

Electronic emanations. Electromagnetic emissions from computers, communications, electronics, wiring, and related equipment.

Electronic Entry Control Systems (EECS). Electronic devices that automatically verify authorization for a person to enter or exit a controlled area.

Electronic Security System (ESS). An integrated system that encompasses interior and exterior sensors, closed circuit television systems for assessment of alarm conditions, Electronic Entry Control Systems, data transmission media, and alarm reporting systems for monitoring, control, and display of various alarm and system information.

Emergency. Any natural or human-caused situation that results in or may result in substantial injury or harm to the population or substantial damage to or loss of property.

Emergency Alert System (EAS). A communications system of broadcast stations and interconnecting facilities authorized by the Federal Communications Commission (FCC). The system provides the president and other national, state, and local officials the means to broadcast emergency information to the public before, during, and after disasters.

Emergency Environmental Health Services. Services required to correct or improve damaging environmental health effects on humans, including inspection for food contamination, inspection for water contamination, and vector control; providing for sewage and solid waste inspection and disposal; cleanup and disposal of hazardous materials; and sanitation inspection for emergency shelter facilities.

Emergency Medical Services (EMS). Services including personnel, facilities, and equipment required to ensure proper medical care for the sick and injured from the time of injury to the time of final disposition, including medical disposition within a hospital, temporary medical facility, or special care facility; release from the site; or declared dead. Further, Emergency Medical Services specifically include those services immediately required to ensure proper medical care and specialized treatment for patients in a hospital and coordination of related hospital services.

Emergency Mortuary Services. Services required to assure adequate death investigation, identification, and disposition of bodies; removal, temporary storage, and transportation of bodies to temporary morgue facilities; notification of next of kin; and coordination of mortuary services and burial of unclaimed bodies.

Emergency Operations Center (EOC). The protected site from which state and local civil government officials coordinate, monitor, and direct emergency response activities during an emergency.

Emergency Operations Plan (EOP). A document that describes how people and property will be protected in disaster and disaster threat situations; details who is responsible for carrying out specific actions; identifies the personnel, equipment, facilities, supplies, and other resources available for use in the disaster; and outlines how all actions will be coordinated.

Emergency Planning Zones (EPZ). Areas around a facility for which planning is needed to ensure prompt and effective actions are taken to protect the health and safety of the public if an accident or disaster occurs. In the Radiological Emergency Preparedness Program, the two EPZs are: **Plume Exposure Pathway** (ten-mile EPZ). A circular geographic zone (with a ten-mile radius centered at the nuclear power plant) for which plans are developed to protect the public against exposure to radiation emanating from a radioactive plume caused as a result of an accident at the nuclear power plant. **Ingestion Pathway** (fifty-mile EPZ). A circular geographic zone (with a fifty-mile radius centered at the nuclear power plant) for which plans are developed to protect the public from the ingestion of water or food contaminated as a result of a nuclear power plant accident. In the Chemical Stockpile Emergency Preparedness Program (CSEPP), the EPZ is divided into three concentric circular zones: **Immediate Response Zone** (IRZ). A circular zone ranging from ten to fifteen kilometers (six to nine miles) from the potential chemical event source, depending on the stockpile location on-post. Emergency response plans developed for the IRZ must provide for the most rapid and effective protective actions possible, because the IRZ will have the highest concentration of agent and the least amount of warning time. **Protective Action Zone** (PAZ). An area that extends beyond the IRZ to approximately sixteen to fifty kilometers (ten to thirty miles) from the stockpile location. The PAZ is that area where public protective actions may still be necessary in case of an accidental release of chemical agent, but where the available warning and response time is such that most people could evacuate. However, other responses (e.g., sheltering) may be appropriate for institutions and special populations that could not evacuate within the available time. **Precautionary Zone** (PZ). The outermost portion of the EPZ for CSEPP, extending from the PAZ outer boundary to a distance where the risk of adverse impacts to humans is negligible. Because of the increased warning and response time available for implementation of response actions in the PZ, detailed local emergency planning is not required, although Consequence Management planning may be appropriate.

Emergency Public Information (EPI). Information that is disseminated primarily in anticipation of an emergency or at the actual time of an emergency and, in addition to providing information frequently directs actions, instructs, and transmits direct orders.

Emergency Response Team (ERT). An interagency team, consisting of the lead representative from each federal department or agency assigned primary responsibility for an ESF and key members of the FCO's staff, formed to assist the FCO in carrying out his or her coordination responsibilities.

Emergency Response Team Advance Element (ERT-A). For federal disaster response and recovery activities under the Stafford Act, the portion of the ERT that is first deployed to the field to respond to a disaster incident. The ERT-A is the nucleus of the full ERT.

Emergency Response Team National (ERT-N). An ERT that has been established and rostered for deployment to catastrophic disasters where the resources of the FEMA Region have been, or are expected to be, overwhelmed.

Emergency Support Function (ESF). In the Federal Response Plan (FRP), a functional area of response activity established to facilitate the delivery of federal assistance required during the immediate response phase of a disaster to save lives, protect property and public health, and to maintain public safety. ESFs represent those types of federal assistance that the state will most likely need because of the impact of a catastrophic or significant disaster on its own resources and response capabilities, or because of the specialized or unique nature of the assistance required. ESF missions are designed to supplement state and local response efforts.

Emergency Support Team (EST). An interagency group operating from FEMA Headquarters. The EST oversees the national-level response support effort under the FRP and coordinates activities with the ESF primary and support agencies in supporting federal requirements in the field.

Entity-wide security. Planning and management that provides a framework and continuing cycle of activity for managing risk, developing security policies, assigning responsibilities, and monitoring the adequacy of the entity's physical and cyber security controls.

Entry control point. A continuously or intermittently manned station at which entry to sensitive or restricted areas is controlled.

Escarpment. Also known as a scarp, with respect to topographic effects, a cliff or steep slope generally separating two levels or gently sloping areas.

Evacuation. Organized, phased, and supervised dispersal of people from dangerous or potentially dangerous areas.

Evacuation, mandatory or directed. This is a warning to persons within the designated area that an imminent threat to life and property exists and individuals MUST evacuate in accordance with the instructions of local officials.

Evacuation, spontaneous. Residents or citizens in the threatened areas observe an emergency event or receive unofficial word of an actual or perceived threat and, without receiving instructions to do so, elect to evacuate the area. Their movement, means, and direction of travel are unorganized and unsupervised.

Evacuation, voluntary. This is a warning to persons within a designated area that a threat to life and property exists or is likely to exist in the immediate future. Individuals issued this type of warning or order are NOT required to evacuate; however, it would be to their advantage to do so.

Exclusion area. A restricted area containing a security interest. Uncontrolled movement permits direct access to the item. See controlled area and limited area.

Exclusion zone. An area around an asset that has controlled entry with highly restrictive access. See controlled area.

Explosives disposal container. A small container into which small quantities of explosives may be placed to contain their blast pressures and fragments if the explosive detonates.

Exposure. The characteristics of the ground roughness and surface irregularities in the vicinity of a building.

F

Facial recognition. A biometric technology that is based on features of the human face.

Federal Coordinating Officer (FCO). The person appointed by the FEMA director to coordinate federal assistance in a presidentially declared emergency or major disaster.

Federal Response Plan (FRP). The FRP establishes a process and structure for the systematic, coordinated, and effective delivery of federal assistance to address the consequences of any major disaster or emergency.

Fiber optics. A method of data transfer by passing bursts of light through a strand of glass or clear plastic.

Field of view. The visible area in a video picture.

First responder. Local police, fire, and emergency medical personnel who first arrive on the scene of an incident and take action to save lives, protect property, and meet basic human needs.

Flash flood. Follows a situation in which rainfall is so intense and severe and runoff so rapid that it precludes recording and relating it to stream stages and other information in time to forecast a flood condition.

Flood. A general and temporary condition of partial or complete inundation of normally dry land areas from overflow of inland or tidal waters, unusual or rapid accumulation or runoff of surface waters, or mudslides/mudflows caused by accumulation of water.

Forced entry. Entry to a denied area achieved through force to create an opening in fence, walls, doors, and such, or to overpower guards.

Fragment retention film (FRF). A thin, optically clear film applied to glass to minimize the spread of glass fragments when the glass is shattered.

Frangible construction. Building components that are designed to fail to vent blast pressures from an enclosure in a controlled manner and direction.

G

Glazing. Glass or transparent or translucent plastic sheet used in windows, doors, and skylights.

Glazing, impact-resistant. Glazing that has been shown by an approved test method to withstand the impact of wind-borne missiles likely to be generated in wind-borne debris regions during design winds.

Grid wire sensor. An intrusion detection sensor that uses a grid of wires to cover a wall or fence. An alarm is sounded if the wires are cut.

H

Hand geometry. A biometric technology that is based on characteristics of the human hand.

Hazard. A source of potential danger or adverse condition.

Hazard mitigation. Any action taken to reduce or eliminate the long-term risk to human life and property from hazards. The term is sometimes used in a stricter sense to mean cost-effective measures to reduce the potential for damage to a facility or facilities from a disaster event.

Hazardous material (HazMat). Any substance or material that, when involved in an accident and released in sufficient quantities, poses a risk to people's health, safety, or property. These substances and materials include explosives, radioactive materials, flammable liquids or solids, combustible liquids or solids, poisons, oxidizers, toxins, and corrosive materials.

High-hazard areas. Geographic locations that, for planning purposes, have been determined through historical experience and vulnerability analysis to be likely to experience the effects of a specific hazard (e.g., hurricane, earthquake, hazardous materials accident, etc.), resulting in vast property damage and loss of life.

High-risk target. Any material resource or facility that, because of mission sensitivity, ease of access, isolation, and symbolic value, may be an especially attractive or accessible terrorist target.

Human-caused hazard. Human-caused hazards are technological hazards and terrorism. They are distinct from natural hazards primarily in that they originate from human activity. Within the military services, the term threat is typically used for human-caused hazard. See definitions of technological hazards and terrorism for further information.

Hurricane. A tropical cyclone, formed in the atmosphere over warm ocean areas, in which wind speeds reach seventy-four miles per hour or more and blow in a large spiral around a relatively calm center or "eye." Circulation is counter-clockwise in the Northern Hemisphere and clockwise in the Southern Hemisphere.

Hurricane-prone regions. Areas vulnerable to hurricanes; in the United States and its territories defined as:

1. The U.S. Atlantic Ocean and Gulf of Mexico coasts where the basic wind speed is greater than ninety miles per hour, and
2. Hawaii, Puerto Rico, Guam, U.S. Virgin Islands, and American Samoa.

I

Impact analysis. A management level analysis that identifies the impacts of losing the entity's resources. The analysis measures the effect of resource loss and escalating losses over time in order to provide the entity with reliable data upon which to base decisions on hazard mitigation and continuity planning.

Importance factor. A factor that accounts for the degree of hazard to human life and damage to property. The importance factor adjusts the mean recurrence interval. Importance factors are given in ASCE 7.

Incident Command System (ICS). A standardized organizational structure used to command, control, and coordinate the use of resources and personnel that have responded to the scene of an emergency. The concepts and principles for ICS include common terminology, modular organization, integrated communication, unified command structure, consolidated action plan, manageable span of control, designated incident facilities, and comprehensive resource management.

International terrorism. Violent acts or acts dangerous to human life that are a violation of the criminal laws of the United States or any state, or that would be a criminal violation if committed within the jurisdiction of the United States or any state. These acts appear to be intended to intimidate or coerce a civilian population, influence the policy of a government by intimidation or coercion, or affect the conduct of a government by assassination or kidnapping. International terrorist acts occur outside the United States, or transcend national boundaries in terms of the means by which they are accomplished, the persons they appear intended to coerce or intimidate, or the locale in which their perpetrators operate or seek asylum.

Intrusion Detection System (IDS). The combination of components, including sensors, control units, transmission lines, and monitor units, integrated to operate in a specified manner.

Isolated fenced perimeters. Fenced perimeters with 100 feet or more of space outside the fence that is clear of obstruction, making approach obvious.

J

Jersey barrier. A protective concrete barrier initially and still used as a highway divider that now also functions as an expedient method for traffic speed control at entrance gates and to keep vehicles away from buildings.

Joint Information Center (JIC). A central point of contact for all news media near the scene of a large-scale disaster. News media representatives are kept informed of activities and events by Public Information Officers who represent all participating federal, state, and local agencies that are collocated at the JIC.

Joint Interagency Intelligence Support Element (JIISE). An interagency intelligence component designed to fuse intelligence information from the various agencies participating in a response to a WMD threat or incident within an FBI JOC. The JIISE is an expanded version of the investigative/intelligence component that is part of the standardized FBI command post structure. The JIISE manages five functions, including: security, collections management, current intelligence, exploitation, and dissemination.

Joint Operations Center (JOC). Established by the LFA under the operational control of the federal OSC, as the focal point for management and direction of on-site activities, coordination/establishment of state requirements/priorities, and coordination of the overall federal response.

L

Laminated glass. A flat lite of uniform thickness consisting of two monolithic glass plies bonded together with an interlayer material. Many different interlayer materials are used in laminated glass.

Layers of protection. A traditional approach in security engineering using concentric circles extending out from an area to be protected as demarcation points for different security strategies.

Lead Federal Agency (LFA). The agency designated by the president to lead and coordinate the overall federal response is referred to as the LFA and is determined by the type of emergency. In general, an LFA establishes operational structures and procedures to assemble and work with agencies providing direct support to the LFA in order to provide an initial assessment of the situation, develop an action plan, monitor and update operational priorities, and ensure each agency exercises its concurrent and distinct authorities under U.S. law and supports the LFA in carrying out the president's relevant policy. Specific responsibilities of an LFA vary, according to the agency's unique statutory authorities.

Level of protection (LOP). The degree to which an asset is protected against injury or damage from an attack.

Liaison. An agency official sent to another agency to facilitate interagency communications and coordination.

Limited area. A restricted area within close proximity of a security interest. Uncontrolled movement may permit access to the item. Escorts and other internal restrictions may prevent access to the item. See controlled area and exclusion area.

Line of sight (LOS). Direct observation between two points with the naked eye or handheld optics.

M

Magnetic lock. An electromagnetic lock that unlocks a door when power is removed.

Magnetic stripe. A card technology that uses a magnetic stripe on the card to encode data used for unique identification of the card.

Main wind-force resisting system. An assemblage of structural elements assigned to provide support and stability for the overall structure. The system generally receives wind loading from more than one surface.

Microwave motion sensor. An intrusion detection sensor that uses microwave energy to sense movement within the sensor's field of view. These sensors work similar to radar by using the Doppler Effect to measure a shift in frequency.

Mitigation. Those actions taken to reduce the exposure to and impact of an attack or disaster.

Motion detector. An intrusion detection sensor that changes state based on movement in the sensor's field of view.

Mutual Aid Agreement. A pre-arranged agreement developed between two or more entities to render assistance to the parties of the agreement.

N

Natural hazard. Naturally occurring events such as floods, earthquakes, tornadoes, tsunami, coastal storms, landslides, and wildfires that strike populated areas. A natural event is a hazard when it has the potential to harm people or property (FEMA 386-2, Understanding Your Risks). The risks of natural hazards may be increased or decreased as a result of human activity; however, they are not inherently human-induced.

Natural protective barriers. Natural protective barriers are mountains and deserts, cliffs and ditches, water obstacles, or other terrain features that are difficult to traverse.

Non-exclusive zone. An area around an asset that has controlled entry, but shared or less restrictive access than an exclusive zone.

Non-persistent agent. An agent that, upon release, loses its ability to cause casualties after ten to fifteen minutes. It has a high evaporation rate, is lighter than air, and will disperse rapidly. It is considered to be a short-term hazard; however, in small, unventilated areas, the agent will be more persistent.

Nuclear, biological, or chemical weapons. Also called Weapons of Mass Destruction (WMD). Weapons that are characterized by their capability to produce mass casualties.

O

On-Scene Coordinator (OSC). The federal official pre-designated by the EPA and U.S. Coast Guard to coordinate and direct response and removals under the National Oil and Hazardous Substances Pollution Contingency Plan.

Openings. Apertures or holes in the building envelope that allow air to flow through the building envelope and that are designed as "open" during design winds. A door that is intended to be in the closed position during a windstorm would not be considered an opening. Glazed openings are also not typically considered an opening. However, if the building is located in a wind-borne debris region and the glazing is not impact-resistant or protected with an impact-resistant covering, the glazing is considered an opening.

Open systems architecture. A term borrowed from the IT industry to claim that systems are capable of interfacing with other systems from any vendor, which also uses open system architecture. The opposite would be a proprietary system.

Organizational areas of control. Controls consist of the policies, procedures, practices, and organization structures designed to provide reasonable assurance that business objectives will be achieved and that undesired events will be prevented or detected and corrected.

P

Passive infrared motion sensor. A device that detects a change in the thermal energy pattern caused by a moving intruder and initiates an alarm when the change in energy satisfies the detector's alarm-criteria.

Passive vehicle barrier. A vehicle barrier that is permanently deployed and does not require response to be effective.

Perimeter barrier. A fence, wall, vehicle barrier, landform, or line of vegetation applied along an exterior perimeter used to obscure vision, hinder personnel access, or hinder or prevent vehicle access.

Persistent agent. An agent that, upon release, retains its casualty-producing effects for an extended period of time, usually anywhere from thirty minutes to several days. A persistent agent usually has a low evaporation rate and its vapor is heavier than air; therefore, its vapor cloud tends to hug the ground. It is considered to be a long-term hazard. Although inhalation hazards are still a concern, extreme caution should be taken to avoid skin contact as well.

Physical security. The part of security concerned with measures/concepts designed to safeguard personnel; to prevent unauthorized access to equipment, installations, materiel, and documents; and to safeguard them against espionage, sabotage, damage, and theft.

Plume. Airborne material spreading from a particular source; the dispersal of particles, gases, vapors, and aerosols into the atmosphere.

Polycarbonate glazing. A plastic glazing material with enhanced resistance to ballistics or blast effects.

Preliminary Damage Assessment (PDA). A mechanism used to determine the impact and magnitude of damage and the resulting unmet needs of individuals, businesses, the public sector, and the community as a whole. Information collected is used by the state as a basis for the governor's request for a presidential declaration, and by FEMA to document the recommendation made to the president in response to the governor's request. PDAs are made by at least one state and one federal representative. A local government representative familiar with the extent and location of damage in the community often participates; other state and federal agencies and voluntary relief organizations also may be asked to participate, as needed.

Preparedness. Establishing the plans, training, exercises, and resources necessary to enhance mitigation of and achieve readiness for response to, and recovery from all hazards, disasters, and emergencies, including WMD incidents.

Pressure mat. A mat that generates an alarm when pressure is applied to any part of the mat's surface, such as when someone steps on the mat. Pressure mats can be used to detect an intruder approaching a protected object, or they can be placed by doors and windows to detect entry.

Primary asset. An asset that is the ultimate target for compromise by an aggressor. Primary gathering building. Inhabited buildings routinely occupied by fifty or more personnel. This designation applies to the entire portion of a building that meets the population density requirements for an inhabited building.

Progressive collapse. A chain reaction failure of building members to an extent disproportionate to the original localized damage. Such damage may result in upper floors of a building collapsing onto lower floors.

Protective measures. Elements of a protective system that protect an asset against a threat. Protective measures are divided into defensive and detection measures.

Proximity sensor. An intrusion detection sensor that changes state based on the close distance or contact of a human to the sensor. These sensors often measure the change in capacitance as a human body enters the measured field.

Public Information Officer (PIO). A federal, state, or local government official responsible for preparing and coordinating the dissemination of emergency public information.

R

Recovery. The long-term activities beyond the initial crisis period and emergency response phase of disaster operations that focus on returning all systems in the community to a normal status or to reconstitute these systems to a new condition that is less vulnerable.

Regional Operations Center (ROC). The temporary operations facility for the coordination of federal response and recovery activities located at the FEMA Regional Office (or Federal Regional Center) and led by the FEMA Regional Director or Deputy Director until the DFO becomes operational. After the ERT-A is deployed, the ROC performs a support role for federal staff at the disaster scene.

Resource Management. Those actions taken by a government to: identify sources and obtain resources needed to support disaster response activities; coordinate the supply, allocation, distribution, and delivery of resources so that they arrive where and when most needed; and maintain accountability for the resources used.

Response. Executing the plan and resources identified to perform those duties and services to preserve and protect life and property as well as provide services to the surviving population.

Restricted area. Any area with access controls that is subject to these special restrictions or controls for security reasons.

Retinal pattern. A biometric technology that is based on features of the human eye.

RF data transmission. A communications link using radio frequency to send or receive data.

S

Safe haven. Secure areas within the interior of the facility. A safe haven should be designed such that it requires more time to penetrate by aggressors than it takes for the response force to reach the protected area to rescue the occupants. It may be a haven from a physical attack or air-isolated haven from CBR contamination.

Secondary asset. An asset that supports a primary asset and whose compromise would indirectly affect the operation of the primary asset.

Secondary hazard. A threat whose potential would be realized as the result of a triggering event that of itself would constitute an emergency (e.g., dam failure might be a secondary hazard associated with earthquakes).

Security analysis. The method of studying the nature of and the relationship between assets, threats, and vulnerabilities.

Segregation of duties. Policies, procedures, and an organizational structure established so that one individual cannot control key aspects of physical or computer-related operations and thereby conduct unauthorized actions or gain unauthorized access to minimum essential infrastructure resource elements.

Shelter in place. When evacuation from a building or home is hazardous, the process of staying in place and creating a barrier between yourself and potentially contaminated air outside, usually by sealing a room.

Shielded wire. Wire with a conductive wrap used to mitigate electromagnetic emanations.

Stand-off distance. A distance maintained between a building or portion thereof and the potential location for an explosive detonation or other threat.

Storm surge. A dome of sea water created by the strong winds and low barometric pressure in a hurricane that causes severe coastal flooding as the hurricane strikes land.

Structural protective barriers. Manmade devices (e.g., fences, walls, floors, roofs, grills, bars, roadblocks, signs, or other construction) used to restrict, channel, or impede access.

Superstructure. The supporting elements of a building above the foundation.

T

Terrorism. The unlawful use of force and violence against persons or property to intimidate or coerce a government, the civilian population, or any segment thereof, in furtherance of political or social objectives.

Thermally tempered glass (TTG). Glass that is heat-treated to have a higher tensile strength and resistance to blast pressures, although with a greater susceptibility to airborne debris.

Threat analysis. A continual process of compiling and examining all available information concerning potential threats and human-caused hazards. A common method to evaluate terrorist groups is to review the factors of existence, capability, intentions, history, and targeting.

Tornado. A local atmospheric storm, generally of short duration, formed by winds rotating at very high speeds, usually in a counter-clockwise direction. The vortex, up to several hundred yards wide, is visible to the observer as a whirlpool-like column of winds rotating about a hollow cavity or funnel. Winds may reach 300 miles per hour or higher.

Toxic-free area. An area within a facility in which the air supply is free of toxic chemical or biological agents.

Tsunami. Sea waves produced by an undersea earthquake. Such sea waves can reach a height of 80 feet and can devastate coastal cities and low-lying coastal areas.

Two-person rule. A security strategy that requires two people to be present in or gain access to a secured area to prevent unobserved access by any individual.

U

Unobstructed space. Space around an inhabited building without obstruction large enough to conceal explosive devices 150 mm (six inches) or greater in height.

V

Vertical rod. Typical door hardware often used with a crash bar to lock a door by inserting rods vertically from the door into the doorframe.

Vulnerability. Any weakness that can be exploited by an aggressor or, in a nonterrorist threat environment, make an asset susceptible to hazard damage.

W

Warning. The alerting of emergency response personnel and the public to the threat of extraordinary danger and the related effects that specific hazards may cause.

Watch. Indication in a defined area that conditions are favorable for the specified type of severe weather (e.g., flash flood watch, severe thunderstorm watch, tornado watch, tropical storm watch).

Waterborne contamination. Chemical, biological, or radiological agent introduced into and fouling a water supply.

Weapons-grade material. Nuclear material considered most suitable for a nuclear weapon. It usually connotes uranium enriched to above 90 percent uranium-235 or plutonium with greater than about 90 percent plutonium-239.

Weapons of Mass Destruction (WMD). Any device, material, or substance used in a manner, in a quantity or type, or under circumstances showing an intent to cause death or serious injury to persons, or significant damage to property. An explosive, incendiary, or poison gas, bomb, grenade, rocket having a propellant charge of more than four ounces, or a missile having an explosive incendiary charge of more than 0.25 ounce, or mine or device similar to the above; poison gas; weapon involving a disease organism; or weapon that is designed to release radiation or radioactivity at a level dangerous to human life.

Wind-borne debris regions. Areas within hurricane-prone regions located:

1. Within one mile of the coastal mean high water line where the basic wind speed is equal to or greater than 110 mph and in Hawaii; or
2. In areas where the basic wind speed is equal to or greater than 120 mph

Wind speed, basic. A three-second gust speed at thirty-three feet above the ground in Exposure C. (Exposure C is flat open terrain with scattered obstructions having heights generally less than thirty feet.) Note: Since 1995, ASCE 7 has used a three-second peak gust measuring time. A three-second peak gust is the maximum instantaneous speed with a duration of approximately three seconds. A three-second peak gust speed could be associated with a given windstorm (e.g., a particular storm could have a forty mile per hour peak gust speed), or a three-second peak gust speed could be associated with a design-level event (e.g., the basic wind speed prescribed in ASCE 7).

Index

access: control, 279; for post-event restoration, 242–43

ACM. *See* asbestos containing material

ADA. *See* Americans with Disabilities Act

ADAAG. *See* Americans with Disabilities Accessibility Guidelines

AEDs. *See* Automated External Defibrillators

after hours, emergency management team working, 182

aftershock, 43, 45, 49

alarm systems: audible, 194, 217; design for, 290; distinctive tones for, 217–18; EAPs and, 194–96; maintenance of, 195; NFPA regulations for, 196; OSHA requirements with, 194, 196, 217–18; smoke alarms, 67, 290; testing, 195–96; understanding, 194–95; visual, 194

Alfred P. Murrah Building, Oklahoma City, bombing of 1995, 96–97, 278–79

alternate contractors, 184

alternative heating sources, safety with, 68

American Heart Association, 239–40

American Red Cross, 142, 239

Americans with Disabilities Accessibility Guidelines (ADAAG), 194

Americans with Disabilities Act (ADA), 172, 174–75, 222, 225

announced evacuations, employee training and, 211

announcements, emergency, 217–19

anthrax (*Bacillus anthracis*), 119–20

anthrax letter attacks of 2001, 109

areas of refuge, ADA and, 225

Artful Persuasion (Mills), 159

asbestos containing material (ACM), 254

asbestos contamination, 254–55

ASDSO. *See* Association of State Dam Safety Officials

assistance devices, evacuations and, 223–25

Association of State Dam Safety Officials (ASDSO), 38, 169

ATF. *See* Bureau of Alcohol, Tobacco, Firearms, and Explosives

Atropine, 121

audible alarm systems, 194, 217

Aum Shinrikyo, 121

authority, EAPs establishing, 161

Automated External Defibrillators (AEDs), 234, 237–39

automatic sprinkler systems. *See* sprinkler systems

avalanches. *See* winter storms

Bacillus anthracis (anthrax), 119–20

bacteria, 110

Base Flood Elevation (BFE), 37

bathroom water conservation, 81

batteries, stocking, 186, 188, *188*

BBP. *See* bloodborne pathogens

Beverly Hills Supper Club fire of 1977, 66
BFE. *See* Base Flood Elevation
biological agents. *See* chemical, biological, radiological agents
blackouts, 148–50
blast-resistant glass, 281
blizzards, 87–88. *See also* winter storms
blizzard warning, 89
bloodborne pathogens (BBP), 234
Bloodborne Pathogen Standard, of OSHA, 143
bollards, design for, 291
bomb search: command center for, 105; decision to conduct, 100–101; preparation for, 101; procedure for, 101, *102–4*, 104–5; radios for, 105; tools for, 101
bomb threats: advice during, 100; advice for explosions, 106–7; Alfred P. Murrah Building, Oklahoma City, bombing of 1995, 96–97, 278–79; checklist for, 98, *99*, 100; debris from explosions and, 107; design for resistance to, 279–80, 291–92; evacuation decisions for, 100; fires from explosions and, 107; frequency of, 95; IS and, 95–96; preparation for, 98; September 11, 2001 attacks, 97–98, 192, 196–97; suspicious packages and letters and, 105–6; World Trade Center bombing of 1993, 96
botulism (*Clostridium botulinum*), 122
BPAT. *See* Building Performance Assessment Team
Bradley, Tom, 146
broken bones, first aid for, 237
building and site mitigation: exterior building perimeter areas and, 278; exterior neighborhood areas and, 280–81; exterior parking and off-site areas and, 278–80; interior limited access areas in, 277; interior public access areas in, 277; point of entry and, 278
building codes, emergency mitigation and, 293
building directory inventory, for evacuation, *312*
building fires. *See* fires
building infrastructure, emergency mitigation and, 273
Building Performance Assessment Team (BPAT), 293–94
building perimeter areas, building and site mitigation and, 278
buildings: asbestos contamination and, 254–55; codes for, 293; critical information for, 190–92; EAPs and use of, 166–68; emergency announcements and, 217–19; emergency floor plans and, 189–90; helicopter rescues and, 214; hurricanes and weaknesses of, 27; structural collapse and, 150–52; tsunamis and re-entering, 56. *See also* shelters
Bureau of Alcohol, Tobacco, Firearms, and Explosives (ATF), 98
burning laws, local, 72
burn victims, first aid for, 235–36
businesses: EAPs and evaluation of, 161–62; fires and, 73–75; interruption costs for, 162–63

CAD. *See* computer-aided design
California Brownouts and Blackouts of 2000 and 2001, 149
California's seven year drought from 1987-1994, 76
carbon monoxide, 123
cardiopulmonary resuscitation (CPR), 233, 234, 239–40
cars, winterizing, 92–93
car-washing water conservation, 83

catering, post-event restoration and, 252
Centers for Disease Control and
  Prevention (CDC), 111, 113
Centers for Medicare and Medicaid
  Services, 297
chain of command, 161, 164, 227–29,
  265
"Chain of Survival," 239
chemical, biological, radiological agents
  (CBR): advice following biological
  attack, 119; advice following chemical
  attack, 118–19; advice for attack from,
  112–13; anthrax and, 119–20; anthrax
  letter attacks of 2001, 109; biological
  agents defined, 110; biological agents
  dispersal methods, 110; botulism and,
  122; categories of, 111–12; chemical
  agents defined, 109–10; chemical threat
  signals, 117–18; clean air and chemical
  attack, 118; contamination indications
  for, 116–17; first aid for chemical
  exposure, 237; HVAC system spreading
  biological agents, 111, 220; indoor-
  outdoor air exchange rate and, 114;
  mustard gas and, 121; natural filtering
  and, 115; nerve agents and, 121; online
  resources for, 113; preparation for
  attacks from, 112; protective action plan
  for, 115; rise of, 108–9; "sealing the
  room" for, 113–14; sheltering in place
  for, 113–16; smallpox and *variola* virus
  and, 120; warning signs of, 116
chemical burns, 129, 235
chemical disposal, 127–28
chemical emergencies, household, 127–29
chemical incidents: definition of, 123; first
  aid for, 129; General Chemical incident
  of 1993, 125; household chemical
  emergencies, 127–29; injuries from,
  129; Love Canal chemical incident of
  1976, 124–25; preparation for, 125–27;

reporting, 126; sheltering in place for,
  126; warning properties of, 123
chemical inventory list, 174, *174*
Chicago, high-rise safety and, 214–15
chimneys, fire preparation and, 67
civil disturbance and demonstrations:
  definition of, 145; events triggering,
  147; Los Angeles Riots of 1992,
  145–46; preparation for, 147–48;
  public relations and, 148; World Trade
  Organization Protests in Seattle of 1999,
  146–47
cladding design, 286–87
clean air, CBR attack and need for, 118
Clean Air Act Amendments, Section
  112(r), 124
Clinton, Bill, 184
Clostridium botulinum (botulism), 122
clothing, 90, 246
CMU. *See* concrete masonry unit
cold and hot contingency centers, 196–97
Columbine High School incident of 1999,
  139
columns, design for, 283, 285
command centers: for bomb search, 105;
  EAPs and, 197; post-event restoration
  and, 248–49
command post leader, in evacuations, 228
commercial facilities, EAPs and, 167
communication: with customers and
  stakeholders, 267; design and, 291;
  emergency plan and needs with,
  325–27; with employees, 266; with
  families, 266–67; forums for, 264;
  with government agencies, 267; with
  insurance providers, 267; with media,
  264–66; post-event restoration and,
  263–69; sample internal memo for,
  268–69; sample press release for, 267–
  68; sample questions for, 264
computer-aided design (CAD), 292

concrete masonry unit (CMU), 286–87

Congressional Research Service (CRS), 299

Consolidated Edison Electric Company, 148

contingency centers, hot and cold, 196–97

Contractor Availability Form: alternate contractors in, 184; hurricanes and, 30, *30*

contractors, EAPs and, 184–86

correspondence log, for post-event restoration, 249, *250*

costs: of business interruption, 162–63; of drills, 216; of drought, 75; EAPs and identification of, 157–58; EAPs and justification of, 158; of first aid, 233; of Hurricane Katrina, 6; from lack of emergency preparedness plans, 9; of post-event restoration, 251; price compared to, 202; risk assessment matrix and, 169–70, *170*; of weather disasters, 6

CPR. *See* cardiopulmonary resuscitation

Crime Prevention through Environmental Design (CPTED), 280, 339

criminal intent, 137

crisis response box, 330

critical building information, for EPAs, 190–92

CRS. *See* Congressional Research Service

customer/client violence, 137

customer communication, post-event restoration and, 267

cutaneous anthrax, 119–20

damage assessment, 243–45

dams, flood risks with, 38, 169

data security, 198–99

data storage, off-site, 198–99

DBT. *See* design basis threat

DDDR. *See* deter, detect, delay, response

debris flow: advice during, 62; advice following, 63; definition of, 60–61; heightened threat of, 62; land mismanagement causing, 61; preparation for, 61–62; from volcano eruptions, 56, 59

dedicated emergency elevators, 290

defibrillators. *See* automated external defibrillators

delay, 156, 276

deluge sprinkler system, 75, 192

demonstrations. *See* civil disturbance and demonstrations

Denny, Reginald, 145

departmental evacuation template, for hospital emergency preparedness, *313*

Department of Education (DOE), 318

design: access control and, 279; alarm systems, smoke alarms and, 290; bollards and, 291; bomb threat resistance and, 279–80, 291–92; CAD for, 292; cladding, 286–87; columns and, 283, 285; communication and, 291; CPTED and, 280, 339; dedicated emergency elevators and, 290; emergency generators and, 288–89; emergency mitigation and guidelines for, 271–73; evacuation routes and, 288; exterior frame and, 282–84; exterior walls and, 286–87; FEMA on educational facilities and, 337–38; Fire Control Center and, 289; floor system and, 284–85; fuel storage and, 289; information and, 272; interdependencies and, 272–73; interior columns and, 285; interior walls and, 285–86; mechanical and electrical systems and, 287–88; operations and, 272; parking and, 279; people and, 271–72; planters, green space and, 291–92; roof system and, 284; for school emergency preparedness,

317–18, 337–39; smoke-control systems and, 291; sprinkler, standpipe systems and, 290; storm shutters and, 282; transformers and, 289; ventilation systems and, 289; windows and doors and, 281–82. *See also* building and site mitigation; emergency mitigation

design basis threat (DBT), 274–75

detection, 156, 276

deter, detect, delay, response (DDDR), 276

deterrence, 156, 276

diesel emergency generators, 201–2

disabled person, ADA definition of, 175

Disaster Mitigation Act of 2000, 184

disasters: aid for, 8–9; definition of, 4; emergencies compared to, 4–5; Hurricane Katrina as example of, 5; NOAA weather radios for, 6–7; simulations of, 215–16; warnings for, 7–8. *See also specific disasters*

disposal of chemicals, 127–28

DOE. *See* Department of Education

domestic terrorism, 3

doors, design for, 281–82

drills: cost of, 216; for earthquakes, 46; evacuation, 213; evaluating performance of, 231; minimizing interruptions and down time in evacuation, 216–17; pre-evacuation, 209; reentry following, 230–31; refusal to participate in evacuation, 229–30; walk-through, 208

driving, during winter storms, 92–93

"drop-to-shock" window, 238–39

drought: business planning for, 79–80; California's seven year drought from 1987-1994, 76; cost of, 75; definition of, 75; extreme heat and, 76; HI and, 76–77, *77*; NDMC and, 77–79; Southern drought from 1998-2000, 76;

U.S. Drought Monitor and, 77–78, *78*. *See also* water conservation

drowning, from tsunamis, 51

dry pipe sprinkler system, 75, 92, 192

dry thunderstorms, wildfires from, 31

dust masks, for volcano eruptions, 59–60

EAP. *See* emergency action plans

Earthquake Hazards Program, of USGS, 45, *45*

earthquakes: advice during, 47–49; advice following, 49–50; aftershocks following, 43, 45; causes of, 43; damage from, 43; definition of, 45; drills for, 46; epicenter of, 45; faults and, 45; food concerns following, 50; injuries from, 49; Loma Prieta earthquake of 1989, 43–44; magnitude of, 45; Northridge, California earthquake of 1989, 44; planning for, 46–47; preparation for, *45*, 45–47; seismic waves and, 45; survival kit for, 47; tsunamis and, 51; volcano eruptions and, 56; water needs and, 48–50

EAS. *See* Emergency Alert System

EBS. *See* Emergency Broadcast System

edge beams, 283–84

educational facilities, 3; EAPs and, 167–68; evacuation of, 231; FEMA and design of, 337–38. *See also* school emergency preparedness

electrical burns, 235

electrical power, hurricanes and loss of, 26

electrical system design, 287–88

electrical wiring, fire preparation and, 66–67

Electric Power Research Institute (EPRI), 149

elevators: design for dedicated emergency, 290; evacuations and, 222–23; vulnerabilities of, 303 emergencies, 4–5. *See also specific emergencies*

emergency account number, 251–52

emergency action plans (EAPs): ADA responsibilities for, 174–75; alarm systems and, 194–96; annual review of, 205–6; authority and chain of command established in, 161; availability and placement of, 181–82; building use and, 166–68; business interruption costs and, 162–63; challenges of creating, 156–57, 178, 179; command centers and, 197; commercial facilities and, 167; costs identified for, 157–58; costs justified for, 158; critical building information for, 190–92; data security and, 198–99; educational facilities and, 167–68; eight steps in developing, 204–5; emergency floor plans and, 189–90; emergency generators and, 200–204; enthusiasm and support for, 211–12; fire extinguishers and, 191; fire suppression systems and, 191–92; geographic location of property and considerations for, 164–66; healthcare facilities and, 168; hearing impairments responsibilities for, 177–78; for hospitals, 155; hot and cold contingency centers and, 196–97; industrial facilities and, 166–67; insurance and, 184; internal and external support for, 183–86; JCAHO inspections and, 162; load shedding and, 202–3; loss of utility and, 199–204; mission critical functions prioritized for, 199–200; mission statement for, 160–61; MSDS responsibilities and, 172–74, *174*; objective and scope of, 157; online hazard maps and databases for, 170; OSHA and business evaluation for, 161–62; OSHA requirements for, 180–81;

OSHA responsibilities of, 171; partner systems responsibilities for, 175–76; positive and negative selling points of, 159–60; pre-planning and, 192–93; presentation of, 158–60; property leased or owned considerations for, 164; purpose of, 180; regular revision of, 181, 209; resources identified for, 157; responsibilities understood for, 171–78; risk determination for, 168–70, *170*; rolling out, 207–8; signage responsibilities and, 172; sprinkler systems and, 192; stages of, 155–56; stocking emergency supplies and, 186, *187–88*, 188; UPS for, 200; Urban Search and Rescue Grid and, 193; vendors and contractors identified for, 184–86; visual impairment responsibilities of, 176–77. *See also* emergency management team; employee training; planning; training, EAP team

Emergency Alert System (EAS), 7–8, 125, 135

emergency announcements, 217–19

Emergency Broadcast System (EBS), 7

emergency floor plans, 189–90

emergency generators: design for, 288–89; diesel, 201–2; EAPs, loss of utility and, 200–204; gasoline, 202; installing, 202; load factor for, 201; load shedding and, 202–3; natural gas, 202; portable, 203–4; procedures for, 203; safety precautions with, 204; testing, 203

Emergency Intervention Team, 333–34

Emergency Management Institute (EMI), 295

emergency management team: after hours work of, 182; identifying team members and responsibilities for, 183; importance of, 182; internal and external support for, 183–86; post-event restoration and activation of, 241–42; vendors and contractors for, 184–86

emergency medical services (EMS), 129

emergency mitigation: building and site mitigation, 277–81; building codes and, 293; building infrastructure identification for, 273; design guidelines for, 271–73; MAT and, 293–95; post-failure analysis and, 292; risk assessment and, 276; structures and, 281–92; threat identification for, 274–75; virtual reality and, 292; vulnerability assessment and, 275–76

emergency oxygen administration, 234

emergency plan, for school emergency preparedness: checklist for, 333; communication needs for, 325–27; customization of, 327; diversity needs and, 328; equipment and supplies for, 329–30; evacuations and, 330–31; existing plans as resources for, 324; implementation of, 329; leadership and, 322–23; mistakes with, 329; openness and partnerships in creation of, 323–24; plain language for, 326; practice for, 332; roles and responsibilities for, 324–25; student release procedures for, 331–32; timetable for, 328

emergency plan template, for hospital emergency preparedness, 310–12, *312–16*

emergency power, hospital emergency preparedness and, 303–4

emergency preparedness plans, 3, 9. *See also* hospital emergency preparedness; school emergency preparedness

emergency response plans, for nuclear power plant incidents, 131

emergency supplies, stocking, 186, *187–88*, 188

EMI. *See* Emergency Management Institute

employee communication, post-event restoration and, 266

employee death, reporting, 259

employee training: announced and unannounced evacuations for, 211; emergency orientation for, 210; evacuations and, 212–17; factors of, 210; support and enthusiasm for, 211–12; tabletop exercises for, 211, 217

empty spray cans, 128

EMS. *See* emergency medical services

envelopes, suspicious, 105–6

Environmental Protection Agency (EPA), 123–24; National Response Center of, 126; oil spill program of, 127; Poison Control of, 128

Environmental Systems Research Institute (ESRI), 170

EP. *See* Evacuation Plan

EPA. *See* Environmental Protection Agency

epicenter, of earthquakes, 45

EPRI. *See* Electric Power Research Institute

equipment maintenance, for winter storms, 91

escape hoods, 115

ESRI. *See* Environmental Systems Research Institute

Evacuation Plan (EP), 300

evacuations: accounting for employees and visitors during, 226–27; areas of refuge and, 225; assistance devices and, 223–25; for bomb threats, 100; building directory inventory for, *312*; for building fires, 67–68; chain of command in, 227–29; Chicago and high-rise safety with, 214–15; command post leader in, 228; departmental evacuation template, *313*; design for, 288; to directly outside

facility, 307–8; disaster simulations and, 215–16; to distant facility, 308; drills for, 213; EAP team and employee training and, 212–17; of educational facilities, 231; elevators and, 222–23; emergency announcements and, 217–19; emergency floor plans and, 189; emergency plan for school emergency preparedness and, 330–31; employee training and announced and unannounced, 211; evaluating performance of, 231; fire brigades and, 220, 227; floor captains and, 219–20, 228; floor key and, 221, *221*; to general public shelter with temporary infirmary, 309–10; group leaders in, 228; healthcare facilities and challenges with, 216–17; helicopter rescues and, 214; hospital emergency preparedness and, 297–98, 307–10; for hurricanes, 23, 26–27; minimizing interruptions and down time in drills for, 216–17; to nearby facility, 308; nuclear power plants and, 135; patient care unit tools for, *314–15*; people with special needs and, 222–25; reentry process after, 230–31; refusal to participate in drills for, 229–30; reverse, 330; roll calls in, 228–29; routes for, 213; runners in, 228; safety considerations with, 226; to shelter designated as medical treatment unit, 308–9; shut down procedures and, 220–22, *221*; staff evacuation template, *316*; staging areas for, 226–27, 331; tabletop exercises and, 217; for tsunamis, 54; for volcano eruptions, 58; wheelchairs and, 223–24; for wildfires, 73
explosions, advice for, 106–7
exterior frame, design for, 282–84
exterior walls, design for, 286–87

external and internal support, for EAPs, 183–86
extreme heat: advice during, 85–86; drought and, 76; first-aid for heat-induced illness from, 86–87; preparation for, 85; terminology for, 84; urban areas and, 84; water consumption for, 85
eye of storm, 27

fall out shelters, 134–35
family communication, post-event restoration and, 266–67
fatigue, injuries and, 242
faults, earthquakes and, 45
Federal Emergency Management Agency (FEMA), 131; BPAT of, 293–94; disaster aid process and programs of, 8–9; educational facility design and, 337–38; floodplains mapped by, 37; online hazard maps and databases of, 170; plain language recommendations of, 326; risk assessment matrix of, 168–70, *170*; spending of, 8; structural collapse search and rescue teams from, 150–52
fire brigades, 74, 220, 227
Fire Control Center, design for, 289
fire extinguishers: EAPs and, 191; installation of, 67; training for, 128
firefighters, MSDS access for, 190
fire-resistant housing measures, 71–72
fires: advice during, 69; advice following, 69–70; Beverly Hills Supper Club fire of 1977, 66; bomb explosions and, 107; businesses and, 73–75; categories of, 65, 191; emergency floor plans and, 189; evacuation routes for, 67–68; first aid for burn victims and, 235–36; food exposure to, 70; frequency of, 65; helicopter rescues and, 214; insurance claims with, 69–70; OSHA

requirements for employers and, 73–74, 180–81; personal safety measures for, 67–69; preparation for, 66–67; smoke inhalation from, 65; sprinkler systems for, 74–75. *See also* wildfires

Fire Safety Director (FSD), 214–15

fire suppression systems, EAPs and, 191–92

FIRM. *See* Flood Insurance Rate Map

first aid: AEDs and, 234, 237–39; for broken bones, 237; for burn victims, 235–36; for chemical exposure, 237; for chemical incidents, 129; costs of, 233; CPR and, 234, 239–40; emergency floor plans and, 189; for heat-induced illness, 86–87; kit, 233–35; OSHA and treatment with, 260–61; training for, 234

first-degree burns, 236

FIS. *See* Flood Insurance Study

flash floods, 20, 31, 35, 39

flash flood warning, 19, 36

flash flood watch, 19, 36

Flood Insurance Rate Map (FIRM), 37

Flood Insurance Study (FIS), 37

floodplains, FEMA mapping, 37

floods: advice during, 39–40; advice following, 40–41; dams and risks for, 38, 169; destruction caused by, 35; flash, 35, 39; Great Chicago Flood of 1992, 35–36; from hurricanes, 20; insurance for, 37, 41; New Orleans Flood of 1995, 36; NOAA weather radios for, 37–38; preparation for, 37–39; property protection options for, 39; risk identification for, 37; riverine, 35; as site-specific hazard, 299; from thunderstorms, 31

flood warning, 19, 36

flood watch, 19, 36, 39–40

floor captains, in evacuations, 219–20, 228

floor plans: emergency, 189–90; location key and, 221, *221*; user-friendly, 220–21

floor system, design and, 284–85

food: catering and, 252; earthquakes and concerns with, 50; fires and exposure of, 70; MREs, 188, *188*, 252; nuclear power plant emergencies and, 136; for post-event restoration, 247; stocking, 186, 188, *188*

foodborne botulism, 122

freezing rain, 89

frostbite, 90

frost/freeze warning, 89

FSD. *See* Fire Safety Director

fuel storage, design for, 289

Fujita scale, for tornadoes, 12, *12*, 13

Fukushima I Nuclear Power Plant disaster of 2011, 132

full-scale exercises, EAP team training and, 209

gasoline emergency generators, 202

General Chemical incident of 1993, 125

General Duty Clause, of OSHA, 140

General Services Administration (GSA), 282

geographic location: EAPs and property considerations with, 164–66; tornado occurrence and, 11; winter storms and, 87

glass, blast-resistant, 281

Good Samaritan Laws, 142

government agency communication, post-event restoration and, 267

government-owned buildings, 3

grants, 9

Great Appalachian Blizzard of 1996, 87–88

Great Chicago Flood of 1992, 35–36

green space, design for, 291–92

Groundhog Day Blizzard of 2011, 88

group leaders, in evacuations, 228
GSA. *See* General Services Administration

"Hands-Only CPR," 240
Harris, Eric, 139
hazard analysis: hospital emergency preparedness and, 305–6; school emergency preparedness and, 336–37
hazard maps and databases, online, 170
HBV. *See* Hepatitis B Virus
HCV. *See* Hepatitis C Virus
healthcare facilities: EAPs and, 168; evacuation challenges with, 216–17; waste disposal and, 303. *See also* hospital emergency preparedness; hospitals
hearing impairments, EAP responsibilities with, 177–78
heat cramps, 84, 86
heat exhaustion, 84, 86
Heat Index (HI), 76–77, *77*, 84
heat-induced illness, first aid for, 86–87
heating sources, 67, 68
heat stroke, *77*, 84, 87
heat wave, 84
Heimlich maneuver, 238
helicopter rescues, 214
Hepatitis B Virus (HBV), 143
Hepatitis C Virus (HCV), 143
HI. *See* Heat Index
high-rise safety, Chicago and, 214–15
Hilo, Hawaii tsunami of 1946, 51–52
HIV. *See* Human Immunodeficiency Virus
homelessness, post-event restoration and, 256
hospital emergency preparedness: building directory inventory for evacuation and, *312*; departmental evacuation template for, *313*; emergency plan template for, 310–12, *312–16*; emergency power and, 303–4; EP for, 300; evacuations and, 297–98, 307–10; hazard analysis and, 305–6; non-structural vulnerability and, 302–4; organizational vulnerability and, 304–5; patient care unit evacuation tools for, *314–15*; requirements for, 297; satellite radiotelephone system and, 298; security concerns for, 300–301, 310; sheltering in place and, 306–7; special challenges for, 298–300; staff evacuation template for, *316*; structural vulnerability and, 301–2
hospitals, 3; EAPs for, 155; loss of utility and, 148. *See also* healthcare facilities
hot and cold contingency centers, 196–97
household chemical emergencies, 127–29
housing aid, 9
Human Immunodeficiency Virus (HIV), 143
Hurricane Andrew of 1992, 21, 245, 248, 262
Hurricane Charley of 2004, 298
Hurricane Georges of 1998, 295
Hurricane Hugo of 1989, 20
Hurricane Katrina of 2005, 5–6, 21–22, 304–5
hurricanes: advice post-storm, 28–29; advice pre-storm and during, 25–27; building weaknesses during, 27; Contractor Availability Form and, 30, *30*; dangerous byproducts of, 19–20; definition of, 18; electrical power loss during, 26; evacuation routes for, 23, 26–27; eye of, 27; floods from, 20; formation of, 17–18; identifying safe shelters for, 23; insurance preparation for damage from, 29; lulls with, 27; planning for, 22–23; post-storm survival kit for, 31; preparation for, 20–21; repairs after, 28; returning home after, 28; Saffir-Simpson intensity scale for, 18–19; season of, 18; storm activities for, 23–25, *24*, *25*; storm surge and

tide from, 19; supplies gathered for, 26; tornadoes associated with, 19. *See also specific hurricanes*

HVAC system, biological agents spread through, 111, 220

Hyatt Regency Walkway Collapse of 1981, 151

hypothermia, 90

ICS. *See* Incident Command System

illness, OSHA examples of, 258

Incident Command System (ICS), 325

indemnity agreement, 186

Indian Ocean tsunami of 2004, 52

indoor-outdoor air exchange rate, CBR and, 114

indoor water conservation, 80–82

industrial facilities, EAPs and, 166–67

infant botulism, 122

inhalation anthrax, 119–20

injuries: broken bones and, 237; from chemical incidents, 129; from earthquakes, 49; fatigue and, 242; from lightning, 34; OSHA and evaluation of, 259–60

installations, non-structural vulnerability and, 302–4

insurance: contractors and, 185–86; EAPs and, 184; emergency account number and, 251–52; fire claims with, 69–70; for floods, 37, 41; hurricane damage and preparation for, 29; indemnity agreement and, 186; misrepresentation and concealment clauses with, 252; post-event restoration and, 244–45; post-event restoration and communication with, 267

interior columns, design for, 285

interior walls, design for, 285–86

internal and external support, for EAPs, 183–86

internal memo, for post-event restoration, 268–69

International Tsunami Information Center (ITIC), 52–53

intestinal anthrax, 119–20

Iran-Iraq war, 1980-1988, 121

Islamic State (IS), 4, 95–96

ITIC. *See* International Tsunami Information Center

Job Accommodation Network (JAN), 225

Joint Commission on Accreditation of Healthcare Organizations (JCAHO), 162, 168, 297

Kaczynski, Ted, 109

Kansas tornadoes of 1999, 13

Kilauea Volcano, Hawaii eruption of 1983, 57

King, Rodney, 145

kitchen water conservation, 81

Klebold, Dylan, 139

KNOX-BOX Rapid Entry System, 190–91

landslides: advice during, 62; advice following, 63; definition of, 60; heightened threat of, 62; land mismanagement causing, 61; preparation for, 61–62; warning signs of, 61–62

laser burns, 236

laundry water conservation, 82

lawn-care water conservation, 82–83

leadership, emergency plan and, 322–23

leased property, EAPs and, 164

Lee, John, 248

letters, suspicious, 105–6

liability, risk assessment matrix and, 169–70, *170*

lightning: injuries from, 34; safety tips for, 34; survivors of, 32; during thunderstorms, 32; wildfires from, 65

limited access areas, building and site mitigation and, 277
load shedding, 202–3
local burning laws, 72
Local Emergency Planning Committees (LEPCs), 125–26
location key, floor plans and, 221, *221*
lockdowns, 330
Locke, Gary, 146
logistics, for post-event restoration, 245–48
Loma Prieta earthquake of 1989, 43–44
Los Angeles Riots of 1992, 145–46
loss of utility: EAPs and, 199–204; emergency generators and, 200–204; hospitals and, 148; mission critical functions prioritized with, 199–200; preparation for, 149–50; UPS and, 200
Louisiana Flood of 1995, 4–5
louvers, 282, 288
Love Canal chemical incident of 1976, 124–25
low-interest loans, 9

magnitude, of earthquakes, 45
malls, 3
Massey, Curtis, 193
Massey Disaster Plans, 193
MAT. *See* Mitigation Assessment Team
Material Safety Data Sheet (MSDS), 126, 237; firefighter access to, 190; OSHA responsibilities for EAPs and, 172–74, *174*
McIlvane, Thomas, 138–39
Meals Ready to Eat (MREs), 188, *188*, 252
mechanical system design, 287–88
media, 264–66
medications: outdated, 128; for post-event restoration, 247
methyl isocyanate (MIC), 124

micro-sized emergency generators, 204
Mills, Harry, 159
misrepresentation and concealment clauses, with insurance, 252
mission statement, for EAPs, 160–61
mitigation. *See* emergency mitigation
Mitigation Assessment Team (MAT), 293–95
Mount St. Helens eruption of 1980, 57
MREs. *See* Meals Ready to Eat
MSDS. *See* Material Safety Data Sheet
mudflows: advice during, 62; advice following, 63; danger from, 59; definition of, 60–61; heightened threat of, 62; land mismanagement causing, 61; preparation for, 61–62
mustard gas (sulfur mustard), 121

National Climatic Data Center (NCDC), 6
National Drought Mitigation Center (NDMC), 77–79
National Fire Protection Association (NFPA), 191, 196, 293
National Flood Insurance Program (NFIP), 62
National Hurricane Center, 18
National Institute for the Certification of Engineering Technologies (NICET), 195
National Institute of Standards and Technology (NIST), 223
National Inventory of Dams (NID), 38
National Oceanic and Atmospheric Administration (NOAA), 77; weather radios of, 6–7, 37–38, 54
National Park Service (NPS), 71
National Response Center, of EPA, 126
National Safety Council, 142
National Training and Education (NTE), 295
National Tsunami Warning Center (NTWC), 52–53

National Weather Service (NWS), 6, 52; HI of, 76–77, *77*

natural events, 5, 11. *See also* debris flow; drought; earthquakes; extreme heat; fires; floods; hurricanes; landslides; mudflows; thunderstorms; tornadoes; tsunamis; volcano eruptions; wildfires; winter storms

natural filtering, CBR and, 115

natural gas emergency generators, 202

NCDC. *See* National Climatic Data Center

NDMC. *See* National Drought Mitigation Center

Needlestick Safety Prevention Act, 143

neighborhood areas, building and site mitigation and, 280–81

nerve agents, 121

New Orleans Flood of 1995, 36

New York Blackout of 1977, 148–49

New York Stock Exchange (NYSE), 198–99

NFIP. *See* National Flood Insurance Program

NFPA. *See* National Fire Protection Association

NICET. *See* National Institute for the Certification of Engineering Technologies

NID. *See* National Inventory of Dams

911, workplace medical emergencies and, 142

NIST. *See* National Institute of Standards and Technology

NOAA. *See* National Oceanic and Atmospheric Administration

non-natural events, 5, 95. *See also* blackouts; bomb threats; chemical, biological, radiological agents; chemical incidents; civil disturbance and demonstrations; loss of utility; nuclear power plants; nuclear weapons; school shootings; structural collapse; terrorism; workplace medical emergencies; workplace violence

nonstructural vulnerability, hospital emergency preparedness and, 302–4

Northridge, California earthquake of 1989, 44

NPS. *See* National Park Service

NRC. *See* Nuclear Regulatory Commission

NTE. *See* National Training and Education

NTWC. *See* National Tsunami Warning Center

nuclear power plants: advice during emergency with, 135–36; DBT and, 275; emergency response plans for, 131; evacuation and, 135; fall out shelters and, 134–35; food and, 136; Fukushima I Nuclear Power Plant disaster of 2011, 132; preparation for emergency with, 133–35; radiation exposure and, 132–33; safety of, 131; terminology for, 134; Three Mile Island nuclear disaster of 1979, 132; warning systems for, 133

Nuclear Regulatory Commission (NRC), 131

nuclear weapons, 131–32, 134–35

nursing home emergency preparedness, 297–98. *See also* hospital emergency preparedness

NWS. *See* National Weather Service

NYSE. *See* New York Stock Exchange

Occupational Safety and Health Act (OSHA), 168; alarm systems and requirements of, 194, 196, 217–18; Bloodborne Pathogen Standard of, 143; EAP requirements of, 180–81; EAP responsibilities with, 171; EAPs and business evaluation with, 161–62; employee death reporting requirements of, 259; fire brigades and, 220; fires and employer requirements of, 73–74, 180–81; first aid treatment according to, 260–61; Form 300 (Log of Work-related Injuries and Illnesses), 257–59; Form 300A (Summary of Work-related Injuries and Illnesses), 258; Form 301 (Injury and Illness Incident Report), 257; General Duty Clause of, 140; illness examples from, 258; injury evaluations and, 259–60; MSDS responsibilities of, 172–74, *174*; PPE requirements of, 255; signage responsibilities and, 172; state plans of, 171; workplace violence categories of, 137–38; workplace violence requirements addressed by, 139–40

office buildings. *See* buildings

off-site data storage, 198–99

off-site parking, 279

oil spill program, of EPA, 127

Oklahoma/Kansas tornadoes of 1999, 13

oleum, 75, 125

online hazard maps and databases, 170

organizational vulnerability, hospital emergency preparedness and, 304–5

orientation training, EAP team training and, 208, 209

OSHA. *See* Occupational Safety and Health Act

outdated medications, 128

outdoor water conservation, 82–83

owned property, EAPs and, 164

Pacific Tsunami Warning Center (PTWC), 52–53

packages, suspicious, 105–6

PACM. *See* Presumed asbestos containing material

Palm Beach Community College (PBCC), 340

parking and off-site areas, building and site mitigation and, 278–80

partner systems, EAP responsibilities with, 175–76

patient care unit evacuation tools, for hospital emergency preparedness, *314–15*

PBCC. *See* Palm Beach Community College

Pentagon, 282

people with special needs, evacuations and, 222–25

personal protective equipment (PPE), 244, 255

personal relationship violence, 137–38

physical security plans, 3

PIO. *See* public information officer

plain language, for emergency plans, 326

planning: drought and business, 79–80; for earthquakes, 46–47; for hurricanes, 22–23; importance of, 10; for school emergency preparedness, 318–20. *See also* emergency action plans

planters, design for, 291–92

point of entry, building and site mitigation and, 278

poison control, 128

poisoning, 258

pools, water conservation for, 83

portable emergency generators, 203–4

post-event restoration: access for, 242–43; asbestos contamination and, 254–55; catering and, 252; challenges of, 241; clothing for, 246; command centers and, 248–49; communication and, 263–69; correspondence log for, 249, *250*; costs of, 251; customer and stakeholder communication and, 267; damage assessment and, 243–45; emergency account number and, 251–52; emergency management team activation for, 241–42; employee assistance with, 255–56; employee communication and, 266; environmental issues with, 253–55; family communication and, 266–67; food and water for, 247; government agency communication and, 267; homelessness and, 256; insurance and salvage decisions in, 244–45; insurance communication and, 267; logistics for, 245–48; media communication and, 264–66; medications for, 247; monitoring progress of, 262–63; PPE for, 244, 255; preparation for, 245; project manager for, 262; risk management for, 263; safety and, 257–61, 263; sample internal memo for, 268–69; sample press release for, 267–68; security and, 261–62; sleeping accommodations and, 253; stress and, 262–63; theft and, 261; toiletries for, 246–47

post-failure analysis, emergency mitigation and, 292

PPE. *See* personal protective equipment

pre-evacuation drills, EAP team training and, 209

preparation: for bomb search, 101; for bomb threats, 98; for CBR attacks, 112; for chemical incidents, 125–27; for civil disturbance and demonstrations, 147–48; for earthquakes, *45*, 45–47; for extreme heat, 85; for fires, 66–67; for floods, 37–39; for household chemical emergencies, 127–29; for hurricanes, 20–21; for landslide, debris flow, or mudflow, 61–62; for loss of utility, 149–50; need for, 9–10; for nuclear power plant emergencies, 133–35; for post-event restoration, 245; for terrorism, 108; for thunderstorms, 32–33; for tornadoes, 14; for tsunamis, 52–54; for volcano eruptions, 57–58; for wildfires, 71–72; for winter storms, 89; winter storms and business, 90–92

pre-planning, EAPs and, 192–93

press release, for post-event restoration, 267–68

Presumed asbestos containing material (PACM), 254

price, cost compared to, 202

principal, as leader, 323

probability, risk assessment matrix and, 169–70, *170*

project manager, for post-event restoration, 262

property, EAPs and: building use and, 166–68; geographic location considerations for, 164–66; leased or owned considerations for, 164

protective action plan, for CBR attacks, 115

protests. *See* civil disturbance and demonstrations

PTWC. *See* Pacific Tsunami Warning Center

public access areas, building and site mitigation and, 277

public address system, emergency announcements and, 218–19

public information officer (PIO), 319, 325

public relations, civil disturbance and demonstrations and, 148

radiation exposure, 131, 132–33

radiological agents. *See* chemical, biological, radiological agents

radios, for bomb search, 105

recovery, 156, 276; school emergency preparedness and, 333–35, 339–42

Red Cross. *See* American Red Cross

re-evaluation, 156

respiratory illness, 258

response, 156
reverse evacuation, 330
rioting. *See* civil disturbance and demonstrations
risk: dams and flood, 38, 169; EAPs and determination of, 168–70, *170*; floods and identification of, 37; post-event restoration and management of, 263; school emergency preparedness and, 317; wildfires and level of, 70–71
risk assessment, 276
risk assessment matrix, 168–70, *170*
Risk Management Plans (RMPs), 124
riverine floods, 35
RMPs. *See* Risk Management Plans
roll calls, in evacuations, 228–29
roof system, design for, 284
routes, for evacuations, 213
Royal Oak Postal Facility incident of 1991, 138–39
runners, in evacuations, 228

Safe Room, 14–15
safety: with alternative heating sources, 68; Chicago and high-rise, 214–15; emergency generators and, 204; evacuations and considerations for, 226; fires and measures for personal, 67–69; lightning and tips for, 34; media and, 265; of nuclear power plants, 131; post-event restoration and, 257–61, 263; thunderstorms and tips for, 34; wildfires and measures for personal, 72
safety clause, indemnity agreement and, 186
Saffir-Simpson hurricane intensity scale, 18–19
salvage decisions, post-event restoration and, 244–45
SAME. *See* Specific Area Message Encoding

Sarin, 121
satellite radiotelephone system, 298
SBA. *See* Small Business Administration
SCBAs. *See* self-contained breathing apparatuses
Schell, Paul, 146
school emergency preparedness: CPTED and, 339; design for, 317–18, 337–39; emergency plan for, 322–33; hazard analysis and, 336–37; planning process for, 318–20; prevention and mitigation for, 320–22; recovery and, 333–35, 339–42; risk and, 317; site inspection and impact records for, 339–42; students as threats and, 322; threat assessment for, 321–22. *See also* educational facilities; emergency plan, for school emergency preparedness
school shootings, 317–18
Schrader, Gerhard, 121
"sealing the room," 113–14
search and rescue teams, from FEMA, 150–52
second-degree burns, 236
security: hospital emergency preparedness and, 300–301, 310; post-event restoration and, 261–62
seismic waves, earthquakes and, 45
self-contained breathing apparatuses (SCBAs), 223
September 11, 2001 attacks, 97–98, 192, 196–97
severe thunderstorm warning, 32
severe thunderstorm watch, 32
SFHAs. *See* Special Flood Hazard Areas
sheltering in place, 113–16, 126, 306–7, 330–31
shelters: evacuations to general public shelter with temporary infirmary, 309–10; evacuations to shelter designated as

medical treatment unit, 308–9; fall out, 134–35; hurricanes and identifying safe, 23; wind, 14–15. *See also* buildings

shut down procedures, evacuations and, 220–22, *221*

signage responsibilities, EAPs and, 172

Silverstein Properties, 252

simulations, disaster, 215–16

skin disorders, 258

sleeping accommodations, post-event restoration and, 253

sleet, 89

Small Business Administration (SBA), 9

smallpox, 120

smoke alarms: design for, 290; installation of, 67

smoke-control systems, design for, 291

smoke inhalation: elevators and, 223; from fires, 65

Soman, 121

Southern drought from 1998-2000, 76

spandrel beams, 283–84

Special Flood Hazard Areas (SFHAs), 37

special needs, evacuations and, 222–25

Specific Area Message Encoding (SAME), 7

spray cans, empty, 128

sprinkler systems: deluge, 75, 192; design for, 290; dry pipe, 75, 192; EAPs and, 192; fires and types of, 74–75; testing, 192; wet pipe, 75, 192; winter storms and maintenance of, 92

staff evacuation template, hospital emergency preparedness, *316*

staging areas, for evacuations, 226–27, 331

stakeholder communication, post-event restoration and, 267

standpipes, design for, 290

stocking emergency supplies, 186, *187–88*, 188

"stop, drop, and roll," 69

storm activities, for hurricanes, 23–25, *24, 25*

storm shutters, 282

storm surge, 20

storm tide, 20

stress, post-event restoration and, 262–63

structural collapse, 150–52

structural vulnerability, hospital emergency preparedness and, 301–2

student emergency cards, 331

student release procedures, emergency plan and, 331–32

students, as threats, 322

sulfur mustard (mustard gas), 121

sunburn, 86

sun stroke, 84, 87

Super Outbreak of 1974, 12–13

supplies, stocking, 186, *187–88*, 188

surfacing material, 254

survival kit: for earthquakes, 47; for hurricanes, 31; for tsunamis, 54; for volcano eruptions, 58

suspicious parcels and letters, 105–6

tabletop exercises: EAP team training and, 208, 211; for employee training, 211, 217; evacuations and, 217

Tabun, 121

team, emergency management. *See* emergency management team

telephone tree system, 219

terrorism: definition of, 108; domestic, 3; nuclear weapons and, 131–32; preparation for, 108; September 11, 2001 attacks, 97–98, 192, 196–97

theft, post-event restoration and, 261

thermal burns, 235

thermal system insulation (TSI), 254

third-degree burns, 236

threats: emergency mitigation and, 274–75; school emergency preparedness and assessment of, 321–22; students as, 322

Three Mile Island nuclear disaster of 1979, 132

thunderstorms: advice during, 33–34; dry, 31; facts on, 32; floods from, 31; lightning during, 32; preparation for, 32–33; safety tips for, 34; severe watch and warning for, 32

toiletries, for post-event restoration, 246–47

"Tornado Alley," 13

tornadoes: advice following, 17; definition of, 11; facts on, 11–12; Fujita scale for, 12, *12*, 13; geography and occurrence of, 11; hurricanes associated with, 19; in Oklahoma and Kansas in 1999, 13; preparation for, 14; Safe Room and wind shelters for, 14–15; Super Outbreak of 1974, 12–13; warnings for, 7

tornado warning, 14, 19; advice for, 16–17; definition of, 13

tornado watch, 14, 19; advice for, 15–16; definition of, 13

toxins, 110

training, EAP team: evacuations and, 212–17; full-scale exercises and, 209; meeting goals for, 207; orientation training and, 208; pre-evacuation drills and, 209; tabletop exercises and, 208, 211; updating, 209–10; walk-through drills and, 208

transformers, design for, 289

tropical cyclone, 18

tropical depression, 18

tropical storm, 18

TSI. *See* thermal system insulation

tsunamis: advice during, 55; advice following, 55–56; advisory, 53; beaches avoided during, 55–56; definition of, 51; drowning from, 51; earthquakes and, 51; evacuation routes for, 54; Fukushima I Nuclear Power Plant disaster of 2011 and, 132; Hilo, Hawaii tsunami of 1946, 51–52; Indian Ocean tsunami of 2004, 52; NOAA weather radios for, 54; preparation for, 52–54; re-entering buildings after, 56; survival kit for, 54; warning, 53; watch, 53–54

unannounced evacuations, employee training and, 211

uninterruptible power supply (UPS), 200

Urban Search and Rescue Grid, 193

U.S. Department of Agriculture (USDA), 77

U.S. Drought Monitor, 77–78, *78*

U.S. Fire Safety (USFS), 71

U.S. Geological Survey (USGS): Earthquake Hazards Program of, 45, *45*; Volcano Notification Service of, 58

variola virus, 120

vendors, EAPs and, 184–86

ventilation systems, 289, 303

virtual reality, emergency mitigation and, 292

viruses, 110

visual alarm systems, 194

visual impairments, EAP responsibilities with, 176–77

volcanic ash, 56–57, 59, 60

volcano eruptions: advice during, 58–60; advice following, 60; danger zone in, 59; debris flow from, 56, 59; dust masks for, 59–60; earthquakes and, 56; evacuation routes for, 58; Kilauea Volcano, Hawaii eruption of 1983, 57; Mount St. Helens eruption of 1980, 57; preparation for, 57–58; survival kit for, 58

Volcano Notification Service, of USGS, 58
vulnerability assessment, 275–76

walk-through drills, EAP team training and, 208
waste disposal, healthcare facilities and, 303
water: contamination of, 75; earthquakes and needs for, 48–50; extreme heat and consumption of, 85; for post-event restoration, 247
water conservation: in bathroom, 81; car-washing and, 83; indoor, 80–82; in kitchen, 81; laundry and, 82; lawn-care and, 82–83; outdoor, 82–83; pools and, 83
water sprinkler systems. *See* sprinkler systems
weather disasters, 6–7
weather radios, NOAA, 6–7, 37–38, 54
Western United States wildfires of 2000, 66
wet pipe sprinkler system, 75, 192
WFAS. *See* Wildland Fire Assessment System
wheelchairs, evacuations and, 223–24
wildfires: advice during, 73; from dry thunderstorms, 31; evacuation routes for, 73; fire-resistant housing measures for, 72; from lighting, 65; personal safety measures for, 72; preparation for, 71–72; risk level of, 70–71; rural areas and, 71; Western United States wildfires of 2000, 66. *See also* fires

Wildland Fire Assessment System (WFAS), 71
Willow Island Tower Collapse of 1978, 150–51
Wilson, Pete, 146
windows, design for, 281–82
wind shelters, 14–15
Wind Zone Map, 14
winter storms: advice during, 90; business preparation for, 90–92; clothing for, 90; driving during, 92–93; equipment maintenance for, 91; geography and, 87; Great Appalachian Blizzard of 1996, 87–88; Groundhog Day Blizzard of 2011, 88; preparation for, 89; sprinkler systems maintenance for, 92; terminology for, 89
winter storm warning, 89
winter storm watch, 89
worker-on-worker violence, 137
workplace medical emergencies, 141–43
workplace violence: behavior solutions for, 140; Columbine High School incident of 1999, 139; definition of, 138; environmental solutions for, 140; factors leading to, 138; first responders to, 141; OSHA categories of, 137–38; OSHA requirements for addressing, 139–40; Royal Oak Postal Facility incident of 1991, 138–39
World Trade Center bombing of 1993, 96
World Trade Organization Protests in Seattle of 1999, 146–47
wound botulism, 122